A·N·N·U·A·L E·D·I·T·I·O·N·S

Sociology

Thirty-Third Edition

04/05

EDITOR

Kurt Finsterbusch

University of Maryland, College Park

Kurt Finsterbusch received a bachelor's degree in history from Princeton University in 1957 and a bachelor of divinity degree from Grace Theological Seminary in 1960. His Ph.D. in sociology, from Columbia University, was conferred in 1969. Dr. Finsterbusch is the author of several books, including *Understanding Social Impacts* (Sage Publications, 1980), *Social Research for Policy Decisions* (Wadsworth Publishing, 1980, with Annabelle Bender Motz), and *Organizational Change as a Development Strategy* (Lynne Rienner Publishers, 1987, with Jerald Hage). He is currently teaching at the University of Maryland, College Park, and, in addition to serving as editor for *Annual Editions: Sociology*, he is also editor of *Annual Editions: Social Problems,* and McGraw-Hill/Dushkin's *Taking Sides: Clashing Views on Controversial Social Issues.*

McGraw-Hill/Dushkin

2460 Kerper Blvd., Dubuque, IA 52001

Visit us on the Internet
http://www.dushkin.com

Credits

1. **Culture**
   Unit photo—© 2003 by PhotoDisc, Inc.
2. **Socialization and Social Control**
   Unit photo—© 2003 by PhotoDisc, Inc.
3. **Groups and Roles in Transition**
   Unit photo—© 2003 by Cleo Freelance Photography.
4. **Stratification and Social Inequalities**
   Unit photo—© 2003 by Sweet By & By/Cindy Brown.
5. **Social Institutions: Issues, Crises, and Changes**
   Unit photo—© 2003 by Sweet By & By/Cindy Brown.
6. **Social Change and the Future**
   Unit photo—© 2003 by Sweet By & By/Cindy Brown.

Copyright

Cataloging in Publication Data
Main entry under title: Annual Editions: Sociology. 2004/2005.
1. Sociology—Periodicals. I. Finsterbush, Kurt, *comp*. II. Title: Sociology.
ISBN 0–07–7286155–X   658'.05   ISSN 0277–9315

Thirty-Third Edition

Cover image © Ken Usami/Getty Images
Printed in the United States of America   123456789QPDQPD987654   Printed on Recycled Paper

Editors/Advisory Board

Members of the Advisory Board are instrumental in the final selection of articles for each edition of ANNUAL EDITIONS. Their review of articles for content, level, currentness, and appropriateness provides critical direction to the editor and staff. We think that you will find their careful consideration well reflected in this volume.

To the Reader

In publishing ANNUAL EDITIONS we recognize the enormous role played by the magazines, newspapers, and journals of the public press in providing current, first-rate educational information in a broad spectrum of interest areas. Many of these articles are appropriate for students, researchers, and professionals seeking accurate, current material to help bridge the gap between principles and theories and the real world. These articles, however, become more useful for study when those of lasting value are carefully collected, organized, indexed, and reproduced in a low-cost format, which provides easy and permanent access when the material is needed. That is the role played by ANNUAL EDITIONS.

The new millennium has arrived with difficult new issues such as how to deal with new levels of terrorism, while many of the old issues remain unresolved. There is much uncertainty. Almost all institutions are under stress. The political system is held in low regard because it seems to accomplish so little, to cost so much, and to focus on special interests more than the public good. The economy is in a recession in the short term and in the long term it suffers from foreign competition, trade deficits, economic uncertainties, and a worrisome concentration of economic power in the hands of relatively few multinational corporations. Complaints about the education system continue, because grades K–12 do not teach basic skills well and college costs are too high. Health care is too expensive, many Americans lack health care coverage, and some diseases are becoming resistant to our medicines. The entertainment industry is booming, but many people worry about its impact on values and behavior. News media standards seem to be set by the tabloids. Furthermore, the dynamics of technology, globalization, and identity groups are creating crises, changes, and challenges. Crime rates have declined somewhat, but they are still at high levels. The public is demanding more police, more jails, and tougher sentences, but less government spending. Government social policies seem to create almost as many problems as they solve. Laborers, women, blacks, and many other groups complain of injustices and victimization. The use of toxic chemicals has been blamed for increases in cancer, sterility, and other diseases. Marriage and the family have been transformed, in part by the women's movement and in part by the stress that current conditions create for women who try to combine family and careers. Schools, television, and corporations are commonly vilified. Many claim that morality has declined to shameful levels. Add to all this the problems of population growth, ozone depletion, and global warming, and it is easy to be pessimistic. Nevertheless, crises and problems also create opportunities.

The present generation may determine the course of history for the next 200 years. Great changes are taking place, and new solutions are being sought where old answers no longer work. The issues that the current generation faces are complex and must be interpreted within a sophisticated framework. The sociological perspective provides such a framework. It expects people to act in terms of their positions in the social structure, the political, economic, and social forces operating on them, and the norms that govern the situation.

Annual Editions: Sociology 04/05 should help you to develop the sociological perspective that will enable you to determine how the issues of the day relate to the way that society is structured. The articles provide not only information but also models of interpretation and analysis that will guide you as you form your own views. In addition, both the *topic guide* and the *World Wide Web* pages can be used to further explore the book's topics.

This thirty-third edition of *Annual Editions: Sociology* emphasizes social change, institutional crises, and prospects for the future. It provides intellectual preparation for acting for the betterment of humanity in times of crucial change. The sociological perspective is needed more than ever as humankind tries to find a way to peace, prosperity, health, and well-being that can be maintained for generations in an improving environment. The numerous obstacles that lie in the path of these important goals require sophisticated responses. The goals of this edition are to communicate to students the excitement and importance of the study of the social world and to provoke interest in and enthusiasm for the study of sociology.

Annual Editions: Sociology depends upon reader response in order to develop and change. You are encouraged to return the postage-paid *article rating form* at the back of the book with your opinions about existing articles, recommendations of articles you think have sociological merit for subsequent editions, and advice on how the anthology can be made more useful as a teaching and learning tool.

Kurt Finsterbusch

Kurt Finsterbusch
Editor
Dedicated to Meredith Ramsay for all that she has taught me about issues of great human concern.

Contents

UNIT 1
Culture

Five selections consider what our culture can learn from primitive peoples, what forces are shaping today's cultures and lifestyles, and the impact of crises on culture.

UNIT 2
Socialization and Social Control

Five articles examine the effects of social influences on childhood, personality, and human behavior with regard to the socialization of the individual.

The concepts in bold italics are developed in the article. For further expansion, please refer to the Topic Guide and the Index.

UNIT 3
Groups and Roles in Transition

Eight articles discuss some of the social roles and group relationships that are in transition in today's society. Topics include primary and secondary groups and the reevaluation of social choices.

The concepts in bold italics are developed in the article. For further expansion, please refer to the Topic Guide and the Index.

UNIT 4
Stratification and Social Inequalities

Nine selections discuss the social stratification and inequalities that exist in today's society with regard to the rich, the poor, blacks and gender issues.

The concepts in bold italics are developed in the article. For further expansion, please refer to the Topic Guide and the Index.

UNIT 5
Social Institutions: Issues, Crises, and Changes

Six articles examine several social institutions that are currently in crisis. Selections focus on the political, economic, and social spheres, as well as the overall state of the nation.

The concepts in bold italics are developed in the article. For further expansion, please refer to the Topic Guide and the Index.

UNIT 6
Social Change and the Future

Eight selections disucss the impact that population, technology, environmental stress, and social values will have on society's future.

The concepts in bold italics are developed in the article. For further expansion, please refer to the Topic Guide and the Index.

The concepts in bold italics are developed in the article. For further expansion, please refer to the Topic Guide and the Index.

Topic Guide

This topic guide suggests how the selections in this book relate to the subjects covered in your course. You may want to use the topics listed on these pages to search the Web more easily.

On the following pages a number of Web sites have been gathered specifically for this book. They are arranged to reflect the units of this *Annual Edition*. You can link to these sites by going to the DUSHKIN ONLINE support site at *http://www.dushkin.com/online/*.

ALL THE ARTICLES THAT RELATE TO EACH TOPIC ARE LISTED BELOW THE BOLD-FACED TERM.

UNIT 1
Culture

Unit Selections

1. **The Kindness of Strangers**, Robert V. Levine
2. **The Mountain People**, Colin M. Turnbull
3. **More Moral**, David Whitman
4. **American Culture Goes Global, or Does It?**, Richard Pells
5. **What's So Great About America?**, Dinesh D'Souza

Key Points to Consider

- What do you think are the core values in American society?

- What are the strengths and weaknesses of cultures that emphasize either cooperation or individualism?

- What is the relationship between culture and identity?

- What might a visitor from a primitive tribe describe as shocking and barbaric about American society?

 **Links: www.dushkin.com/online/**
These sites are annotated in the World Wide Web pages.

New American Studies Web
http://www.georgetown.edu/crossroads/asw/

Anthropology Resources Page
http://www.usd.edu/anth/

Human Rights and Humanitarian Assistance
http://www.etown.edu/vl/humrts.html

Sociology Library
http://www.library.upenn.edu/resources/subject/social/sociology/sociology.html

The ordinary, everyday objects of living and the daily routines of life provide a structure to social life that is regularly punctuated by festivals, celebrations, and other special events (both happy and sad). These routine and special times are the stuff of culture, for culture is the sum total of all the elements of one's social inheritance. Culture includes language, tools, values, habits, science, religion, literature, and art.

It is easy to take one's own culture for granted, so it is useful to pause and reflect on the shared beliefs and practices that form the foundations for our social life. Students share beliefs and practices and thus have a student culture. Obviously the faculty has one also. Students, faculty, and administrators share a university culture. At the national level, Americans share an American culture. These cultures change over time and especially between generations. As a result, there is much variety among cultures across time and across nations, tribes, and groups. It is fascinating to study these differences and to compare the dominant values and signature patterns of different groups.

The two articles in the first subsection deal with some of the variety among cultures. In the first the author studies the differences between various places in the prevalence of helping behavior and then tries to explain these differences. The second article, by Colin Turnbull, reports how the Ik tribe suffered the loss of its tribal lands and was forced to live in a harsh environment. This environmental change caused a terrifying change in its culture. When a society's technology is very primitive, its environment has a profound impact on its social structure and culture. We would expect, therefore, that such a momentous change in the tribe's environment would require some interesting adaptations. The change that occurred, however, was shocking. Literally all aspects of life changed for the tribe's members in a disturbingly sinister way. Moreover, the experience of this tribe leads Turnbull to question some of the individualistic tendencies of America.

In the next subsection, David Whitman attacks the moral decline thesis. He shows that most moral indicators have improved in the last 25 years. Drug and alcohol use, heavy drinking and drunk driving, cheating on taxes, political corruption, and crime have declined noticeably. Controlling for inflation, charitable giving has increased 50 percent. Church attendance and religion-based behavior have not declined. Though a few trends in moral indicators are negative, most are positive and the vast improvement on some social issues, such as discrimination, leads Whitman to conclude that America is more moral today than it was 25 years ago.

The culture of America continues to have an impact on the world. In fact, many people throughout the world are critical of American culture and thus are angered by its worldwide influence. Osama bin Laden is the most famous of such critics. In the next article, Richard Pells acknowledges that American culture has a considerable impact around the world, but challenges the thesis that the culture of America is Americanizing the world as many critics argue. He points out that much of American culture is imported and has spread throughout the world because it has incorporated foreign styles and ideas. The final article of this section argues that America has much to be proud about. Its author, Dinesh D'Souza, is an immigrant himself so he can see America both as an outsider and as an insider. He is able to identify many wonderful aspects of America that amaze and attract foreigners. He emphasizes the whole population's sense of equality and freedom of choice, in addition to the wealth that even the poor have here, when compared to the poor in other countries.

The Kindness of Strangers

People's willingness to help someone during a chance encounter on a city street varies considerably around the world

Robert V. Levine

I'll never forget a lesson that I learned as a boy growing up in New York City. One day, when I was perhaps six years old, I was walking with my father on a crowded midtown street. All of a sudden, the normal flow of pedestrian traffic backed up as people tried to avoid a large object on the sidewalk. To my astonishment, the object turned out to be a human being, a man lying unconscious against a building. Not one of the passing herd seemed to notice that the obstacle was a man. Certainly no one made eye contact. As we shuffled by, my father—the model of a loving, caring gentleman—pointed to a bottle in a paper bag and told me that the poor soul on the sidewalk "just needed to sleep it off." When the drunken man began to ramble senselessly, my father warned me not to go near, saying "You never know how he'll react." I soon came to see that day's lesson as a primer for urban adaptation.

Yet many years later I had a very different experience while visiting a market in Rangoon. I had spent the previous 12 months traveling in poor Asian cities, but even by those standards this was a scene of misery. In addition to being dreadfully poor, the residents had to contend with the sweltering climate, ridiculously dense crowds and a stiff wind blowing dust everywhere. Suddenly a man carrying a huge bag of peanuts called out in pain and fell to the ground. I then witnessed an astonishing piece of choreography. Appearing to have rehearsed their motions many times, a half dozen sellers ran from their stalls to help, leaving unattended what may have been the totality of their possessions. One put a blanket under the man's head; another opened his shirt; a third questioned him carefully about the pain; a fourth fetched water; a fifth kept onlookers from crowding around too closely; a sixth ran for help. Within minutes, a doctor arrived, and two other locals joined in to assist. The performance could have passed for a final exam at paramedic school.

The Good, the Bad and the Ugly

Rousseau wrote that "cities are the sink of the human race." But as my experiences in New York and Rangoon make clear, not all cities are the same. Places, like individuals, have their own personalities. Which environments most foster altruism? In which cities is a person in need likely to receive help? I have spent most of the past 15 years systematically exploring these questions.

My students and I have traveled across the United States and much of the world to observe where passersby are most likely to aid a stranger. In each of the cities we surveyed, we conducted five different field experiments. Our studies focused on simple acts of assistance, as opposed to Oskar Schindler-like heroism: Is an inadvertently dropped pen retrieved by a passing pedestrian? Does a man with an injured leg receive assistance picking up a fallen magazine? Will a blind person be helped across a busy intersection? Will someone try to make change for a quarter (or its foreign equivalent) when asked? Do people take the time to mail a stamped and addressed letter that has apparently been lost?

Our first studies were done in the early 1990s, when my students and I visited 36 cities of various sizes in different regions of the United States. The results did nothing to dispel my childhood impressions of New York. In an assessment that combined the results of these five experiments, New York came out dead last—36th out of 36. When we included a sixth measure of kindness toward strangers (per capita contribution to United Way), New York only moved up to 35th on the list. Overall, we found that people in small and medium-sized cities in the Southeast were the most helpful and that residents of large Northeastern and West Coast cities were the least.

One of the advantages of testing so many places is that we could see how other social, economic and environmen-

An illustration from a Victorian-era children's Bible depicts the famous story Jesus is said to tell in Luke 10:25–37: A man is attacked by thieves and left injured by the roadside; the only one to come to his aid is a passing Samaritan, a member of a group despised by Jews of that era. This parable about the willingness of one stranger to help another is especially relevant in modern times, because so many people live in cities and are surrounded daily by people they do not know. How likely is one to encounter a "good Samaritan" today? The author and his students probed that question and found that the answer varies considerably from place to place.

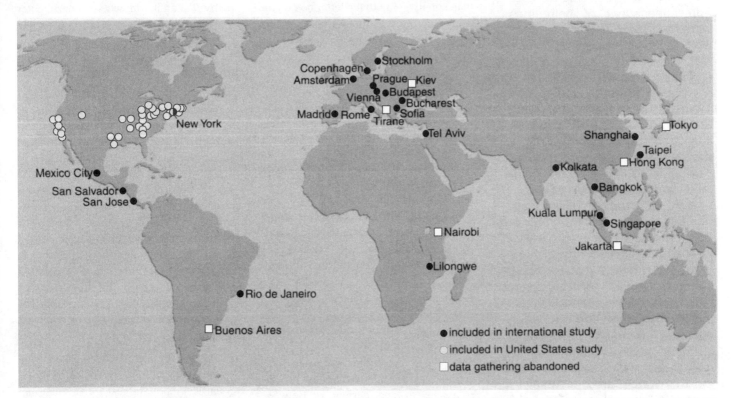

Figure 1. Tests of helpfulness span the globe. The author's 1994 study of helping was limited to 36 U.S. cities *(light gray, yellow)*, but his more recent work includes 23 cities *(black, red)*, 22 of them located in other countries. In a few places, attempts to gather information about helpfulness of strangers had to be abandoned *(square, blue)*.

tal indicators correlated with our experimental results. Far and away the best predictor, we found, was population density. This parameter was more closely tied to the helpfulness of a city than were the crime rate, the pace of life, the prevailing economic conditions or environmental stressors—say, noise or air pollution. We could readily make a case that, overall, people in more crowded cities were much less likely to take the time to help. New York was Exhibit A.

This finding is, of course, easy enough to understand. Crowding brings out the worst in us. Urban critics have demonstrated that squeezing too many people into too small a space leads, paradoxically enough, to alienation, anonymity and social isolation. Ultimately, people feel less responsible for their behavior toward others—especially strangers. Previous research had shown that city dwellers are more likely to do one another harm. Our study indicated that they are also less likely to do one another good and that this apathy increases with the degree of crowding.

But do all big cities exhibit this pattern? It was no surprise to find that densely packed cities like New York do not measure up to the communitarian standards of their smaller and calmer counterparts in the Southeast and Midwest. But as my experience in Rangoon showed, one comes across pockets of village cohesiveness in the most urban places. How do big-city dwellers from various countries compare? In particular, how does New York measure up to other large cities worldwide?

To answer these questions, for six summers Ara Norenzayan and more than 20 other adventurous students from my university worked with me to carry out five separate experiments in large cities around the world. In all, we ran nearly 300 trials of helpfulness that involved feigning blindness, dropped more than 400 pens, approached some 500 people while pretending to have a hurt leg or to be in need of change, and strategically lost almost 800 letters. To relate our findings to the situation in the United States, we used results for the same five

experiments carried out in New York during our earlier study.

Problems in Translation

Psychologists who mount elaborate field studies are keenly aware that observing what doesn't work in experiments is sometimes as instructive as observing what does. True to this rule, our first noteworthy finding was that ways of measuring helping do not always translate cleanly across cultures. Two experiments in particular—those that involved asking for change and losing letters—simply do not have the same functional meaning in many countries that they have in the United States.

The lost-letter test was the most troublesome. This experiment entails leaving stamped, addressed envelopes in a visible location on the street and then recording the percentage of these letters that get delivered. One problem we encountered was that people literally ran away from the letters in some cities. In Tel Aviv, in particular, where unclaimed packages have all too often turned out to contain bombs, people actively avoided our sus-

Three measures of helpfulness were found to translate reasonably well between cultures. For one test, the experimenter would drop a pen, apparently by accident and seemingly without noticing, at a moment when a stranger approaching the sidewalk would see it fall. If this person pointed out the dropped pen to the experimenter, a positive result was entered in the tally, which gauged the helpfulness of 424 people in all. In a second set of tests, the experimenter donned a leg brace and walked with a limp. when a passerby approached within 20 feet, the experimenter would drop several magazines on the sidewalk, seemingly by accident, and then struggle to pick them up. If the passing stranger helped gather up the magazines or even offered to help, the trial was scored positively. A total of 493 people were tested in this way. For a third test, the experimenter would feign blindness and approach the curb at a busy intersection just as the traffic light facing him turned green. He would then wait on the sidewalk for a passerby to offer aid. If one did so while the light was still green, the experiment would be scored positively; if not, it would be scored negatively. The author and his students completed a total of 281 trials of this nature.

picious-looking envelopes. In El Salvador, our experimenter was informed about a popular scam in which shysters were intentionally dropping letters: When a good Samaritan picked one up, a con man appeared, announcing that he had lost the letter and that it contained cash (it didn't), then demanding the money back with enough insistence to intimidate the mild-mannered. Not surprisingly, very few letters were touched in El Salvador.

In many developing countries, we found that local mailboxes are either unattended or nonexistent. As a result, mailing a letter in these places requires walking to a central post office, rather than simply going to the letter box on the nearest corner. In Tirane, Albania (where we eventually gave up our attempts to gather data), we were warned not to bother with this experiment, because even if a letter were posted, it probably wouldn't arrive at its destination. (Of course, postal unreliability is also a factor in some more affluent nations.) And most problematic of all, in several countries we found that letters and postal communication are irrelevant to many residents' lives. In retrospect, we should have known better and been less ethnocentric when we designed the experiment. After all, what can one expect in India, for example, where the illiteracy rate is 52 percent?

The asking-for-change experiment also encountered a variety of problems in translation. In this study, the experimenter would ask someone walking in the opposite direction for change for a quarter (in the United States) or the equivalent in other currencies. Between monetary inflation and the widespread use of prepaid telephone cards, however, we learned that the need for particular coins has disappeared in many parts of the world. In Tel Aviv, for example, no one seemed to understand why a person might require small change. In Calcutta (a city that has now officially changed its name to Kolkata), our experimenter had difficulty finding anyone who had small-value bills and coins—reflecting a general shortage all over India at that time. In Buenos Aires, capital of the struggling Argentine economy, we wondered how to score the response of a person who replied that he was so broke that he couldn't even make change. In a few cities, people were afraid to exchange any money with strangers. In Kiev (another city for which we eventually gave up collecting data), where thieves run rampant, visitors are warned never to open a purse or wallet on the street.

In the end, we limited our cross-national comparisons to the tests in which the experimenter pretended to be blind, to have an injured leg or to accidentally drop a pen. Even these situations, we found, occasionally suffered in translation. In the hurt-leg trials, for example, we learned that a mere leg brace was sometimes insufficient to warrant sympathy. Take Jakarta, where experimenter Widyaka Nusapati reported that people don't usually bother to help someone with a minor leg injury. Perhaps if the limb were missing, Nusapati observed, the test might be valid there.

We found that in some cities, such as Tokyo and in parts of the United States, traffic light controls give off distinctive sounds so that the visually impaired will know when it is safe to walk, making it less likely that people would consider a blind person crossing an intersection as someone in need of aid. And, in a curious twist, the experimenter in Tokyo felt so compelled by the surrounding norms of civility that he found it nearly impossible to fake blindness or a hurt leg to attract well-meaning helpers. As a result, Tokyo could not be included in our final ranking.

Despite these difficulties, we ran the three tests successfully in 23 different countries—the largest cross-national comparison of helping ever conducted. What we found suggests a world of difference in the willingness of urbanites to reach out to strangers. In the blind-person experiment, for example, subjects in five cities—Rio de Janeiro, San Jose (Costa Rica, not California), Lilongwe, Madrid and Prague—helped the pedestrian across the street on every occasion, whereas in Kuala Lumpur and Bangkok help was offered less than half the time. If you have a hurt leg in downtown San Jose, Kolkata or Shanghai, our results show that you are more than three times more likely to receive help picking up a fallen magazine than if you are struggling on the streets of New York or Sofia. And if you drop your pen behind you in New York, you have less than one-third the chance that you do in Rio of ever seeing it again.

The two highest-ranking cities are in Latin America: Rio and San Jose. Overall, we found that people in Portuguese- and Spanish-speaking cities tended to be among the most helpful: The other three such cities on our list, Madrid, San Salvador and Mexico City, each scored well above average. Considering that some of these places suffer from long-term political instability, high crime rates and a potpourri of other social, economic and environmental ills, these positive results are noteworthy.

Social psychologist Aroldo Rodrigues, who is currently a colleague of mine at California State University, Fresno, spent most of his career as a leading scholar at universities in the most helpful city of all, Rio. Rodrigues was not surprised by our results. "There is an important word in Brazil: 'simpático,'" Rodrigues explains. "The term has no equivalent in English. It refers to a range of desirable social qualities—to be friendly, nice, agreeable and good-natured, a person who is fun to be with and pleasant to deal with. Mind you, simpático doesn't mean that a person is necessarily honest or moral. It is a social quality. Brazilians, especially the Cariocas of Rio, want very much to be seen as simpático. And going out of one's way to assist strangers is part of this image." This Brazilian social script also extends to the Hispanic cultures in our study, where a simpático personality is held in equally high regard.

There were other notable trends, although each had its exceptions. Helping rates tended to be high in countries with low economic productivity (low gross domestic product per capita—that is, less purchasing power for each citizen), in cities with a slow pace of life (as measured by pedestrian walking speeds) and in cultures that emphasize the value of social harmony. This city "personality" is consistent with the simpático hypothesis. People in communities where social obligations take priority over individual achievement tend to be less economically productive, but they show more willingness to assist others. This trend did not, however, hold for all of the cities in our study. Pedestrians in the fast-paced, first-world cities of Copenhagen and Vienna, for example, were very kind to strangers, whereas their counterparts in slower-paced Kuala Lumpur were not helpful at all. These exceptions make clear that even city dwellers with a fast pace of life and a focus on economic achievement are capable of finding time for strangers in need and that a slow pace of life is no guarantee that people will invest their leisure time in practicing social ideals.

Start Spreading the News

New York may not have ranked lowest in our global study, as it had in our earlier tests of helpful acts in various U.S. cities, but it came close. Overall, New Yorkers placed 22nd in our list of 23. They ranked 22nd on tests of whether people would retrieve a dropped pen and of whether they would assist someone with a hurt leg. They came out a little below the average (13th) when it came to helping a blind person to cross the street.

We also learned that there may be a difference between helping and civility. In places where people walked fast, they were less likely to be civil even when they did offer assistance. In New York, helping gestures often had a particularly hard edge. During the dropped-pen experiment, for example, helpful New Yorkers would typically call to the experimenter that he had dropped his pen, then quickly move on in the opposite direction. In contrast, helpers in laid-back Rio—where a leisurely gait and simpático personality are ways of life—were more likely to return the pen personally, sometimes running to catch up with the experimenter. In the blind-person trials, helpful New Yorkers would often wait until the light turned green, tersely announce that it was safe to cross and then quickly walk ahead. In the friendlier cities, helpers were more likely to offer to walk the experimenter across the street, and they sometimes asked if he then needed further assistance. Indeed, one of our experimenters' problems in these place was how to separate from particularly caring strangers.

In general, it seemed as though New Yorkers are willing to offer help only when they could do so with the assurance of no further contact, as if to say "I'll meet my social obligation but, make no mistake, this is as far as we go together." How much of this attitude is motivated by fear and how much by simply not wanting to waste time is hard to know. But in more helpful cities, like Rio, it often seemed to us that human contact is the very motive for helping. People were more likely to give aid with a smile and to welcome the "thank you" our experimenter returned.

Perhaps the most dramatic example of uncivil helping involved one of the tests

we attempted and then abandoned, the lost-letter experiment. In many cities, I received envelopes that had clearly been opened. In almost all of these cases, the finder had then resealed it or mailed it in a new envelope. Sometimes they attached notes, usually apologizing for opening our letter. Only from New York did I receive an envelope which had its entire side ripped and left open. On the back of the letter the helper had scribbled, in Spanish: "Hijo de puta ir[r]esposable"—which I discovered when it was translated for me, makes a very nasty accusation about my mother. Below that was added a straightforward English-language expletive, which I could readily understand. It is interesting to picture this angry New Yorker, perhaps cursing my irresponsibility all the while he was walking to the mailbox, yet for some reason feeling compelled to take the time to perform his social duty for a stranger he already hated. Ironically, this rudely returned letter counted in the helping column in scoring New York. A most antipático test subject, as the Brazilians would say.

Compare this response to those in Tokyo, where several finders hand-delivered the letters to their addressees. Or, consider a note I received on the back of a returned letter from the most helpful city in our earlier study of U.S. cities, Rochester, New York:

Hi. I found this on my windshield where someone put it with a note saying they found it next to my car. I thought it was a parking ticket. I'm putting this in the mailbox 11/19. Tell whoever sent this to you it was found on the bridge near/across from the library and South Ave. Garage about 5 p.m. on 11/18.

P. S. Are you related to any Levines in New Jersey or Long Island? L. L.

A Special Attitude?

Do our results mean that New Yorkers are less kind people—less caring on the inside—than city dwellers in more helpful places? Not at all. The New Yorkers to whom we spoke gave many good reasons for their reluctance to help strang-

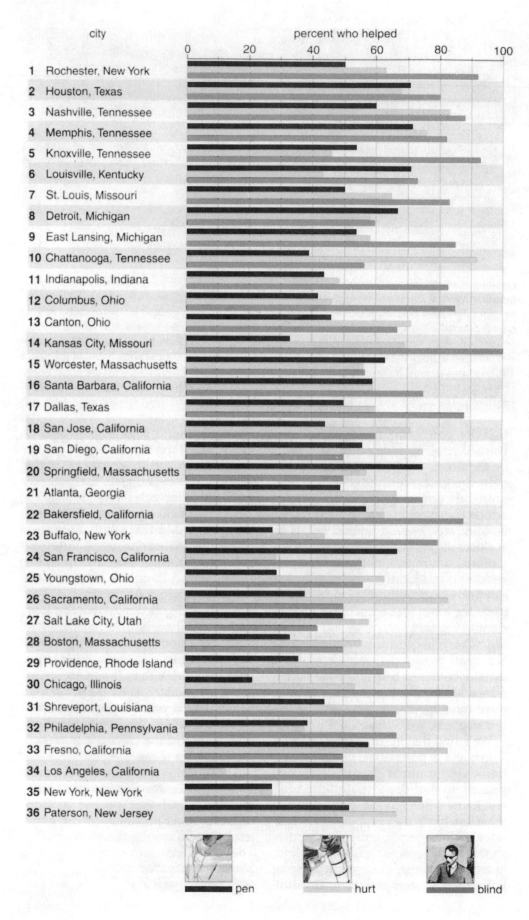

Figure 2. Author's 1994 study measured the general level of helpfulness in 36 U.S. cities. The published ranking was based on five experiments of helpfulness and on per-capita contribution to United Way, a popular charity campaign. (The final ranking differs somewhat when giving to United Way is not factored in. In that case, New York moves to the very bottom of the list.) The author's attempts to extend the same analysis to foreign cities proved problematic, because some of the experiments did not translate well to other cultures. Only three of the experimental yardsticks proved readily applicable in most places: willingness to help someone who had dropped a pen (upper bar), willingness to help someone with an injured leg (middle bar) and willingness to help a blind person (lower bar).

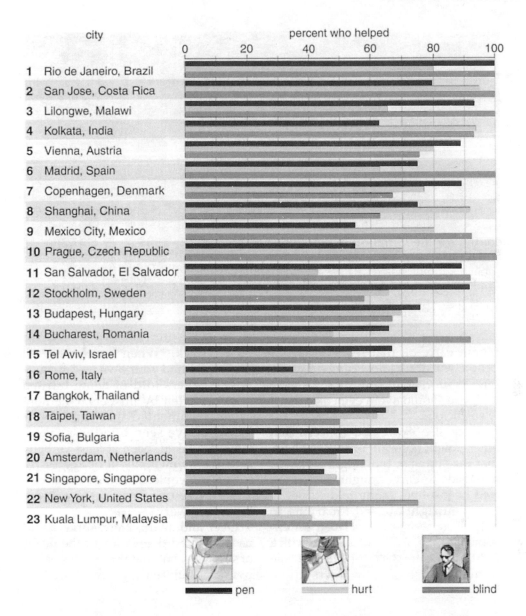

Figure 3. Ranking of cities around the world (by the same three measures show in Figure 2) places Rio first and Kuala Lampur last. It is, however, unlikely that these results reflect any real variation in human nature from country to country. Rather, the author posits, people are more or less likely to offer help to a stranger depending on the place they happen to be in at that moment.

ers. Most, like me, had been taught early on that reaching out to people you don't know can be dangerous. To survive in New York, we were told, you should avoid even the vaguely suspicious.

Some also expressed concern that others might not want unsolicited help, that the stranger, too, might be afraid of outside contact or might feel patronized or insulted. Many told stories of being outright abused for trying to help. One woman described an encounter with a frail, elderly man with a red-tipped cane who appeared unable to manage crossing an intersection. When she gently offered assistance, he barked back, "When I want help I'll ask for it. Mind your own f---ing business." Others told of being burned once too often by hustlers. One nonhelper commented that "most New Yorkers have seen blindness faked, lameness faked, been at least verbally accosted by mentally ill or aggressive homeless people. This does not necessar-

ily make one immune or callous, but rather, wary."

Over and again, New Yorkers told us they cared deeply about the needs of strangers, but that the realities of city living prohibited their reaching out. People spoke with nostalgia for the past, when they would routinely pick up hitchhikers or arrange a meal for a hungry stranger. Many expressed frustration—even anger—that life today deprived them of the satisfaction of feeling like good Samaritans.

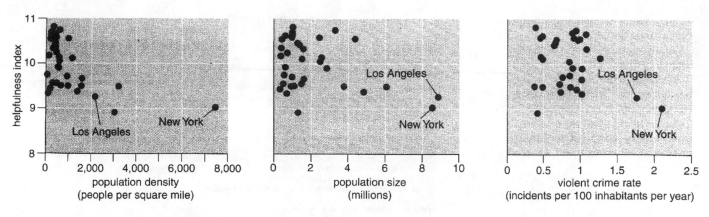

Figure 4. What accounts for the variation in helpfulness? The author's 1994 study of U.S. cities suggests that the key parameter may be population density: Cities having more than about 1,500 people per square mile tend to show comparatively low levels of helpfulness (left). Two of those unfriendly cities, New York and Los Angeles, are also especially large (middle) and have high rates of violent crime (right), factors that might also contribute to the lack of helpfulness one finds on the street. The other cities tested show no obvious correlation between size or crime rate and the prevailing level of helpfulness. Credit: David Schneider/American Scientist.

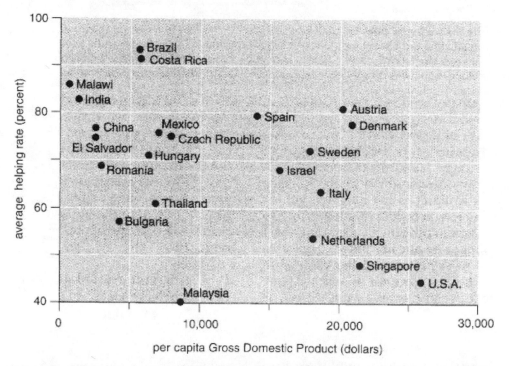

Figure 5. Economic productivity appears to have some influence on the degree of helpfulness one can expect. People generally show the highest level of helpfulness in places with low economic productivity (gauged here by the per-capita Gross Domestic Product after a correction to compensate for relative purchasing power in different countries). Similarly, those in places with high economic productivity typically rank low in measures of helpfulness. The helpfulness values plotted represent the results for one major city in each of these countries. Credit: David Schneider/American Scientist.

These explanations may simply be the rationalizations of uncharitable citizens trying to preserve their self-image. But I do not think this is the case. The bulk of the evidence indicates that helping tends to be less dependent on the nature of the local people than it is on the characteristics of the local environment. And investigators have demonstrated that seemingly minor changes in situation can drastically affect helping—above and beyond the personalities or moral beliefs of the people involved. It is noteworthy that studies show the location where one was raised has less to do with helping than the place one currently lives. In other words, Brazilians and New Yorkers are both more likely to offer help in Ipanema than they are in Manhattan.

Yet the cause of civility in cities like New York and Kuala Lumpur may not be hopeless. Just as characteristics of the situation may operate against helping, there are ways to modify the environment so as to encourage it. Experiments have shown, for example, that reversing the anonymity and diffusion of responsibility that characterize life in some cities—by increasing personal accountability, or simply by getting people to address one another by name—boosts helping. In a 1975 experiment at a New York beach, Thomas Moriarity, then a social psychologist at New York University, found that only 20 percent of people intervened when a man (actually one of the experimenters) blatantly stole a portable radio off of the temporarily abandoned blanket next to them. But when the owner of the radio simply asked her neighbors to keep an eye on the radio while she was gone, 95 percent of those who agreed stepped in to stop the snatcher.

Inducing a bit of guilt—by making people aware that they could be doing more—also seems to make a difference. Perhaps most promising is the observation that helping can be effectively taught. Psychologists have found, for example, that children who are exposed to altruistic characters on television tend to mimic them. And, because prosocial exemplars in real life often induce others to

follow suit, any increases in helping are potentially self-perpetuating.

> New Yorkers earned a reputation for callousness in 1964 when Catherine ("Kitty") Genovese was killed on this street in Kew Gardens, Queens, while making her way home from her job. Dozens of people in the surrounding buildings heard her screams as she was repeatedly attacked over an interval of 32 minutes, but none came to her aid and she died of stab wounds. This tragic episode inspired much self-analysis among the city's residents. The author's interviews of New Yorkers who proved unwilling to help in simple experiments suggest some of the factors that prevent well-meaning people from aiding strangers.

Might a kinder environment eventually raise the level of helpfulness in New York? This city is leading a nationwide trend and currently enjoying a wave of crime reduction. (Statistics indicate that fewer New Yorkers are doing each other injury today than in the recent past.) Could diminished worries over street crime free more people to step forth and offer one another aid, strangers included? Our experiments do not address variations over time, but I suspect that little will change. After all, the reduction in the number of harm-doers does not necessarily imply that there will be greater quantity of altruism practiced. And there is little doubt that the drunk man I watched people sidestep when I was six would be even less likely to receive help from a passing stranger today.

A little more than a century ago, author John Habberton may have had New Yorkers in mind when he wrote that "nowhere in the world are there more charitable hearts with plenty of money behind them than in large cities, yet nowhere else is there more suffering." Perhaps good Samaritans are indeed living in New York in large numbers but are hiding behind protective screens. To strangers in need of help, it would make little difference, thoughts being less important than actions. The bottom line: One's prospects for being helped by a stranger are bleaker in New York than they are in Rio, Mexico City or Shanghai. Indeed, you're more likely to receive assistance from someone you don't know just about anywhere else in world.

Bibliography

Clark, M. S. (ed.) 1991. *Prosocial Behavior*. Newbury Park, Calif.: Sage.

Levine, R. V. 1990. The pace of life. *American Scientist* 78:450–459.

Levine, R. 1997. *A Geography of Time*. New York: BasicBooks.

Levine, R. V., T. S. Martinez, G. Brase and K. Sorenson. 1994. Helping in 36 U.S. Cities. *Journal of Personality and Social Psychology* 67:69–82.

Levine, R. V., and A. Norenzayan. 1999. The pace of life in 31 countries. *Journal of Cross-cultural Psychology* 30:178–205.

Levine, R. V., A. Norenzayan and K. Philbrick. 2001. Cross-cultural differences in helping strangers. *Journal of Cross-cultural Psychology* 32:543–560.

Milgram, S. 1970. The experience of living in cities. *Science* 167:1461–1468.

Moriarity, T. 1975. Crime, commitment, and the responsive bystander: Two field experiments. *Journal of Personality and Social Psychology* 31:370–376.

Links to Internet resources for further exploration of "The Kindness of Strangers" are available on the *American Scientist* Web site: http://www.americanscientist.org/articles/05articles/levine.html

Robert V. Levine received his doctorate from New York University in 1974. Except for brief visiting appointments in Brazil, Japan and Sweden, he has spent the past three decades working at California State University in Fresno, *where he teaches and does research in the Department of Psychology. In addition to numerous scholarly articles, Levine has authored two popular books, the most recent being* The Power of Persuasion: How We're Bought and Sold *(John Wiley & Sons, 2003).*

Address: Department of Psychology, 5310 N. Campus Drive, M/S PH11, California State University, Fresno, CA 93740-8019. Internet: robertle@csufresno.edu

The Mountain People

Colin M. Turnbull

In what follows, there will be much to shock, and the reader will be tempted to say, "how primitive, how savage, how disgusting," and, above all, "how inhuman." The first judgments are typical of the kind of ethno- and egocentricism from which we can never quite escape. But "how inhuman" is of a different order and supposes that there are certain values inherent in humanity itself, from which the people described here seem to depart in a most drastic manner. In living the experience, however, and perhaps in reading it, one finds that it is oneself one is looking at and questioning; it is a voyage in quest of the basic human and a discovery of his potential for inhumanity, a potential that lies within us all.

Just before World War II the Ik tribe had been encouraged to settle in northern Uganda, in the mountainous northeast corner bordering on Kenya to the east and Sudan to the north. Until then they had roamed in nomadic bands, as hunters and gatherers, through a vast region in all three countries. The Kidepo Valley below Mount Morungole was their major hunting territory. After they were confined to a part of their former area, Kidepo was made a national park and they were forbidden to hunt or gather there.

The concept of family in a nomadic society is a broad one; what really counts most in everyday life is community of residence, and those who live close to each other are likely to see each other as effectively related, whether there is any kinship bond or not. Full brothers, on the other hand, who live in different parts of the camp may have little concern for each other.

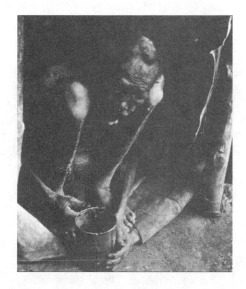

It is not possible, then, to think of the family as a simple, basic unit. A child is brought up to regard any adult living in the same camp as a parent, and age-mate as a brother or sister. The Ik had this essentially social attitude toward kinship, and it readily lent itself to the rapid and disastrous changes that took place following the restriction of their movement and hunting activities. The family simply ceased to exist.

It is a mistake to think of small-scale societies as "primitive" or "simple." Hunters and gatherers, most of all, appear simple and straightforward in terms of their social organization, yet that is far from true. If we can learn about the nature of society from a study of small-scale societies, we can also learn about human relationships. The smaller the society, the less emphasis there is on the formal system and the more there is on interpersonal and intergroup relations. Security is seen in terms of these rela-tionships, and so is survival. The result, which appears so deceptively simple, is that hunters frequently display those characteristics that we find so admirable in man: kindness, generosity, consideration, affection, honesty, hospitality, compassion, charity. For them, in their tiny, close-knit society, these are necessities for survival. In our society anyone possessing even half these qualities would find it hard to survive, yet we think these virtues are inherent in man. I took it for granted that the Ik would possess these same qualities. But they were as unfriendly, uncharitable, inhospitable and generally mean as any people can be. For those positive qualities we value so highly are no longer functional for them; even more than in our own society they spell ruin and disaster. It seems that, far from being basic human qualities, they are luxuries we can afford in times of plenty or are mere mechanisms for survival and security. Given the situation in which the Ik found themselves, man has no time for such luxuries, and a much more basic man appears, using more basic survival tactics.

Turnbull had to wait in Kaabong, a remote administration outpost, for permission from the Uganda government to continue to Pirre, the Ik water hole and police post. While there he began to learn the Ik language and became used to their constant demands for food and tobacco. An official in Kaabong gave him, as a "gift," 20 Ik workers to build a house and a road up to it. When they arrived at Pirre, however, wages for the workers were negotiated by wily Atum, "the senior of all the Ik on Morungole."

The police seemed as glad to see me as I was to see them. They hungrily

asked for news of Kaabong, as though it were the hub of the universe. They had a borehole and pump for water, to which they said I was welcome, since the water holes used by the Ik were not fit for drinking or even for washing. The police were not able to tell me much about the Ik, because every time they went to visit an Ik village, there was nobody there. Only in times of real hunger did they see much of the Ik, and then only enough to know that they were hungry.

The next morning I rose early, but even though it was barely daylight, by the time I had washed and dressed, the Ik were already outside. They were sitting silently, staring at the Land Rover. As impassive as they seemed, there was an air of expectancy, and I was reminded that these were, after all, hunters, and the likelihood was that I was their morning's prey. So I left the Land Rover curtains closed and as silently as possible prepared a frugal breakfast.

Atum was waiting for me. He said that he had told all the Ik that Iciebam [friend of the Ik] had arrived to live with them and that I had given the workers a "holiday" so they could greet me. They were waiting in the villages. They were very hungry, he added, and many were dying. That was probably one of the few true statements he ever made, and I never even considered believing it.

There were seven villages in all. Village Number One was built on a steep slope, and even the houses tilted at a crazy angle. Atum rapped on the outer stockade with his cane and shouted a greeting, but there was no response. This was Giriko's village, he said, and he was one of my workers.

"But I thought you told them to go back to their villages," I said.

"Yes, but you gave them a holiday, so they are probably in their fields," answered Atum, looking me straight in the eye.

At Village Number Two there was indisputably someone inside, for I could hear loud singing. The singing stopped, a pair of hands gripped the stockade and a craggy head rose into view, giving me an undeniably welcoming smile. This was Lokelea. When I asked him what he had been singing about, he answered, "Because I'm hungry."

Village Number Three, the smallest of all, was empty. Village Number Four had only 8 huts, as against the 12 or so in Lokelea's village and the 18 in Giriko's. The outer stockade was broken in one section, and we walked right in. We ducked through a low opening and entered a compound in which a woman was making pottery. She kept on at her work but gave us a cheery welcome and laughed her head off when I tried to speak in Icietot. She willingly showed me details of her work and did not seem unduly surprised at my interest. She said that everyone else had left for the fields except old Nangoli, who, on hearing her name mentioned, appeared at a hole in the stockade shutting off the next compound. Nangoli mumbled toothlessly at Losike, who told Atum to pour her some water.

As we climbed up to his own village, Number Five, Atum said that Losike never gave anything away. Later I remembered that gift of water to Nangoli. At the time I did not stop to think that in

this country a gift of water could be a gift of life.

Atum's village had nearly 50 houses, each within its compound within the stout outer stockade. Atum did not invite me in.

A hundred yards away stood Village Number Six. Kauar, one of the workers, was sitting on a rocky slab just outside the village. He had a smile like Losike's, open and warm, and he said he had been waiting for me all morning. He offered us water and showed me his own small compound and that of his mother.

Coming up from Village Number Seven, at quite a respectable speed, was a blind man. This was Logwara, emaciated but alive and remarkably active. He had heard us and had come to greet me, he said, but he added the inevitable demand for tobacco in the same breath. We sat down in the open sunlight. For a brief moment I felt at peace.

After a short time Atum said we should start back and called over his shoulder to his village. A muffled sound came from within, and he said, "That's my wife, she is very sick—and hungry." I offered to go and see her, but he shook his head. Back at the Land Rover I gave Atum some food and some aspirin, not knowing what else to give him to help his wife.

I was awakened well before dawn by the lowing of cattle. I made an extra pot of tea and let Atum distribute it, and then we divided the workers into two teams. Kauar was to head the team building the house, and Lokelatom, Losike's husband, was to take charge of the road workers.

While the Ik were working, their heads kept turning as though they were expecting something to happen. Every now and again one would stand up and peer into the distance and then take off into the bush for an hour or so. On one such occasion, after the person had been gone two hours, the others started drifting off. By then I knew them better; I looked for a wisp of smoke and followed it to where the road team was cooking a goat. Smoke was a giveaway, though, so they economized on cooking and ate most food nearly raw. It is a curious hangover from what must once have been a moral code that Ik will offer food if surprised in the act of eating, though they now go to enormous pains not to be so surprised.

I was always up before dawn, but by the time I got up to the villages they were always deserted. One morning I followed the little *oror* [gulley] up from *oror a pirre'i* [Ravine of Pirre] while it was still quite dark, and I met Lomeja on his way down. He took me on my first illicit hunt in Kidepo. He told me that if he got anything he would share it with me and with anyone else who managed to join us but that he certainly would not take anything back to his family. "Each one of them is out seeing what he can get

for himself, and do you think they will bring any back for me?"

Lomeja was one of the very few Ik who seemed glad to volunteer information. Unlike many of the others, he did not get up and leave as I approached. Apart from him, I spent most of my time, those days, with Losike, the potter. She told me that Nangoli, the old lady in the adjoining compound, and her husband, Amuarkuar, were rather peculiar. They helped each other get food and water, and they brought it back to their compound to eat together.

I still do not know how much real hunger there was at that time, for most of the younger people seemed fairly well fed, and the few skinny old people seemed healthy and active. But my laboriously extracted genealogies showed that there were quite a number of old people still alive and allegedly in these villages, though they were never to be seen. Then Atum's wife died.

Atum told me nothing about it but kept up his demands for food and medicine. After a while the beady-eyed Lomongin told me that Atum was selling the medicine I was giving him for his wife. I was not unduly surprised and merely remarked that that was too bad for his wife. "Oh no," said Lomongin, "she has been dead for weeks."

It must have been then that I began to notice other things that I suppose I had chosen to ignore before. Only a very few of the Ik helped me with the language. Others would understand when it suited them and would pretend they did not understand when they did not want to listen. I began to be forced into a similar isolationist attitude myself, and although I cannot say I enjoyed it, it did make life much easier. I even began to enjoy, in a peculiar way, the company of the silent Ik. And the more I accepted it, the less often people got up and left as I approached. On one occasion I sat on the *di* [sitting place] by Atum's rain tree for three days with a group of Ik, and for three days not one word was exchanged.

The work teams were more lively, but only while working. Kauar always played and joked with the children when they came back from foraging. He used to volunteer to make the two-day walk into Kaabong and the even more tiring

two-day climb back to get mail for me or to buy a few things for others. He always asked if he had made the trip more quickly than the last time.

Then one day Kauar went to Kaabong and did not come back. He was found on the last peak of the trail, cold and dead. Those who found him took the things he had been carrying and pushed his body into the bush. I still see his open, laughing face, see him giving precious tidbits to the children, comforting some child who was crying, and watching me read the letters he carried so lovingly for me. And I still think of him probably running up that viciously steep mountainside so he could break his time record and falling dead in his pathetic prime because he was starving.

Once I settled down into my new home, I was able to work more effectively. Having recovered at least some of my anthropological detachment, when I heard the telltale rustling of someone at my stockade, I merely threw a stone. If when out walking I stumbled during a difficult descent and the Ik shrieked with laughter, I no longer even noticed it.

Anyone falling down was good for a laugh, but I never saw anyone actually trip anyone else. The adults were content to let things happen and then enjoy them; it was probably conservation of energy. The children, however, sought their pleasures with vigor. The best game of all, at this time, was teasing poor little Adupa. She was not so little—in fact she should have been an adult, for she was nearly 13 years old—but Adupa was a little mad. Or you might say she was the only sane one, depending on your point of view. Adupa did not jump on other people's play houses, and she lavished enormous care on hers and would curl up inside it. That made it all the more jump-on-able. The other children beat her viciously.

Children are not allowed to sleep in the house after they are "put out," which is at about three years old, four at the latest. From then on they sleep in the open courtyard, taking what shelter they can against the stockade. They may ask for permission to sit in the doorway of their parents' house but may not lie down or sleep there. "The same thing applies to old people," said Atum, "if they can't build a house of their own and, of course, *if* their children let them stay in their compounds."

I saw a few old people, most of whom had taken over abandoned huts. For the first time I realized that there really was starvation and saw why I had never known it before: it was confined to the aged. Down in Giriko's village the old ritual priest, Lolim, confidentially told me that he was sheltering an old man who had been refused shelter by his son. But Lolim did not have enough food for himself, let alone his guest; could I… I liked old Lolim, so, not believing that Lolim had a visitor at all, I brought him a double ration that evening. There was rustling in the back of the hut, and Lolim helped ancient Lomeraniang to the entrance. They shook with delight at the sight of the food.

When the two old men had finished eating, I left; I found a hungry-looking and disapproving little crowd clustered outside. They muttered to each other about wasting food. From then on I brought food daily, but in a very short time Lomeraniang was dead, and his son refused to come down from the village above to bury him. Lolim scratched a hole and covered the body with a pile of stones he carried himself, one by one.

Hunger was indeed more severe than I knew, and, after the old people, the children were the next to go. It was all quite impersonal—even to me, in most cases, since I had been immunized by the Ik themselves against sorrow on their behalf. But Adupa was an exception. Her madness was such that she did not know just how vicious humans could be. Even worse, she thought that parents were for loving, for giving as well as receiving. Her parents were not given to fantasies. When she came for shelter, they drove her out; and when she came because she was hungry, they laughed that Icien laugh, as if she had made them happy.

Adupa's reactions became slower and slower. When she managed to find food—fruit peels, skins, bits of bone, half-eaten berries—she held it in her hand and looked at it with wonder and delight. Her playmates caught on quickly; they put tidbits in her way and watched her simple drawn little face wrinkle in a smile. Then as she raised her

hand to her mouth, they set on her with cries of excitement, fun and laughter, beating her savagely over the head. But that is not how she died. I took to feeding her, which is probably the cruelest thing I could have done, a gross selfishness on my part to try to salve my own rapidly disappearing conscience. I had to protect her, physically, as I fed her. But the others would beat her anyway, and Adupa cried, not because of the pain in her body but because of the pain she felt at the great, vast, empty wasteland where love should have been.

It was *that* that killed her. She demanded that her parents love her. Finally they took her in, and Adupa was happy and stopped crying. She stopped crying forever because her parents went away and closed the door tight behind them, so tight that weak little Adupa could never have moved it.

The Ik seem to tell us that the family is not such a fundamental unit as we usually suppose, that it is not essential to social life. In the crisis of survival facing the Ik, the family was one of the first institutions to go, and the Ik as a society have survived.

The other quality of life that we hold to be necessary for survival—love—the Ik dismiss as idiotic and highly dangerous. But we need to see more of the Ik before their absolute lovelessness becomes truly apparent.

In this curious society there is one common value to which all Ik hold tenaciously. It is *ngag*, "food." That is the one standard by which they measure right and wrong, goodness and badness. The very word for "good" is defined in terms of food. "Goodness" is "the possession of food," or the "*individual* possession of food." If you try to discover their concept of a "good man," you get the truly Icien answer: one who has a full stomach.

We should not be surprised, then, when the mother throws her child out at three years old. At that age a series of *rites de passage* begins. In this environment a child has no chance of survival on his own until he is about 13, so children from age bands. The junior band consists of children between three and seven, the senior of eight- to twelve-year-olds. Within the band each child seeks another close to him in age for defense against the older children. There friendships are temporary, however, and inevitably there comes a time when each turns on the one that up to then had been the closest to him; that is the *rite de passage*, the destruction of that fragile bond called friendship. When this has happened three or four times, the child is ready for the world.

The weakest are soon thinned out, and the strongest survive to achieve leadership of the band. Such a leader is eventually driven out, turned against by his fellow band members. Then the process starts all over again; he joins the senior age band as its most junior member.

The final *rite de passage* is into adulthood, at the age of 12 or 13. By then the candidate has learned the wisdom of acting on his own, for his own good, while acknowledging that on occasion it is profitable to associate temporarily with others.

One year in four the Ik can count on a complete drought. About this time it began to be apparent that there were going to be two consecutive years of drought and famine. Men as well as women took to gathering what wild fruits and berries they could find, digging up roots, cutting grass that was going to seed, threshing and eating the seed.

Old Nangoli went to the other side of Kidepo, where food and water were more plentiful. But she had to leave her husband, Amuarkuar, behind. One day he appeared at my *odok* and asked for water. I gave him some and was going to get him food when Atum came storming over and argued with me about wasting water. In the midst of the dispute Amuarkuar quietly left. He wandered over to a rocky outcrop and lay down there to rest. Nearby was a small bundle of grass that evidently he had cut and had been dragging painfully to the ruins of his village to make a rough shelter. The grass was his supreme effort to keep a home going until Nangoli returned. When I went over to him, he looked up and smiled and said that my water tasted good. He lay back and went to sleep with a smile on his face. That is how Amuarkuar died, happily.

There are measures that can be taken for survival involving the classical institutions of gift and sacrifice. These are weapons, sharp and aggressive. The object is to build up a series of obligations so that in times of crisis you have a number of debts you can recall; with luck one of them may be repaid. To this end, in the circumstances of Ik life, considerable sacrifice would be justified, so you have the odd phenomenon of these otherwise singularly self-interested people going out of their way to "help" each other. Their help may very well be resented in the extreme, but is done in such a way that it cannot be refused, for it has already been given. Someone may hoe another's field in his absence or rebuild his stockade or join in the building of a house.

The danger in this system was that the debtor might not be around when collection was called for and, by the same token, neither might the creditor. The future was too uncertain for this to be anything but one additional survival measure, though some developed it to a fine technique.

There seemed to be increasingly little among the Ik that could by any stretch of the imagination be called social life, let alone social organization. The family does not hold itself together; economic interest is centered on as many stomachs as there are people; and cooperation is merely a device for furthering an interest that is consciously selfish. We often do the same thing in our so-called "altruistic" practices, but we tell ourselves it is for the good of others. The Ik have dispensed with the myth of altruism. Though they have no centralized leadership or means of physical coercion, they do hold together with remarkable tenacity.

In our world, where the family has also lost much of its value as a social unit and where religious belief no longer binds us into communities, we maintain order only through coercive power that is ready to uphold a rigid law and through an equally rigid penal system. The Ik, however, have learned to do without coercion, either spiritual or physical. It seems that they have come to a recognition of what they accept as man's basic selfishness, of his natural determination to survive as an individual before all else. This they consider to be man's basic right, and they allow others to pursue that right without recrimination.

In large-scale societies such as our own, where members are individual beings rather than social beings, we rely on law for order. The absence of both a common law and a common belief would surely result in lack of any community of behavior; yet Ik society is not anarchical. One might well expect religion, then, to play a powerful role in Icien life, providing a source of unity.

The Ik, as may be expected, do not run true to form. When I arrived, there were still three ritual priests alive. From them and from the few other old people, I learned something of the Ik's belief and practice as they had been before their world was so terribly changed. There had been a powerful unity of belief in Didigwari—a sky god—and a body of ritual practice reinforcing secular behavior that was truly social.

Didigwari himself is too remote to be of much practical significance to the Ik. He created them and abandoned them and retreated into his domain somewhere in the sky. He never came down to earth, but the *abang* [ancestors] have all known life on earth; it is only against them that one can sin and only to them that one can turn for help, through the ritual priest.

While Morungole has no legends attached to it by the Ik, it nonetheless figures in their ideology and is in some ways regarded by them as sacred. I had noticed this by the almost reverential way in which they looked at it—none of the shrewd cunning and cold appraisal with which they regarded the rest of the world. When they talked about it, there was a different quality to their voices. They seemed incapable of talking about Morungole in any other way, which is probably why they talked about it so very seldom. Even that weasel Lomongin became gentle the only time he talked about it to me. He said, "If Atum and I were there, we would not argue. It is a good place." I asked if he meant that it was full of food. He said yes. "Then why do Ik never go there?" "They do go there." "But if hunting is good there, why not live there?" "We don't hunt there, we just go there." "Why?" "I told you, it is a good place." If I did not understand him, that was my fault; for once he was doing his best to communicate something to me. With others it was the same. All agreed that it was "a good place." One added, "That is the Place of God."

Lolim, the oldest and greatest of the ritual priests, was also the last. He was not much in demand any longer, but he was still held in awe, which means kept at a distance. Whenever he approached a *di*, people cleared a space for him, as far away from themselves as possible. The Ik rarely called on his services, for they had little to pay him with, and he had equally little to offer them. The main things they did try to get out of him were certain forms of medicine, both herbal and magical.

Lolim said that he had inherited his power from his father. His father had taught him well but could not give him the power to hear the *abang*—that had to come from the *abang* themselves. He had wanted his oldest son to inherit and had taught him everything he could. But his son, Longoli, was bad, and the *abang* refused to talk to him. They talked instead to his oldest daughter, bald Nangoli. But there soon came the time when all the Ik needed was food in their stomachs, and Lolim could not supply that. The time came when Lolim was too weak to go out and collect the medicines he needed. His children all refused to go except Nangoli, and then she was jailed for gathering in Kidepo Park.

Lolim became ill and had to be protected while eating the food I gave him. Then the children began openly ridiculing him and teasing him, dancing in front of him and kneeling down so that he would trip over them. His grandson used to creep up behind him and with a pair of hard sticks drum a lively tattoo on the old man's bald head.

I fed him whenever I could, but often he did not want more than a bite. Once I found him rolled up in his protective ball, crying. He had had nothing to eat for four days and no water for two. He had asked his children, who all told him not to come near them.

The next day I saw him leaving Atum's village, where his son Longoli lived. Longoli swore that he had been giving his father food and was looking after him. Lolim was not shuffling away; it was almost a run, the run of a drunken man, staggering from side to side. I called to him, but he made no reply, just a kind of long, continuous and horrible moan. He had been to Longoli to beg him to let him into his compound because he knew he was going to die in a few hours, Longoli calmly told me afterward. Obviously Longoli could not do a thing like that: a man of Lolim's importance would have called for an enormous funeral feast. So he refused. Lolim begged Longoli then to open up Nangoli's *asak* for him so that he could die in *her* compound. But Longoli drove him out, and he died alone.

Atum pulled some stones over the body where it had fallen into a kind of hollow. I saw that the body must have lain parallel with the *oror*. Atum answered without waiting for the question: "He was lying looking up at Mount Meraniang."

Insofar as ritual survived at all, it could hardly be said to be religious, for it did little or nothing to bind Icien society together. But the question still remained: Did this lack of social behavior and communal ritual or religious expression mean that there was no community of belief?

Belief may manifest itself, at either the individual or the communal level, in what we call morality, when we behave according to certain principles supported by our belief even when it seems against our personal interest. When we call ourselves moral, however, we tend to ignore that ultimately our morality benefits us even as individuals, insofar as we are social individuals and live in a society. In the absence of belief, law takes over and morality has little role. If there was such a thing as an Icien morality, I had not yet perceived it, though traces of a moral past remained. But it still remained a possibility, as did the existence of an unspoken, unmanifest belief that might yet reveal itself and provide a basis for the reintegration of society. I was somewhat encouraged in this hope by the unexpected flight of old Nangoli, widow of Amuarkuar.

When Nangoli returned and found her husband dead, she did an odd thing: she grieved. She tore down what was left of their home, uprooted the stockade, tore up whatever was growing in her little field. Then she fled with a few belongings.

Some weeks later I heard that she and her children had gone over to the Sudan and built a village there. This migration was so unusual that I decided to see whether this runaway village was different.

Lojieri led the way, and Atum came along. One long day's trek got us there. Lojieri pulled part of the brush fence aside, and we went in and wandered around. He and Atum looked inside all the huts, and Lojieri helped himself to tobacco from one and water from another. Surprises were coming thick and fast. That households should be left open and untended with such wealth inside… That there should have been such wealth, for as well as tobacco and jars of water there were baskets of food, and meat was drying on racks. There were half a dozen or so compounds, but they were separated from each other only by a short line of sticks and brush. It was a village, and these were homes, the first and last I was to see.

The dusk had already fallen, and Nangoli came in with her children and grandchildren. They had heard us and came in with warm welcomes. There was no hunger here, and in a very short time each kitchen hearth had a pot of food cooking. Then we sat around the central fire and talked until late, and it was another universe.

There was no talk of "how much better it is here than there"; talk revolved around what had happened on the hunt that day. Loron was lying on the ground in front of the fire as his mother made gentle fun of him. His wife, Kinimei, whom I had never seen even speak to him at Pirre, put a bowl of fresh-cooked berries and fruit in front of him. It was all like a nightmare rather than a fantasy, for it made the reality of Pirre seem all the more frightening.

The unpleasantness of returning was somewhat alleviated by Atum's suffering on the way up the stony trail. Several times he slipped, which made Lojieri and me laugh. It was a pleasure to move rapidly ahead and leave Atum gasping behind so that we could be sitting up on the *di* when he finally appeared and could laugh at his discomfort.

The days of drought wore on into weeks and months and, like everyone else, I became rather bored with sickness and death. I survived rather as did the young adults, by diligent attention to my own needs while ignoring those of others.

More and more it was only the young who could go far from the village as hunger became starvation. Famine relief had been initiated down at Kasile, and those fit enough to make the trip set off. When they came back, the contrast between them and the others was that between life and death. Villages were villages of the dead and dying, and there was little difference between the two. People crawled rather than walked. After a few feet some would lie down to rest, but they could not be sure of ever being able to sit up again, so they mostly stayed upright until they reached their destination. They were going nowhere, these semianimate bags of skin and bone; they just wanted to be with others, and they stopped whenever they met. Perhaps it was the most important demonstration of sociality I ever saw among the Ik. Once they met, they neither spoke nor did anything together.

Early one morning, before dawn, the village moved. In the midst of a hive of activity were the aged and crippled, soon to be abandoned, in danger of being trampled but seemingly unaware of it. Lolim's widow, Lo'ono, whom I had never seen before, also had been abandoned and had tried to make her way

16

down the mountainside. But she was totally blind and had tripped and rolled to the bottom of the *oror a pirre'i;* there she lay on her back, her legs and arms thrashing feebly, while a little crowd laughed.

At this time a colleague was with me. He kept the others away while I ran to get medicine and food and water, for Lo'ono was obviously near dead from hunger and thirst as well as from the fall. We treated her and fed her and asked her to come back with us. But she asked us to point her in the direction of her son's new village. I said I did not think she would get much of a welcome there, and she replied that she knew it but wanted to be near him when she died. So we gave her more food, put her stick in her hand and pointed her the right way. She suddenly cried. She was crying, she said, because we had reminded her that there had been a time when people had helped each other, when people had been kind and good. Still crying, she set off.

The Ik up to this point had been tolerant of my activities, but all this was too much. They said that what we were doing was wrong. Food and medicine were for the living, not the dead. I thought of Lo'ono. And I thought of other old people who had joined in the merriment when they had been teased or had a precious morsel of food taken from their mouths. They knew that it was silly of them to expect to go on living, and, having watched others, they knew that the spectacle really was quite funny. So they joined in the laughter. Perhaps if we had left Lo'ono, she would have died laughing. But we prolonged her misery for no more than a few brief days. Even worse, we reminded her of when things had been different, of days when children had cared for parents and parents for children. She was already dead, and we made her unhappy as well. At the time I was sure we were right, doing the only "human" thing. In a way we *were*—we were making life more comfortable for ourselves. But now I wonder if the Ik way was not right, if I too should not have laughed as Lo'ono flapped about, then left her to die.

Ngorok was a man at 12. Lomer, his older brother, at 15 was showing signs of strain; when he was carrying a load, his face took on a curious expression of pain

that was not physical pain. Giriko, at 25 was 40, Atum at 40 was 65, and the very oldest, perhaps a bare 50, were centenarians. And I, at 40, was younger than any of them, for I still enjoyed life, which they had learned was not "adult" when they were 3. But they retained their will to survive and so offered grudging respect to those who had survived for long.

Even in the teasing of the old there was a glimmer of hope. It denoted a certain intimacy that did not exist between adjacent generations. This is quite common in small-scale societies. The very old and the very young look at each other as representing the future and the past. To the child, the aged represent a world that existed before their own birth and the unknown world to come.

And now that all the old are dead, what is left? Every Ik who is old today was thrown out at three and has survived, and in consequence has thrown his own children out and knows that they will not help him in his old age any more than he helped his parents. The system has turned one full cycle and is now self-perpetuating; it has eradicated what we know as "humanity" and has turned the world into a chilly void where man does not seem to care even for himself, but survives. Yet into this hideous world Nangoli and her family quietly returned because they could not bear to be alone.

For the moment abandoning the very old and the very young, the Ik as a whole must be searched for one last lingering trace of humanity. They appear to have disposed of virtually all the qualities that we normally think of as differentiating us from other primates, yet they survive without seeming to be greatly different from ourselves in terms of behavior. Their behavior is more extreme, for we do not start throwing our children out until kindergarten. We have shifted responsibility from family to state, the Ik have shifted it to the individual.

It has been claimed that human beings are capable of love and, indeed, are dependent upon it for survival and sanity. The Ik offer us an opportunity for testing this cherished notion that love is essential to survival. If it is, the Ik should have it.

Love in human relationships implies mutuality, a willingness to sacrifice the

self that springs from a consciousness of identity. This seems to bring us back to the Ik, for it implies that love is self-oriented, that even the supreme sacrifice of one's life is no more than selfishness, for the victim feels amply rewarded by the pleasure he feels in making the sacrifice. The Ik, however, do not value emotion above survival, and they are without love.

But I kept looking, for it was the one thing that could fill the void their survival tactics had created; and if love was not there in some form, it meant that for humanity love is not a necessity at all, but a luxury or an illusion. And if it was not among the Ik, it meant that mankind can lose it.

The only possibility for any discovery of love lay in the realm of interpersonal relationships. But they were, each one, simply alone, and seemingly content to be alone. It was this acceptance of individual isolation that made love almost impossible. Contact, when made, was usually for a specific practical purpose having to do with food and the filling of a stomach, a single stomach. Such contacts did not have anything like the permanence or duration required to develop a situation in which love was possible.

The isolation that made love impossible, however, was not completely proof against loneliness, I no longer noticed normal behavior, such as the way people ate, running as they gobbled, so as to have it all for themselves. But I did notice that when someone was making twine or straightening a spear shaft, the focus of attention for the spectators was not the person but the action. If they were caught watching by the one being watched and their eyes met, the reaction was a sharp retreat on both sides.

When the rains failed for the second year running, I knew that the Ik as a society were almost certainly finished and that the monster they had created in its place, that passionless, feelingless association of individuals, would spread like a fungus, contaminating all it touched. When I left, I too had been contaminated. I was not upset when I said good-bye to old Loiangorok. I told him I had left a sack of *posho* [ground corn meal] with the police for him, and I said I would send money for more when that ran out.

17

He dragged himself slowly toward the *di* every day, and he always clutched a knife. When he got there, or as far as he could, he squatted down and whittled at some wood, thus proving that he was still alive and able to do things. The *posho* was enough to last him for months, but I felt no emotion when I estimated that he would last one month, even with the *posho* in the hands of the police. I underestimated his son, who within two days had persuaded the police that it would save a lot of bother if he looked after the *posho*. I heard later that Loiangorok died of starvation within two weeks.

So, I departed with a kind of forced gaiety, feeling that I should be glad to be gone but having forgotten how to be glad. I certainly was not thinking of returning within a year, but I did. The following spring I heard that rain had come at last and that the fields of the Ik had never looked so prosperous, nor the country so green and fertile. A few months away had refreshed me, and I wondered if my conclusions had not been excessively pessimistic. So, early that summer, I set off to be present for the first harvests in three years.

I was not surprised too much when two days after my arrival and installation at the police post I found Logwara, the blind man, lying on the roadside bleeding, while a hundred yards up other Ik were squabbling over the body of a hyena. Logwara had tried to get there ahead of the others to grab the meat and had been trampled on.

First I looked at the villages. The lush outer covering concealed an inner decay. All the villages were like this to some extent, except for Lokelea's. There the tomatoes and pumpkins were carefully pruned and cleaned, so that the fruits were larger and healthier. In what had been my own compound the shade trees had been cut down for firewood, and the lovely hanging nests of the weaver birds were gone.

The fields were even more desolate. Every field without exception had yielded in abundance, and it was a new sensation to have vision cut off by thick crops. But every crop was rotting from sheer neglect.

The Ik said that they had no need to bother guarding the fields. There was so much food they could never eat it all, so why not let the birds and baboons take some? The Ik had full bellies; they were good. The *di* at Atum's village was much the same as usual, people sitting or lying about. People were still stealing from each other's fields, and nobody thought of saving for the future.

It was obvious that nothing had really changed due to the sudden glut of food except that interpersonal relationships had deteriorated still further and that Icien individualism had heightened beyond what I thought even Ik to be capable of.

The Ik had faced a conscious choice between being humans and being parasites and had chosen the latter. When they saw their fields come alive, they were confronted with a problem. If they reaped the harvest, they would have to store grain for eating and planting, and every Ik knew that trying to store anything was a waste of time. Further, if they made their fields look too promising, the government would stop famine relief. So the Ik let their fields rot and continued to draw famine relief.

The Ik were not starving any longer; the old and infirm had all died the previous year, and the younger survivors were doing quite well. But the famine relief was administered in a way that was little short of criminal. As before, only the young and well were able to get down from Pirre to collect the relief; they were given relief for those who could not come and told to take it back. But they never did—they ate it themselves.

The facts are there, though those that can be read here form but a fraction of what one person was able to gather in under two years. There can be no mistaking the direction in which those facts point, and that is the most important thing of all, for it may affect the rest of mankind as it has affected the Ik. The Ik have "progressed," one might say, since the change that has come to them came with the advent of civilization to Africa. They have made of a world that was alive a world that is dead—a cold, dispassionate world that is without ugliness because it is without beauty, without hate because it is without love, and without any realization of truth even, because it simply is. And the symptoms of change in our own

society indicate that we are heading in the same direction.

Those values we cherish so highly may indeed be basic to human society but not to humanity, and that means that the Ik show that society itself is not indispensable for man's survival and that man is capable of associating for purposes of survival without being social. The Ik have replaced human society with a mere survival system that does not take human emotion into account. As yet the system i[s] imperfect, for although survival is assured, it is at a minimal level and there is still competition between individuals. With our intellectual sophistication and advanced technology we should be able to perfect the system and eliminate competition, guaranteeing survival for a given number of years for all, reducing the demands made upon us by a social system, abolishing desire and consequently that ever-present and vital gap between desire and achievement, treating us, in a word, as individuals with one basic individual right—the right to survive.

Such interaction as there is within this system is one of mutual exploitation. That is how it already is with the Ik. In our own world the mainstays of a society based on a truly social sense of mutuality are breaking down, indicating that perhaps society as we know it has outworn its usefulness and that by clinging to an outworn system we are bringing about our own destruction. Family, economy, government and religion, the basic categories of social activity and behavior, no longer create any sense of social unity involving a shared and mutual responsibility among all members of our society. At best they enable the individual to survive as an individual. It is the world of the individual, as is the world of the Ik.

The sorry state of society in the civilized world today is in large measure due to the fact that social change has not kept up with technological change. This mad, senseless, unthinking commitment to technological change that we call progress may be sufficient to exterminate the human race in a very short time even without the assistance of nuclear warfare. But since we have already become individualized and desocialized, we say that extermination will not come in our time, which shows about as much sense of family devotion as one might expect from the Ik.

Even supposing that we can avert nuclear holocaust or the almost universal famine that may be expected if population keeps expanding and pollution remains unchecked, what will be the cost if not the same already paid by the Ik? They too were driven by the need to survive, and they succeeded at the cost of their humanity. We are already beginning to pay the same price, but we not only still have the choice (though we may not have the will or courage to make it), we also have the intellectual and technological ability to avert an Icien end. Any change as radical as will be necessary is not likely to bring material benefits to the present generation, but only then will there be a future.

The Ik teach us that our much vaunted human values are not inherent in humanity at all but are associated only with a particular form of survival called society and that all, even society itself, are luxuries that can be dispensed with. That does not make them any less wonderful, and if man has any greatness, it is surely in his ability to maintain these values, even shortening an already pitifully short life rather than sacrifice his humanity. But that too involves choice, and the Ik teach us that man can lose the will to make it. That is the point at which there is an end to truth, to goodness and to beauty, an end to the struggle for their achievement, which gives life to the individual and strength and meaning to society. The Ik have relinquished all luxury in the name of individual survival, and they live on as a people without life, without passion, beyond humanity. We pursue those trivial, idiotic technological encumbrances, and all the time we are losing our potential for social rather than individual survival, for hating as well as loving, losing perhaps our last chance to enjoy life with all the passion that is our nature.

Anthropologist Colin M. Turnbull, author of The Forest People *and* The Lonely Africans, *went to study the Ik of Uganda, who he believed were still primarily hunters, in order to compare them with other hunting-and-gathering societies he had studied in totally different environments. He was surprised to discover that they were no longer hunters but primarily farmers, well on their way to starvation and something worse in a drought-stricken land.*

America's moral non-decline.

MORE MORAL

By David Whitman

By the time the Lewinsky scandal erupted, three out of four Americans already believed that moral values had weakened in the past quarter-century. Now, thanks to Bill Clinton's Oval Office high jinks, the case that moral standards are eroding seems stronger than ever. In his new bestseller *The Death of Outrage*, William Bennett argues that the lack of public outcry over the president's adultery and prevarication is but one more sign that people's "commitment to long-standing American ideals has been enervated." Al Gore would disagree with Bennett's analysis of Clinton, but he, too, believes that "there is indeed a spiritual crisis in modern civilization."

Yet, for all the bipartisan hand-wringing about moral decline, there is surprisingly little evidence that Americans *act* more immorally today than they did a quarter-century ago. In fact, just the opposite seems to be true—as even a few conservatives are beginning to concede. In the current issue of the right-leaning magazine *The American Enterprise*, editor-in-chief Karl Zinsmeister urges fellow conservatives not "to accuse the American people of becoming morally rotten. Especially when there exist abundant data suggesting that the residents of our land are actually becoming *less* morally rotten." It is still true, of course, that millions of citizens continue to err and sin, and that the culture now has a surfeit of coarseness, from noxious rap lyrics to the "Jerry Springer Show." But, if one looks beyond the anecdotes, the picture of how people behave is unexpectedly encouraging.

Compared with their predecessors of a quarter-century ago, Americans today are less likely to drink to excess, take drugs, rely on the dole, drive drunk, or knowingly evade paying taxes. They give more money to charity and spend as much or more time in church. And they are more likely than their predecessors to do good Samaritan work among the poor, sick, and elderly. Despite fears of random violence, FBI reports suggest that fewer people were murdered by strangers in 1997 (2,067) than in 1977 (about 2,500), even though the U.S. population grew by 47 million during that time. The dramatic drop in the number of Americans victimized by murder, burglary, and theft represents another well-known illustration of moral progress, but there are many more.

For example, Americans now donate significantly more money to charity than they did a generation ago, as Everett Carll Ladd, director of the Roper Center for Public Opinion Research, documents in a forthcoming book. Adjusted for inflation, Americans gave about $525 per adult to charity in 1996. That is 50 percent more than Americans on average donated in 1970 ($349) and roughly triple what people gave in 1950 ($179). Starting in 1977, pollsters also began regularly asking adults whether they were involved in charity or social services, such as helping the poor, the sick, or the elderly. The ranks of those participating roughly doubled from 26 percent in 1977 to 54 percent in 1995. Volunteer work by college students is up, too. In 1998, 74 percent of college freshmen had done volunteer work the preceding year, the highest such figure since researchers started tracking it in 1984.

Charity has often gone hand in hand with religion, so perhaps it is not surprising to learn that religious faith, too, is not in decline. On the contrary, America remains a deeply religious nation, with a reinvigorated evangelical movement. In 1997, the Gallup Poll replicated one of its earliest surveys on Americans' religious practices from 1947. The 50-year update found that the same percentage of Americans pray (90 percent), believe in God (96 percent), and attend church once a week. One of the few differences between the two eras was that Americans were actually more likely to give grace or give thanks aloud in 1997 than in 1947 (63 percent compared with 43 percent).

Both adults and teens are now as likely to belong to a church or synagogue as their counterparts were 25 years ago, and they attend religious services a bit more often. Two months ago, at the start of December, 42 percent of adults reported attending a service at a church or synagogue the previous week—a tad higher than the 40 percent or so who said they had attended services in 1972, 1950, and 1940. As the political scientist Seymour Martin Lipset writes in his book *American Exceptionalism,* "Religious affiliation and belief in America are much higher in the twentieth century than in the nineteenth, and have not decreased in the post–World War II era."

While everyone "knows" that cheating on tests has exploded in recent decades, the few studies that have looked at trends over time suggest a different picture. A 1996 analysis by Donald McCabe and Linda Klebe Trevino of Rutgers University at nine state universities did find that cheating on tests and exams increased significantly from 1963 to 1993. But serious cheating on written work, such as plagiarism and turning in work done by others, had declined slightly, leading the researchers to conclude that "the dramatic upsurge in cheating heralded by the media was not found."

Cheating on taxes also appears to be no worse than in the recent past. Since 1973, the Internal Revenue Service has tracked the "voluntary compliance rate," a figure used to describe the percentage of total tax liability that individuals and corporations pay voluntarily. In 1992, the voluntary compliance rate for the individual income tax was roughly 83 percent, a hair higher than in 1973.

As for another vice—drug use—Americans seem to be doing better, not worse. Use of illicit drugs peaked in 1979, when 14.1 percent of the population reported having used an illicit drug the previous month, more than double the 1997 figure of 6.4 percent. Cocaine use peaked in 1985; Americans were four times as likely to use cocaine then as they are today. The trends are similar among high school seniors (though marijuana use has risen since 1992).

At the same time, heavy alcohol consumption, binge drinking, and drunken driving have all declined. Heavy alcohol use—defined as having five or more drinks on the same occasion on each of five or more days in the previous months—at its lowest point since 1985, when the federal government first started tracking the figure. In 1985, 8.3 percent of the population were heavy drinkers compared with 5.4 percent in 1997, a drop of about a third. The decline in drunken driving has been equally marked. In 1997, the number of people killed in alcohol-related crashes dropped to less than 40 percent of all traffic fatalities for the first time since the government started tracking this statistic in 1975. Americans consumed about as much alcohol per person in 1995 as in 1945—and drank substantially less than in 1970.

For all the talk of scandal, and despite the official statistics, political corruption seems to be waning, too. In 1996, 952 individuals were indicted in federal prosecutions for public corruption, more than triple the number in 1975. Yet most historians believe the apparent rise in corruption stems from the proliferation of special prosecutors and inspector generals, not from a real upsurge in unethical conduct. New disclosure rules, government intercessions in allegedly corrupt unions, a law enforcement crackdown on the mob, the disappearance of Tammany Hall–style urban political machines and "good-time Charlie" governors, and a more watchful press all seem to have reduced bribes, hush money, and other blatant types of political corruption. Even William Bennett concedes in *The Death of Outrage* that "in general, politics today is less corrupt than perhaps at any point in American history."

Granted, not all the news on the moral front is good. One institution that undeniably weakened in the past quarter-century is the family. Since the early '70s, out-of-wedlock childbearing has skyrocketed. Child abuse and neglect have risen, too—thanks mainly to the advent of crack—and most noncustodial parents still don't pay their child support.

Yet other much-lamented changes in family life do not really demonstrate a rise (or fall) in collective virtue. The surge in divorce suggests that Americans now lack a sense of commitment, but most divorced couples do not think they are acting immorally—more often, they think they have done the right thing by ending a troubled marriage. Many couples similarly defend cohabitation, once deemed to be "living in sin," as a sensible trial run at marriage.

Some moral behavior that has improved in the past quarter-century, particularly the reduction in criminality and drug-taking, is still worse today than it was in the 1950s. But, even when stacked up against the "good ol' days," there are plenty of signs of moral progress. In the 1950s, well over half of the nation's black population lived under almost apartheid-like conditions through much of the South. Millions of women faced sexual discrimination and were denied the right to pursue a calling of their own. Society treated the elderly shabbily, with more than one in three living in poverty (compared with one in ten today). The disabled faced blatant, ugly bigotry, as did homosexuals.

Why hasn't the news about moral progress reached the public? In part, the reason is that it is often thought that people were more moral in earlier eras. Back in 1939, a Gallup Poll showed that 62 percent of the population believed that Americans were happier and more contented in the horse-and-buggy days; a survey taken by Elmo Roper two years earlier found that half of the population felt religion was then losing its influence on American life as well.

But part of the explanation for the public disbelief is that Americans experience an "optimism gap." When members of the public voice distress about family breakdown they are almost always referring to other people's families. Yet the vast majority of citizens do not have serious moral qualms about themselves or their families. Surveys show that most people think they are more moral than the average American, and members of the public repeatedly describe their own families as happy ones with strong ties.

In 1997, *U.S. News & World Report* conducted a revealing survey of 1,000 adults who were asked to rate the chances that various celebrities would one day get into heaven. Topping the list of famous people bound for heaven was Mother Teresa, who had not yet died. Nearly 80 percent of those polled thought it likely that the Nobel Peace Prize winner would one day get her wings. But the survey's most startling finding was that the individuals voted most likely to get into heaven were, well, those being polled. Eighty-seven percent felt that they were heaven-bound, compared with 79 percent who thought the same of Mother Teresa.

Most Americans, in short, hold a generous opinion of their own morals, even while they remain acutely aware of others' failings. But, if Americans can convince themselves that they are bound for heaven, it may also be time to acknowledge that the rest of the nation is not making a beeline for purgatory.

DAVID WHITMAN is a senior writer at *U.S. News & World Report* and the author of *The Optimism Gap: The I'm OK—They're Not Syndrome and the Myth of American Decline* (Walker and Company).

American Culture Goes Global, or Does It?

By RICHARD PELLS

Since September 11, newspaper and magazine columnists and television pundits have told us that it is not only the economic power of the United States or the Bush administration's "unilateralist" foreign policy that breeds global anti-Americanism. Dislike for the United States stems also, they say, from its "cultural imperialism." We have been hearing a good deal about how American mass culture inspires resentment and sometimes violent reactions, not just in the Middle East but all over the world.

Yet the discomfort with American cultural dominance is not new. In 1901, the British writer William Stead published a book called, ominously, *The Americanization of the World*. The title captured a set of apprehensions—about the disappearance of national languages and traditions, and the obliteration of the unique identities of countries under the weight of American habits and states of mind—that persists today.

More recently, globalization has become the main enemy for academics, journalists, and political activists who loathe what they see as a trend toward cultural uniformity. Still, they usually regard global culture and American culture as synonymous. And they continue to insist that Hollywood, McDonald's, and Disneyland are eradicating regional and local eccentricities—disseminating images and subliminal messages so beguiling as to drown out competing voices in other lands.

Despite those allegations, the cultural relationship between the United States and the rest of the world over the past 100 years has never been one-sided. On the contrary, the United States was, and continues to be, as much a consumer of foreign intellectual and artistic influences as it has been a shaper of the world's entertainment and tastes.

That is not an argument with which many foreigners (or even many Americans) would readily agree. The clichés about America's cultural "hegemony" make it difficult for most people to recognize that modern global culture is hardly a monolithic entity foisted on the world by the American media.

Neither is it easy for critics of Microsoft or AOL Time Warner to acknowledge that the conception of a harmonious and distinctively American culture—encircling the globe, implanting its values in foreign minds—is a myth.

In fact, as a nation of immigrants from the 19th to the 21st centuries, and as a haven in the 1930s and '40s for refugee scholars and artists, the United States has been a recipient as much as an exporter of global culture. Indeed, the influence of immigrants and African-Americans on the United States explains why its culture has been so popular for so long in so many places. American culture has spread throughout the world because it has incorporated foreign styles and ideas. What Americans have done more brilliantly than their competitors overseas is repackage the cultural products we receive from abroad and then retransmit them to the rest of the planet. In effect, Americans have specialized in selling the dreams, fears, and folklore of other people back to them. That is why a global mass culture has come to be identified, however simplistically, with the United States.

Americans, after all, did not invent fast food, amusement parks, or the movies. Before the Big Mac, there were fish and chips. Before Disneyland, there was Copenhagen's Tivoli Gardens (which Walt Disney used as a prototype for his first theme park, in Anaheim, a model later re-exported to Tokyo and Paris).

Nor can the origins of today's international entertainment be traced only to P.T. Barnum or Buffalo Bill. The roots of the new global culture lie as well in the European modernist assault, in the early 20th century, on 19th-century literature, music, painting, and architecture—particularly in the modernist refusal to honor the traditional boundaries between high and low culture. Modernism in the arts was improvisational, eclectic, and irreverent. Those traits have also been characteristic of, but not peculiar to, mass culture.

The hallmark of 19th-century culture, in Europe and also in Asia, was its insistence on defending the purity of literature, classical music, and representational painting against the intrusions of folklore and popular amusements. No one confused Tolstoy with dime novels, opera with Wild West shows, the Louvre with Coney Island. High culture was supposed to be educational, contemplative, and uplifting—a way of preserving the best in human civilization.

Such beliefs didn't mean that a Dickens never indulged in melodrama, or that a Brahms disdained the use of popular songs. Nor did Chinese or Japanese authors and painters refuse to draw on oral or folkloric traditions. But the 19th-century barriers between high and low culture were resolutely, if imperfectly, maintained.

The artists of the early 20th century shattered what seemed to them the artificial demarcations between different cultural forms. They also challenged the notion that culture was a means of intellectual or moral improvement. They did so by emphasizing style and craftsmanship at the expense of philosophy, religion, or ideology. They deliberately called attention to language in their novels, to optics in their paintings, to the materials in and function of their architecture, to the structure of music instead of its melodies.

And they wanted to shock their audiences. Which they succeeded in doing. Modern painting and literature—with its emphasis on visually distorted nudes, overt sexuality, and meditations on violence—was attacked for being degrading and obscene, and for appealing to the baser instincts of humanity. In much the same way, critics would later denounce the vulgarity of popular culture.

Although modernism assaulted the conventions of 19th-century high culture in Europe and Asia, it inadvertently accelerated the growth of mass culture in the United States. Indeed, Americans were already receptive to the blurring of cultural boundaries. In the 19th century, symphony orchestras in the United States often included band music in their programs, and opera singers were asked to perform both Mozart and Stephen Foster.

So, for Americans in the 20th century, Surrealism, with its dreamlike associations, easily lent itself to the wordplay and psychological symbolism of advertising, cartoons, and theme parks. Dadaism ridiculed the snobbery of elite cultural institutions and reinforced, instead, an existing appetite (especially among the immigrant audiences in the United States) for low-class, anti-bourgeois nickelodeons and vaudeville shows. Stravinsky's experiments with atonal (and thus unconventional and unmelodic) music validated the rhythmic innovations of American jazz. Writers like Hemingway, detesting the rhetorical embellishments of 19th-century prose, invented a terse, hard-boiled language, devoted to reproducing as authentically as possible the elemental qualities of personal experience. That laconic style became a model for modern journalism, detective fiction, and movie dialogue.

All of those trends provided the foundations for a genuinely new culture. But the new culture turned out to be neither modernist nor European. Instead, the United States transformed what was still a parochial culture, appealing largely to the young and the rebellious in Western society, into a global phenomenon.

The propensity of Americans to borrow modernist ideas, and to transform them into a global culture, is clearly visible in the commercial uses of modern architecture. The European Bauhaus movement—intended in the 1920s as a socialist experiment in working-class housing—eventually provided the theories and techniques for the construction of skyscrapers and vacation homes in the United States. But the same architectural ideas were then sent back to Europe after World War II as a model for the reconstruction of bombed-out cities like Rotterdam, Cologne, and Frankfurt. Thus, the United States converted what had once been a distinctive, if localized, rebellion by Dutch and German architects into a generic "international style."

But it is in popular culture that the reciprocal relationship between America and the rest of the world can best be seen. There are many reasons for the ascendancy of American mass culture. Certainly, the ability of American-based media conglomerates to control the production and distribution of their products has been a major stimulus to the worldwide spread of American entertainment. But the power of American capitalism is not the only, or even the most important, explanation for the global popularity of America's movies and television shows.

The effectiveness of English as a language of mass communications has been essential to the acceptance of American culture. Unlike, for example, German, Russian, or Chinese, the simple structure and grammar of English, along with its tendency to use shorter, less-abstract words and more-concise sentences, are all advantageous for the composers of song lyrics, ad slogans, cartoon captions, newspaper headlines, and movie and TV dialogue. English is thus a language exceptionally well-suited to the demands and spread of American mass culture.

American musicians and entertainers have followed modernist artists like Picasso and Braque in drawing on elements from high and low culture.

Another factor is the size of the American audience. A huge domestic market has made it possible for many American filmmakers and TV executives to retrieve most of their production costs and make a profit within the borders of the United States. That economic cushion has enabled them to spend more money on stars, sets, special effects, location shooting, and merchandising—the very ingredients that attract international audiences as well.

Yet even with such advantages, America's mass culture may not be all that American. The American audience is not only large; because of the influx of immigrants and refugees, it is also international in its complexion. The heterogeneity of America's population—its regional, ethnic, religious, and racial diversity—has forced the media, since the early years of the 20th century, to experiment with messages, images, and story lines that have a broad multicultural appeal. The Hollywood studios, mass-circulation magazines, and television networks have had to learn how to speak to a variety of groups and classes at home. That has given them the techniques to appeal to an equally diverse audience abroad. The American domestic market has, in essence, been a laboratory, a place to develop cultural products that can then be adapted to the world market.

An important way that the American media have succeeded in transcending internal social divisions, national borders, and language barriers is by mixing up cultural styles. American musicians and entertainers have followed the example of modernist artists like Picasso and Braque in drawing on elements from high and low culture, combining the sacred and the profane. Advertisers have adapted the techniques of Surrealism and Abstract Expressionism to make their products more intriguing. Composers like Aaron Copland, George Gershwin, and Leonard Bernstein incorporated folk melodies, religious hymns, blues, gospel songs, and jazz into their symphonies, concertos, operas, and ballets. Indeed, an art form as quintessentially American as jazz evolved during the 20th century into an amalgam of African, Caribbean, Latin American, and modernist European music. That blending of forms in America's mass culture has enhanced its appeal to multiethnic domestic and international audiences by capturing their varied experiences and tastes.

NOWHERE ARE FOREIGN INFLUENCES more evident than in the American movie industry. For better or worse, Hollywood became, in the 20th century, the cultural capital of the modern world. But it was never an exclusively American capital. Like past cultural centers—Florence, Paris, Vienna—Hollywood has functioned as an international community, built by immigrant entrepreneurs and drawing on the talents of actors, directors, writers, cinematographers, editors, and costume and set designers from all over the world. The first American movie star, after all, was Charlie Chaplin, whose comic skills were honed in British music halls.

Moreover, during much of the 20th century, American moviemakers thought of themselves as acolytes, entranced by the superior works of foreign directors. In the 1920s, few American directors could gain admittance to a European pantheon that included Sergei Eisenstein, F.W. Murnau, G.W. Pabst, Fritz Lang, and Carl Dreyer. The postwar years, from the 1940s to the mid-'60s, were once again a golden age of filmmaking in Britain, Sweden, France, Italy, Japan, and India. An extraordinary generation of foreign directors—Ingmar Bergman, Federico Fellini, Michelangelo Antonioni, François Truffaut, Jean-Luc Godard, Akira Kurosawa, Satyajit Ray—were the world's most celebrated auteurs.

Nevertheless, it is one of the paradoxes of the European and Asian cinemas that their greatest success was in spawning American imitations. After the release, in 1967, of *Bonnie and Clyde* (originally to have been directed by Truffaut or Godard), the newest geniuses—Francis Ford Coppola, Martin Scorsese, Robert Altman, Steven Spielberg, Woody Allen—were American. They may have owed their improvisational methods and autobiographical preoccupations to Italian neo-Realism and the French New Wave. But who, in any country, needed to see another *La Dolce Vita* when you could enjoy *Nashville*? Why try to decipher *Jules and Jim* or *L'Avventura* when you could see *Annie Hall* or *The Godfather*? Wasn't it conceivable that *The Seven Samurai* might not be as powerful or as disturbing a movie as *The Wild Bunch*?

It turned out that foreign filmmakers had been too influential for their own good. They helped revolutionize the American cinema, so that, after the 1960s and '70s, it became hard for any other continent's film industry to match the worldwide popularity of American movies.

Once again, however, we need to remember that Hollywood movies have never been just American. To take another example, American directors, in all eras, have emulated foreign artists and filmmakers by paying close attention to the style and formal qualities of a movie, and to the need to tell a story visually. Early-20th-century European painters wanted viewers to recognize that they were looking at lines and color on a canvas rather than at a reproduction of the natural world. Similarly, many American films—from the multiple narrators in *Citizen Kane*, to the split-screen portrait of how two lovers imagine their relationship in *Annie Hall*, to the flashbacks and flash-forwards in *Pulp Fiction*, to the roses blooming from the navel of Kevin Spacey's fantasy dream girl in *American Beauty*—deliberately remind the audience that it is watching a movie instead of a play or a photographed version of reality. American filmmakers (not only in the movies but also on MTV) have been willing to use the most sophisticated techniques of editing and camera work, much of it inspired by European directors, to create a modernist collage of images that captures the speed and seductiveness of life in the contemporary world.

Hollywood's addiction to modernist visual pyrotechnics is especially evident in the largely nonverbal style of many of its contemporary performers. The tendency to mumble was not always in vogue. In the 1930s and '40s, the sound and meaning of words were important not only in movies but also on records and the radio. Even though some homegrown stars, like John Wayne and Gary Cooper, were famously terse, audiences could at least hear and understand what they were saying. But the centrality of language in the films of the 1930s led, more often, to a dependence in Hollywood on British actors (like Cary Grant), or on Americans who sounded vaguely British (like Katharine Hepburn and Bette Davis). It is illustrative of how important foreign (especially British) talent was to Hollywood in an earlier era that the two most famous Southern belles in American fiction and drama—Scarlett O'Hara and Blanche DuBois—were played in the movies by Vivien Leigh.

The verbal eloquence of pre-World War II acting, in both movies and the theater, disappeared after 1945. After Marlon Brando's revolutionary performance in *A Streetcar Named Desire*, in the 1947 stage version and the 1951 screen version, the model of American acting became inarticulateness—a brooding and halting introspection that one doesn't find in the glib and clever heroes or heroines of the screwball comedies and gangster films of the '30s. Brando was trained in the Method, an acting technique originally developed in Stanislavsky's Moscow Art Theater in prerevolutionary Russia, then imported to New York by members of the Group Theater during the 1930s. Where British actors, trained in Shakespeare, were taught to subordinate their personalities to the role as written, the Method encouraged actors to improvise, to summon up childhood memories, and to explore their inner feelings, often at the expense of what the playwright or screenwriter intended. Norman Mailer once said that Brando, in his pauses and his gazes into the middle distance, always seemed to be searching for a better line than the one the writer had composed. In effect, what Brando did (along with his successors and imitators, from James Dean to Warren Beatty to Robert De Niro) was to lead a revolt against the British school of acting, with its reverence for the script and the written (and spoken) word.

Thus, after World War II, the emotional power of American acting lay more in what was not said, in what could not even be communicated in words. The Method actor's reliance on physical mannerisms and even silence in interpreting a role has been especially appropriate for a cinema that puts a premium on the inexpressible. Indeed, the influence of the Method, not only in the United States but also abroad (where it was reflected in the acting styles of Jean-Paul Belmondo and Marcello Mastroianni), is a classic example of how a foreign idea, originally meant for the stage, was adapted in postwar America to the movies, and then conveyed to the rest of the world as a paradigm for both cinematic and social behavior. More important, the Method's disregard for language permitted global audiences—even those not well-versed in English—to understand and appreciate what they were watching in American films.

FINALLY, American culture has imitated not only the modernists' visual flamboyance, but also their emphasis on personal expression and their tendency to be apolitical and anti-ideological. The refusal to browbeat an audience with a social message has accounted, more than any other factor, for the worldwide popularity of American entertainment. American movies, in particular, have customarily focused on human relationships and private feelings, not on the problems of a particular time and place. They tell tales about romance, intrigue, success, failure, moral conflicts, and survival. The most memorable movies of the 1930s (with the exception of *The Grapes of Wrath*) were comedies and musicals about mismatched people falling in love, not socially conscious films dealing with issues of poverty and unemployment. Similarly, the finest movies about World War II (like *Casablanca*) or the Vietnam War (like *The Deer Hunter*) linger in the mind long after those conflicts have ended because they explore their characters' intimate emotions rather than dwelling on headline events.

Such intensely personal dilemmas are what people everywhere wrestle with. So Europeans, Asians, and Latin Americans flocked to *Titanic* (as they once did to *Gone With the Wind*) not because it celebrated American values, but because people all over the world could see some part of their own lives reflected in the story of love and loss.

America's mass culture has often been crude and intrusive, as its critics—from American academics like Benjamin Barber to German directors like Wim Wenders—have always complained. In their eyes, American culture is "colonizing" everyone else's subconscious, reducing us all to passive residents of "McWorld."

But American culture has never felt all that foreign to foreigners. And, at its best, it has transformed what it received from others into a culture that everyone, everywhere, can embrace, a culture that is both emotionally and, on occasion, artistically compelling for millions of people throughout the world.

So, despite the current hostility to America's policies and values—in Europe and Latin America as well as in the Middle East and Asia—it is important to recognize how familiar much of American culture seems to people abroad. If anything, our movies, television shows, and theme parks have been less "imperialistic" than cosmopolitan. In the end, American mass culture has not transformed the world into a replica of the United States. Instead, America's dependence on foreign cultures has made the United States a replica of the world.

Richard Pells is a professor of history at the University of Texas at Austin. His books include Not Like Us: How Europeans Have Loved, Hated, and Transformed American Culture Since World War II (*Basic Books, 1997*).

Originally published in *The Chronicle of Higher Education*, April 12, 2002, pp. B7, B9. © 2002 by Richard Pells. Reprinted by permission.

What's So Great About America?

By Dinesh D'Souza

The newcomer who sees America for the first time typically experiences emotions that alternate between wonder and delight. Here is a country where *everything works*: The roads are paper-smooth, the highway signs are clear and accurate, the public toilets function properly, when you pick up the telephone you get a dial tone. You can even buy things from the store and then take them *back* if you change your mind. For the Third World visitor, the American supermarket is a marvel to behold: endless aisles of every imaginable product, 50 different types of cereal, multiple flavors of ice cream, countless unappreciated inventions like quilted toilet paper, fabric softener, roll-on deodorant, disposable diapers.

The immigrant cannot help noticing that America is a country where the poor live comparatively well. This fact was dramatized in the 1980s, when CBS television broadcast an anti-Reagan documentary, "People Like Us," which was intended to show the miseries of the poor during an American recession. The Soviet Union also broadcast the documentary, with the intention of embarrassing the Reagan administration. But it had the opposite effect. Ordinary people across the Soviet Union saw that the poorest Americans had television sets and cars. They arrived at the same conclusion that I witnessed in a friend of mine from Bombay who has been trying unsuccessfully to move to the United States for nearly a decade. I asked him, "Why are you so eager to come to America?" He replied, "Because I really want to live in a country where the poor people are fat."

The point is that the United States is a country where the ordinary guy has a good life. This is what distinguishes America from so many other countries. Everywhere in the world, the rich person lives well. Indeed, a good case can be made that if you are rich, you live better in countries other than America, because you enjoy the pleasures of aristocracy. In India, where I grew up, the wealthy have innumerable servants and toadies groveling before them and attending to their every need.

In the United States, on the other hand, the social ethic is egalitarian, regardless of wealth. For all his riches, Bill Gates could not approach a homeless person and say, "Here's a $100 bill. I'll give it to you if you kiss my feet."

Most likely the homeless guy would tell Gates to go to hell. The American view is that the rich guy may have more money, but he isn't in any fundamental sense better than you are. The American janitor or waiter sees himself as performing a service, but he doesn't see himself as inferior to those he serves. And neither do the customers see him that way: They are generally happy to show him respect and appreciation on a plane of equality. America is the only country in the world where we call the waiter "Sir," as if he were a knight.

The moral triumph of America is that it has extended the benefits of comfort and affluence, traditionally enjoyed by very few, to a large segment of society. Very few people in America have to wonder where their next meal is coming from. Even sick people who don't have money or insurance will receive medical care at hospital emergency rooms. The poorest American girls are not humiliated by having to wear torn clothes. Every child is given an education, and most have the chance to go on to college. The common man can expect to live long enough and have enough free time to play with his grandchildren.

Ordinary Americans not only enjoy security and dignity, but also comforts that other societies reserve for the elite. We now live in a country where construction workers regularly pay $4 for a cappuccino, where maids drive nice cars, where plumbers take their families on vacation to Europe. As Irving Kristol once observed, there is virtually no restaurant in America to which a CEO can go to lunch with the absolute assurance that he will not find his secretary also dining there. Given the standard of living of the ordinary American, it is no wonder that socialist or revolutionary schemes have never found a wide constituency in the United States. As Werner Sombart observed, all socialist utopias in America have come to grief on roast beef and apple pie.

Thus it is entirely understandable that people would associate the idea of America with a better life. For them, money is not an end in itself; money is the means to a longer, healthier, and fuller life. Money allows them to purchase a level of security, dignity, and comfort not available in other countries. Money also frees up time for family life, community involvement, and spiritual pursuits, and so provides moral as well as material gains.

Yet even this offers an incomplete picture of why America is so appealing to so many outsiders. Let me illustrate with the example of my own life. Not long ago, I asked myself: What would my existence have been like had I never come to the United States, if I had stayed in India? Materially, my life has improved, but not in a fundamental sense. I grew up in a middle-class family in Bombay. My father was a chemical engineer; my mother, an office secretary. I was raised without great luxury, but neither did I lack for anything. My standard of living in America is higher, but it is not a radical difference. My life has changed far more dramatically in other ways.

Had I remained in India, I would probably have lived my entire existence within a one-mile radius of where I was born. I would undoubtedly have married a woman of my identical religious, socioeconomic, and cultural background. I would almost certainly have become a medical doctor, an engineer, or a software programmer. I would have socialized within my ethnic community and had few real friends outside that group. I would have a whole set of opinions that could be predicted in advance; indeed, they would not be very different from what my father believed, or his father before him. In sum, my destiny would to a large degree have been given to me.

Instead, I came to Arizona in 1978 as a high-school exchange student, then a year later enrolled at Dartmouth College. There I fell in with a group of students who were actively involved in politics; soon I had switched my major from economics to English literature. My reading included books like Plutarch's *Moralia*; Hamilton, Madison, and Jay's *Federalist Papers*; and Evelyn Waugh's *Brideshead Revisited*. They transported me to places a long way from home and implanted in my mind ideas that I had never previously considered. By the time I graduated, I decided that I should become a writer. America permits many strange careers: This is a place where you can become, say, a comedian. That is very different from most places.

If there is a single phrase that encapsulates life in the Third World, it is that "birth is destiny." A great deal of importance is attached to what tribe you come from, whether you are male or female, and whether you are the eldest son or not. Once your tribe, caste, sex and family position have been established at birth, your life takes a course that is largely determined for you.

In America, by contrast, you get to write the script of your own life. When your parents say to you, "What do you want to be when you grow up?" the question is open ended, it is you who supply the answer. Your parents can advise you: "Have you considered law school?" "Why not become the first doctor in the family?" It is considered very improper, however, for them to try to force your decision. Indeed, American parents typically send their teenage children away to college where they live on their own and learn independence. This is part of the process of forming your mind, choosing a field of interest for yourself, and developing your identity.

It is not uncommon in the United States for two brothers who come from the same gene pool and were raised in similar circumstances to do quite different things: The eldest becomes a gas station attendant, the younger moves up to be vice president at Oracle; the eldest marries his high-school sweetheart and raises four kids; the youngest refuses to settle down; one is the Methodist that he was raised to be, the other becomes a Christian Scientist. What to be, where to live, whom to marry, what to believe, what religion to practice—these are all decisions that Americans make for themselves.

In America your destiny is not prescribed; it is constructed. Your life is like a blank sheet of paper and you are the artist. This notion of being the architect of your own destiny is the incredibly powerful idea that is behind the worldwide appeal of America. Young people especially find the prospect of authoring their own lives irresistible. The immigrant discovers that America permits him to break free of the constraints that have held him captive, so that the future becomes a landscape of his own choosing.

If there is a single phrase that captures this, it is "the pursuit of happiness." As writer V. S. Naipaul notes, "much is contained" in that simple phrase: "the idea of the individual, responsibility, choice, the life of the intellect, the idea of vocation, perfectibility, and achievement. It is an immense human idea. It cannot be reduced to a fixed system. It cannot generate fanaticism. But it is known [around the world] to exist; and because of that, other more rigid systems in the end blow away."

But where did the "pursuit of happiness" come from? And why has it come in America to mean something much more than simple selfishness? America's founders were religious men. They believed that political legitimacy derives from God. Yet they were determined not to permit theological differences to become the basis for political conflict.

The American system refused to establish a national church, instead recognizing all citizens as free to practice their own religion. From the beginning the United States was made up of numerous sects. The Puritans dominated in Massachusetts, the Anglicans in Virginia, the Catholics were concentrated in Maryland, so it was in every group's interest to "live and let live." The ingenuity of the American solution is evident in Voltaire's remark that where there is one religion, you have tyranny; where there are two, you have religious war; but where they are many, you have freedom.

One reason the American founders were able to avoid religious oppression and conflict is that they found a way to channel people's energies away from theological quarrels and into commercial activity. The American system is founded on property rights and trade, and *The Federalist* tells us that protection of the obtaining of property is "the first object of government." The founders reasoned that people who are working assiduously to better their condition are not likely to go around spearing their neighbors.

Capitalism gives America a this-worldly focus that allows death and the afterlife to recede from everyday view. Along with their heavenly aspirations, the gaze of the people is shifted to earthly progress. This "lowering of the sights" convinces many critics that American capitalism is a base, degraded system and that the energies that drive it are crass and immoral.

These modern critiques draw on some very old prejudices. In the ancient world, labor was generally despised. The Greeks looked down on merchants and traders as low-lifes. "The gentleman understands what is noble," Confucius writes in his *Analects*, "the small man understands what is profitable." In the Indian caste system the *vaisya* or trader occupies nearly the lowest rung of the ladder—one step up from the despised "untouchable." The Muslim historian Ibn Khaldun suggests that even gain by conquest is preferable to gain by trade, because conquest embodies the virtues of courage and manliness. In these traditions, the honorable life is devoted to philosophy or the priesthood or military valor. "Making a living" was considered a necessary, but undignified, pursuit. Far better to rout your adversary, kill the men, enslave the women and children, and make off with a bunch of loot than to improve your lot by buying and selling stuff.

Drawing on the inspiration of philosophers like John Locke and Adam Smith, the American founders altered this moral hierarchy. They argued that trade based on consent and mutual gain was preferable to plunder. The founders established a regime in which the self-interest of entrepreneurs and workers would be directed toward serving the wants and needs of others. In this view, the ordinary life, devoted to production, serving the customer, and supporting a family, is a noble and dignified endeavor. Hard work, once considered a curse, now becomes socially acceptable, even honorable. Commerce, formerly a degraded thing, now becomes a virtue.

Of course the founders recognized that in both the private and the public sphere, greedy and ambitious people can pose a danger to the well-being of others. Instead of trying to outlaw these passions, the founders attempted a different approach. As the fifty-first book of *The Federalist* puts it, "Ambition must be made to counteract ambition." In a free society, "the security for civil rights [consists] in the multiplicity of interests." The framers of the Constitution reasoned that by setting interests against each other, by making them compete, no single one could become strong enough to imperil the welfare of the whole.

In the public sphere the founders took special care to devise a system that would minimize the abuse of power. They established limited government, in order that the power of the state would remain confined. They divided authority between the national and state governments. Within the national framework, they provided for separation of powers, so that the legislature, executive, and judiciary would each have its own domain of authority. They insisted upon checks and balances, to enhance accountability.

The founders didn't ignore the importance of virtue, but they knew that virtue is not always in abundant supply. According to Christianity, the problem of the bad person is that his will is corrupted, a fault endemic to human nature. America's founders knew they could not transform human nature, so they devised a system that would thwart the schemes of the wicked and channel the energies of flawed persons toward the public good.

The experiment that the founders embarked upon more than two centuries ago has largely succeeded in achieving its goals. Tribal and religious battles such as we see in Lebanon, Mogadishu, Kashmir, and Belfast don't happen here. Whites and African Americans have lunch together. Americans of Jewish and Palestinian descent collaborate on software problems and play racquetball after work. Hindus and Muslims, Serbs and Croats, Turks and Armenians, Irish Catholics and British Protestants, all seem to have forgotten their ancestral differences and joined the vast and varied American parade. Everybody wants to "make it," to "get ahead," to "hit it big." And even as they compete, people recognize that somehow they are all in this together, in pursuit of some great, elusive American dream. In this respect America is a glittering symbol to the world.

America's founders solved two great problems which are a source of perennial misery and conflict in many other societies—the problem of scarcity, and the problem of religious and tribal conflict. They invented a new regime in which citizens would enjoy a wide range of freedoms—economic freedom, political freedom, and freedom of speech and religion—in order to shape their own lives and pursue happiness. By protecting religion and government from each other, and by directing the energies of the citizens toward trade and commerce, the American founders created a rich, dynamic, and peaceful society. It is now the hope of countless millions all across the world.

Dinesh D'Souza, Rishwain Fellow at the Hoover Institution, is author of What's So Great About America, *from which this is adapted.*

UNIT 2

Socialization and Social Control

Unit Selections

Key Points to Consider

- What are the major differences between the ways that boys and girls are socialized?

- How can the ways in which children are socialized in America be improved?

- Why is socialization a lifelong process?

- What are the principal factors that make people what they are?

- What are the major ways to reduce crime in the United States, and how effective are they?

- How can the recently revealed problem of pedophilia in the Roman Catholic Church be explained?

 **Links: www.dushkin.com/online/**
These sites are annotated in the World Wide Web pages.

Center for Leadership Studies
   http://www.situational.com
Crime Times
   http://www.crime-times.org
Ethics Updates/Lawrence Hinman
   http://ethics.acusd.edu
National Institute on Drug Abuse (NIDA)
   http://165.112.78.61/
Sexual Assault Information Page
   http://web.archive.org/web//http://www.cs.utk.edu/~bartley/saInfoPage.html*

Why do we behave the way we do? Three forces are at work: biology, socialization, and the human will or internal decision maker. The focus in sociology is on socialization, which is the conscious and unconscious process whereby we learn the norms and behavior patterns that enable us to function appropriately in our social environment. Socialization is based on the need to belong, because the desire for acceptance is the major motivation for internalizing the socially approved attitudes and behaviors. Fear of punishment is another motivation. It is utilized by parents and institutionalized in the law enforcement system. The language we use, the concepts we apply in thinking, the images we have of ourselves, our gender roles, and our masculine and feminine ideals are all learned through socialization. Socialization may take place in many contexts. The most basic socialization takes place in the family, but churches, schools, communities, the media, and workplaces also play major roles in the process.

The first subsection deals with issues concerning the basic influences on the development of our character and behavior patterns. First, Matt Ridley reviews the latest science on the nature versus nurture debate. It is clear that both are important and now we are learning that there is an interaction between genes and the environment. Ridley explains that "genes are not static blueprints that dictate our destiny. How they are expressed— where and when they are turned on or off and for how long—is affected by changes in the womb, by the environment and by other factors." Ridley also explains many other differences. In the next article, Hara Estroff Marano reviews the literature on the genetic differences between men and women, including mental, sexual, health, emotional, and psychological differences. For example, did you know that women have more gray brain matter and men have more white brain matter? Gray matter provides concentrated processing power and more thought linking capability. White matter helps spatial reasoning and allows a single mindedness.

The next subsection deals with crime, law enforcement, and social control—major concerns today because crime and violence seem to be out of control. In the first article in this subsection, Gene Stephens describes crime trends throughout the world but focuses on the United States. Overall crime rates in the United States were the highest in the Western world in 1980 but have fallen in the United States and increased in many other nations so that several Western countries now have higher rates. Nevertheless, the U.S. murder rate is still the highest. Stephens presents three competing explanations for the crime decline in the United States: 1) greater success of the justice system in catching and locking up criminals, 2) the lowering of the percent of the population in the high crime ages, 3) the greater prevalence and success of community based approaches.

In the next article Jennifer Roback Morse argues that "for some people, prisons are a substitute for parents... [for] without parents — two of them, married to each other, working together as a team a child is more likely to end up in the criminal justice system." A key role of parents is to help a child develop a conscience and self—control, and two loving married parents do this job the best. Morse shows that dealing with criminals is very costly for society and indirectly the failure of many marriages contributes substantially to these costs. In the final article, Clifton Leaf describes the prevalence, impacts, and punishment of white—collar crime with an emphasis on securities and commodities fraud. White collar crime is fairly common, seldom punished, fines are light and jail time is short, and is responsible for hundreds of times the financial loss of theft and burglary.

WHAT MAKES YOU WHO YOU ARE

Which is stronger—nature or nurture?
The latest science says genes and your
experience interact for your whole life

By MATT RIDLEY

THE PERENNIAL DEBATE ABOUT NATURE AND NURTURE—which is the more potent shaper of the human essence?—is perennially rekindled. It flared up again in the London *Observer* of Feb. 11, 2001. REVEALED: THE SECRET OF HUMAN BEHAVIOR, read the banner headline. ENVIRONMENT, NOT GENES, KEY TO OUR ACTS. The source of the story was Craig Venter, the self-made man of genes who had built a private company to read the full sequence of the human genome in competition with an international consortium funded by taxes and charities. That sequence—a string of 3 billion letters, composed in a four-letter alphabet, containing the complete recipe for building and running a human body—was to be published the very next day (the competition ended in an arranged tie). The first analysis of it had revealed that there were just 30,000 genes in it, not the 100,000 that many had been estimating until a few months before.

Details had already been circulated to journalists under embargo. But Venter, by speaking to a reporter at a biotechnology conference in France on Feb. 9, had effectively broken the embargo. Not for the first time in the increasingly bitter rivalry over the genome project, Venter's version of the story would hit the headlines before his rivals'. "We simply do not have enough genes for this idea of biological determinism to be right," Venter told the *Observer*. "The wonderful diversity of the human species is not hard-wired in our genetic code. Our environments are critical."

In truth, the number of human genes changed nothing. Venter's remarks concealed two whopping nonsequiturs: that fewer genes implied more environmental influences and that 30,000 genes were too few to explain human nature, whereas 100,000 would have been enough. As one scientist put it to me a few weeks later, just 33 genes, each coming in two varieties (on or off), would be enough to make every human being in the world unique. There are more than 10 billion combinations that could come from flipping a coin 33 times, so 30,000 does not seem such a small number after all. Besides, if fewer genes meant more free will, fruit flies would be freer than we are, bacteria freer still and viruses the John Stuart Mill of biology.

Fortunately, there was no need to reassure the population with such sophisticated calculations. People did not weep at the humiliating news that our genome has only about twice as many genes as a worm's. Nothing had been hung on the number 100,000, which was just a bad guess.

But the human genome project—and the decades of research that preceded it—did force a much more nuanced understanding of how genes work. In the early days, scientists detailed how genes encode the various proteins that make up the cells in our bodies. Their more sophisticated and ultimately more satisfying discovery—that gene expression can be modified by experience—has been gradually emerging since the 1980s. Only now is it dawning on scientists what a big and general idea it implies: that learning itself consists of nothing more than switching genes on and off. The more we lift the lid on the genome, the more vulnerable to experience genes appear to be.

This is not some namby-pamby, middle-of-the-road compromise. This is a new understanding of the fundamental building blocks of life based on the discovery that genes are not immutable things handed down from our parents like Moses' stone tablets but are active participants in our lives, designed to take their cues from everything that happens to us from the moment of our conception.

Early Puberty
Girls raised in FATHERLESS HOUSE-HOLDS experience puberty earlier. Apparently the change in timing is the reaction of a STILL MYSTERIOUS set of genes to their ENVIRONMENT. Scientists don't know how many SETS OF GENES act this way

For the time being, this new awareness has taken its strongest hold among scientists, changing how they think about everything from the way bodies develop in the womb to how new species emerge to the inevitability of homosexuality in some people. (More on all this later.) But eventually, as the general population becomes more attuned to this interdependent view, changes may well occur in areas as diverse as education, medicine, law and religion. Dieters may learn precisely which combination of fats, carbohydrates and proteins has the greatest effect on their individual waistlines. Theologians may develop a whole new theory of free will based on the observation that learning expands our capacity to choose our own path. As was true of Copernicus's observation 500 years ago that the earth orbits the sun, there is no telling how far the repercussions of this new scientific paradigm may extend.

To appreciate what has happened, you will have to abandon cherished notions and open your mind. You will have to enter a world in which your genes are not puppet masters pulling the strings of your behavior but puppets at the mercy of your behavior, in which instinct is not the opposite of learning, environmental influences are often less reversible than genetic ones, and nature is designed for nurture.

Fear of snakes, for instance, is the most common human phobia, and it makes good evolutionary sense for it to be instinctive. Learning to fear snakes the hard way would be dangerous. Yet experiments with monkeys reveal that their fear of snakes (and probably ours) must still be acquired by watching another individual react

with fear to a snake. It turns out that it is easy to teach monkeys to fear snakes but very difficult to teach them to fear flowers. What we inherit is not a fear of snakes but a predisposition to learn a fear of snakes—a nature for a certain kind of nurture.

Before we dive into some of the other scientific discoveries that have so thoroughly transformed the debate, it helps to understand how deeply entrenched in our intellectual history the false dichotomy of nature vs. nurture became. Whether human nature is born or made is an ancient conundrum discussed by Plato and Aristotle. Empiricist philosophers such as John Locke and David Hume argued that the human mind was formed by experience; nativists like Jean-Jacques Rousseau and Immanuel Kant held that there was such a thing as immutable human nature.

It was Charles Darwin's eccentric mathematician cousin Francis Galton who in 1874 ignited the nature-nurture controversy in its present form and coined the very phrase (borrowing the alliteration from Shakespeare, who had lifted it from an Elizabethan schoolmaster named Richard Mulcaster). Galton asserted that human personalities were born, not made by experience. At the same time, the philosopher William James argued that human beings have more instincts than animals, not fewer.

In the first decades of the 20th century, nature held sway over nurture in most fields. In the wake of World War I, however, three men recaptured the social sciences for nurture: John B. Watson, who set out to show how the conditioned reflex, discovered by Ivan Pavlov, could explain human learning; Sigmund Freud, who sought to explain the influence of parents and early experiences on young minds; and Franz Boas, who argued that the origin of ethnic differences lay with history, experience and circumstance, not physiology and psychology.

Homosexuality
GAY MEN are more likely to have OLDER BROTHERS than either gay women or heterosexual men. It may be that a FIRST MALE FETUS triggers an immune reaction in the mother, ALTERING THE EXPRESSION of key gender genes

Galton's insistence on innate explanations of human abilities had led him to espouse eugenics, a term he coined. Eugenics was enthusiastically adopted by the Nazis to justify their campaign of mass murder against the disabled and the Jews. Tainted by this association, the idea of innate behavior was in full retreat for most of the middle years of the century. In 1958, however, two men began the counterattack on behalf of nature. Noam Chomsky, in his review of a book by the behaviorist B.F. Skinner, argued that it was impossible to learn human language by trial and error alone; human beings must come already equipped with an innate grammatical skill. Harry Harlow did a simple experiment that showed that a baby monkey prefers a soft, cloth model of a mother to a hard, wire-frame mother, even if the wire-frame mother provides it with all its milk; some preferences are innate.

Fast-forward to the 1980s and one of the most stunning surprises to greet scientists when they first opened up animal genomes: fly geneticists found a small group of genes called the hox genes that seemed to set out the body plan of the fly during its early development—telling it roughly where to put the head, legs, wings and so on. But then colleagues studying mice found the same hox genes, in the same order, doing the same job in Mickey's world—telling the mouse where to put its various parts. And when scientists looked in our genome, they found hox genes there too.

Hox genes, like all genes, are switched on and off in different parts of the body at different times. In this way, genes can have subtly different effects, depending on where, when and how they are switched on. The switches that control this process—stretches of DNA upstream of genes—are known as promoters.

Small changes in the promoter can have profound effects on the expression of a hox gene. For example, mice have short necks and long bodies; chickens have long necks and short bodies. If you count the vertebrae in the necks and thoraxes of mice and chickens, you will find that a mouse has seven neck and 13 thoracic vertebrae, a chicken 14 and seven, respectively. The source of this difference lies in the promoter attached to HoxC8, a hox gene that helps shape the thorax of the body. The promoter is a 200-letter paragraph of DNA, and in the two species it differs by just a handful of letters. The effect is to alter the expression of the HoxC8 gene in the development of the chicken embryo. This means the chicken makes thoracic vertebrae in a different part of the body than the mouse. In the python, HoxC8 is expressed right from the head and goes on being expressed for most of the body. So pythons are one long thorax; they have ribs all down the body.

Divorce

If a **FRATERNAL TWIN** gets divorced, there's a **30% CHANCE** that his or her twin will get divorced as well. If the twins are **IDENTICAL**, however, one sibling's divorce **BOOSTS THE ODDS** to 45% that the other will split

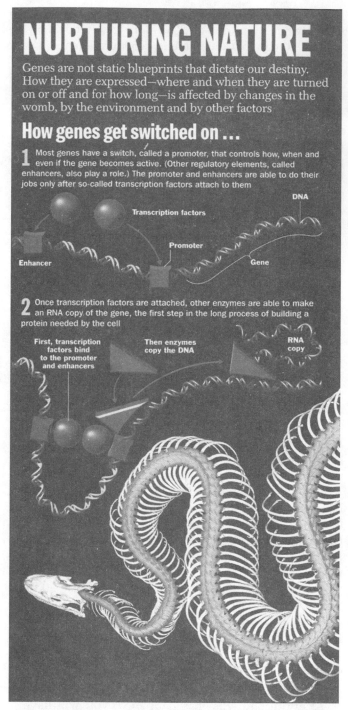

NURTURING NATURE

Genes are not static blueprints that dictate our destiny. How they are expressed—where and when they are turned on or off and for how long—is affected by changes in the womb, by the environment and by other factors

How genes get switched on ...

1 Most genes have a switch, called a promoter, that controls how, when and even if the gene becomes active. (Other regulatory elements, called enhancers, also play a role.) The promoter and enhancers are able to do their jobs only after so-called transcription factors attach to them

Transcription factors

DNA

Enhancer

Promoter

Gene

2 Once transcription factors are attached, other enzymes are able to make an RNA copy of the gene, the first step in the long process of building a protein needed by the cell

First, transcription factors bind to the promoter and enhancers

Then enzymes copy the DNA

RNA copy

(continued)

To make grand changes in the body plan of animals, there is no need to invent new genes, just as there's no need to invent new words to write an original novel (unless your name is Joyce). All you need do is switch the same ones on and off in different patterns. Suddenly, here is a mechanism for creating large and small evolutionary changes from small genetic differences. Merely by adjusting the sequence of a promoter or adding a new one, you could alter the expression of a gene.

In one sense, this is a bit depressing. It means that until scientists know how to find gene promoters in the vast

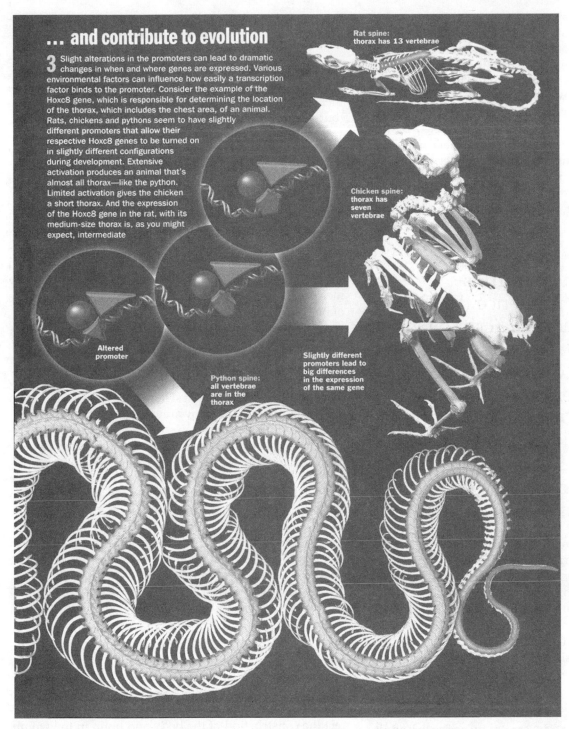

... and contribute to evolution

3 Slight alterations in the promoters can lead to dramatic changes in when and where genes are expressed. Various environmental factors can influence how easily a transcription factor binds to the promoter. Consider the example of the Hoxc8 gene, which is responsible for determining the location of the thorax, which includes the chest area, of an animal. Rats, chickens and pythons seem to have slightly different promoters that allow their respective Hoxc8 genes to be turned on in slightly different configurations during development. Extensive activation produces an animal that's almost all thorax—like the python. Limited activation gives the chicken a short thorax. And the expression of the Hoxc8 gene in the rat, with its medium-size thorax is, as you might expect, intermediate

Rat spine:
thorax has 13 vertebrae

Chicken spine:
thorax has
seven
vertebrae

Altered
promoter

Slightly different
promoters lead to
big differences
in the expression
of the same gene

Python spine:
all vertebrae
are in the
thorax

(continued) Sources: Cooduvalli S. Shashikant, Pennsylvania State University and other associates of Frank Ruddle, Yale University; Anne Burke, Wesleyan University; M.J. Cohn and C. Tickle, University of Reading, Britain

Photos: TED THAI FOR-TIME; TIME Graphic by Joe Lertola

text of the genome, they will not learn how the recipe for a chimpanzee differs from that for a person. But in another sense, it is also uplifting, for it reminds us more forcefully than ever of a simple truth that is all too often forgotten: bodies are not made, they grow. The genome is not a blueprint for constructing a body. It is a recipe for baking a body. You could say the chicken embryo is marinated for a shorter time in the HoxC8 sauce than the mouse embryo is. Likewise, the development of a certain human behavior takes a certain time and occurs in a certain order, just as the cooking of a perfect souffle requires not just the right ingredients but also the right amount of cooking and the right order of events.

How does this new view of genes alter our understanding of human nature? Take a look at four examples.

LANGUAGE   Human beings differ from chimpanzees in having complex, grammatical language. But language does not spring fully formed from the brain; it must be learned from other language-speaking human beings. This capacity to learn is written into the human brain by genes that open and close a critical window during which learning takes place. One of those genes, FoxP2, has recently been discovered on human chromosome 7 by Anthony Monaco and his colleagues at the Wellcome Trust Centre for Human Genetics in Oxford. Just having the FoxP2 gene, though, is not enough. If a child is not exposed to a lot of spoken language during the critical learning period, he or she will always struggle with speech.

Crime Families
GENES may influence the way people respond to a "crimogenic" ENVIRONMENT. How else to explain why the BIOLOGICAL children of criminal parents are more likely than their ADOPTED children to break the LAW?

LOVE   Some species of rodents, such as the prairie vole, form long pair bonds with their mates, as human beings do. Others, such as the montane vole, have only transitory liaisons, as do chimpanzees. The difference, according to Tom Insel and Larry Young at Emory University in Atlanta, lies in the promoter upstream of the oxytocin- and vasopressin-receptor genes. The insertion of an extra chunk of DNA text, usually about 460 letters long, into the promoter makes the animal more likely to bond with its mate. The extra text does not create love, but perhaps it creates the possibility of falling in love after the right experience.

ANTISOCIAL BEHAVIOR   It has often been suggested that childhood maltreatment can create an antisocial adult. New research by Terrie Moffitt of London's Kings College on a group of 442 New Zealand men who have been followed since birth suggests that this is true only for a genetic minority. Again, the difference lies in a promoter that alters the activity of a gene. Those with high-active monoamine oxidase A genes were virtually immune to the effects of mistreatment. Those with low-active genes were much more antisocial if maltreated, yet—if anything—slightly less antisocial if not maltreated. The low-active, mistreated men were responsible for four times their share of rapes, robberies and assaults. In other words, maltreatment is not enough; you must also have the low-active gene. And it is not enough to have the low-active gene; you must also be maltreated.

HOMOSEXUALITY   Ray Blanchard at the University of Toronto has found that gay men are more likely than either lesbians or heterosexual men to have older brothers (but not older sisters). He has since confirmed this observation in 14 samples from many places. Something about occupying a womb that has held other boys occasionally results in reduced birth weight, a larger placenta and a greater probability of homosexuality. That something, Blanchard suspects, is an immune reaction in the mother, primed by the first male fetus, that grows stronger with each male pregnancy. Perhaps the immune response affects the expression of key genes during brain development in a way that boosts a boy's attraction to his own sex. Such an explanation would not hold true for all gay men, but it might provide important clues into the origins of both homosexuality and heterosexuality.

TO BE SURE, EARLIER SCIENTIFIC DISCOVERIES HAD HINTED AT the importance of this kind of interplay between heredity and environment. The most striking example is Pavlovian conditioning. When Pavlov announced his famous experiment a century ago this year, he had apparently discovered how the brain could be changed to acquire new knowledge of the world—in the case of his dogs, knowledge that a bell foretold the arrival of food. But now we know how the brain changes: by the real-time expression of 17 genes, known as the CREB genes. They must be switched on and off to alter connections among nerve cells in the brain and thus lay down a new long-term memory. These genes are at the mercy of our behavior, not the other way around. Memory is in the genes in the sense that it uses genes, not in the sense that you inherit memories.

In this new view, genes allow the human mind to learn, remember, imitate, imprint language, absorb culture and express instincts. Genes are not puppet masters or blueprints, nor are they just the carriers of heredity. They are active during life; they switch one another on and off; they respond to the environment. They may direct the construction of the body and brain in the womb, but then almost at once, in response to experience, they set about dismantling and rebuilding what they have made. They are both the cause and the consequence of our actions.

Will this new vision of genes enable us to leave the nature-nurture argument behind, or are we doomed to reinvent it in every generation? Unlike what happened in previous eras, science is explaining in great detail precisely how genes and their environment—be it the womb, the classroom or pop culture—interact. So perhaps the pendulum swings of a now demonstrably false dichotomy may cease.

ANCIENT QUARREL

How much of who we are is learned or innate is an argument with a fruitful but fractious pedigree

Nature We may be destined to be bald, mourn our dead, seek mates, fear the dark	**Nurture** But we can also learn to love tea, hate polkas, invent alphabets and tell lies
IMMANUEL KANT His philosophy sought a native morality in the mind	**JOHN LOCKE** Considered the mind of an infant to be a tabula rasa, or blank slate
FRANCIS GALTON Math geek saw mental and physical traits as innate	**IVAN PAVLOV** Trained dogs to salivate at the sound of the dinner bell
KONRAD LORENZ Studied patterns of instinctive behavior in animals	**SIGMUND FREUD** Felt we are formed by mothers, fathers, sex, jokes and dreams
NOAM CHOMSKY Argued that human beings are born with a capacity for grammar	**FRANZ BOAS** Believed chance and environs are key to cultural variation

It may be in our nature, however, to seek simple, linear, cause-and-effect stories and not think in terms of circular causation, in which effects become their own causes. Perhaps the idea of nature via nurture, like the ideas of quantum mechanics and relativity, is just too counterintuitive for human minds. The urge to see ourselves in terms of nature versus nurture, like our instinctual ability to fear snakes, may be encoded in our genes.

Matt Ridley is an Oxford-trained zoologist and science writer whose latest book is Nature via Nurture *(HarperCollins)*

The New Sex Scorecard

TALKING OPENLY ABOUT SEX DIFFERENCES IS NO LONGER AN EXERCISE IN POLITICAL INCORRECTNESS; IT IS A NECESSITY IN FIGHTING DISEASE AND FORGING SUCCESSFUL RELATIONSHIPS. AT 109 AND COUNTING, *PT* EXAMINES THE TALLY.

By Hara Estroff Marano

Get out the spittoon. Men produce twice as much saliva as women. Women, for their part, learn to speak earlier, know more words, recall them better, pause less and glide through tongue twisters.

Put aside Simone de Beauvoir's famous dictum, "One is not born a woman but rather becomes one." Science suggests otherwise, and it's driving a whole new view of who and what we are. Males and females, it turns out, are different from the moment of conception, and the difference shows itself in every system of body and brain.

It's safe to talk about sex differences again. Of course, it's the oldest story in the world. And the newest. But for a while it was also the most treacherous. Now it may be the most urgent. The next stage of progress against disorders as disabling as depression and heart disease rests on cracking the binary code of biology. Most common conditions are marked by pronounced gender differences in incidence or appearance.

Although sex differences in brain and body take their inspiration from the central agenda of reproduction, they don't end there. "We've practiced medicine as though only a woman's breasts, uterus and ovaries made her unique—and as though her heart, brain and every other part of her body were identical to those of a man," says Marianne J. Legato, M.D., a cardiologist at Columbia University who spearheads the new push on gender differences. Legato notes that women live longer but break down more.

Do we need to explain that difference doesn't imply superiority or inferiority? Although sex differences may provide ammunition for David Letterman or the Simpsons, they unfold in the most private recesses of our lives, surreptitiously molding our responses to everything from stress to space to speech. Yet there are some ways the sexes are becoming more alike—they are now both engaging in the same kind of infidelity, one that is equally threatening to their marriages.

Everyone gains from the new imperative to explore sex differences. When we know why depression favors women two to one, or why the symptoms of heart disease literally hit women in the gut, it will change our understanding of how our bodies and our minds work.

The Gene Scene

Whatever sets men and women apart, it all starts with a single chromosome: the male-making Y, a puny thread bearing a paltry 25 genes, compared with the lavish female X, studded with 1,000 to 1,500 genes. But the Y guy trumps. He has a gene dubbed Sry, which, if all goes well, instigates an Olympic relay of development. It commands primitive fetal tissue to become testes, and they then spread word of masculinity out to the provinces via their chief product, testosterone. The circulating hormone not only masculinizes the body but affects the developing brain, influencing the size of specific structures and the wiring of nerve cells.

25%
of females experience daytime sleepiness, versus 18% of males

But sex genes themselves don't cede everything to hormones. Over the past few years, scientists have come to believe that they too play ongoing roles in gender-flavoring the brain and behavior.

Females, it turns out, appear to have backup genes that protect their brains from big trouble. To level the genetic playing field between men and women, nature normally shuts off one of the two X chromosomes in every cell in females. But about 19 percent of genes escape inactivation; cells get a double dose of some X genes. Having fall-back genes may explain why females are far less subject than males to mental disorders from autism to schizophrenia.

What's more, which X gene of a pair is inactivated makes a difference in the way female and male brains respond to things, says neurophysiologist Arthur P. Arnold, Ph.D., of the University of California at Los Angeles. In some cases, the X gene donated by Dad is nullified; in other cases it's the X from Mom. The parent from whom a woman gets her working genes determines how robust her genes are. Paternal genes ramp up the genetic volume, maternal genes tune it down. This is known as genomic imprinting of the chromosome.

For many functions, it doesn't matter which sex genes you have or from whom you get them. But the Y chromosome itself spurs the brain to grow extra dopamine neurons, Arnold says. These nerve cells are involved in reward and motivation, and dopamine release underlies the pleasure of addiction and novelty seeking. Dopamine neurons also affect motor skills and go awry in Parkinson's disease, a disorder that afflicts twice as many males as females.

XY makeup also boosts the density of vasopressin fibers in the brain. Vasopressin is a hormone that both abets and minimizes sex differences; in some circuits it fosters parental behavior in males; in others it may spur aggression.

Sex on the Brain

Ruben Gur, Ph.D., always wanted to do the kind of psychological research that when he found something new, no one could say his grandmother already knew it. Well, "My grandmother couldn't tell you that women have a higher percentage of gray matter in their brains," he says. Nor could she explain how that discovery resolves a long-standing puzzle.

99%
of girls play with dolls at age 6, versus 17% of boys

Gur's discovery that females have about 15 to 20 percent more gray matter than males suddenly made sense of another major sex difference: Men, overall, have larger brains than women (their heads and bodies are larger), but the sexes score equally well on tests of intelligence.

Gray matter, made up of the bodies of nerve cells and their connecting dendrites, is where the brain's heavy lifting is done. The female brain is more densely packed with neurons and dendrites, providing concentrated processing power—and more thought-linking capability.

The larger male cranium is filled with more white matter and cerebrospinal fluid. "That fluid is probably helpful," says Gur, director of the Brain Behavior Laboratory at the University of Pennsylvania. "It cushions the brain, and men are more likely to get their heads banged about."

White matter, made of the long arms of neurons encased in a protective film of fat, helps distribute processing throughout the brain. It gives males superiority at spatial reasoning. White matter also carries fibers that inhibit "information spread" in the cortex. That allows a single-mindedness that spatial problems require, especially difficult ones. The harder a spatial task, Gur finds, the more circumscribed the right-sided brain activation in males, but not in females. The white matter advantage of males, he believes, suppresses activation of areas that could interfere with work.

The white matter in women's brains is concentrated in the corpus callosum, which links the brain's hemispheres, and enables the right side of the brain to pitch in on language tasks. The more difficult the verbal task, the more global the neural participation required—a response that's stronger in females.

Women have another heady advantage—faster blood flow to the brain, which offsets the cognitive effects of aging. Men lose more brain tissue with age, especially in the left frontal cortex, the part of the brain that thinks about consequences and provides self-control.

"You can see the tissue loss by age 45, and that may explain why midlife crisis is harder on men," says Gur. "Men have the same impulses but they lose the ability to consider long-term consequences." Now, there's a fact someone's grandmother may have figured out already.

Minds of Their Own

The difference between the sexes may boil down to this: dividing the tasks of processing experience. Male and female minds are innately drawn to different aspects of the world around them. And there's new evidence that testosterone may be calling some surprising shots.

Women's perceptual skills are oriented to quick—call it intuitive—people reading. Females are gifted at detecting the feelings and thoughts of others, inferring intentions, absorbing contextual clues and responding in emotionally appropriate ways. They empathize. Tuned to others, they more readily see alternate sides of an argument. Such empathy fosters communication and primes females for attachment.

Women, in other words, seem to be hard-wired for a top-down, big-picture take. Men might be programmed to look at things from the bottom up (no surprise there).

Men focus first on minute detail, and operate most easily with a certain detachment. They construct rules-based analyses of the natural world, inanimate objects and events. In the coinage of Cambridge University psychologist Simon Baron-Cohen, Ph.D., they systemize.

The superiority of males at spatial cognition and females' talent for language probably subserve the more basic difference of systemizing versus empathizing. The two mental styles manifest in the toys kids prefer (humanlike dolls versus mechanical trucks); verbal impatience in males (ordering rather than negotiating); and navigation (women personalize space by finding landmarks; men see a geometric system, taking directional cues in the layout of routes).

26%
of males say they have extramarital sex without being emotionally involved, versus 3% of females

Almost everyone has some mix of both types of skills, although males and females differ in the degree to which one set predominates, contends Baron-Cohen. In his work as director of Cambridge's Autism Research Centre, he finds that children and adults with autism, and its less severe variant Asperger syndrome, are unusual in both dimensions of perception. Its victims are "mindblind," unable to recognize people's feelings. They also have a peculiar talent for systemizing, obsessively focusing on, say, light switches or sink faucets.

Autism overwhelmingly strikes males; the ratio is ten to one for Asperger. In his new book, *The Essential Difference: The Truth About the Male and Female Brain*, Baron-Cohen argues that autism is a magnifying mirror of maleness.

The brain basis of empathizing and systemizing is not well understood, although there seems to be a "social brain," nerve circuitry dedicated to person perception. Its key components lie on the left side of the brain, along with language centers generally more developed in females.

Baron-Cohen's work supports a view that neuroscientists have flirted with for years: Early in development, the male hormone testosterone slows the growth of the brain's left hemisphere and accelerates growth of the right.

Testosterone may even have a profound influence on eye contact. Baron-Cohen's team filmed year-old children at play and measured the amount of eye contact they made with their mothers, all of whom had undergone amniocentesis during pregnancy. The researchers looked at various social factors—birth order, parental education, among others—as well as the level of testosterone the child had been exposed to in fetal life.

Baron-Cohen was "bowled over" by the results. The more testosterone the children had been exposed to in the womb, the less able they were to make eye contact at 1 year of age. "Who would have thought that a behavior like eye contact, which is so intrinsically social, could be in part shaped by a biological factor?" he asks. What's more, the testosterone level during fetal life also influenced language skills. The higher the prenatal testosterone level, the smaller a child's vocabulary at 18 months and again at 24 months.

Lack of eye contact and poor language aptitude are early hallmarks of autism. "Being strongly attracted to systems, together with a lack of empathy, may be the core characteristics of individuals on the autistic spectrum," says Baron-Cohen. "Maybe testosterone does more than affect spatial ability and language. Maybe it also affects social ability." And perhaps autism represents an "extreme form" of the male brain.

Depression: Pink—and Blue, Blue, Blue

This year, 19 million Americans will suffer a serious depression. Two out of three will be female. Over the course of their lives, 21.3 percent of women and 12.7 percent of men experience at least one bout of major depression.

The female preponderance in depression is virtually universal. And it's specific to unipolar depression. Males and females suffer equally from bipolar, or manic, depression. However, once depression occurs, the clinical course is identical in men and women.

The gender difference in susceptibility to depression emerges at 13. Before that age, boys, if anything, are a bit more likely than girls to be depressed. The gender difference seems to wind down four decades later, making depression mostly a disorder of women in the child-bearing years.

As director of the Virginia Institute for Psychiatric and Behavioral Genetics at Virginia Commonwealth University, Kenneth S. Kendler, M.D., presides over "the best natural experiment that God has given us to study gender differences"—thousands of pairs of opposite-sex twins. He finds a significant difference between men and women in their response to low levels of adversity. He says, "Women have the capacity to be precipitated into depressive episodes at lower levels of stress."

Adding injury to insult, women's bodies respond to stress differently than do men's. They pour out higher levels of stress hormones and fail to shut off production readily. The female sex hormone progesterone blocks the normal ability of the stress hormone system to turn itself off. Sustained exposure to stress hormones kills brain cells, especially in the hippocampus, which is crucial to memory.

It's bad enough that females are set up biologically to internally amplify their negative life experiences. They are prone to it psychologically as well, finds University of Michigan psychologist Susan Nolen-Hoeksema, Ph.D.

Women ruminate over upsetting situations, going over and over negative thoughts and feelings, especially if they have to do with relationships. Too often they get caught in downward spirals of hopelessness and despair.

It's entirely possible that women are biologically primed to be highly sensitive to relationships. Eons ago it might have helped alert them to the possibility of abandonment while they were busy raising the children. Today, however, there's a clear downside. Ruminators are unpleasant to be around, with their oversize need for reassurance. Of course, men have their own ways of inadvertently fending off people. As pronounced as the female tilt to depression is the male excess of alcoholism, drug abuse and antisocial behaviors.

The Incredible Shrinking Double Standard

Nothing unites men and women better than sex. Yet nothing divides us more either. Males and females differ most in mating psychology because our minds are shaped by and for our reproductive mandates. That sets up men for sex on the side and a more casual attitude toward it.

Twenty-five percent of wives and 44 percent of husbands have had extramarital intercourse, reports Baltimore psychologist Shirley Glass, Ph.D. Traditionally for men, love is one thing and sex is . . . well, sex.

90%
of males and females agree that infidelity is always wrong, 20–25% of all marital fights are about jealousy

In what may be a shift of epic proportions, sexual infidelity is mutating before our very eyes. Increasingly, men as well as women are forming deep emotional attachments before they even slip into an extramarital bed together. It often happens as they work long hours together in the office.

"The sex differences in infidelity are disappearing," says Glass, the doyenne of infidelity research. "In my original 1980 study, there was a high proportion of men who had intercourse with almost no emotional involvement at all—nonrelational sex. Today, more men are getting emotionally involved."

One consequence of the growing parity in affairs is greater devastation of the betrayed spouse. The old-style strictly sexual affair never impacted men's marital satisfaction. "You could be in a good marriage and still cheat," reports Glass.

Liaisons born of the new infidelity are much more disruptive—much more likely to end in divorce. "You can move away from just a sexual relationship but it's very difficult to break an attachment," says Rutgers University anthropologist Helen Fisher, Ph.D. "The betrayed partner can probably provide more exciting sex but not a different kind of friendship."

It's not that today's adulterers start out unhappy or looking for love. Says Glass: "The work relationship becomes so rich and the stuff at home is pressurized and child-centered. People get involved insidiously without planning to betray."

Any way it happens, the combined sexual-emotional affair delivers a fatal blow not just to marriages but to the traditional male code. "The double standard for adultery is disappearing," Fisher emphasizes. "It's been around for 5,000 years and it's changing in our lifetime. It's quite striking. Men used to feel that they had the right. They don't feel that anymore."

LEARN MORE ABOUT IT:

Eve's Rib: The New Science of Gender-Specific Medicine and How It Can Save Your Life. Marianne J. Legato, M.D. (*Harmony Books, 2002*).

Not "Just Friends": Protect Your Relationship from Infidelity and Heal the Trauma of Betrayal. Shirley P. Glass, Ph.D. (*The Free Press, 2003*).

Male, Female: The Evolution of Human Sex Differences. David C. Geary, Ph.D. (*American Psychological Association, 1998*).

THE CRIMINAL MENACE

SHIFTING GLOBAL TRENDS

GENE STEPHENS

Crime in the United States is bottoming out after a steep slide downward during the past decade. But crime in many other nations—particularly in eastern and parts of western Europe—has continued to climb. In the United States, street crime overall remains near historic lows, prompting some analysts to declare life in the United States safer than it has ever been. In fact, statistics show that, despite terrorism, the world as a whole seems to be becoming safer. This is in sharp contrast to the perceptions of Americans and others, as polls indicate they believe the world gets more dangerous every day.

CURRENT CRIME RATES AROUND THE WORLD

Although the United States still has more violent crime than other industrialized nations and still ranks high in overall crime, the nation has nevertheless been experiencing a decline in crime numbers. Meanwhile, a number of European countries are catching up; traditionally low-crime societies, such as Denmark and Finland, are near the top in street crime rates today. Other countries that weren't even on the crime radar—such as Japan—are also experiencing a rise in crime.

Comparing crime rates across countries is difficult. Different definitions of crimes, among other factors, make official crime statistics notoriously unreliable. However, the periodic World Crime Survey, a UN initiative to track global crime rates, may offer the most reliable figures currently available:

• *Overall crime (homicide, rape, major assault, robbery) and property crime.* The United States in 1980 clearly led the Western world in overall crime and ranked particularly high in property crime. A decade later, statistics show a marked decline in U.S. property crime. By 2000, overall crime rates for the U.S.

dropped below those of England and Wales, Denmark, and Finland, while U.S. property-crime rates also continued to decline.

• *Homicide.* The United States had consistently higher homicide rates than most Western nations from 1980 to 2000. In the 1990s, the U.S. rate was cut almost in half, but the 2000 rate of 5.5 homicides per 100,000 people was still higher than all nations except those in political and social turmoil. Colombia, for instance, had 63 homicides per 100,000 people; South Africa, 51.

• *Rape.* In 1980 and 1990, U.S. rape rates were higher than those of any Western nation, but by 2000, Canada took the lead. The lowest reported rape rates were in Asia and the Middle East.

• *Robbery* has been on a steady decline in the United States over the past two decades. As of 2000, countries with more reported robberies than the United States included England and Wales, Portugal, and Spain. Countries with fewer reported robberies include Germany, Italy, and France, as well as Middle Eastern and Asian nations.

• *Burglary,* usually considered the most serious property crime, is lower in the United States today than it was in 1980. As of 2000, the United States had lower burglary rates than Australia, Denmark, Finland, England and Wales, and Canada. It had higher reported burglary rates than Spain, Korea, and Saudi Arabia.

• *Vehicle theft* declined steadily in the United States from 1980 to 2000. The 2000 figures show that Australia, England and Wales, Denmark, Norway, Canada, France, and Italy all have higher rates of vehicle theft.

Overall, the United States has experienced a downward trend in crime while other Western nations, and even industrialized non-Western nations, are witnessing higher numbers. What's behind the U.S. decreases? Some analysts believe that tougher laws, enforcement, and incarceration policies have lowered crime in the United States. They point to "three-strikes" legislation, mandatory incarceration for offenses such as drug possession and domestic violence, and tougher street-level enforcement. The reason many European countries are suffering higher crime rates, analysts argue, is because of their fewer laws and more-lenient enforcement and sentencing.

Other analysts argue that socioeconomic changes—such as fewer youth in the crime-prone 15- to 25-year old age group, a booming economy, and more community care of citizens—led to the drop in U.S. crime. They now point out that the new socioeconomic trends of growing unemployment, stagnation of wages, and the growing numbers in the adolescent male population are at work in today's terror-wary climate and may signal crime increases ahead.

Still other analysts see community-oriented policing (COP) problem-oriented policing (POP), and restorative justice (mediation, arbitration, restitution, and community service instead of criminal courts and incarceration) as the nexus of recent and future crime control successes.

U.S. CRIME TREND

Just which crime fighting tactics have effected this U.S. crime trend is a matter of debate. Three loose coalitions offer their views:

Getting tough works. "There is, in fact, a simple explanation for America's success against crime: The American justice system now does a better job of catching criminals and locking them up," writes Eli Lehrer, senior editor of *The American Enterprise.* Lehrer says local control of policing was probably what made a critical difference between the United States and European countries where regional and national systems predominate. He holds that local control allowed police to use enforcement against loitering and other minor infractions to keep the streets clean of potential lawbreakers. He acknowledges that "positive loitering"—stickers or a pat on the back for well-behaved juveniles—was the other side of the successful effort. In addition, more people have since been imprisoned for longer periods of time, seen by "get-tough" advocates as another factor in safer streets today.

Demographics rule. Some criminologists and demographers see the crime decrease as a product of favorable socioeconomic population factors in the mid- through late-1990s. High employment rates, with jobs in some sectors going unfilled for lack of qualified candidates, kept salaries growing. Even the unemployed went back to school to gain job skills. By the end of the decade the older students filled the college classrooms, taking up the slack left by the lower numbers in the traditional student age group. In such times, both violent and property crimes have usually dropped, as economic need decreased and frustration and anger subsided.

"Get-tough" theorists hold that 200 crimes a year could be prevented for each criminal taken off the streets but criminologist Albert Reiss counters that most offenders work in groups and are simply replaced when one leaves.

If demographic advocates are right, then the next few years could see a boom in street crime in the United States due to a combination of growing unemployment, stagnant wages, and

state and local governments so strapped for funds that social programs and even education are facing major cutbacks.

Community-based approaches succeed. Whereas the "get-tough" advocates mention community policing as a factor in the crime decrease, this third group sees the service aspects (rather than strict enforcement) of COP combined with the emerging restorative-justice movement as being the catalyst for success in crime prevention and control.

More criminologists believe street crime is a product of socioeconomic conditions interacting on young people, primarily adolescent males. Usually their crimes occur in interaction with others in gangs or groups, especially when law-abiding alternatives (youth athletic programs, tutors, mentors, community centers, social clubs, after-school programs) are not available. Thus, any chance of success in keeping crime rates low on a long-term basis depends on constant assessment of the community and its needs to maintain a nurturing environment.

COP and POP coordinate community cohesion by identifying problems that will likely result in crime and by simply improving the quality of life in the neighborhoods. The key: partnerships among police, citizens, civic and business groups, public and private social-service agencies, and government agencies. Combined with an ongoing needs analysis in recognition of constantly changing community dynamics, the partnerships can quickly attack any problem or situation that arises.

A restorative-justice movement has grown rapidly but stayed below the radar screen in the United States. In many communities, civil and criminal incidents are more likely to be handled through mediation or arbitration, restitution, community service, and reformation/reintegration than in civil or criminal courts. The goal, besides justice for all, is the development of a symbolic relationship and reconciliation within the community, since more than 90% of all street offenders return to the same community.

LESSONS FOR THE FUTURE OF CRIME PREVENTION AND CONTROL

All schools of thought on why street crime is decreasing have a commonality: proactive prevention rather than reactive retribution. Even the method to achieve this goal is not really in question—only the emphasis.

Since the 1980s, progressive police agencies in the United States have adhered to the "Broken Windows" and "Weed and Seed" philosophies taken from the work of criminologists James Q. Wilson and George L. Keeling. Broken windows are a metaphor for failure to establish and maintain acceptable standards of behavior in the community. The blame, according to Wilson and Keeling, lay primarily in the change in emphasis by police from being peace officers who seek to capture criminals. They argue that, in healthy communities, informal but widely understood rules were maintained by citizens and police, often using extralegal ("move on") or arrest for minor infractions (vagrancy, loitering, pandering). It was, then, this citizen-police partnership that worked to stem community deterioration and disorder, which unattended, would lead to crime.

"Weeding" involved using street-sweeping ordinances to clean the streets of the immediate problems (drunks, drug addicts, petty thieves, panhandlers). "Seeding" involved taking a breather while these offenders were in jail and establishing "opportunity" programs designed to make the community viable and capable of self-regulating its behavioral controls (job training, new employers, day care nurseries in schools, after-school programs, tutors and mentors, civic pride demonstrations, tenant management of housing projects). In the early years, the "weed" portion was clearly favored; in the early 1990s, "seed" programs based on analysis of the specific needs of the individual community were developed and spread—about the time the crime rates began to plunge.

The Weed and Seed programs in the United States imparted the following lessons:

• Proactive prevention must be at the core of any successful crime-control strategy.
• Each community must have an ongoing needs assessment carried out by a police-citizen partnership.
• A multitude of factors—from laws and neighborhood standards to demographics and socioeconomic needs—must be considered in the assessment process.
• Weed and seed must be balanced according to specific needs—somewhat different in each community.
• When crime does occur, community-based restorative justice should be used to provide restitution to victims and community while reforming and then reintegrating the offender as a law-abiding citizen of the community.

NEW APPROACHES FOR THE EMERGING CRIME LANDSCAPE

Twenty-first-century crime is going to require new approaches to prevention and control. Street crime dominated the attention of the justice system in the twentieth century, but recent excesses of corporations, costing stockholders and retirees literally billions of dollars, do not fit into the street-crime paradigm. Nor do political or religious-motivated terrorism, Internet fraud, deception, theft, harassment, pedophilia, and terrorism on an information highway without borders, without ownership, and without jurisdiction. Now attention must—and will—be paid to white-collar crimes, infotech and biotech crimes, and terrorism.

Surveys find that a large majority of corporations have been victims of computer-assisted crimes. Polls of citizens find high rates of victimization by Internet offenses ranging from identity theft to fraud, hacking to harassment. U.S. officials have maintained since the late 1990s that it is just a matter of time until there is a "Pearl Harbor" on the Internet (such as shutting down medical services networks, power grids, or financial services nationwide or even worldwide).

DOOMSDAY SCENARIOS

Following the attacks by terrorists on September 11, 2001, and later strikes abroad, doomsday scenarios have abounded, with release of radio-active or biological toxins being the most frightening. Attempts to shoot down an Israeli commercial airliner with a shoulder-held missile launcher further increased anxiety.

Clearly these crimes against victims generally unknown to the attacker and often chosen randomly cannot be stopped by community policing alone, although vigilant community partners often can spot suspicious activity and expose possible criminals and terrorists. Early response to this dilemma was to pass more laws, catch more offenders, and thus deter future incidents. This is the same response traditionally taken to street crime—the one being abandoned in preference to proactive prevention methods (COP and restorative justice.) Clearly, prevention has to be the first and most important strategy for dealing with the new threats.

Two major approaches will evolve over the next few years. First, national and international partnerships will be necessary to cope with crimes without borders. In 2000, a task force of agents from 32 U.S. communities, the federal government, and 13 other nations conducted the largest-ever crackdown on child pornography exchanged internationally over the Internet. Coordinated by the U.S. Customs Service, the raid resulted in shutting down an international child-pornography ring that used secret Internet chat rooms and sophisticated encryption to exchange thousands of sexually explicit images of children as young as 18 months. It is this type of coordinated transnational effort that will be necessary to cope with infotech and biotech crime and terrorism.

Second, the focus of prevention must change from opportunity reduction to desire reduction. Crime-prevention specialists have long used the equation, Desire + Opportunity = Crime. Prevention programs have traditionally focused on reducing opportunity through target hardening. Locks, alarms, high-intensity lighting, key control, and other methods have been used, along with neighborhood crime watches and citizen patrols.

Little attention has been paid to desire reduction, in large part because of the atomistic approach to crime. Specifically, an offender's criminal behavior is viewed as a result of personal choice. Meanwhile, criminologists and other social scientists say crime is more likely to be a product of the conditions under which the criminal was reared and lived—yet there were no significant efforts to fix this root of the problem. Instead, the criminal-justice system stuck to target hardening, catching criminals, and exacting punishment.

Quashing conditions that lead to a desire to commit crime is especially necessary in light of the apparent reasons terrorists and international criminals attack: religious fervor heightened by seeing abject poverty, illiteracy, and often homelessness and hunger all around while also seeing others live in seeming splendor.

The opportunity to reduce crime and disorder is at hand. The strategies outlined above will go a long way toward that lofty goal as will new technologies. A boom in high-tech development has brought about new surveillance and tracking gadgetry, security machines that see through clothing and skin, cameras and listening devices that see and hear through walls and ceilings, "bugs" that can be surreptitiously placed on individuals and biometric scanners that can identify suspects in large crowds. On the other hand, there are also the technologies that could take away our freedom, particularly our freedom of speech and movement. Some in high government positions believe loss of privacy and presumption of innocence is the price we must pay for safety.

For many it is too high a price. One group that urges judicious use of technology within the limitations of civil liberties protected by the U.S. Constitution is the Society of Police Futurists International (PFI)—a collection primarily of police officials from all over the world dedicated to improving the professional field of policing by taking a professional futurist's approach to preparing for the times ahead. While definitely interested in staying on the cutting edge of technology and even helping to guide its development, PFI debates the promises and perils of each new innovation on pragmatic and ethical grounds. Citizens need to do the same.

Mr. Stephens is a professor emeritus in the Department of Criminology and Criminal Justice at the University of South Carolina. From "Global Trends in Crime," by Gene Stephens, The Futurist, *May–June 2003, pages 40–46.*

Parents or Prisons

By JENNIFER ROBACK MORSE

FOR SOME PEOPLE, prisons are a substitute for parents. This apparent overstatement is shorthand for two more precise points. First, without parents—two of them, married to each other, working together as a team—a child is more likely to end up in the criminal justice system at some point in his life. Without parents, prison becomes a greater probability in the child's life. Second, if a child finds himself in the criminal justice system, either in his youth or adulthood, the prison will perform the parental function of supervising and controlling that person's behavior.

Of course, prison is a pathetic substitute for genuine parents. Incarceration provides extreme, tightly controlled supervision that children typically outgrow in their toddler years and does so with none of the love and affection that characterize normal parental care of small children. But that is what is happening: The person has failed to internalize the self-command necessary for living in a reasonably free and open society at the age most people do. Since he cannot control himself, someone else must control him. If he becomes too much for his parents, the criminal justice system takes over.

These necessary societal interventions do not repair the loss the child has sustained by the loss of a relationship with his parents. By the time the penal system steps in, the state is engaged in damage control. A child without a conscience, a child without self-control, is a lifelong problem for the rest of society.

> ## A child without a conscience or self-control is a lifelong problem for the rest of society.

A free society needs people with consciences. The vast majority of people must obey the law voluntarily. If people don't conform themselves to the law, someone will either have to compel them to do so or protect the public when they do not. It costs a great deal of money to catch, convict, and incarcerate lawbreakers—not to mention that the surveillance and monitoring of potential criminals tax everybody's freedom if habitual lawbreakers comprise too large a percentage of the population.

The basic self-control and reciprocity that a free society takes for granted do not develop automatically. Conscience development takes place in childhood. Children need to develop empathy so they will care whether they hurt someone or whether they treat others fairly. They need to develop self-control so they can follow through on these impulses and do the right thing even if it might benefit them to do otherwise.

All this development takes place inside the family. Children attach to the rest of the human race through their first relationships with their parents. They learn reciprocity, trust, and empathy from these primal relationships. Disrupting those foundational relations has a major negative impact on children as well as on the people around them. In particular, children of single parents—or completely absent parents—are more likely to commit crimes.

Without two parents, working together as a team, the child has more difficulty learning the combination of empathy, reciprocity, fairness, and self-command that people ordinarily take for granted. If the child does not learn this at home, society will have to manage his behavior in some other way. He may have to be rehabilitated, incarcerated, or otherwise restrained. In this case, prisons will substitute for parents.

The observation that there are problems for children growing up in a disrupted family may seem to be old news. Ever since Barbara Defoe Whitehead famously pronounced "Dan Quayle Was Right" (*Atlantic Monthly*, April 1993), the public has become more aware that single motherhood is not generally glamorous in the way it is sometimes portrayed on television. David Blankenhorn's *Fatherless America* (Basic Books, 1995) depicted a country that is fragmenting along family lines. Blankenhorn argued, and continues to argue in his work at the Institute for American Values, that the primary determinant of a person's life chances is whether he grew up in a household with his own father.

Since these seminal works, it has become increasingly clear that the choice to become a single parent is not strictly a private choice. The decision to become an unmarried mother or the decision to disrupt an existing family does not meet the economist's definition of "private." These choices regarding family structure have significant spillover effects on other people. We can no longer deny that such admittedly very personal decisions have an impact on people other than the individuals who choose.

There are two parts to my tale. The first concerns the impact of being raised in a single-parent household on the children. The second involves the impact that those children have on the rest of society.

Current events

THE TWO PARTS of my story were juxtaposed dramatically on the local page of the *San Diego Union-Tribune* one Wednesday morning at the end of January. "Dangling Foot Was Tip-Off," explained the headline. A security guard caught two teenaged boys attempting to dump their "trash" into the dumpster of the gated community he was responsible for guarding. The guard noticed what looked like a human foot dangling out of the bag. He told the boys he wanted to see what was in it. They refused. As a private security guard, he had no authority to arrest or detain the pair. He took their license plate number and a description of the duo and called authorities.

The "trash" proved to be the dismembered body of the boys' mother. They had strangled her, chopped off her head and hands, and ultimately dumped her body in a ravine in Orange County. The boys were half-brothers. The elder was 20 years old. His father had committed suicide when the boy was an infant. The younger boy was 15. His father had abandoned their mother. As of this writing, the older boy, Jason Bautista, was being held in lieu of $1 million bail. The younger, Matthew Montejo, was being held in juvenile hall.

At first glance, the second news item seems unrelated to the first. On the same page of the newspaper, a headline read, "Mayor Wants 20% Budget Cuts." This particular mayor presides over the city of Oceanside, the same city where the brothers tried to dump their mother's body. In nearby Vista, the mayor's "State of the City Address Warns of Possible Deep Cuts." In Carlsbad, one freeway exit to the south, the city's finances were "Called Good Now, Vulnerable in Future." All these mayors were tightening their cities' belts in response to severe budget cuts proposed by California Governor Gray Davis. The governor expects to reduce virtually every budget category in the state budget except one: the Department of Corrections.

Therein lies the tale: These stories are connected by more than just the date and time of their reportage. The increase in serious crimes by younger and younger offenders is absorbing a greater percentage of state resources, necessarily crowding out other services. The Bautista brothers and others like them do have something to do with the budget woes of state and local governments.

Several other high-profile cases of juvenile crime fit this pattern. Alex and Derek King, aged 12 and 13 respectively, bludgeoned their sleeping father to death with a baseball bat and set fire to the house to hide the evidence. The mother of the King brothers had not lived with them for the seven years prior to the crime. Derek had been in foster care for most of those years until his behavior, including a preoccupation with fire, became too difficult for his foster parents to handle. The murder took place two months after Derek was returned to his father's custody.

John Lee Malvo, the youthful assistant in the Beltway Sniper case, came to the United States with his mother from Jamaica. His biological father has not seen him since 1998. His mother evidently had a relationship with John Allen Mohammed, who informally adopted her son. Mohammed himself, probably the mastermind if not the triggerman in the serial sniper case, was also a fatherless child. According to one of his relatives, Mohammed's mother died when he was young; his grandfather and aunt raised him because his dad was not around.

While these high-profile cases dramatize the issues at stake, excessive focus on individual cases like these can be a distraction. As more information about the Bautista family comes in, for instance, a variety of mitigating or confounding circumstances might emerge to suggest that factors other than living in a single-parent home accounted for the horrible crime. A family history of mental illness, perhaps, or maybe a history of child abuse by the mother toward the children may surface as contributing factors. And indeed, many of the most gruesome crimes are committed not by fatherless children in single-mother households, but by motherless boys, growing up in a father-only household. Some, such as John Lee Malvo, had essentially no household at all. But these confounding factors should not distract us from the overwhelming evidence linking single parents or absent parents to the propensity to commit crimes.

The statistical evidence

THIS RESULT HAS been found in numerous studies. The National Fatherhood Initiative's *Father Facts*, edited in 2002 by Wade Horn and Tom Sylvester, is the best one-stop shopping place for this kind of evidence. Of the many studies reviewed there, a representative one was reported in the *Journal of Marriage and the Family* in May 1996. Researchers Chris Couglin and Samuel Vuchinich found that being in stepparent or single-parent households more than doubled the risk of delinquency by age 14. Similarly, a massive 1993 analysis of the underclass by M. Anne Hill and June O'Neill, published by Baruch College's Center for the Study of Business and Government, found that the likelihood that a young male will engage in criminal activity increases substantially if he is raised without a father.

These studies, like most in this area, attempted to control for other, confounding factors that might be correlated with living in a single-parent household. If single mothers have less money than married mothers, then perhaps poverty is the fundamental problem for their children. But even taking this possibility into account, the research still shows that boys who grew up outside of intact marriages were, on average, more likely than other boys to end up in jail.

Another set of studies found that the kids who are actually in the juvenile justice system disproportionately come from disrupted families. The Wisconsin Department of Health and Social Services, in a 1994 report entitled "Family Status of Delinquents in Juvenile Correctional Facilities in Wisconsin," found that only 13 percent came from families in which the biological mother and father were married to each other. By contrast, 33 percent had parents who were either divorced or separated, and 44 percent had parents who had never married. The 1987 *Survey of Youth in Custody*, published by the U.S. Bureau of Justice Statistics, found that 70 percent of youth in state reform institutions across the U.S. had grown up in single- or no-parent situations.

Causal links

THERE ARE SEVERAL plausible links between single parenthood and criminal behavior. The internal dynamic of a one-parent household is likely to be rather different from that of a two-parent household. Two parents can supervise the child's behavior more readily than one. Misbehavior can continue undetected and uncorrected for longer periods of time until it becomes more severe and more difficult to manage.

Likewise, the lowered level of adult input partially accounts for the lowered educational attainments of children of single parents. Such families report parents spending less time supervising homework and children spending less time doing homework. Not surprisingly, kids in these families have inferior grades and drop out of school more frequently. Leaving school increases the likelihood of a young person becoming involved in criminal behavior. It is similarly no surprise that adolescents who are left home alone to supervise themselves after school find more opportunities to get into trouble. Finally, the percentage of single-parent families in a neighborhood is one of the strongest predictors of the neighborhood's crime rate. In fact, Wayne Osgood and Jeff Chambers, in their 2000 article in the journal *Criminology*, find that father absence is more significant than poverty in predicting the crime rate.

These kinds of factors are easy enough to understand. A more subtle connection between the fractured family and criminal behavior is the possibility that the child does not form strong human attachments during infancy. A child obviously cannot attach to an absent parent. If the one remaining parent is overwhelmed or exhausted or preoccupied, the child may not form a proper attachment even to that parent. Full-fledged attachment disorder is often found among children who have spent a substantial fraction of their infancy in institutions or in foster care. (Think of Derek King.)

An attachment-disordered child is the truly dangerous sociopath, the child who doesn't care what anyone thinks, who does whatever he can get away with. Mothers and babies ordinarily build their attachments by being together. When the mother responds to the baby's needs, the baby can relax into her care. The baby learns to trust. He learns that human contact is the great good that ensures his continued existence. He learns to care about other people. He comes to care where his mother is and how she responds to him. Eventually, he will care what his mother thinks of him.

> *Usually, the parents win the race between the growth of the child's body and that of his conscience.*

This process lays the groundwork for the development of the conscience; caring what she thinks of him allows him to internalize her standards of good conduct. As he gets older, bigger, and stronger, his mother can set limits on his behavior without physically picking him up and carrying him out of trouble. Mother's raised eyebrow from across the room can be a genuine deterrent against misbehavior. As he matures, she doesn't even need to be present. He simply remembers what she wants him to do. Ultimately, he doesn't explicitly think about his parents' instructions. Without even considering punishments or approval, his internal voice reminds him, "We don't do that sort of thing." He has a conscience.

In most families, the parents win the race between the growth of the child's body and that of his conscience. By the time a child is too large and strong to muscle around, he had better have some self-command. If he doesn't, somebody will have to monitor his behavior all the time. He'll lie and steal and sneak. Punishments won't have much impact. He will become more sophisticated at calculating what he wants to try to get away with.

If the parents weren't abusive to begin with, they can become so at this point. They may keep trying to step up the penalties without realizing that the penalties aren't the point. The problem is that the child isn't listening to any inner voice of conscience. The child shouldn't even be thinking about the severity of penalties. The child ought to be thinking, "I am not the kind of person who even considers doing that."

Mental illness and genetics

ONE ALTERNATIVE hypothesis is that a family history of mental illness provides the causal relationship between crime and family structure. People who have a family history of certain kinds of mental illness may also have a higher propensity to become single parents. The same mental instability that contributes to a higher propensity to commit crimes may also make it more difficult for the person to form and sustain long-term relationships such as marriage.

A number of studies examine the relationship between single parenthood and some kinds of mental and emotional problems. A Swedish study by Gunilla Ringback Weitoft, Anders Hjern, Bengt Haglund, and Mans Rosen, released in January 2003 in the British medical journal *Lancet*, considered the impact of single-parent households on adolescents. This study explicitly took account of the family's history of mental illness. The Swedish adolescent children of single-parent households were twice as likely to abuse drugs or alcohol, twice as likely to attempt suicide, and about one and a half times as likely to suffer from a psychiatric illness. Parental history of mental illness accounted for very little of the variation in these various adolescent problems.

An extensive study of British data, reported by Andrew Cherlin and colleagues in the April 1998 issue of the *American Sociological Review*, also establishes a link between living in a single-parent household and some kinds of emotional problems over the child's entire lifetime. These researchers found that having divorced parents increases the likelihood of a wide range of problems, including depression, anxiety, phobias, and obsessions, over the entire lifetime. In addition, these children are more likely to be aggressive and disobedient during childhood.

The increased likelihood of aggressive behavior is confirmed in a variety of American studies, including Michael Workman and John Beer's 1992 study in *Psychological Reports* and Nancy Vaden-Kiernan's 1995 study in the *Journal of Abnormal Child Psychology*. Not every instance of aggressive behavior is criminal behavior, of course, but it is fair to say that something that increases the likelihood of aggression probably raises the possibility of some kinds of crime.

The cost of controlling people

PEOPLE WHO DO not control themselves have to be controlled by outside forces. This very costly business may, for a while, be hidden from the public eye. The family absorbs the costs. A single mother, for instance, may try to enlist the help of her parents or other extended family members if she has a truly out-of-control child. The family, however it is structured, rearranges itself to protect itself from the child who is disruptive, defiant, or violent. The family has to provide extremely tight supervision or else bear the brunt of the child's behavior.

If the behavior gets serious enough, the criminal justice system will be called into action. People outside the family then have to manage the child's behavior. These people might include some combination of police officers, prison guards, social workers, psychiatrists, judges, and parole officers, depending on the child's age and the seriousness of his crimes. All these people have to be paid, either by the family or by the taxpayers. When the public sector gets involved, the costs become visible to the rest of society.

> *When the public sector gets involved, the costs become visible to the rest of society.*

These costs add up. In California, for instance, the corrections budget has doubled since the 1960s as a percentage of the state's budget. By 2002–03, the prison system accounted for about 6 percent of the state budget, or more than $5.2 billion, an amount greater than what the state spends on transportation. Despite the current California budget crisis forcing cutbacks in most areas, the Department of Corrections is gaining a small boost of $40 million.

Some critics have claimed that these increases are political paybacks: The California Correctional Peace Officers Association has been one of the governor's biggest campaign contributors. This charge has some plausibility, since most of the increases in the department's budget are going to personnel costs. But being a prison guard is not a particularly pleasant job, and somebody, as they say, has to do it. Many of the facilities are in remote, unattractive parts of the state where attracting workers presents a continuing challenge. For instance, the Pelican Bay maximum-security prison in the far north of California is considered, if I may use the term, "godforsaken." The all-male facility recently had to use an ob-gyn as a primary care physician due to the difficulty of attracting an internal medicine doctor there.

While it may be easy for some to conclude that Davis is courting favor with his contributors, the teachers unions are also powerful political players in California, and education faces unprecedented cuts. The Department of Corrections spends $26,700 per adult inmate per year. Nobody seriously wants the governor to empty the prisons to save money.

Other critics claim that California's prison costs have escalated because the system is too tough on criminals. These critics cite the "Three Strikes" law, which requires a lifetime of incarceration for criminals with three offenses, no matter how trivial. Because of the law, an unprecedented number of relatively young people will spend the rest of their lives in prison at taxpayer expense.

Although such a law seems harsh, we should remember why we have a Three Strikes law in the first place: Richard Allen Davis. The sociopathic, unrepentant killer of Polly Klaas had a long history of criminal behavior. He had been recently released from prison when he stole Polly from her own bedroom and killed her. In the courtroom, he not only showed no remorse for his crime, he shouted obscenities at her parents. The people of California were sickened by the thought that a person so obviously dangerous should ever have been released.

As it happens, Richard Allen Davis was part of a disrupted family. His parents divorced when he was nine years old. He had virtually no contact with his mother after that. His father was often absent from the home and would leave his children with his own mother or with his different wives.

Think how much the state would save for every young person who can go on to create a life of his own.

We could pose the question of costs to the taxpayer in this way: Suppose the kids in the juvenile justice system were functioning well enough that they could be a reasonably normal part of society. They could then be in the educational system instead of in the juvenile justice system. Look at the per-person cost of incarceration for a year, compared with the cost of education.

The California Youth Authority is the juvenile branch of California's criminal justice system. The system works with youngsters in a variety of settings, including camps, schools, and residential treatment facilities. According to the state Legislative Analysts Office, the state spends approximately $49,200 per year per person on these programs.

If that same young person could function normally in society, he would cost taxpayers about $8,568 per year while in K–12 education. If he went on to the community college system, he would cost about $4,376—or about a tenth of the cost of a year under the jurisdiction of the Youth Authority. If he went to the prestigious University of California system, he would cost the state $17,392. Think how much the state would save for every young person who can go on to create a life of his own rather than have to have his every move controlled or monitored by someone else.

The educational system represents an investment; the state's expenditures are likely to be repaid over the years by its graduates when they become productive citizens. By contrast, the money spent on incarceration has little prospect of turning the individual into a more productive citizen. These expenditures merely neutralize the negative impact on society of an individual who can't or won't control himself.

Statistics and probabilities

SOME MIGHT RESPOND that they personally are acquainted with many wonderful children of single parents. The parents are loving and giving; the children are thriving. But these anecdotal cases are not decisive. For every such story, we could produce a counter-story of a struggling single-parent family that fits the more distressing profile. The mother is a lovely person who did her best, but the boy got out of hand in his teenage years. Or the mother started out as a lovely person, but she became preoccupied with her new boyfriend or her job troubles. Her parents are heartbroken because they can see that their grandchildren are headed for trouble.

Besides, it is important to understand what statistical evidence does and does not prove. To say that a child of a single mother is twice as likely to commit a crime as the child of married parents is not to say that each and every child of every unwed mother will commit crimes or that no child of married parents will ever commit crimes. It is simply to say that growing up with unmarried parents is a significant risk factor.

Nor does saying that single-parent households are a risk factor diminish the possibility that some propensity for criminal activity might be genetically determined. Some individuals may well have a genetic propensity for aggression or for mental instability—or even for sociopathic behavior. These individuals are surely at higher than average risk for criminal activity, whether their parents are married or not. But the claim that some sociopaths are born does not preclude the possibility that some sociopaths are made. It makes sense to minimize the risk factors over which we can exercise a reasonable amount of control.

Some of the causal links between single-parent households and criminal behavior are better established than others. The causal connection between dropping out of school and higher probability of criminal behavior seems pretty straightforward and is well-documented. The link from single-parent households to attachment disorder is a weaker causal connection with a lower probability. But because a lifetime without a conscience is such a serious problem, it makes sense to try to lower the risk.

Look at it this way: When the evidence linking smoking with lung cancer first came to light, many people wanted to minimize that link. People with a serious addiction felt it was impossible for them to give up smoking. They didn't necessarily welcome the arrival of accurate information about a ship that had already sailed. "I know someone who smoked for a lifetime and never had cancer," skeptics replied. And indeed, that could be true. Smokers do not all die of smoking-related illness.

However, looking at the vast sweep of the evidence, enough people do die of smoking-related illnesses that smoking can safely be classified as a serious risk factor. And it is a choice-related risk factor, unlike genetic predispositions toward disease that might increase the likelihood of contracting lung cancer. It makes sense to have public health campaigns to educate the public about the risks associated with smoking, even though people irredeemably addicted to smoking might prefer not to be afflicted with this guilt- and anxiety-provoking information. Similarly, there is now enough evidence about the risks associated with growing up in a single-parent household that people are entitled to accurate information about those risks.

What to do?

No serious person would claim that the government can or should take over marriage as a matter for "public" regulation and control, even if there are significant externalities to some behaviors. At a minimum, though, the government ought to refrain from counterproductive policies that discourage family formation or encourage family dissolution. The current regime of no-fault divorce, for example, really amounts to unilateral divorce.

Divorce imposes large costs on children. A unilateral divorce also imposes costs on the person who wants to preserve the marriage. Such people are willing to exert effort to stay married, but they don't even have the opportunity to state this case in court. These injured parties, adults and children alike, can never be made fully whole as the law would ordinarily require in a tort. It is a distortion of the idea of freedom to claim that no-fault divorce is the only policy consistent with individual liberty. Even a purely economic theory suggests that the imposition of costs on third parties should not be allowed to occur willy-nilly. Common decency requires that people who impose costs on others at least offer an account of themselves. The law should do no less.

But real policy recommendations have to go well beyond the reach of the law. In matters relating to the family, the dichotomy between "private" and "public," so familiar in policymaking circles, does not really work; these are not mutually exhaustive categories. We need an additional analytical category: "social."

Family matters are first and foremost social matters because a family is a little society. The larger society is built in crucial ways upon the little society of the family. The family is more than a collection of individuals who make quasi-market exchanges with each other. And families are not miniature political institutions. The label of "social" also points us in the right direction for solutions. The most important tools for building up the family are not primarily economic and political, but social and cultural. Accurate information is a necessary educational tool in reversing the culture of despair around the institution of marriage.

A young woman needs to know that the decision to have a child by herself is a decision that exposes her and her child to a lifetime of elevated risks: of poverty, of lower education, of depression, and of prison. Getting and staying married may seem formidable to a young pregnant woman because marriage is filled with a hundred irritations and difficulties. She might think it simpler to strike out alone rather than to put up with the innumerable adjustments and accommodations that are inevitable in married life. And it is easier for us to remain uninvolved in such a decision. But we are not doing the young person any favors by acting as if we are ignorant of the likely consequences of her choices. The time-honored American ethos of "live and let live" has metamorphosed into a categorical imperative to keep our mouths shut.

For years we have heard that single parenthood is an alternative lifestyle choice that doesn't affect anyone but the person who chooses it. We have been instructed that society should loosen the stigma against it in order to promote individual freedom of choice. We have been scolded for being insufficiently sensitive to the plight of single mothers if we utter any criticism of their decisions. At the urging of various activist groups, the government and society at large have been developing a posture of neutrality among family arrangements. There are no better or worse forms of family, we are told. There are no "broken families," only "different families."

The premise behind this official posture of neutrality is false. The decision to become a single parent or to disrupt an existing family does affect people outside the immediate household. These words may seem harsh to adults who have already made crucial life decisions, but it is time to be candid. We need to create a vocabulary for lovingly, but firmly and without apology, telling young people what we know. Surely, telling the truth is no infringement on anyone's liberty. Young people need to have accurate information about the choices they face. For their own sake—and for ours.

Jennifer Roback Morse is a research fellow at the Hoover Institution, Stanford University. She is the author of Love and Economics: Why the Laissez-Faire Family Doesn't Work (*Spence Publishing, 2001*).

ENOUGH IS ENOUGH

WHITE-COLLAR CRIMINALS: THEY LIE THEY CHEAT THEY STEAL AND THEY'VE BEEN GETTING AWAY WITH IT FOR TOO LONG

BY CLIFTON LEAF

Arthur Levitt, the tough-talking former chairman of the Securities and Exchange Commission, spoke of a "multitude of villains." Red-faced Congressmen hurled insults, going so far as to compare the figures at the center of the Enron debacle unfavorably to carnival hucksters. The Treasury Secretary presided over a high-level working group aimed at punishing negligent CEOs and directors. Legislators from all but a handful of states threatened to sue the firm that bollixed up the auditing, Arthur Andersen. There was as much handwringing, proselytizing, and bloviating in front of the witness stand as there was shredding behind it.

It took a late-night comedian, though, to zero in on the central mystery of this latest corporate shame. After a parade of executives from Enron and Arthur Andersen flashed on the television monitor, Jon Stewart, anchor of *The Daily Show*, turned to the camera and shouted, "Why aren't all of you in jail? And not like white-guy jail—*jail* jail. With people by the weight room going, 'Mmmmm.'"

It was a pitch-perfect question. And, sadly, one that was sure to get a laugh.

Not since the savings-and-loan scandal a decade ago have high crimes in the boardroom provided such rich television entertainment. But that's not for any lack of malfeasance. Before Enronitis inflamed the public, gigantic white-collar swindles were rolling through the business world and the legal system with their customary regularity. And though they displayed the full creative range of executive thievery, they had one thing in common: Hardly anyone ever went to prison.

Regulators alleged that divisional managers at investment firm Credit Suisse First Boston participated in a "pervasive" scheme to siphon tens of millions of dollars of their customers' trading profits during the Internet boom of 1999 and early 2000 by demanding excessive trading fees. (For one 1999 quarter the backdoor bonuses amounted to as much as a fifth of the firm's total commissions.) Those were the facts, as outlined by the

SEC and the National Association of Securities Dealers in a high-profile news conference earlier this year. But the January news conference wasn't to announce an indictment. It was to herald a settlement, in which CSFB neither admitted nor denied wrongdoing. Sure, the SEC concluded that the investment bank had failed to observe "high standards of commercial honor," and the company paid $100 million in fines and "disgorgement," and CSFB itself punished 19 of its employees with fines ranging from $250,000 to $500,000. But whatever may or may not have happened, no one was charged with a crime. The U.S. Attorney's office in Manhattan dropped its investigation when the case was settled. Nobody, in other words, is headed for the hoosegow.

A month earlier drugmaker ICN Pharmaceuticals actually pleaded guilty to one count of criminal fraud for intentionally misleading investors—over many years, it now seems—about the FDA approval status of its flagship drug, ribavirin. The result of a five-year grand jury investigation? A $5.6 million fine and the company's accession to a three-year "probationary" period. Prosecutors said that not only had the company deceived investors, but its chairman, Milan Panic, had also made more than a million dollars off the fraud as he hurriedly sold shares. He was never charged with insider trading or any other criminal act. The SEC is taking a firm stand, though, "seeking to bar Mr. Panic from serving as a director or officer of any publicly traded company." Tough luck.

And who can forget those other powerhouse scandals, Sunbeam and Waste Management? The notorious Al "Chainsaw" Dunlap, accused of zealously fabricating Sunbeam's financial statements when he was chief executive, is facing only civil, not criminal, charges. The SEC charged that Dunlap and his minions made use of every accounting fraud in the book, from "channel stuffing" to "cookie jar reserves." The case is now in the discovery phase of trial and likely to be settled; he has denied wrongdoing. (Earlier Chainsaw rid himself of a class-

Schemers and scams: a brief history of bad business

It takes some pretty spectacular behavior to get busted in this country for a white-collar crime. But the business world has had a lot of overachievers willing to give it a shot.

by Ellen Florian

1920: The Ponzi scheme

Charles Ponzi planned to arbitrage postal coupons—buying them from Spain and selling them to the U.S. Postal Service at a profit. To raise capital, he outlandishly promised investors a 50% return in 90 days. They naturally swarmed in, and he paid the first with cash collected from those coming later. He was imprisoned for defrauding 40,000 people of $15 million.

1929: Albert Wiggin

In the summer of 1929, Wiggin, head of Chase National Bank, cashed in by shorting 42,000 shares of his company's stock. His trades, though legal, were counter to the interests of his shareholders and led to passage of a law prohibiting executives from shorting their own stock.

1930: Ivar Krueger, the Match King

Heading companies that made two-thirds of the world's matches, Krueger ruled—until the Depression. To keep going, he employed 400 off-the-books vehicles that only he understood, scammed his bankers, and forged signatures. His empire collapsed when he had a stroke.

1938: Richard Whitney

Ex-NYSE president Whitney propped up his liquor business by tapping a fund for widows and orphans of which he was trustee and stealing from the New York Yacht Club and a relative's estate. He did three years' time.

1961: The electrical cartel

Executives of GE, Westinghouse, and other big-name companies conspired to serially win bids on federal projects. Seven served time—among the first imprisonments in the 70-year history of the Sherman Antitrust Act.

1962: Billie Sol Estes

A wheeler-dealer out to corner the West Texas fertilizer market, Estes built up capital by mortgaging nonexistent farm gear. Jailed in 1965 and paroled in 1971, he did the mortgage bit again, this time with nonexistent oil equipment. He was re-jailed in 1979 for tax evasion and did five years.

1970: Cornfeld and Vesco

Bernie Cornfeld's Investors Overseas Service, a fund-of-funds outfit, tanked in 1970, and Cornfeld was jailed in Switzerland. Robert Vesco "rescued" IOS with $5 million and then absconded with an estimated $250 million, fleeing the U.S. He's said to be in Cuba serving time for unrelated crimes.

1983: Marc Rich

Fraudulent oil trades in 1980–1981 netted Rich and his partner, Pincus Green, $105 million, which they moved to offshore subsidiaries. Expecting to be indicted by U.S. Attorney Rudy Giuliani for evading taxes, they fled to Switzerland, where tax evasion is not an extraditable crime. Clinton pardoned Rich in 2001.

1986: Boesky and Milken and Drexel Burnham Lambert

The Feds got Wall Streeter Ivan Boesky for insider trading, and then Boesky's testimony helped them convict Drexel's Michael Milken for market manipulation. Milken did two years in prison, Boesky 22 months. Drexel died.

1989: Charles Keating and the collapse of Lincoln S&L

Keating was convicted of fraudulently marketing junk bonds and making sham deals to manufacture profits. Sentenced to 12½ years, he served less than five. Cost to taxpayers: $3.4 billion, a sum making this the most expensive S&L failure.

(continued)

Schemers and Scams (continued)

1991: BCCI	1991: Salomon Brothers	1995: Nick Leeson and Barings Bank	1995: Bankers Trust	1997: Walter Forbes
The Bank of Credit & Commerce International got tagged the "Bank for Crooks & Criminals International" after it came crashing down in a money-laundering scandal that disgraced, among others, Clark Clifford, advisor to four Presidents.	Trader Paul Mozer violated rules barring one firm from bidding for more than 35% of the securities offered at a Treasury auction. He did four months' time. Salomon came close to bankruptcy. Chairman John Gutfreund resigned.	A 28-year-old derivatives trader based in Singapore, Leeson brought down 233-year-old Barings by betting Japanese stocks would rise. He hid his losses—$1.4 billion—for a while but eventually served more than three years in jail.	Derivatives traders misled clients Gibson Greetings and Procter & Gamble about the risks of exotic contracts they entered into. P&G sustained about $200 million in losses but got most of it back from BT. The Federal Reserve sanctioned the bank.	Only months after Cendant was formed by the merger of CUC and HFS, cooked books that created more than $500 million in phony profits showed up at CUC. Walter Forbes, head of CUC, has been indicted on fraud charges and faces trial this year.

1997: Columbia/HCA	1998: Waste Management	1998: Al Dunlap	1999: Martin Frankel	2000: Sotheby's and Al Taubman
This Nashville company became the target of the largest-ever federal investigation into healthcare scams and agreed in 2000 to an $840 million Medicare-fraud settlement. Included was a criminal fine—rare in corporate America—of $95 million.	Fighting to keep its reputation as a fast grower, the company engaged in aggressive accounting for years and then tried straight-out books cooking. In 1998 it took a massive charge, restating years of earnings.	He became famous as "Chainsaw Al" by firing people. But he was then axed at Sunbeam for illicitly manufacturing earnings. He loved overstating revenues—booking sales, for example, on grills neither paid for nor shipped.	A financier who siphoned off at least $200 million from a series of insurance companies he controlled, Frankel was arrested in Germany four months after going on the lam. Now jailed in Rhode Island—no bail for this guy—he awaits trial on charges of fraud and conspiracy.	The world's elite were ripped off by years of price-fixing on the part of those supposed bitter competitors, auction houses Sotheby's and Christie's. Sotheby's chairman, Taubman, was found guilty of conspiracy last year. He is yet to be sentenced.

action shareholder suit for $15 million, without admitting culpability.) Whatever the current trial's outcome, Dunlap will still come out well ahead. Sunbeam, now under bankruptcy protection, gave him $12.7 million in stock and salary during 1998 alone. And if worse comes to worst, he can always tap the stash he got from the sale of the disemboweled Scott Paper to Kimberly-Clark, which by Dunlap's own estimate netted him a $100 million bonanza.

Sunbeam investors, naturally, didn't fare as well. When the fraud was discovered internally, the company was forced to restate its earnings, slashing half the reported profits from fiscal 1997. After that embarrassment, Sunbeam shares fell from $52 to $7 in just six months—a loss of $3.8 billion in market cap. Sound familiar?

The auditor in that case, you'll recall, was Arthur Andersen, which paid $110 million to settle a civil action. According to an SEC release in May, an Andersen partner authorized unqualified audit opinions even though "he was aware of many of the

company's accounting improprieties and disclosure failures." The opinions were false and misleading. But nobody is going to jail.

At Waste Management, yet another Andersen client, income reported over six years was overstated by $1.4 billion. Andersen coughed up $220 million to shareholders to wipe its hands clean. The auditor, agreeing to the SEC's first antifraud injunction against a major firm in more than 20 years, also paid a $7 million fine to close the complaint. Three partners were assessed fines, ranging from $30,000 to $50,000, as well. (You guessed it. Not even home detention.) Concedes one former regulator familiar with the case: "Senior people at Andersen got off when we felt we had the goods." Andersen did not respond to a request for comment.

The list goes on—from phony bookkeeping at the former Bankers Trust (now part of Deutsche Bank) to allegations of insider trading by a former Citigroup vice president. One employee of California tech firm nVidia admitted that he cleared

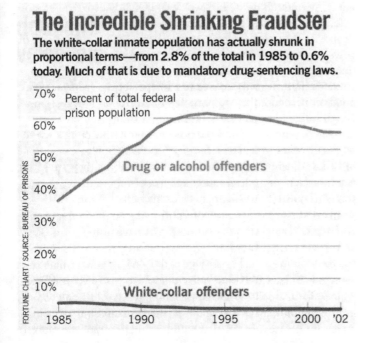

The Incredible Shrinking Fraudster

The white-collar inmate population has actually shrunk in proportional terms—from 2.8% of the total in 1985 to 0.6% today. Much of that is due to mandatory drug-sentencing laws.

Percent of total federal prison population

Drug or alcohol offenders

White-collar offenders

1985 · 1990 · 1995 · 2000 · '02

FORTUNE CHART / SOURCE: BUREAU OF PRISONS

nearly half a million dollars in a single day in March 2000 from an illegal insider tip. He pleaded guilty to criminal charges, paid fines, and got a 12-month grounding at home.

The problem will not go away until white-collar thieves face a consequence they're actually scared of: time in jail.

While none of those misbehaviors may rise to Enronian proportions, at least in terms of salacious detail, taken en masse they say something far more distressing. The double standard in criminal justice in this country is starker and more embedded than many realize. Bob Dylan was right: Steal a little, and they put you in jail. Steal a lot, and you're likely to walk away with a lecture and a court-ordered promise not to do it again.

Far beyond the pure social inequity—and that would be bad enough, we admit—is a very real dollar-and-cents cost, a doozy of a recurring charge that ripples through the financial markets. As the Enron case makes abundantly clear, white-collar fraud is not a victimless crime. In this age of the 401(k), when the retirement dreams of middle-class America are tied to the integrity of the stock market, crooks in the corner office are everybody's problem. And the problem will not go away until white-collar thieves face a consequence they're actually scared of: time in jail.

The U.S. regulatory and judiciary systems, however, do little if anything to deter the most damaging Wall Street crimes. Interviews with some six dozen current and former federal prosecutors, regulatory officials, defense lawyers, criminologists, and high-ranking corporate executives paint a disturbing pic-

ture. The already stretched "white-collar" task forces of the FBI focus on wide-ranging schemes like Internet, insurance, and Medicare fraud, abandoning traditional securities and accounting offenses to the SEC. Federal securities regulators, while determined and well trained, are so understaffed that they often have to let good cases slip away. Prosecutors leave scores of would-be criminal cases referred by the SEC in the dustbin, declining to prosecute more than half of what comes their way. State regulators, with a few notable exceptions, shy away from the complicated stuff. So-called self-regulatory organizations like the National Association of Securities Dealers are relatively toothless; trade groups like the American Institute of Certified Public Accountants stubbornly protect their own. And perhaps worst of all, corporate chiefs often wink at (or nod off to) overly aggressive tactics that speed along the margins of the law.

LET'S START WITH THE NUMBERS. WALL STREET, AFTER ALL, IS about numbers, about playing the percentages. And that may be the very heart of the problem. Though securities officials like to brag about their enforcement records, few in America's top-floor suites and corporate boardrooms fear the local sheriff. They know the odds of getting caught.

The U.S. Attorneys' Annual Statistical Report is the official reckoning of the Department of Justice. For the year 2000, the most recent statistics available, federal prosecutors say they charged 8,766 defendants with what they term white-collar crimes, convicting 6,876, or an impressive 78% of the cases brought. Not bad. Of that number, about 4,000 were sentenced to prison—nearly all of them for less than three years. (The average time served, experts say, is closer to 16 months.)

But that 4,000 number isn't what you probably think it is. The Justice Department uses the white-collar appellation for virtually every kind of fraud, says Henry Pontell, a leading criminologist at the University of California at Irvine, and co-author of *Big-Money Crime: Fraud and Politics in the Savings and Loan Crisis.* "I've seen welfare frauds labeled as white-collar crimes," he says. Digging deeper into the Justice Department's 2000 statistics, we find that only 226 of the cases involved securities or commodities fraud.

And guess what: Even those are rarely the highfliers, says Kip Schlegel, chairman of the department of criminal justice at Indiana University, who wrote a study on Wall Street law-breaking for the Justice Department's research wing. Many of the government's largest sting operations come from busting up cross-state Ponzi schemes, "affinity" investment scams (which prey on the elderly or on particular ethnic or religious groups), and penny-stock boiler rooms, like the infamous Stratton Oakmont and Sterling Foster. They are bad seeds, certainly. But let's not kid ourselves: They are not corporate-officer types or high-level Wall Street traders and bankers—what we might call *starched*-collar criminals. "The criminal sanction is generally reserved for the losers," says Schlegel, "the scamsters, the low-rent crimes."

Statistics from the Federal Bureau of Prisons, up to date as of October 2001, make it even clearer how few white-collar criminals are behind bars. Of a total federal inmate population of

The SEC's Impressive Margins

Did someone say "resource problem"? The SEC is, in fact, a moneymaking machine. The U.S. Treasury keeps fees and penalties. Disgorgements go into a fund for fraud victims.

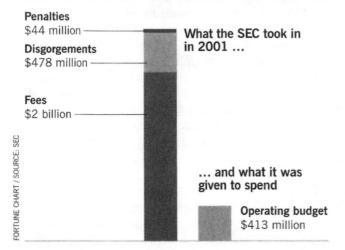

Penalties
$44 million

Disgorgements
$478 million

Fees
$2 billion

FORTUNE CHART / SOURCE: SEC

What the SEC took in in 2001 ...

... and what it was given to spend

Operating budget
$413 million

156,238, prison authorities say only 1,021 fit the description—which includes everyone from insurance schemers to bankruptcy fraudsters, counterfeiters to election-law tamperers to postal thieves. Out of those 1,000 or so, well more than half are held at minimum-security levels—often privately managed "Club Feds" that are about two steps down the comfort ladder from Motel 6.

And how many of them are the starched-collar crooks who commit securities fraud? The Bureau of Prisons can't say precisely. The Department of Justice won't say either—but the answer lies in its database.

Susan Long, a professor of quantitative methods at the school of management at Syracuse University, co-founded a Web data clearinghouse called TRAC, which has been tracking prosecutor referrals from virtually every federal agency for more than a decade. Using a barrage of Freedom of Information Act lawsuits, TRAC has been able to gather data buried in the Justice Department's own computer files (minus the individual case numbers that might be used to identify defendants). And the data, which follow each matter from referral to the prison steps, tell a story the Justice Department doesn't want you to know.

In the full ten years from 1992 to 2001, according to TRAC data, SEC enforcement attorneys referred 609 cases to the Justice Department for possible criminal charges. Of that number, U.S. Attorneys decided what to do on about 525 of the cases—declining to prosecute just over 64% of them. Of those they did press forward, the feds obtained guilty verdicts in a respectable 76%. But even then, some 40% of the convicted starched-collars didn't spend a day in jail. In case you're wondering, here's the magic number that did: 87.

FIVE-POINT TYPE IS SMALL PRINT, SO TINY THAT ALMOST everyone who remembers the Bay of Pigs or the fall of Saigon will need bifocals to read it. For those who love pulp fiction or the crime blotters in their town weeklies, however, there is no better place to look than in the small print of the *Wall Street Journal*'s B section. Once a month, buried in the thick folds of newsprint, are bullet reports of the NASD's disciplinary actions. February's disclosures about alleged misbehavior, for example, range from the unseemly to the lurid—from an Ohio bond firm accused of systematically overcharging customers and fraudulently marking up trades to a California broker who deposited a client's $143,000 check in his own account. Two senior VPs of a Pittsburgh firm, say NASD officials, cashed out of stock, thanks to timely inside information they received about an upcoming loss; a Dallas broker reportedly converted someone's 401(k) rollover check to his personal use.

In all, the group's regulatory arm received 23,753 customer complaints against its registered reps between the years 1997 and 2000. After often extensive investigations, the NASD barred "for life" during this period 1,662 members and suspended another 1,000 or so for violations of its rules or of laws on the federal books. But despite its impressive 117-page *Sanction Guidelines*, the NASD can't do much of anything to its miscreant broker-dealers other than throw them out of the club. It has no statutory right to file civil actions against rule breakers, it has no subpoena power, and from the looks of things it can't even get the bums to return phone calls. Too often the disciplinary write-ups conclude with a boilerplate "failed to respond to NASD requests for information."

"That's a good thing when they default," says Barry Goldsmith, executive vice president for enforcement at NASD Regulation. "It gives us the ability to get the wrongdoers out quickly to prevent them from doing more harm."

Goldsmith won't say how many cases the NASD passes on to the SEC or to criminal prosecutors for further investigation. But he does acknowledge that the securities group refers a couple of hundred suspected insider-trading cases to its higher-ups in the regulatory chain.

Thus fails the first line of defense against white-collar crime: self-policing. The situation is worse, if anything, among accountants than it is among securities dealers, says John C. Coffee Jr., a Columbia Law School professor and a leading authority on securities enforcement issues. At the American Institute of Certified Public Accountants, he says, "no real effort is made to enforce the rules." Except one, apparently. "They have a rule that they do not take action against auditors until all civil litigation has been resolved," Coffee says, "because they don't want their actions to be used against their members in a civil suit." Lynn E. Turner, who until last summer was the SEC's chief accountant and is now a professor at Colorado State University, agrees. "The AICPA," he says, "often failed to discipline members in a timely fashion, if at all. And when it did, its most severe remedy was just to expel the member from the organization."

Al Anderson, senior VP of AICPA, says the criticism is unfounded. "We have been and always will be committed to enforcing the rules," he says. The next line of defense after the professional associations is the SEC. The central role of this independent regulatory agency is to protect investors in the financial markets by making sure that publicly traded companies

The Odds Against Doing Time

Regulators like to talk tough, but when it comes to actual punishment, all but a handful of Wall Street cheats get off with a slap on the wrist.

What Really Happens
In the ten-year period from 1992 to 2001, SEC officials felt that 609 of its civil cases were egregious enough to merit criminal charges. These were referred to U.S. Attorneys.

Of the initial 609 referrals, U.S. Attorneys have disposed of **525**:

187 defendants were prosecuted:

142 were found guilty:

87 went to jail:

= ten defendants

SOURCE: TRANSACTIONAL RECORDS ACCESS CLEARINGHOUSE

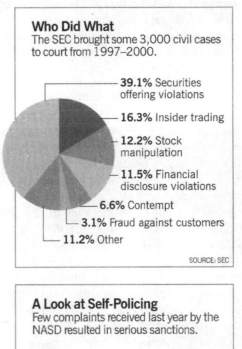

Who Did What
The SEC brought some 3,000 civil cases to court from 1997–2000.

- **39.1%** Securities offering violations
- **16.3%** Insider trading
- **12.2%** Stock manipulation
- **11.5%** Financial disclosure violations
- **6.6%** Contempt
- **3.1%** Fraud against customers
- **11.2%** Other

SOURCE: SEC

A Look at Self-Policing
Few complaints received last year by the NASD resulted in serious sanctions.

Registered reps	675,821
Customer complaints received	5,155
Individuals barred	466
Individuals suspended	346

SOURCE: NASD REGULATION

play by the rules. With jurisdiction over every constituent in the securities trade, from brokers to mutual funds to accountants to corporate filers, it would seem to be the voice of Oz. But the SEC's power, like that of the Wizard, lies more in persuasion than in punishment. The commission can force companies to comply with securities rules, it can fine them when they don't, it can even charge them in civil court with violating the law. But it can't drag anybody off to prison. To that end, the SEC's enforcement division must work with federal and state prosecutors—a game that often turns into weak cop/bad cop.

Nevertheless, the last commission chairman, Arthur Levitt, did manage to shake the ground with the power he had. For the 1997–2000 period, for instance, attorneys at the agency's enforcement division brought civil actions against 2,989 respondents. That figure includes 487 individual cases of alleged insider trading, 365 for stock manipulation, 343 for violations of laws and rules related to financial disclosure, 196 for contempt of the regulatory agency, and another 94 for fraud against customers. In other words, enough bad stuff to go around. What would make them civil crimes, vs. actual handcuff-and-fingerprint ones? Evidence, says one SEC regional director. "In a civil case you need only a preponderance of evidence that there was an intent to defraud," she says. "In a criminal case you have to prove that intent beyond a reasonable doubt."

When the SEC does find a case that smacks of criminal intent, the commission refers it to a U.S. Attorney. And that is where the second line of defense often breaks down. The SEC has the expertise to sniff out such wrongdoing but not the big stick of prison to wave in front of its targets. The U.S. Attorney's office has the power to order in the SWAT teams but often lacks the expertise—and, quite frankly, the inclination—to deconstruct a complex financial crime. After all, it is busy pursuing drug kingpins and terrorists.

And there is also the key issue of institutional kinship, say an overwhelming number of government authorities. U.S. Attorneys, for example, have kissing-cousin relationships with the agencies they work with most, the FBI and DEA. Prosecutors and investigators often work together from the start and know the elements required on each side to make a case stick. That is hardly true with the SEC and all but a handful of U.S. Attorneys around the country. In candid conversations, current and former regulators cited the lack of warm cooperation between the law-enforcement groups, saying one had no clue about how the other worked.

THIRTEEN BLOCKS FROM WALL STREET IS A DIFFERENT KIND of ground zero. Here, in the shadow of the imposing Federalist-style courthouses of lower Manhattan, is a nine-story stone fortress of indeterminate color, somewhere in the unhappy genus of waiting-room beige. As with every federal building these days, there are reminders of the threat of terrorism, but this particular outpost has taken those reminders to the status of a four-bell alarm. To get to the U.S. Attorney's office, a visitor must wind his way through a phalanx of blue police barricades, stop by a kiosk manned by a U.S. marshal, enter a giant white tent with police and metal detectors, and proceed to a bulletproof visitors desk, replete with armed guards. Even if you make it to the third floor, home of the Securities and Commodities Fraud Task Force, Southern District of New York, you'll need an electronic passkey to get in.

This, the office which Rudy Giuliani led to national prominence with his late-1980s busts of junk-bond king Michael Milken, Ivan Boesky, and the Drexel Burnham insider-trading ring, is one of the few outfits in the country that even know how to prosecute complex securities crimes. Or at least one of the few willing to take them on. Over the years it has become the favorite (and at times lone) repository for the SEC's enforcement hit list.

And how many attorneys are in this office to fight the nation's book cookers, insider traders, and other Wall Street thieves? Twenty-five—including three on loan from the SEC. The unit has a fraction of the paralegal and administrative help of even a small private law firm. Assistant U.S. Attorneys do their own copying, and in one recent sting it was Sandy—one of the unit's two secretaries—who did the records analysis that broke the case wide open.

Even this office declines to prosecute more than half the cases referred to it by the SEC. Richard Owens, the newly minted chief of the securities task force and a six-year veteran of the unit, insists that it is not for lack of resources. There are plenty of legitimate reasons, he says, why a prosecutor would choose not to pursue a case—starting with the possibility that there may not have been true criminal intent.

But many federal regulators scoff at such bravado. "We've got too many crooks and not enough cops," says one. "We could fill Riker's Island if we had the resources."

And Owens' office is as good as it gets in this country. In other cities, federal and state prosecutors shun securities cases for all kinds of understandable reasons. They're harder to pull off than almost any other type of case—and the payoff is rarely worth it from the standpoint of local political impact. "The typical state prosecution is for a standard common-law crime," explains Philip A. Feigin, an attorney with Rothgerber Johnson & Lyons in Denver and a former commissioner of the Colorado Securities Division. "An ordinary trial will probably last for five days, it'll have 12 witnesses, involve an act that occurred in one day, and was done by one person." Now hear the pitch coming from a securities regulator thousands of miles away. "Hi. We've never met, but I've got this case I'd like you to take on. The law that was broken is just 158 pages long. It involves only three years of conduct—and the trial should last no more than three months. What do you say?" The prosecutor has eight burglaries or drug cases he could bring in the time it takes to prosecute a single white-collar crime. "It's a completely easy choice," says Feigin.

That easy choice, sadly, has left a glaring logical—and moral—fallacy in the nation's justice system: Suite thugs don't go to jail because street thugs have to. And there's one more thing on which many crime experts are adamant. The double standard makes no sense whatsoever when you consider the damage done by the offense. Sociologist Pontell and his col-

leagues Kitty Calavita, at U.C. Irvine, and Robert Tillman, at New York's St. John's University, have demonstrated this in a number of compelling academic studies. In one the researchers compared the sentences received by major players (that is, those who stole $100,000 or more) in the savings-and-loan scandal a decade ago with the sentences handed to other types of nonviolent federal offenders. The starched-collar S&L crooks got an average of 36.4 months in the slammer. Those who committed burglary—generally swiping $300 or less—got 55.6 months; car thieves, 38 months; and first-time drug offenders, 64.9 months. Now compare the costs of the two kinds of crime: The losses from all bank robberies in the U.S. in 1992 *totaled* $35 million, according to the FBI's Uniform Crime Reports. That's about 1% of the estimated cost of Charles Keating's fraud at Lincoln Savings & Loan.

"Nobody writes an e-mail that says, 'Gee, I think I'll screw the public today.' There's never been a fraud of passion."

"OF ALL THE FACTORS THAT LEAD TO CORPORATE CRIME, NONE comes close in importance to the role top management plays in tolerating, even shaping, a culture that allows for it," says William Laufer, the director of the Zicklin Center for Business Ethics Research at the Wharton School. Laufer calls it "winking." And with each wink, nod, and nudge-nudge, instructions of a sort are passed down the management chain. Accounting fraud, for example, often starts in this way. "Nobody writes an e-mail that says, 'Gee, I think I'll screw the public today,'" says former regulator Feigin. "There's never been a fraud of passion. These things take years." They breed slowly over time.

So does the impetus to fight them. Enron, of course, has stirred an embarrassed Administration and Congress to action. But it isn't merely Enron that worries legislators and the public—it's *another* Enron. Every day brings news of one more accounting gas leak that for too long lay undetected. Wariness about Lucent, Rite Aid, Raytheon, Tyco, and a host of other big names has left investors not only rattled but also questioning the very integrity of the financial reporting system.

And with good reason. Two statistics in particular suggest that no small degree of executive misconduct has been brewing in the corporate petri dish. In 1999 and 2000 the SEC demanded 96 restatements of earnings or other financial statements—a figure that was more than in the previous nine years combined. Then, in January, the Federal Deposit Insurance Corp. announced more disturbing news. The number of publicly traded companies declaring bankruptcy shot up to a record 257, a stunning 46% over the prior year's total, which itself had been a record. These companies shunted $259 billion in assets into protective custody—that is, away from shareholders. And a record 45 of these losers were biggies, companies with assets greater than $1 billion. That might all seem normal in a time of burst bubbles and economic recession. But the number of nonpublic bankruptcies has barely risen. Regulators and plaintiffs lawyers say both restatements and sudden public bankruptcies often signal the presence of fraud.

The ultimate cost could be monumental. "Integrity of the markets, and the willingness of people to invest, are critical to us," says Harvey J. Goldschmid, a professor of law at Columbia since 1970 and soon to be an SEC commissioner. "Widespread false disclosure would be incredibly dangerous. People could lose trust in corporate filings altogether."

So will all this be enough to spark meaningful changes in the system? Professor Coffee thinks the Enron matter might move Congress to take action. "I call it the phenomenon of crash-then-law," he says. "You need three things to get a wave of legislation and litigation: a recession, a stock market crash, and a true villain." For instance, Albert Wiggin, head of Chase National Bank, cleaned up during the crash of 1929 by short-selling his own company stock. "From that came a new securities law, Section 16(b), that prohibits short sales by executives," Coffee says.

But the real issue isn't more laws on the books—it's enforcing the ones that are already there. And that, says criminologist Kip Schlegel, is where the government's action falls far short of the rhetoric. In his 1994 study on securities law-breaking for the Justice Department, Schlegel found that while officials were talking tough about locking up insider traders, there was little evidence to suggest that the punishments imposed—either the incarceration rates or the sentences themselves—were more severe. "In fact," he says, "the data suggest the opposite trend. The government lacks the will to bring these people to justice."

DENNY CRAWFORD SAYS THERE'S AN ALL-TOO-SIMPLE REASON for this. The longtime commissioner of the Texas Securities Board, who has probably put away more bad guys than any other state commissioner, says most prosecutors make the crimes too complicated. "You've got to boil it down to lying, cheating, and stealing," she says, in a warbly voice that sounds like pink lemonade. "That's all it is—the best way to end securities fraud is to put every one of these crooks in jail."

Reprinted from the March 18, 2002, issue of *Fortune*, pp. 62-65 by special permission. © 2002 by Time, Inc.

UNIT 3

Groups and Roles in Transition

Unit Selections

Key Points to Consider

• Is the family in America in crisis? What indicators of family health have worsened and what indicators have improved?

• What factors are influencing women's roles today? How are they changing women's lives?

• When marriages are working badly, should the couple stay together for the kids?

• Is the American male in crisis? If so, why?

• What factors create community? How can they be brought into being under today's conditions? What are the impediments to community? What are the consequences of weak communities? Does the Internet strengthen community?

 **Links: www.dushkin.com/online/**
These sites are annotated in the World Wide Web pages.

American Men's Studies Association
http://www.vix.com/pub/men/orgs/writeups/amsa.html
The Gallup Organization
http://www.gallup.com
Marriage and Family Therapy
http://www.aamft.org/index_nm.asp
The North-South Institute
http://www.nsi-ins.ca/ensi/index.html
PsychNet/American Psychological Association
http://www.apa.org/psychnet/
SocioSite: Feminism and Woman Issues
http://www.pscw.uva.nl/sociosite/TOPICS/Women.html

Primary groups are small, intimate, spontaneous, and personal. In contrast, secondary groups are large, formal, and impersonal. Primary groups include the family, couples, gangs, cliques, teams, and small tribes or rural villages. Primary groups are the main sources that the individual draws upon in developing values and an identity. Secondary groups include most of the organizations and bureaucracies in a modern society and carry out most of its instrumental functions. Often primary groups are formed within secondary groups such as a factory, school, or business.

Urbanization, geographic mobility, centralization, bureaucratization, and other aspects of modernization have had an impact on the nature of groups, the quality of the relationships between people, and individuals' feelings of belonging. The family, in particular, has undergone radical transformation. The greatly increased participation of women in the paid labor force and their increased careerism have led to severe conflicts for women between their work and family roles.

The first subsection of this unit deals with marriage and family in the context of dramatic changes in the culture and the economy. Everyone seems to agree that the family is in trouble, but Stephanie Coontz challenges this viewpoint in the first article in this subsection. She takes issue with the data presented for the decline of marriage and the family thesis and offers evidence that marriage is strong today even though divorce is common. In fact, she argues that today's families are better than families of a century ago in many ways. According to Coontz "the biggest problem facing most families… is not that our families have changed too much but that our institutions have changed too little."

The next two articles look at the current marriage issues. The first analyzes why families are started outside of marriage and the second analyzes the impacts of marriages ending. In the first, James Wilson explores why the "illegitimacy ratio" has risen to 33 percent. Using history and statistics he searches for the major causes. Wilson argues that welfare is a cause, although a small one. The big cause is cultural change, which has removed the stigma both of welfare and of unmarried motherhood. Cultural changes have also weakened the moral underpinnings of marriage. Since Wilson believes in the power of culture he also believes that it is very hard to change the situation. The next article, by Karen Kornbluh, describes the intense time pressures that affect the 70 percent of today's families with children which are headed by two working parents. Many of the pressure problems could be greatly reduced if the work-world was more flexible and provided more options that did not have such heavy costs. Therefore, Kornbluh discusses policies that are needed to address the resulting issues.

The next subsection focuses on sexual behavior and gender roles. In "Now for the Truth About Americans and Sex," Philip Elmer-Dewitt reviews the most authoritative national survey of American sexual behavior conducted to date. Most prior surveys were deeply flawed and often misleading. He points out, among other things, that Americans are more sexually faithful to their spouses than is commonly perceived. In the next article, Evan Thomas reviews the current hot issue of gay marriages. Gay people have demanded and gradually obtained equal rights as citizens. Now they seek to gain the right to officially marry members of the same sex and two states have made gay marriages legal. According to many straight people, however, this is contrary to the true meaning of marriage as an institution so their resistance is strong. Thomas explains the current situation on this issue.

The next article discusses a dramatic way that gender roles are changing. Rather unexpectedly the number of cases of reversal of the gender of the provider role is increasing rapidly (from a small base). It is not uncommon for the wife to make as much or more money than the husband and in a small but growing number of cases she works and he does not. This is a touchy situation and the authors try to show how couples are coping with these changes.

The last subsection of unit 3 looks at cities and communities. The first article in the unit speculates on what might happen when within a half century no group will be a majority in America. Today this is true of Sacramento, California. The authors examine how this situation works out in America's most integrated city. Twenty percent of babies are multiracial and though racial tensions exist, they are relatively minor. In the second article, Amitai Etzioni describes the trends toward greater inequality and diversity in the United States and asks whether these trends threaten the integration of American society. Since the 1960s identity politics have succeeded in reducing past injustices but also have divided the nation along group lines. He then draws on sociological theory to propose ways to build community by reducing inequalities, increasing bonds, and generating stronger value commitments.

THE AMERICAN FAMILY

New research about an old institution challenges the conventional wisdom that the family today is worse off than in the past. Essay by Stephanie Coontz

As the century comes to an end, many observers fear for the future of America's families. Our divorce rate is the highest in the world, and the percentage of unmarried women is significantly higher than in 1960. Educated women are having fewer babies, while immigrant children flood the schools, demanding to be taught in their native language. Harvard University reports that only 4 percent of its applicants can write a proper sentence.

Things were worse at the turn of the last century than they are today. Most workers labored 10 hours a day, six days a week, leaving little time for family life.

There's an epidemic of sexually transmitted diseases among men. Many streets in urban neighborhoods are littered with cocaine vials. Youths call heroin "happy dust." Even in small towns, people have easy access to addictive drugs, and drug abuse by middle-class wives is skyrocketing. Police see 16-year-old killers, 12-year-old prostitutes, and gang members as young as 11.

America at the end of the 1990s? No, America at the end of the 1890s.

The litany of complaints may sound familiar, but the truth is that many things were worse at the start of this century than they are today. Then, thousands of children worked full-time in mines, mills and sweatshops. Most

workers labored 10 hours a day, often six days a week, which left them little time or energy for family life. Race riots were more frequent and more deadly than those experienced by recent generations. Women couldn't vote, and their wages were so low that many turned to prostitution.

DAHLSTROM COLLECTION/TIME INC.

c. 1890 A couple and their six children sit for a family portrait. With smaller families today, mothers spend twice as much time with each kid.

In 1900 a white child had one chance in three of losing a brother or sister before age 15, and a black child had a fifty-fifty chance of seeing a sibling die. Children's-aid groups reported widespread abuse and neglect by parents. Men who deserted or divorced their wives rarely paid child support. And only 6 percent of the children graduated from high school, compared with 88 percent today.

LEWIS HINE/CULVER PICTURES

1915 An Italian immigrant family gathers around the dinner table in an apartment on the East Side of New York City. Today, most families still eat together—but often out.

Why do so many people think American families are facing worse problems now than in the past? Partly it's because we compare the complex and diverse families of the 1990s with the seemingly more standard-issue ones of the 1950s, a unique decade when every long-term trend of the 20th century was temporarily reversed. In the 1950s, for the first time in 100 years, the divorce rate fell while marriage and fertility rates soared, crating a boom in nuclear-family living. The percentage of foreign-born individuals in the country decreased. And the debates over social and cultural issues that had divided Americans for 150 years were silenced, suggesting a national consensus on family values and norms.

Some nostalgia for the 1950s is understandable: Life looked pretty good in comparison with the hardship of the Great Depression and World War II. The GI Bill gave a generation of young fathers a college education and a subsidized mortgage on a new house. For the first time, a majority of men could support a family and buy a home without pooling their earnings with those of other family members. Many Americans built a stable family life on these foundations.

But much nostalgia for the 1950s is a result of selective amnesia—the same process that makes childhood memories of summer vacations grow sunnier with each passing year. The superficial sameness of 1950s family life was achieved through censorship, coercion and discrimination. People with unconventional beliefs faced governmental investigation and arbitrary firings. African Americans and Mexican Americans were prevented from voting in some states by literacy tests that were not ad-

ministered to whites. Individuals who didn't follow the rigid gender and sexual rules of the day were ostracized.

Leave It to Beaver did not reflect the real-life experience of most American families. While many moved into the middle class during the 1950s, poverty remained more widespread than in the worst of our last three recessions. More children went hungry, and poverty rates for the elderly were more than twice as high as today's.

Even in the white middle class, not every woman was as serenely happy with her lot as June Cleaver was on TV. Housewives of the 1950s may have been less rushed than today's working mothers, but they were more likely to suffer anxiety and depression. In many states, women couldn't serve on juries or get loans or credit cards in their own names.

And not every kid was as wholesome as Beaver Cleaver, whose mischievous antics could be handled by Dad at the dinner table. In 1955 alone, Congress discussed 200 bills aimed at curbing juvenile delinquency. Three years later, LIFE reported that urban teachers were being terrorized by their students. The drugs that were so freely available in 1900 had been outlawed, but many children grew up in families ravaged by alcohol and barbiturate abuse.

Rates of unwed childbearing tripled between 1940 and 1958, but most Americans didn't notice because unwed mothers generally left town, gave their babies up for adoption and returned home as if nothing had happened. Troubled youths were encouraged to drop out of high school. Mentally handicapped children were warehoused in institutions like the Home for Idiotic and Imbecilic Children in Kansas, where a woman whose sister had lived there for most of the 1950s once took me. Wives routinely told pollsters that being disparaged or ignored by their husbands was a normal part of a happier than-average marriage.

Many of our worries today reflect how much better we want to be, not how much better we used to be.

Denial extended to other areas of life as well. In the early 1900s, doctors refused to believe that the cases of gonorrhea and syphilis they saw in young girls could have been caused by sexual abuse. Instead, they reasoned, girls could get these diseases from toilet seats, a myth that terrified generations of mothers and daughters. In the 1950s, psychiatrists dismissed incest reports as Oedipal fantasies on the part of children.

Spousal rape was legal throughout the period and wife beating was not taken seriously by authorities. Much of what we now label child abuse was accepted as a normal part of parental discipline. Physicians saw no reason to question parents who claimed that their child's broken bones had been caused by a fall from a tree.

MARGARET BOURKE-WHITE

1937: The Hahn family sits in the living room of a working-class Muncie home, which rents for $10 a month. Class distinctions have eroded over 60 years.

American Mirror

Muncie, Ind. (pop. 67,476), calls itself America's Hometown. But to generations of sociologists it is better known as America's Middletown—the most studied place in the 20th century American landscape. "Muncie has nothing extraordinary about it," says University of Virginia professor Theodore Caplow, which is why, for the past 75 years, researchers have gone there to observe the typical American family. Muncie's averageness first drew sociologists Robert and Helen Lynd in 1924. They returned in 1935 (their follow-up study was featured in a LIFE photo essay by Margaret Bourke-White). And in 1976, armed with the Lynds' original questionnaires, Caplow launched yet another survey of the town's citizens.

Caplow discovered that family life in Muncie was much healthier in the 1970s than in the 1920s. No only were husbands and wives communicating more, but unlike married couples in the 1920s, they were also shopping, eating out, exercising and going to movies and concerts together. More than 90 percent of Muncie's couples characterized their marriages as "happy" or "very happy." In 1929 the Lynds had described partnerships of a drearier kind, "marked by sober accommodation of each partner to his share in the joint undertaking of children, paying off the mortgage and generally 'getting on.' "

Caplow's five-year study, which inspired a six-part PBS series, found that even though more moms were working outside the home, two thirds of them spent at least two hours a day with their children; in 1924 fewer than half did. In 1924 most children expected their mothers to be good cooks and housekeepers, and wanted their fathers to spend time with them and respect their opinions. Fifty years later, expectations of fathers were unchanged, but children wanted the same—time and respect—from their mothers.

This year, Caplow went back to survey the town again. The results (and another TV documentary) won't be released until December 2000.

—*Sora Song*

There are plenty of stresses in modern family life, but one reason they seem worse is that we no longer sweep them under the rug. Another is that we have higher expectations of parenting and marriage. That's a good thing. We're right to be concerned about inattentive parents, conflicted marriages, antisocial values, teen violence and child abuse. But we need to realize that many of our worries reflect how much better we *want* to be, not how much better we *used* to be.

Fathers in intact families are spending more time with their children than at any other point in the past 100 years. Although the number of hours the average woman spends at home with her children has declined since the early 1900s, there has been a decrease in the number of children per family and an increase in individual attention to each child. As a result, mothers today, including working moms, spend almost twice as much time with each child as mothers did in the 1920s. People who raised children in the 1940s and 1950s typically report that their own adult children and grandchildren communicate far better with their kids and spend more time helping with homework than they did—even as they complain that other parents today are doing a worse job than in the past.

Despite the rise in youth violence from the 1960s to the early 1990s, America's children are also safer now than they've ever been. An infant was four times more likely to die in the 1950s than today. A parent then was three times more likely than a modern one to preside at the funeral of a child under the age of 15, and 27 percent more likely to lose an older teen to death.

If we look back over the last millennium, we can see that families have always been diverse and in flux. In each period, families have solved one set of problems only to face a new array of challenges. What works for a family in one economic and cultural setting doesn't work for a family in another. What's helpful at one stage of a family's life may be destructive at the next stage. If there is one lesson to be drawn from the last millennium of family history, it's that families are always having to play catch-up with a changing world.

Take the issue of working mothers. Families in which mothers spend as much time earning a living as they do raising children are nothing new. They were the norm throughout most of the last two millennia. In the 19th century, married women in the United States began a withdrawal from the workforce, but for most families this was made possible only by sending their children out to work instead. When child labor was abolished, married women began reentering the workforce in ever large numbers.

For a few decades, the decline in child labor was greater than the growth of women's employment. The result was an aberration: the male-breadwinner family. In the 1920s, for the first time, a bare majority of American children grew up in families where the husband provided all the income, the wife stayed home full-time, and they and their siblings went to school instead of work. During the 1950s, almost two thirds of children grew up in such

MARK KAUFFMAN

1955 A family poses in Seattle. Husbands today are doing more housework.

increase from 1900 to 1950. Today, 40 percent of all marriages will end in divorce before a couple's 40th anniversary. Yet despite this high divorce rate, expanded life expectancies mean that more couples are reaching that anniversary than ever before.

Families and individuals in contemporary America have more life choices than in the past. That makes it easier for some to consider dangerous or unpopular options. But it also makes success easier for many families that never would have had a chance before—interracial, gay or lesbian, and single-mother families, for example. And it expands horizons for most families.

Women's new options are good not just for themselves but for their children. While some people say that women who choose to work are selfish, it turns out that maternal self-sacrifice is not good for children. Kids do better when their mothers are happy with their lives, whether their satisfaction comes from being a full-time homemaker or from having a job.

Largely because of women's new roles at work, men are doing more at home. Although most men still do less housework than their wives, the gap has been halved since the 1960s. Today, 49 percent of couples say they share childcare equally, compared with 25 percent of 1985.

Men's greater involvement at home is good for their relationships with their parents, and also good for their children. Hands-on fathers make better parents than men who let their wives do all the nurturing and childcare: They raise sons who are more expressive and daughters who are more likely to do well in school, especially in math and science.

The biggest problem is not that our families have changed too much but that our institutions have changed too little.

families, an all-time high. Yet that same decade saw an acceleration of workforce participation by wives and mothers that soon made the dual-earner family the norm, a trend not likely to be reversed in the next century.

What's new is not that women make half their families' living, but that for the first time they have substantial control over their own income, along with the social freedom to remain single or to leave an unsatisfactory marriage. Also new is the declining proportion of their lives that people devote to rearing children, both because they have fewer kids and because they are living longer. Until about 1940, the typical marriage was broken by the death of one partner within a few years after the last child left home. Today, couples can look forward to spending more than two decades together after the children leave.

The growing length of time partners spend with only each other for company has made many individuals less willing to put up with an unhappy marriage, while women's economic independence makes it less essential for them to do so. It is no wonder that divorce has risen steadily since 1900. Disregarding a spurt in 1946, a dip in the 1950s and another peak around 1980, the divorce rate is just where you'd expect to find it, based on the rate of

In 1900, life expectancy was 47 years, and only 4 percent of the population was 65 or older. Today, life expectancy is 76 years, and by 2025, about 20 percent of Americans will be 65 or older. For the first time, a generation of adults must plan for the needs of both their parents and their children. Most Americans are responding with remarkable grace. One in four households gives the equivalent of a full day a week or more in unpaid care to an aging relative, and more than half say they expect to do so in the next 10 years. Older people are less likely to be impoverished or incapacitated by illness than in the past, and they have more opportunity to develop a relationship with their grandchildren.

Even some of the choices that worry us the most are turning out to be manageable. Divorce rates are likely to remain high, but more non-custodial parents are staying in touch with their children. Child-support receipts are up. And a lower proportion of kids from divorced families are exhibiting problems than in earlier decades. Stepfamilies are learning to maximize children's access to supportive adults rather than cutting them off from one side of the family.

Out-of-wedlock births are also high, however, and this will probably continue because the age of first marriage for women has risen to an all-time high of 25, almost five years above what it was in the 1950s. Women who marry at an older age are less likely to divorce, but they have more years when they are at risk—or at choice—for a nonmarital birth.

Nevertheless, births to teenagers have fallen from 50 percent of all nonmarital births in the late 1970s to just 30 percent today. A growing proportion of women who have a nonmarital birth are in their twenties and thirties and usually have more economic and educational resources than unwed mothers of the past. While two involved parents are generally better than one, a mother's personal maturity, along with her educational and economic status, is a better predictor of how well her child will turn out than her marital status. We should no longer assume that children raised by single parents face debilitating disadvantages.

As we begin to understand the range of sizes, shapes and colors that today's families come in, we find that the differences *within* family types are more important than the differences *between* them. No particular family form guarantees success, and no particular form is doomed to fail. How a family functions on the inside is more important than how it looks from the outside.

The biggest problem facing most families as this century draws to a close is not that our families have changed too much but that our institutions have changed too little. America's work policies are 50 years out of date, designed for a time when most moms weren't in the workforce and most dads didn't understand the joys of being involved in childcare. Our school schedules are 150 years out of date, designed for a time when kids needed to be home to help with the milking and haying. And many political leaders feel they have to decide whether to help parents stay home longer with their kids or invest in better childcare, preschool and afterschool programs, when most industrialized nations have long since learned it's possible to do both.

So America's social institutions have some Y2K bugs to iron out. But for the most part, our families are ready for the next millennium.

DIVORCE AND COHABITATION

Why We Don't Marry

JAMES Q. WILSON

Everyone knows that the rising proportion of women who bear and raise children out of wedlock has greatly weakened the American family system. This phenomenon, once thought limited to African Americans, now affects whites as well, so much so that the rate at which white children are born to an unmarried mother is now as high as the rate for black children in the mid-1960s, when Daniel Patrick Moynihan issued his famous report on the Negro family. For whites the rate is one-fifth; for blacks it is over one-half.

Almost everyone—a few retrograde scholars excepted—agrees that children in mother-only homes suffer harmful consequences: the best studies show that these youngsters are more likely than those in two-parent families to be suspended from school, have emotional problems, become delinquent, suffer from abuse, and take drugs. Some of these problems may arise from the economic circumstances of these one-parent families, but the best studies, such as those by Sara McLanahan and Gary Sandefur, show that low income can explain, at most, about half of the differences between single-parent and two-parent families. The rest of the difference is explained by a mother living without a husband.

And even the income explanation is a bit misleading, because single moms, by virtue of being single, are more likely to be poor than are married moms. Now that our social security and pension systems have dramatically reduced poverty among the elderly, growing up with only one parent has dramatically increased poverty among children. In this country we have managed to shift poverty from old folks to young folks. Former Clinton advisor William Galston sums up the matter this way: you need only do three things in this country to avoid poverty—finish high school, marry before having a child, and marry after the age of 20. Only 8 percent of the families who do this are poor; 79 percent of those who fail to do this are poor.

This pattern of children being raised by single parents is now a leading feature of the social life of almost all English-speaking countries and some European ones. The illegitimacy ratio in the late 1990s was 33 percent for the United States, 31 percent for Canada, and 38 percent for the United Kingdom.

Now, not all children born out of wedlock are raised by a single mother. Some, especially in Sweden, are raised by a man and woman who, though living together, are not married; others are raised by a mother who gets married shortly after the birth. Nevertheless, there has been a sharp increase in children who are not only born out of wedlock but are raised without a father. In the United States, the percentage of children living with an unmarried mother has tripled since 1960 and more than doubled since 1970. In England, 22 percent of all children under the age of 16 are living with only one parent, a rate three times higher than in 1971.

Why has this happened? There are two possible explanations to consider: money and culture.

Money readily comes to mind. If a welfare system pays unmarried mothers enough to have their own apartment, some women will prefer babies to husbands. When government subsidizes something, we get more of it. But for many years, American scholars discounted this possibility. Since the amount of welfare paid per mother had declined in inflation-adjusted terms, and since the amount paid in each state showed no correlation with each state's illegitimacy rate, surely money could not have caused the increase in out-of-wedlock births.

This view dominated scholarly discussions until the 1990s. But there are three arguments against it. First, the inflation-adjusted value of welfare benefits was not the key factor. What counted was the inflation-adjusted value of all the benefits an unmarried mother might receive—not only welfare, but also food stamps, public housing, and Medicaid. By adding these in, welfare kept up with inflation.

Second, what counted was not how much money each state paid out, but how much it paid compared with the cost of living in that state. As Charles Murray pointed out, the benefits for a woman in New Orleans ($654 a month) and those for one in San Francisco ($867 a month) made nearly identical contributions to the cost of living, because in New Orleans it cost about two-thirds as much to live as it did in San Francisco.

Third, comparing single-parent families and average spending levels neglects the real issue: how attractive is welfare to a low-income unmarried woman in a given locality? When economist Mark Rosenzweig asked this question of women who are part of the National Longitudinal Survey of Youth—a panel study of people that has been going on since 1979—he found that a 10 percent increase in welfare benefits made the chances that a poor young woman would have a baby out of wedlock before the age of 22 go up by 12 percent. And this was true for whites as well as blacks. Soon other scholars were confirming Rosenzweigs findings. Welfare made a difference.

WELFARE CHILDREN

But how big a difference? AFDC began in 1935, but by 1960 only 4 percent of the children getting welfare had a mother who had never been married; the rest had mothers who were widows or had been separated from their husbands. By 1996 that had changed dramatically: now approximately two-thirds of welfare children had an unmarried mom, and hardly any were the offspring of widows.

Why this change? At least for blacks, one well-known explanation has been offered: men did not marry because there were no jobs for them in the big cities. As manufacturing employment sharply declined in the central cities, William Julius Wilson has argued, blacks were unable to move to the suburbs as fast as the jobs. The unemployed males left behind are not very attractive as prospective husbands to the women they know, and so more and more black women do without marriage.

The argument has not withstood scholarly criticism. First, Mexican Americans, especially illegal immigrants, live in the central city also, but the absence of good jobs has not mattered, even though many Mexicans are poorer than blacks, speak English badly, and if undocumented cannot get good jobs. Nevertheless, the rate of out-of-wedlock births is much lower among these immigrants than it is among African Americans, as W. J. Wilson acknowledges.

Second, Christopher Jencks has shown that there has been as sharp a decline in marriage among employed black men as among unemployed ones, and that the supply of employed blacks is large enough to provide husbands for almost all unmarried black mothers. For these people, as Jencks concludes, "marriage must… have been losing its charms for non-economic reasons."

Moreover, the argument that single-parent families have increased because black men have not been able to move to wherever factory jobs can be found does not explain why such families have grown so rapidly among whites, for whom moving around a city should be no problem. For these whites—and I suspect for many blacks as well—there must be another explanation.

To explain the staggering increase in unmarried mothers, we must turn to culture. In this context, what I mean by culture is simply that being an unmarried mother and living on welfare has lost its stigma. At one time living on the dole was shameful; now it is much less so. As this may not be obvious to some people, let me add some facts that will support it.

STIGMA

Women in rural communities who go on welfare leave it much sooner than the same kind of women who take welfare in big cities, and this is true for both whites and blacks and regardless of the size of their families. The studies that show this outcome offer a simple explanation for it. In a small town, everyone knows who is on welfare, and welfare recipients do not have many friends in the same situation with whom they can associate. But in a big city, welfare recipients are not known to everyone, and each one can easily associate with other women living the same way. In the small town, welfare recipients tell interviewers the same story: "I always felt like I was being watched"; "they treat us like welfare cattle"; people make "nasty comments." But in a big city, recipients had a different story: Everyone "is in the same boat I am"; people "dont look down on you."

American courts have made clear that welfare laws cannot be used to enforce stigma. When Alabama tried in 1960 to deny welfare to an unmarried woman who was living with a man who was not her husband, the U.S. Supreme Court objected. Immorality, it implied, was an outdated notion. The states have no right to limit welfare to a "worthy person," and welfare belongs to the child, not the mother. If the state is concerned about immorality, it will have to rehabilitate the women by other means.

How did stigma get weakened by practice and undercut by law, when Americans—no less than Brits, Canadians, and Australians—favor marriage and are skeptical of welfare?

Let me suggest that beneath the popular support for marriage there has slowly developed, almost unnoticed, a subversion of it, which can be summarized this way: whereas marriage was once thought to be about a social union, it is now about personal preferences. Formerly, law and opinion enforced the desirability of marriage without asking what went on in that union; today, law and opinion enforce the desirability of personal happiness without worrying much about maintaining a formal relationship. Marriage was once a sacrament, then it became a contract, and now it is an arrangement. Once religion provided the sacrament, then the law enforced the contract, and now personal preferences define the arrangement.

The cultural change that made this happen was the same one that gave us science, technology, freedom, and capitalism: the Enlightenment. The Enlightenment—that extraordinary intellectual development that began in eighteenth-century England, Scotland, Holland, and Germany—made human reason the measure of all things, throwing off ancient rules if they fell short. What the king once ordered, what bishops once enforced, what tradition once required was to be set aside in the name of scientific knowledge and personal self-discovery. The Enlightenment's great spokesmen were David Hume, Adam Smith, and Immanuel Kant; its greatest accomplishment was the creation of the United States of America.

I am a great admirer of the Enlightenment. But it entailed costs. I take great pride in the vast expansion in human freedom that the Enlightenment conferred on so many people, but I also know that the Enlightenment spent little time worrying about those cultural habits that make freedom meaningful and constructive. The family was one of these.

THE ENLIGHTENMENT

It was in the world most affected by the Enlightenment that we find both its good and bad legacies. There we encounter both remarkable science and personal self-indulgence. There we find human freedom and high rates of crime. There we find democratic governments and frequent divorces. There we find regimes concerned about the poor and a proliferation of single-parent families.

Single-parent families are most common in those nations—England, America, Canada, Australia, France, the Netherlands—where the Enlightenment had its greatest effect. Such families are far less common in Italy, Spain, Eastern Europe, Russia, the Middle East, China, and Japan. It was in the enlightened nations that nuclear rather than extended families became common, that individual consent and not clan control was the basis of a marriage contract, and that divorce first became legal.

But why did the Enlightenment have its greatest effect on the English-speaking world and on northwestern Europe? I think it was because life in those countries had for so long been arranged in ways that provided fertile ground in which human reason and personal freedom could take root and prosper. Alan Macfarlane, the great English anthropologist, has shown that land in England was individually owned as far back as the thirteenth century and possibly even earlier. There, and in similar countries in northwestern Europe, land ownership had established the basis for a slow assertion of human rights and legal defenses. If you own the land, you have a right to keep, sell, or bequeath it, and you have access to courts that will defend those rights and, in defending them, will slowly add more rights.

LAND OWNERSHIP

Marriage depended on land. Until a young man inherited or bought a piece of property, he was in no position to take a wife. The rule was: no land, no marriage. As a result, English men and women married at a much older age than was true elsewhere. But with the rise of cities and the growth of industrialism, that began to change. Now a man and a woman, already defined by rights that were centuries old, could marry on an income, not on a farm, and so they married at a younger age.

English couples could get married on the basis of their individual consent, without obtaining the formal approval of their parents, though parents still might try to influence these decisions, and among the landed aristocracy such influence was often decisive. But for most people, the old rule of the Roman Catholic church was in force: no marriage was legitimate unless the man and woman freely consented. That rule found its widest observance in countries like England, where individual land ownership and personal rights reinforced it.

In Eastern Europe, to say nothing of the Middle and Far East, a different culture had been created out of a different system for owning land. In many parts of these regions, land lay in the control of families and clans. No individual owned it, and no individual could sell or bequeath it. One man might run the farm, but he did so not on the basis of ownership, but because of his seniority or skill, with the land itself remaining the property of an extended family.

In these places—where courts, unimportant in matters of real estate, tended to be unimportant in other respects as well—human rights were less likely to develop. In clan-based regimes, families often decided what man a woman might marry, and, since family labor worked family-owned land, men and women married at a young age, in hopes of adding many children to the common labor force.

The Enlightenment did not change the family immediately, because everyone took family life for granted. The most important Enlightenment thinkers assumed marriage and denounced divorce. That assumption—and in time that denunciation—slowly lost force, as people gradually experienced the widening of human freedom.

The laws, until well into the twentieth century, made it crystal clear that, though a child might be conceived by an unmarried couple, once born it had to have two parents. There was no provision for the state to pay for a single-parent child, and public opinion strongly and unanimously endorsed that policy.

But by the end of the nineteenth century and the early years of the twentieth, policies changed, and then, slowly, opinion changed. Two things precipitated the change: first, a compassionate desire to help needy children; and second, a determination to end the legal burdens under which women suffered. The first was a powerful force, especially since the aid to needy children was designed to help those who had lost their fathers owing to wars or accidents, as so many did as a consequence of the First World War and of industrial or mining accidents. Slowly, however, a needy child was redefined to include those of any mother without a husband, and not just any who had become a widow.

EMANCIPATION OF WOMEN

The emancipation of women was also a desirable process. In America and England, nineteenth-century women already had more rights than those in most of Europe, but when married they still could not easily own property, file for a divorce, or conduct their own affairs. By the 1920s most of these restrictions had ended, and once women got the vote, there was no chance of these limitations ever being reinstated.

We should therefore not be surprised that the twenties were an enthusiastic display of unchaperoned dating, provocative dress, and exhibitionist behavior. Had it not been for a time-out imposed by the Great Depression and the Second World War, we would no longer be referring to the sixties as an era of self-indulgence; we would be talking about the legacy of the twenties.

The sixties reinstated trends begun half a century earlier, but now without effective opposition. No-fault divorce laws were passed throughout most of the West, the pill and liberalized abortion laws dramatically reduced the chances of unwanted pregnancies, and popular entertainment focused on pleasing the young. As a result, family law, in Carl Schneider's term, lost its moral basis. It was easier to get out of a marriage than a mortgage. This change in culture was made crystal clear by court decisions. At the end of the nineteenth century, the Supreme Court referred to marriage as a "holy estate" and a "sacred obligation." By 1965 the same court described marriage as "an association of two individuals."

People still value marriage; but it is only that value—and very little social pressure or legal obligation—that sustains it.

But there is another part of the cultural argument, and it goes to the question of why African Americans have such high rates of mother-only families. When black scholars addressed this question, as did W. E. B. DuBois in 1908 and E. Franklin Frazier in 1939, they argued that slavery had weakened the black family. When Daniel Patrick Moynihan repeated this argument in 1965, he was denounced for "blaming the victim."

An intense scholarly effort to show that slavery did little harm to African-American families followed that denunciation; instead, what really hurt them was migrating to big cities where they encountered racism and oppression.

SLAVERY

It was an astonishing argument. Slavery, a vast and cruel system of organized repression that, for over two centuries, denied to blacks the right to marry, vote, sue, own property, or take an oath; that withheld from them the proceeds of their own labor; that sold them and their children on the auction block; that exposed them to brutal and unjust punishment: all this misery had little or no effect on family life, but moving as free people to a big city did. To state the argument is to refute it.

But since some people take academic nonsense seriously, let me add that we now know, thanks to such scholars as Orlando Patterson, Steven Ruggles, and Brenda E. Stevenson, that this argument was empirically wrong. The scholars who made it committed some errors. In calculating what percentage of black mothers had husbands, they accepted many women's claims that they were widows, when we now know that such claims were often lies, designed to conceal that the respondents had never been married. In figuring out what proportion of slaves were married, these scholars focused on large plantations, where the chance of having a spouse was high, instead of on small ones, where most slaves lived, and where the chance of having a spouse was low. On these small farms, only about one-fifth of the slaves lived in a nuclear household.

After slavery ended, sharecropping took its place. For the family, this was often no great improvement. It meant that it was very difficult for a black man to own property and thus hard for him to provide for the progress of his children or bequeath to them a financial start in life. Being a tenant farmer also meant that he needed help on the land, and so he often had many children, despite the fact that, without owning the land, he could not provide for their future.

The legacy of this sad history is twofold. First, generations of slaves grew up without having a family, or without having one that had any social and cultural meaning. Second, black boys grew up aware that their fathers were often absent or were sexually active with other women, giving the boys poor role models for marriage. Today, studies show that the African-American boys most likely to find jobs are those who reject, rather than emulate, their fathers; whereas for white boys, those most likely to find work are those who admire their fathers.

What is astonishing today is that so many African Americans are married and lead happy and productive lives. This is an extraordinary accomplishment, of which everyone should be proud. But it is an accomplishment limited to only about half of all black families, and white families seem to be working hard to catch up.

But there remains at least one more puzzle to solve. Culture has shaped how we produce and raise children, but that culture surely had its greatest impact on how educated people think. Yet the problem of weak, single-parent families is greatest among the least educated people. Why should a culture that is so powerfully shaped by upper-middle-class beliefs have so profound an effect on poor people? If some intellectuals have devalued marriage, why should ordinary people do so? If white culture has weakened marriage, why should black culture follow suit?

I suspect that the answer may be found in Myron Magnet's book *The Dream and the Nightmare*. When the haves remake a culture, the people who pay the price are the have-nots. Let me restate his argument with my own metaphor. Imagine a game of crack-the-whip, in which a line of children, holding hands, starts running in a circle. The first few children have no problem keeping up, but near the end of the line the last few must run so fast that many fall down. Those children who did not begin the turning suffer most from the turn.

There are countless examples of our cultural crack-the-whip. Heroin and cocaine use started among elites and then spread down the social scale. When the elites wanted to stop, they could hire doctors and therapists; when the poor wanted to stop, they could not hire anybody. The elites endorsed community-based centers to treat mental illness, and so mental hospitals were closed down. The elites hired psychiatrists; the poor slept on the streets. People who practiced contraception endorsed loose sexuality in writing and movies; the poor practiced loose sexuality without contraception. Divorce is more common among the affluent than the poor. The latter, who can't afford divorce, deal with unhappy marriages by not getting married in the first place. My only trivial quarrel with Magnet is that I believe these changes began a century ago and even then built on more profound changes that date back centuries.

Now you probably expect me to tell you what we can do about this, but if you believe, as I do, in the power of culture, you will realize that there is very little one can do. As a University of Chicago professor once put it, if you succeed in explaining why something is so, you have probably succeeded in explaining why it must be so. He implied what is in fact often the case: change is very hard.

The remarkable fact is that today so many Americans value marriage, get married, and want their children to marry. Many often cohabit, but when a child arrives most get married. The ones who don't make their children suffer. But to many people the future means more cohabitation—more "relationships"—and fewer marriages. Their goal is Sweden, where marriage is slowly going out of style.

The difficulty with cohabitation as opposed to marriage has been brilliantly laid out by Linda Waite and Maggie Gallagher in their book *The Case for Marriage*. In it they show that married people, especially men, benefit greatly from marriage: they are healthier, live longer, and are less depressed. But many young men today have not absorbed that lesson. They act as if sex is more important than marriage, worry more about scoring than dating, and are rewarded by their buddies when they can make it with a lot of young women. To them, marriage is at best a long-term benefit, while sex is an immediate preoccupation. This fact supplies us with a sober lesson: the sexual revolution—one that began nearly a century ago but was greatly hastened by the 1960s—was supposed to help make men and women equal. Instead it has helped men, while leaving many women unmarried spectators watching *Sex and the City* on HBO.

One could imagine an effort to change our culture, but one must recognize that there are many aspects of it that no one, least of all I, wants to change. We do not want fewer freedoms or less democracy. Most of us, myself included, do not want to change any of the gains women have made in establishing their moral and legal standing as independent actors with all the rights that men once enjoyed alone. We can talk about tighter divorce laws, but it is not easy to design one that both protects people from ending a marriage too quickly with an easy divorce and at the same time makes divorce for a good cause readily available.

The right and best way for a culture to restore itself is for it to be rebuilt, not from the top down by government policies, but from the bottom up by personal decisions. On the side of that effort, we can find churches—or at least many of them—and the common experience of adults that the essence of marriage is not sex, or money, or even children: it is commitment.

Mr. Wilson teaches at Pepperdine University. From "Why We Don't Marry," by James Q. Wilson, City Journal, *Winter 2002, pages 46–55.*

THE PARENT TRAP

*Working American parents have twenty-two fewer hours a week
to spend with their kids than they did thirty years ago.
Here's how to help the new "juggler family"*

BY KAREN KORNBLUH

The American family changed dramatically over the last decades of the twentieth century. In the postwar years up to the early 1970s a single breadwinner—working forty hours a week, often for the same employer, until retirement—generally earned enough to support children and a spouse. Today fully 70 percent of families with children are headed by two working parents or by an unmarried working parent. The traditional family—one breadwinner and one homemaker—has been replaced by the "juggler family," and American parents have twenty-two fewer hours a week to spend with their kids than they did in 1969. As a result, millions of children are left in unlicensed day care or at home with the TV as a babysitter.

Yet the nation clings to the ideal of the 1950s family; many of our policies for and cultural attitudes toward families are relics of a time when Father worked and Mother was home to mind the children. Every time a working parent has to risk a job to take a sick child to the doctor, and every time parents have to leave their children home alone or entrust them to inadequate supervision, families are paying the price for our outdated policies.

The 1950s family is not coming back anytime soon, however, in part because the economic conditions that supported it no longer exist. Starting in the 1970s de-industrialization, corporate restructuring, and globalization led to stagnating wages and greater economic insecurity. Many women went to work to help make ends meet. Indeed, conservatives who lament that feminism undermined the traditional family model overlook the fact that the changing economic environment made that model financially impossible for most American families.

These days most women and men—across all income levels—expect to remain in the workplace after having children. Thus to be decent parents, workers now need greater flexibility than they once did. Yet good part-time or flex-time jobs remain rare. Whereas companies have embraced flexibility in virtually every other aspect of their businesses (inventory control, production schedules, financing), full-time workers' schedules remain inflexible. Employers often demand that high-level workers be available around the clock, and hourly workers can be fired for refusing overtime. Moreover, many employees have no right to a minimum number of sick or vacation days: more than a third of all working parents—and an even larger percentage of low-income parents—lack both sick and vacation leave. Though the Family and Medical Leave Act of 1993 finally guaranteed that workers at large companies could take a leave of absence for the birth or adoption of a baby, or for the illness of a family member, that leave is unpaid. This means that the United States is one of only two countries in the Organization for Economic Cooperation and Development without paid maternity leave—and the other country, Australia, is actively considering providing it.

Many parents who need flexibility find themselves shunted into part-time, temporary, on-call, or contract jobs with reduced wages and career opportunities and, often, no benefits. A full quarter of American workers are in these jobs. Only 15 percent of women and 12 percent of men in such jobs receive health insurance from their employers. In other developed countries health benefits are often government-provided, and therefore not contingent on full-time employment. The United States is the only advanced industrial nation that relies on a voluntary employer-based system to provide health insurance and retirement benefits to its citizens.

Our nation has also failed to respond to the need for affordable, high-quality child care. Schools still operate on an agrarian schedule, closing at three every day and for more than two months in the summer. After-school-care programs are relatively scarce, and day-care standards are uneven. (Training requirements for hairdressers and manicurists are currently more stringent than those for child-care workers.) And the expense of day care—which

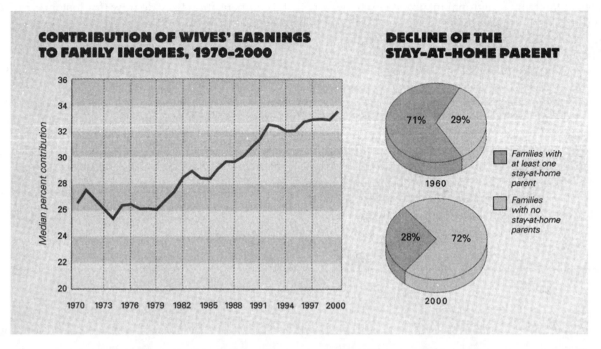

CONTRIBUTION OF WIVES' EARNINGS TO FAMILY INCOMES, 1970-2000

DECLINE OF THE STAY-AT-HOME PARENT

1960

71% 29%

2000

28% 72%

Families with at least one stay-at-home parent

Families with no stay-at-home parents

CHART DATA SOURCES: (LEFT) THE ECONOMIC POLICY INSTITUTE. (RIGHT) U.S. CENSUS BUREAU; BUREAU OF LABOR STATISTICS

is often more than the tuition at a state college—is borne almost entirely by parents alone. In stark contrast, most European nations view child care as a national responsibility and publicly subsidize it. In France, for instance, day-care centers and preschools are heavily subsidized—and staffed by qualified child-care workers whose education is financed by the government.

A sensible modern family policy—that supports rather than undermines today's juggler family—would have three components. The first is paid leave. No American worker should have to fear losing a job or suffering a reduction in pay because he or she needs to care for a child or a parent. Every worker should be entitled to at least a minimum number of days of paid leave for personal illness or that of a family member, or to care for a new child. In September, California adopted the first law in the country that provides workers with paid family and medical leave, up to six weeks' worth.

The second component of a smart family policy is high-quality child care. The United States is practically alone among developed countries in leaving day care almost entirely to the private market. At a minimum, U.S. day-care facilities must be held to higher standards than they are now, and parents should be eligible for subsidies, so that they do not have to shoulder the cost of this care all on their own. In addition, preschool and after-school programs should be universally available.

The third and most important component is more fundamental: we should sever the link between employers and basic benefits. In today's labor market, when working parents need maximum flexibility and people move

frequently from job to job, it no longer makes sense to rely on employers for the provision of health insurance and pensions. The link between them is an industrial-era relic that often denies benefits and tax subsidies to parents who require nonstandard working arrangements. We need a new approach to our social-insurance system, one in which control and responsibility lie with individuals, not their employers, and in which government subsidies are granted based on an individual's ability to pay, rather than on whether he or she works full time, part time, or flex time. Unlinking benefits from employment could do wonders for the American family: parents could have the flexibility of part-time work with the benefits that today accompany full-time work.

How to unlink pensions from employment—by providing universal 401(k) accounts that offer government subsidies to the poorest workers—is addressed elsewhere in this issue (see "Spendthrift Nation," page 102). Unlinking health care from employment could be accomplished in a number of ways. One way would be to expand Medicare to cover all citizens, not just the elderly, thus creating a single-payer system. But a better approach would be to create a system of mandatory self-insurance, with government subsidies for low-income workers and for people taking time off to care for family members. Creating such a system—one that ensures that everyone is covered while keeping costs low—could not be done easily or quickly, of course, but there are precedents. Switzerland, for instance, provides universal health-care coverage without relying on a single-payer system. Another model can be found closer to home: auto insurance, which almost all American states require car owners to have. In the health-care version of this model everyone would either choose a plan from a regional insurance exchange or be enrolled in a default plan by the government. Participating health-insurance providers would be required to offer a "basic" plan—with a minimum level of coverage—and to cover anyone who applied. Federal subsidies would ensure that no one spent more than a fixed percentage of income on basic health insurance.

Though the government would have to subsidize those who cannot afford to pay for a basic plan on their own, this cost could be largely offset by redirecting both the funds currently spent on Medicaid and the nearly $100 billion that workers get in tax breaks through their employer-provided health insurance. Employers should welcome the change, because although they would likely continue to provide employees with the same level of to-tal compensation they do now (for instance, by increasing wages), they would be relieved of the administrative burdens and the restrictions of flexibility imposed by the current social-insurance system.

For the past few decades both Democrats and Republicans have tried to lay claim to the "pro-family" mantle. Neither party, however, has offered a coherent plan for giving American parents the security and the flexibility they need. A plan that offers both would appeal powerfully to the many voters who are having such difficulty balancing their work and family obligations.

Karen Kornbluh, a fellow at the New America Foundation and the director of its Work and Family Program, was previously the deputy chief of staff at the U.S. Department of the Treasury.

Now for the Truth About Americans and
SEX

The first comprehensive survey since Kinsey smashes some of our most intimate myths

PHILIP ELMER-DEWITT

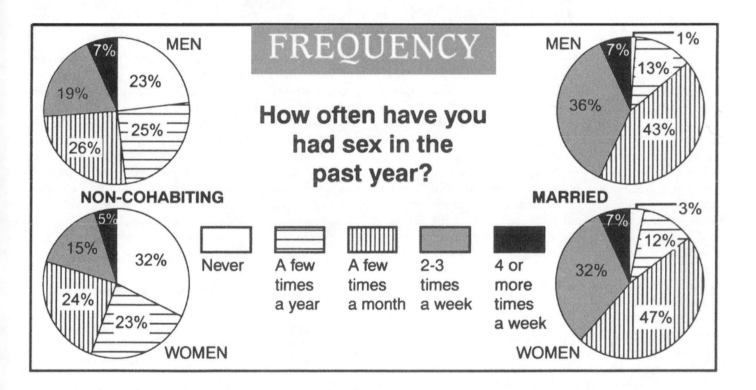

FREQUENCY

How often have you had sex in the past year?

MEN

NON-COHABITING
23% 25% 26% 19% 7%

WOMEN
32% 23% 24% 15% 5%

MEN

MARRIED
1% 13% 43% 36% 7%

WOMEN
3% 12% 47% 32% 7%

Never | A few times a year | A few times a month | 2-3 times a week | 4 or more times a week

Is THERE A LIVING, BREATHING ADULT WHO hasn't at times felt the nagging suspicion that in bedrooms across the country, on kitchen tables, in limos and other venues too scintillating to mention, other folks are having more sex, livelier sex, better sex? Maybe even that quiet couple right next door is having more fun in bed, and more often. Such thoughts spring, no doubt, from a primal anxiety deep within the human psyche. It has probably haunted men and women since the serpent

pointed Eve toward the forbidden fruit and urged her to get with the program.

Still, it's hard to imagine a culture more conducive to feelings of sexual inadequacy than America in the 1990s. Tune in to the soaps. Flip through the magazines. Listen to Oprah. Lurk in the seamier corners of cyberspace. What do you see and hear? An endless succession of young, hard bodies preparing for, recovering from or engaging in constant, relentless copulation. Sex is every-

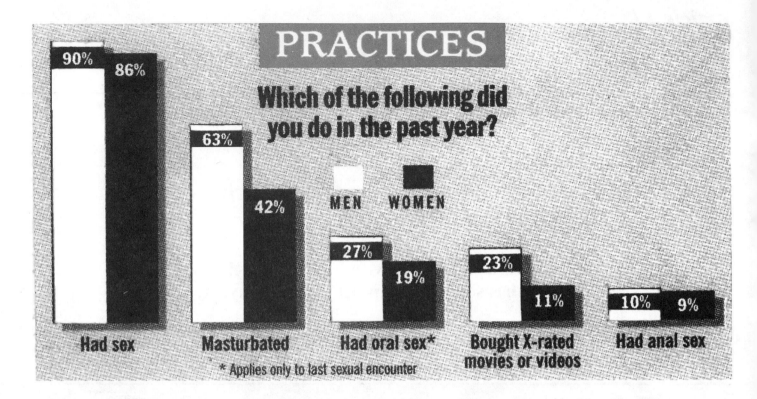

PRACTICES

Which of the following did you do in the past year?

MEN   WOMEN

Had sex 90% 86%

Masturbated 63% 42%

Had oral sex* 27% 19%

Bought X-rated movies or videos 23% 11%

Had anal sex 10% 9%

* Applies only to last sexual encounter

where in America—and in the ads, films, TV shows and music videos it exports abroad. Although we know that not every ZIP code is a Beverly Hills, 90210, and not every small town a Peyton Place, the impression that is branded on our collective subconscious is that life in the twilight of the 20th century is a sexual banquet to which everyone else has been invited.

Just how good is America's sex life? Nobody knows for sure. Don't believe the magazine polls that have Americans mating energetically two or three times a week. Those surveys are inflated from the start by the people who fill them out: *Playboy* subscribers, for example, who brag about their sex lives in reader-survey cards. Even the famous Kinsey studies—which caused such a scandal in the late 1940s and early '50s by reporting that half of American men had extramarital affairs—were deeply flawed. Although Alfred Kinsey was a biologist by training (his expertise was the gall wasp), he compromised science and took his human subjects where he could find them: in boardinghouses, college fraternities, prisons and mental wards. For 14 years he collared hitchhikers who passed through town and quizzed them mercilessly. It was hardly a random cross section.

Now, more than 40 years after Kinsey, we finally have some answers. A team of researchers based at the University of Chicago has released the long-awaited results of what is probably the first truly scientific survey of who does what with whom in America and just how often they do it.

The findings—based on face-to-face interviews with a random sample of nearly 3,500 Americans, ages 18 to 59, selected using techniques honed through decades of po-

litical and consumer polling—will smash a lot of myths. "Whether the numbers are reassuring or alarming depends on where you sit," warns Edward Laumann, the University of Chicago sociologist who led the research team. While the scientists found that the spirit of the sexual revolution is alive and well in some quarters—they found that about 17% of American men and 3% of women have had sex with at least 21 partners—the overall impression is that the sex lives of most Americans are about as exciting as a peanut-butter-and-jelly sandwich.

Among the key findings:

- Americans fall into three groups. One-third have sex twice a week or more, one-third a few times a month, and one-third a few times a year or not at all.

- Americans are largely monogamous. The vast majority (83%) have one or zero sexual partners a year. Over a lifetime, a typical man has six partners; a woman, two.

- Married couples have the most sex and are the most likely to have orgasms when they do. Nearly 40% of married people say they have sex twice a week, compared with 25% for singles.

- Most Americans don't go in for the kinky stuff. Asked to rank their favorite sex acts, almost everybody (96%) found vaginal sex "very or somewhat appealing." Oral sex ranked a distant third, after an activity that many may not have realized was a sex act: "Watching partner undress."

- Adultery is the exception in America, not the rule. Nearly 75% of married men and 85% of married women say they have never been unfaithful.
- There are a lot fewer active homosexuals in America than the oft-repeated 1 in 10. Only 2.7% of men and 1.3% of women report that they had homosexual sex in the past year.

THE FULL RESULTS OF THE NEW SURVEY ARE SCHEDULED to be published next week as *The Social Organization of Sexuality* (University of Chicago; $49.95), a thick, scientific tome co-authored by Laumann, two Chicago colleagues—Robert Michael and Stuart Michaels—and John Gagnon, a sociologist from the State University of New York at Stony Brook. A thinner companion volume, *Sex in America: A Definitive Survey* (Little, Brown; $22.95), written with New York Times science reporter Gina Kolata, will be in bookstores this week.

54% of men think about sex daily. 19% of women do

But when the subject is sex, who wants to wait for the full results? Even before the news broke last week, critics and pundits were happy to put their spin on the study.

"It doesn't ring true," insisted Jackie Collins, author of *The Bitch*, *The Stud* and other potboilers. "Where are the deviants? Where are the flashers? Where are the sex maniacs I see on TV every day?"

"I'm delighted to hear that all this talk about rampant infidelity was wildly inflated," declared postfeminist writer Camille Paglia. "But if they're saying the sexual revolution never happened, that's ridiculous."

"Positively, outrageously stupid and unbelievable," growled *Penthouse* publisher Bob Guccione. "I would say five partners a year is the average for men."

"Totally predictable," deadpanned Erica Jong, author of the 1973 sex fantasy *Fear of Flying*. "Americans are more interested in money than sex."

"Our Puritan roots are deep," said *Playboy* founder Hugh Hefner, striking a philosophical note. "We're fascinated by sex and afraid of it."

"Two partners? I mean, come on!" sneered *Cosmopolitan* editor Helen Gurley Brown. "We advise our Cosmo girls that when people ask how many partners you've had, the correct answer is always three, though there may have been more."

Europeans seemed less surprised—one way or the other—by the results of the survey. The low numbers tend to confirm the Continental caricature of Americans as flashy and bold onscreen but prone to paralysis in bed. Besides, the findings were pretty much in line with recent studies conducted in England and France that also found low rates of homosexuality and high rates of marital fidelity. (The French will be gratified by what a comparison of these surveys shows: that the average Frenchman and -woman has sex about twice as often as Americans do.)

If the study is as accurate as it purports to be, the results will be in line with the experience of most Americans. For many, in fact, they will come as a relief. "A lot of people think something is wrong with them when they don't have sexual feelings," says Toby, a 32-year-old graduate student from Syracuse, New York, who, like 3% of adult Americans (according to the survey), has never had sex. "These findings may be liberating for a lot of people. They may say, 'Thank God, I'm not as weird as I thought.'"

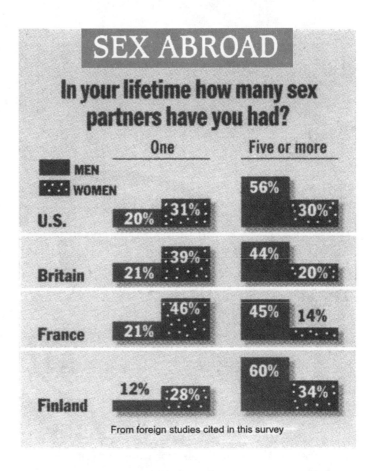

Scientists, on the whole, praise the study. "Any new research is welcome if it is well done," says Dr. William Masters, co-author of the landmark 1966 study Human Sexual Response. By all accounts, this one was very well done. But, like every statistical survey, it has its weaknesses. Researchers caution that the sample was too limited to reveal much about small subgroups of the population—gay Hispanics, for example. The omission of people over 59 is regrettable, says Shirley Zussman, past president of the American Association of Sex Educators, Counselors and Therapists: "The older population is more sexually active than a 19-year-old thinks, and it's good for both 19-year-olds and those over 59 to know that."

PARTNERS

How many sexual partners have you had since age 18?

MEN · WOMEN

3% HIGH SCHOOL GRADUATES (both sexes)

ALL COLLEGE GRADUATES (both sexes)

None · 1 · 2-4 · 5-10 · 11-20 · 21 or more

The Chicago scientists admit to another possible defect: "There is no way to get around the fact some people might conceal information," says Stuart Michaels of the Chicago team, whose expertise is designing questions to get at those subjects people are most reluctant to discuss. The biggest hot button, he says, is homosexuality. "This is a stigmatized group. There is probably a lot more homosexual activity going on than we could get people to talk about."

The 2nd most appealing sex act: seeing partner undress

It was, in large part, to talk about homosexual activity that the study was originally proposed. The project was conceived in 1987 as a response to the AIDS crisis. To track the spread of the AIDS virus—and to mount an effective campaign against it—government researchers needed good data about how much risky sexual behavior (anal sex, for example) was really going on. But when they looked for scientific data about sex, they found little besides Kinsey and Masters and Johnson.

So the National Institutes of Health issued a formal request for a proposal, tactfully giving it the bland title "Social and Behavioral Aspects of Fertility Related Behavior" in an attempt to slip under the radar of right-wing politicians. But the euphemism fooled no one—least of all Jesse Helms. In the Reagan and Bush era, any government funding for sex research was suspect, and the Senator from North Carolina was soon lobbying to have the project killed. The Chicago team redesigned the study

several times to assuage conservative critics, dropping the questions about masturbation and agreeing to curtail the interview once it was clear that a subject was not at high risk of contracting AIDS. But to no avail. In September 1991 the Senate voted 66 to 34 to cut off funding.

The vote turned out to be the best thing that could have happened—at least from the point of view of the insatiably curious. The Chicago team quickly rounded up support from private sources, including the Robert Wood Johnson, Rockefeller and Ford foundations. And freed of political constraints, they were able to take the survey beyond behavior related to AIDS transmission to tackle the things inquiring minds really want to know: Who is having sex with whom? How often do they do it? And when they are behind closed doors, what exactly do they do?

The report confirms much of what is generally accepted as conventional wisdom. Kids *do* have sex earlier now: by 15, half of all black males have done it; by 17, the white kids have caught up to them. There *was* a lot of free sex in the '60s: the percentage of adults who have racked up 21 or more sex partners is significantly higher among the fortysomething boomers than among other Americans. And AIDS *has* put a crimp in some people's sex lives: 76% of those who have had five or more partners in the past year say they have changed their sexual behavior, by either slowing down, getting tested or using condoms faithfully.

But the report is also packed with delicious surprises. Take masturbation, for example. The myth is that folks are more likely to masturbate if they don't have a sex partner. According to the study, however, the people who masturbate the most are the ones who have the most sex. "If you're having sex a lot, you're thinking about sex a lot," says Gagnon. "It's more like Keynes (wealth begets wealth) and less like Adam Smith (if you spend it on this, you can't spend it on that)."

Or take oral sex. Not surprisingly, both men and women preferred receiving it to giving it. But who would have guessed that so many white, college-educated men would have done it (about 80%) and so few blacks (51%)? Skip Long, a 33-year-old African American from Raleigh, North Carolina, thinks his race's discomfort with oral sex may owe much to religious teaching and the legacy of slavery: according to local legend, it was something slaves were required to do for their masters. Camille Paglia is convinced that oral sex is a culturally acquired preference that a generation of college students picked up in the '70s from seeing Linda Lovelace do it in *Deep Throat*, one of the first—and last—X-rated movies that men and women went to see together. "They saw it demonstrated on the screen, and all of a sudden it was on the map," says Paglia. "Next thing you knew, it was in *Cosmo* with rules about how to do it."

More intriguing twists emerge when sexual behavior is charted by religious affiliation. Roman Catholics are the most likely to be virgins (4%) and Jews to have the most sex partners (34% have had 10 or more). The women most likely to achieve orgasm each and every time (32%) are, believe it or not, conservative Protestants. But Catholics edge out mainline Protestants in frequency of intercourse. Says Father Andrew Greeley, the sociologist-priest and writer of racy romances: "I think the church will be surprised at how often Catholics have sex and how much they enjoy it."

Among women 29% always had an orgasm during sex

But to concentrate on the raw numbers is to miss the study's most important contribution. Wherever possible, the authors put those figures in a social context, drawing on what they know about how people act out social scripts, how they are influenced by their social networks and how they make sexual bargains as if they were trading economic goods and services. "We were trying to make people think about sex in an entirely different way," says Kolata. "We all have this image, first presented by Freud, of sex as a riderless horse, galloping out of control. What we are saying here is that sex is just like any other social behavior: people behave the way they are rewarded for behaving."

Kolata and her co-authors use these theories to explain why most people marry people who resemble them in terms of age, education, race and social status, and why the pool of available partners seems so small—especially for professional women in their 30s and 40s. "You can still fall in love across a crowded room," says Gagnon. "It's just that society determines whom you're in the room with."

That insight, applied to AIDS, leads the Chicago team to a conclusion that is sure to get them into trouble. America's AIDS policy, they say, has been largely misdirected. Although AIDS spread quickly among intravenous drug users and homosexuals, the social circles these groups travel in are so rigidly circumscribed that it is unlikely to spread widely in the heterosexual population. Rather than pretend that AIDS affects everyone, they say, the government would be better advised to concentrate its efforts on those most at risk.

That's a conclusion that will not sit well with AIDS activists or with many health-policy makers. "Their message is shocking and flies against the whole history of this epidemic," says Dr. June Osborn, former chair of the National Commission on AIDS. "They're saying we don't have to worry if we're white, heterosexual adults. That gets the public off the hook and may keep parents from talking to their kids about sex. The fact is, teens are at enormous risk for experimentation."

Of married people, 94% were faithful in the past year

Other groups will find plenty here to make a fuss about. Interracial couples are likely to take offense at the author's characterization of mixed-race marriages as unlikely to succeed. And right-to-life activists who believe abortion is widely used as a cruel form of birth control are likely to be unconvinced by the finding that 72% of the women who have an abortion have only one.

Elsewhere in the study, the perceptual gulf between the sexes is reminiscent of the scene in *Annie Hall* where Woody Allen tells his psychiatrist that he and Annie have sex "hardly ever, maybe three times a week," and she tells hers that they do it "constantly; I'd say three times a week." In the Chicago study, 54% of the men say they think about sex every day or several times a day. By contrast, 67% of the women say they think about it only a few times a week or a few times a month. The disconnect is even greater when the subject turns to forced sex. According to the report, 22% of women say they have been forced to do sexual things they didn't want to, usually by someone they loved. But only 3% of men admit to ever forcing themselves on women. Apparently men and women have very different ideas about what constitutes voluntary sex.

But the basic message of *Sex in America* is that men and women have found a way to come to terms with each other's sexuality—and it is called marriage. "Our study," write the authors, "clearly shows that no matter how sexually active people are before and between marriages... marriage is such a powerful social institution that, essentially, married people are all alike—they are faithful to their partners as long as the marriage is intact."

Americans, it seems, have come full circle. It's easy to forget that as recently as 1948, Norman Mailer was still

HOMOSEXUALITY

MEN

2.7%
In the
past year

7.1%
Since
puberty

1.3%

3.8%

Have you had sex with someone of your gender?

Are you sexually attracted to people of the same gender?

6.2%

4.4%

WOMEN

using the word fug in his novels. There may have been a sexual revolution—at least for those college-educated whites who came of age with John Updike's swinging *Couples*, Philip Roth's priapic *Portnoy* and Jong's *Fear of Flying*—but the revolution turned out to have a beginning, a middle and an end. "From the time of the Pill to Rock Hudson's death, people had a sense of freedom," says Judith Krantz, author of *Scruples*. "That's gone."

It was the first survey—Kinsey's—that got prudish America to talk about sex, read about sex and eventually watch sex at the movies and even try a few things (at least once). Kinsey's methods may have been less than perfect,

but he had an eye for the quirky, the fringe, the bizarre. The new report, by contrast, is a remarkably conservative document. It puts the fringe on the fringe and concentrates on the heartland: where life, apparently, is ruled by marriage, monogamy and the missionary position. The irony is that the report Jesse Helms worked so hard to stop has arrived at a conclusion that should make him proud. And it may even make the rest of us a bit less anxious about what's going on in that bedroom next door.

—Reported by Wendy Cole/Chicago, John F. Dickerson/New York and Martha Smilgis/Los Angeles

The War Over Gay Marriage

In a landmark decision, the Supreme Court affirms gay privacy and opens the way to a revolution in family life

IT WAS A HOMEY SCENE. STANDING in their warm kitchen on a winter's day in 2001, Julie and Hillary Goodridge, a couple for 16 years, played the old Beatles song "All You Need Is Love" for their young daughter, Annie. Hillary asked Annie if she knew any people who loved each other. The little girl rattled off the names of her mothers' married friends, heterosexuals all. "What about Mommy and Ma?" asked Hillary. "Well," the child replied, "if you loved each other you'd get married."

That did it. "My heart just dropped," said Hillary. The gay couple headed for the Massachusetts Department of Public Health to get a marriage license. Julie was optimistic, Hillary less so. "I thought we'd be led away in handcuffs," Hillary recalled. Blood tests and $30 in hand, they anxiously asked for an application. "No, you're not allowed to," responded the woman behind the counter. "I'll need two grooms first." Hillary and Julie asked to speak to the department's director. The woman politely told them, "No, you can't get married, and there's nothing you can do about it."

Actually, there was. With the help of the Gay & Lesbian Advocates & Defenders (GLAD), Hillary and Julie sued for the right to be legally wed. Any day now, the Massachusetts Supreme Judicial Court is expected to decide their case. No court in America has ever recognized gay marital vows. But last week Hillary and Julie—and every gay person who wants to be married or adopt a child or hold a job or receive a government benefit or simply enjoy the right to be respected—received a tremendous boost from the highest court in the land.

The outcome of *Lawrence et al. v. Texas*, handed down on the final day of the Supreme Court's 2002–2003 term, was not unexpected. In a Houston apartment five years ago, Tyron Garner and John Geddes Lawrence had been arrested by police for performing a homosexual act and fined $200. By a 6–3 vote, the high court struck down the Texas anti-sodomy law. In some ways, the Supreme Court was just catching up to public opinion. In 1986, in *Bowers v. Hardwick*, a decision that lived in infamy among gays in America, the court had upheld a Georgia anti-sodomy law. At the time, 25 states had such laws. Some 17 years later, only four states banned sodomy between homosexuals (an additional nine states had laws, on the books but rarely enforced, barring sodomy between any sexual partners).

Advocates have had to deal with what one called 'the ick factor'—the revulsion some heterosexuals feel about homosexuals.

What stunned court watchers—and what promises to change forever the status of homosexuals in America—was the far reach of the court's reasoning. Gays "are entitled to respect for their private lives," said Justice Anthony Kennedy, reading from his majority opinion from the high court's mahogany bench. His voice was quiet and he seemed a little nervous, but his words rang with lasting meaning. Under the due-process clause of the 14th Amendment of the Constitution, Kennedy ruled, gays were entitled to a right of privacy. "The state cannot demean their existence or control their destiny by making their private sexual conduct a crime," said Kennedy. In the crowded courtroom, some of the gay activists and lawyers silently but visibly wept as they listened.

Justice Kennedy's ruling in the *Lawrence* case "may be one of the two most important opinions of the last 100 years," says David Garrow, legal scholar at Emory University and Pulitzer Prize-winning biographer of Martin Luther King Jr. "It's the most libertarian majority opinion ever issued by the Supreme Court. It's arguably bigger than *Roe v. Wade*," said Garrow, referring to the 1973 Supreme Court decision giving women a right to abortion. At least in symbolic terms, Garrow put the decision on a par with *Brown v. Board of Education*, the landmark 1954

A Winding Road
A look back at the highs and lows of gay rights:

1895 The writer Oscar Wilde is convicted for "gross indecency between males."

1924 The first formal U.S. gay-activist group is founded in Chicago.

1969 Patrons of Stonewall Inn resist a police raid in what's considered birth of the gay-rights movement.

1975 Former NFL player Dave Kopay announces he's gay—the first pro athlete to do so.

1977 Anita Bryant mounts national crusade to block gay rights.

1986 Supreme Court rules in *Bowers* that sodomy is a crime.

1987 ACT UP is born, taking up the fight against AIDS.

1993 Military adopts "don't ask, don't tell" policy for gays.

1993 Thousands of gay-rights supporters march on Washington.

1996 High court: gays enjoy equal rights under the Constitution.

1997 Ellen DeGeneres's TV-show character comes out.

2000 Vermont allows gay couples to form civil unions.

2001 Federal judge upholds law banning gay adoption.

2003 An openly gay Episcopal bishop is elected in N.H.

will encounter fierce resistance from people and institutions that still regard homosexuality as morally deviant. The battle—over gay marriage, gay adoption, gays in the military and gays in the workplace—will be fought out court to court, state to state for years to come. Nonetheless, there is no question that the *Lawrence* case represents a sea change, not just in the Supreme Court, a normally cautious institution, but also in society as a whole.

In 1986, when the court had ruled in the *Bowers* case, Justice Byron White curtly dismissed the argument that the Constitution protected the right of homosexuals to have sex in their own homes. Writing for the majority of justices, White had called such an assertion "facetious." But social norms have been transformed over the past two decades. How mainstream is the idea of "gay rights"? Of the six justices who voted to strike down laws against homosexual sodomy, four were appointed by Republican presidents. (Kennedy, David Souter and John Paul Stevens all subscribed to a right of privacy for gays; Justice Sandra Day O'Connor stuck to the narrower ground that it was unfair to punish gays but not heterosexuals for sodomy.) Polls showed that the justices have public opinion behind them: some six out of 10 Americans believe that homosexual sex between consenting adults should be legal.

One veteran gay activist could sense the change in the attitudes of the justices. Kevin Cathcart, executive director of the Lambda Legal Defense and Education Fund, has been part of a small but determined circle of lawyers plotting gay-rights strategy since 1984. In the past, he had to deal with what he called the "ick factor"—the revulsion some heterosexuals feel about homosexual acts. "The Kennedy opinion not only does not have an ick factor," says Cathcart, "but is almost an apology for the ick factor 17 years ago."

One justice was still full of disgust. In a biting, sarcastic voice, Justice Antonin Scalia read his dissent from the bench. He denounced his colleagues for "taking sides in the culture war." He accused the court's majority of having "largely signed on to the so-called homosexual agenda." Most Americans, Scalia warned, "do not want persons who openly engage in homosexual conduct as partners in their business, as scout-masters for their children, as teachers in their children's schools, or as boarders in their homes." Scalia predicted that the court's decision would cause "a massive disruption of the current social order" by calling into question the government's right to legislate morality. While noting the majority's statement that the case did not involve gay marriage, Scalia scoffed, "Do not believe it."

Scalia's fulmination was impressive, but (as even he might privately concede) it was also an overstatement of the legal and political reality, at least for the immediate future. While gays can now claim some constitutional protection—their new right to privacy under the *Lawrence* decision—the federal government and the states can override those rights if they have a good enough reason,

ruling declaring that separate was not equal in the nation's public schools.

But it may be years before the ripple effects of *Lawrence* are felt. Just as schools were still segregated in parts of the South a decade after the *Brown* decision, it is likely that attempts to give gays true legal equality with heterosexuals a "legitimate state interest." Thus, national security could trump privacy in the military and preserve the Pentagon's "don't ask, don't tell" policy on gays. Or the state's interest in preserving "traditional institutions"—like marriage between different-sex couples—might overcome a homosexual's right to not be "demeaned," as Justice Kennedy put it. After *Lawrence*, gays can no longer be branded as criminals. But that does not mean they will enjoy all the rights of "straight" citizens. The current Supreme Court has shown, albeit erratically, a federalist streak: it will not lightly trample "states' rights"—that is, second-guess the power of states to make up their own rules, especially if popular opinion is running strong.

Inevitably, politics will play a role. Some conservative groups were apoplectic. "People of faith are not going to lie down and allow their faith to be trampled because a politically correct court has run amok," promised the Rev. Lou Sheldon, president of the Traditional Values Coalition. He offered a hint of the battles that lie ahead when a vacancy opens up on the high court. "In this court, you do not have friends of the Judeo-Christian standard. We know who our friends are. And we know who needs to be replaced," said Sheldon. Sandy Rios, president of the Concerned Women for America, predicted moral Armageddon. "We're opening up a complete Pandora's box," she said. Some conservatives, including Justice Scalia, warned that the court's decision would undermine laws barring bigamy, incest and prostitution.

> Blood tests and $30 in hand,
> the Goodridges asked for a license.
> 'No,' the clerk told the women.
> 'I'll need two grooms first.'

Maybe. But states will still be able to ban sexual practices that are obviously hurtful or exploitative of women or minors. Nonetheless, the fear of legalized wantonness will quickly become a campaign issue. Last week the White House—which decided not to file a brief in the case—was taking cover; White House spokesman Ari Fleischer defensively mumbled that gay rights were a matter for the states to decide. Bush's political handlers were fearful of alienating either gay voters or the legion of Christian conservatives who provided Bush with his electoral base in 2000. "Bush officials apparently think homosexual activists make better leaders than the conservative activists who delivered millions of votes," taunted Bob Knight, director of the conservative Culture and Family Institute.

The fight over gay rights could easily become a "wedge issue" in the 2004 presidential campaign, though Democrats, too, will be wary of getting ahead of public opinion. For the most part, gay rights will be fought out at the local and state level. The struggle will be protracted

and there may be a real backlash. An overview of the main battlegrounds:

Gay Marriage. Although gay couples routinely have commitment ceremonies and The New York Times wedding pages now run photos of gay and lesbian pairings, no state in the country recognizes or grants gay marriages. (Churches are badly split, with some denominations honoring same-sex unions and others vehemently opposing them.) Vermont comes the closest of any state with "civil unions" that bestow many of the same rights and responsibilities as marriage, but give it a different name—for purely political reasons. A few other states, most notably Massachusetts and California, seem to be edging toward the recognition of gay marriage, either by legislation or judicial fiat. But the stronger movement, at least for now, appears to be in the other direction. Some 37 states—and the federal government—have adopted "Defense of Marriage Acts," which define marriage as applying only to a man and a woman, and—significantly—bar recognition of same-sex marriage from other states.

These laws will inevitably be challenged in the courts under the *Lawrence* decision. On June 11, a court in Ontario, Canada, ruled that same-sex marriages are legal (they are also legal in the Netherlands and Belgium). Last weekend in Toronto, during the city's Gay Pride celebration, the city's marriage office stayed open for extended hours. A dozen of the first 200 customers were Americans who had driven across the border. Legal experts are divided over whether a gay couple with a Canadian marriage license will be recognized back in the States, but they are sure that sooner or later the issue of gay marriage will wind up in the Supreme Court, though probably not for several years.

By then the court may be, as the saying goes, following the election returns. Gary Bauer, the president of American Values and a former presidential candidate, warned that if the Republicans do not take a stand against gay marriage in the 2004 election, then GOP "family values" activists might just sit home rather than work for the party. On the other hand, Bush may pick up votes from libertarians and Republican moderates (the "soccer moms") if he is seen as being compassionate or tolerant of different sexual orientations.

Adoption and Custody. Most states now permit single gays to adopt children. Resistance to gay adoption has waned as studies show that children raised by gays look a lot like those raised by straights—and are no more or less likely to be gay. Still, only 11 states permit same-sex couples to adopt children. The rest of the states are a patchwork of conflicting rules. Florida, swayed by Anita Bryant's 1977 "Save the Children" campaign, is the most restrictive, banning adoption by any gay or lesbian individuals. That law, based largely on moral disapproval, seems vulnerable after *Lawrence*.

The most immediate impact of *Lawrence* will be on custody battles. One Virginia judge, for instance, asked a lesbian to detail her homosexual acts in court testimony and

Marriage is one thing. But what happens when partners part?
For gay couples splitting up, it's still a legal 'no man's land.'

Breaking Up Is Hard to Do

BY DEBRA ROSENBERG

When Texans Russell Smith and John Anthony traveled to Vermont to join in a civil union in February 2002, they had all the romantic intentions of any couple exchanging "I do's." But like the 50 percent of Americans whose marriages end in divorce, Smith and Anthony later decided to call it quits. Because the two had shared business deals, Smith worried he might one day face financial obligations from his ex. So he filed for divorce in a Texas court. Though a district judge initially agreed to grant one, Texas Attorney General Greg Abbott intervened. He feared granting a divorce would signal that the state recognized the union in the first place—a step Texas and other states aren't yet willing to take. "A judge cannot grant a divorce where no marriage existed," Abbott argued. The judge reversed the divorce and the couple was forced to hash things out on their own. "They were just wanting to legally terminate this relationship," says Anthony's lawyer, Tommy Gunn. "Obviously the divorce route did not work."

If gay couples think it's tough to get married, they may find it's even harder to split up. Few want to think about it on the way to the altar, but "we're not immune to relationship problems," says David Buckel, an attorney who directs the marriage project at Lambda Legal. Though all it takes is a romantic weekend to tie the knot under Canada's just-passed same-sex marriage law or get linked by civil union in Vermont, both places require at least one member of the couple to establish residency for a year before granting a divorce or official dissolution. Of the roughly 5,000 civil unions performed so far in Vermont, the only state that legally recognizes the same-sex commitments, 85 percent went to out-of-staters.

That has left other states grappling with what to do when civil unions sour—and whether standard divorce laws can apply. A West Virginia family-court judge agreed to use divorce laws to dissolve a civil union there last year. But Connecticut courts dismissed the divorce case filed by Glen Rosengarten, who decided to end his 15-year relationship shortly after he and his partner got a civil union in Vermont. Dying of AIDS, Rosengarten wanted to preserve his estate for children from an earlier marriage, says his lawyer Gary I. Cohen. "He had incredible anxiety about it—he really wanted closure in his life," Cohen says. Rosengarten appealed to the state Supreme Court, but died before the case was heard. Medical bills ate up his estate, so inheritance became a moot point too.

Without access to divorce, all the benefits gay couples get with a civil union—shared property, adoption rights, insurance—must be undone one by one. If they can't dissolve the union, they may not be free to enter into a new union or marriage, either. "It shoves gay people into a no man's land where they have to fight it out for themselves," says Evan Wolfson, director of Freedom to Marry. "Because it's not marriage, people don't have one of the automatic protections that comes with marriage." Gay couples can't hope to erase the pain that comes with parting. But after last week, there's at least a chance they may one day get a little more help when things fall apart.

With PAT WINGERT

then told her she would lose her child because her behavior was immoral. That sort of reasoning will likely no longer pass constitutional muster.

Gays in the Workplace, Schools and the Military. Big employers have already gotten the message. In 1992 only one of the Fortune 500 companies offered benefits to gay partners. Today the number is 197, including 27 of the top 50. Unfounded worries about getting tagged with massive AIDS bills have been replaced by top companies' desire to compete for gay workers.

Schools and the military will be slower going. Teachers fear harassment or retribution if they support student efforts to form "gay-straight alliances" (even so, there are some 1,700 pro-tolerance clubs in 50 states). The Pentagon will argue that "unit cohesion" will suffer if gays are openly tolerated in the military. Part of the underlying legal basis for the armed services' restrictive "don't ask, don't tell" policy, a federal anti-sodomy law, is likely to

be struck down. Still, the courts are very reluctant to interfere with the military.

PRAYERFUL PROTEST AT THE HIGH COURT
Critics share Scalia's view that the decision hurts the state's right to legislate morality

Despite the challenges ahead, the alliance of gay lawyers who have been working for two decades to overturn discriminatory laws can feel the ground shifting beneath their feet. Last week Susan Sommer, the supervising attorney at the Lambda Legal Defense and Education Fund, went to an early court hearing in a case aimed at overturning New Jersey's ban on gay marriages. The U.S. Supreme Court's ruling in *Lawrence* "didn't come up," she noted. "But now I feel like when I walk in the courtroom I've got a powerful symbol on our side, the ringing words of Justice Kennedy that *Bowers v. Hardwick* had demeaned gay people."

Lambda is trying to soften up public opinion with town-hall meetings designed to show that gay families are good for the community. "The town halls we're doing tell people, 'Hey, we're just like anyone else—a middle-class, hometown suburban couple that's been called bor-ing'," says Cindy Meneghin, 45, who with her partner, Maureen Kilian, also 45, and their two children, Joshua, 10, and Sarah, 8, are suing to be recognized as a legal fam-ily in New Jersey. "You can't look at our beautiful, charm-ing kids and not notice that we're a family, and the myths start tumbling down. What we've found is that people get to know us as people with families and kids, that I coach soccer and take pictures, and Maureen is the best dessert maker in town, and, oh yes, Maureen and Cindy are a gay couple."

At their home in the liberal Boston enclave of Jamaica Plain, Julie and Hillary Goodridge (who adopted the common last name from Hillary's grandmother because it sounded "positive") have found acceptance—except for the time a bunch of high-school kids urinated on their car and yelled "Dyke!" Last week Julie sat down with their daughter, Annie, to explain the *Lawrence* decision. "I had to do it without talking about sodomy," said Julie. "I mean, she's only 7 and three quarters!" "The Supreme Court made an important decision yesterday," Julie told Annie. "They said it was OK for lesbians and gays to love each other." "That's good," said Annie. But she still wants her parents to be married.

This story was reported by T. TRENT GEGAX, DEBRA ROSENBERG, PAT WINGERT, MARK MILLER, MARTHA BRANT, STUART TAY-LOR JR., TAMARA LIPPER, JOHN BARRY, REBECCA SINDER-BRAND, SARAH CHILDRESS and JULIE SCELFO. It was written by EVAN THOMAS.

She Works, He Doesn't

She's got an advanced degree, A HIGH-PAYING JOB and a boss who loves her. He just got a pink slip. Or maybe her career has more EARNING POTENTIAL. Or maybe he's THE NURTURING ONE. The number of American families in which the SOLE WAGE EARNER is the woman is small, but many economists think it's growing.

BY PEG TYRE AND DANIEL MCGINN

SINCE THE BEGINNING OF TIME, ANTHROPOLOGISTS BELIEVE, women have been programmed to seek a mate who can provide for a family—whether that means dragging the mastodon back to the cave or making the payments on the Volvo. So when Laurie Earp walked down the aisle, she joined hands with a man most brides would consider a good catch: a lawyer. "By marrying a lawyer," she says, "I thought he'd be able to bring in money." Freed from the need to earn a big paycheck, Laurie imagined herself in a part-time job, one that allowed her to spend long afternoons with their children.

54%
of Americans know a couple where the woman is clearly the major wage earner and the man's career is secondary, according to the NEWSWEEK Poll.

For a time the Earps realized that vision. Jonathan earned a six-figure salary as a lawyer at Napster, while Laurie worked leisurely hours as a fund-raising consultant. But last May Jonathan was laid off; he still can't find work. So, reluctantly, Laurie has become the breadwinner. On a recent evening their son, Dylan, 5, skipped through their home in Oakland, Calif., praising how well his stay-at-home dad cares for him. But Dylan is the only one pleased with the turnabout. "This is not the life I wanted," says Laurie, who's heading off to an after-dinner meeting with clients. Meanwhile, Jonathan spends his days doing housework and preparing badly cooked dinners. "I hate it all," he says.

Men who identify with their jobs are HIT HARDEST. Younger couples—the ones who GREW UP LISTENING to 'Free to Be... You and Me'—tend to take the turnabout more IN STRIDE.

Like several million American families, the Earps are experiencing the quiet, often painful transformation that takes place when Dad comes home with a severance package. The unemployment rate hit 6 percent last month, and while that's low by historical standards, some economists say it underestimates the difficulties facing laid-off workers—especially white-collar men who've been victimized by corporate downsizings. Despite Alan Greenspan's predictions of rosier times on the horizon, some experts talk of a growing problem of "underemployment" that goes beyond the nation's 8.8 million jobless. Their numbers include people forced to accept part-time work, all those newfound "consultants" who are playing computer solitaire but producing little income, and "discouraged workers" who've given up job hunting altogether.

The good news, at least for the 1.7 million unemployed men who are married, is that their wives are better equipped than any generation in history to pick up the financial slack. Women are currently earning more college degrees and M.B.A.s than men. In 1983, women made up 34 percent of high-paying "executive, administrative and managerial" occupations; in 2001 they were nearly half of that category. They've also weathered the recession better than men, because traditionally female industries like health care and education have suffered less than male-dominated businesses like manufacturing. Although the average woman's wage still trails a man's (78 cents to the dollar), enough women are breaking into better-paying professions that in 30.7 percent of married households with a working wife, the wife's earnings exceeded the husband's in 2001. Many of these women were born and bred for the office; they wouldn't want it any other way.

Laurie and Jonathan Earp: Oakland, Calif.

SHE
While her husband was at Napster, Laurie worked part time and hung out with her kids. Now she's ratcheted up her hours. "It's a lot of stress," she says.

HE
He's the main caregiver, runs the house and is also trying to start a small business making notecards for kids' lunchboxes. He misses his old life: "I make bad dinners," he says.

Within these homes, some of the husbands have voluntarily dialed back their careers (or quit work entirely) to care for kids and live off their wives' income. Some experts use a new phrase to describe high-income female providers: Alpha Earners. For some families, this shift works wonderfully; for others (especially those forced into it by layoffs), it creates tensions. Regardless, it's a trend we'd better get used to. Like runners passing the baton in a track event, many 21st-century couples will take turns being the primary breadwinner and the domestic god or goddess as their careers ebb and flow. Says marriage historian Stephanie Coontz: "These couples are doing, in a more extreme form, what most couples will have to do in the course of their working lives."

Most experts believe the number of families converting to the "Mr. Mom" lifestyle remains quite small. According to the Bureau of Labor Statistics, just 5.6 percent of married couples feature a wife who works and a husband who doesn't. But that information is misleading: most of those nonworking husbands are retired, disabled or full-time students, not househusbands who care for the kids. On the other hand, many of the men who have put their careers on the back burner to watch the kids still have part-time or entrepreneurial gigs of some sort, so they

Sandra and Tom Núñez: Dallas, Texas

SHE
A software engineer for IBM, Sandra's still feeding their infant daughter, Ava, in the wee hours. She's glad Tom quit his job. "I'd rather have him here," she says.

HE
Was a vet's assistant, but the money wasn't worth the time away. Their son, Andrew, now 3, was ill, and Tom didn't want the boy in day care. "He's not going to suffer," he says.

---

don't show up in that number. So to better understand the Alpha Earner phenomenon, some researchers focus instead on those households where the wife outearns the husband. They're crunching the data to eliminate men who are retirees or students, and to seek families where the wife's career appears dominant (by finding, say, households where the wife earns 60 percent or more of the family income). Until the 1990s these numbers were tiny. But University of Maryland demographer Suzanne Bianchi recently began analyzing new 2001 data. Her initial results suggest that 11 percent of marriages feature an Alpha Earner wife. There's probably one in your neighborhood: in the NEWSWEEK Poll, 54 percent of Americans said they "personally know a couple where the woman is clearly the major wage earner and the man's career is secondary."

The shift is showing up more frequently in pop culture, too. "Friends" fans spent much of this season watching Monica support her unemployed husband, Chandler. (To recycle an old Thursday-night catchphrase: "Not that there's anything wrong with that.") Eddie Murphy hits theaters this week in "Daddy Day Care," in which he plays a laid-off dad whose wife becomes the primary breadwinner. In the bookstores, Alpha Earners are at the heart of Allison Pearson's novel "I Don't Know How She Does It" and "The Bitch in the House," a collection of feminist essays. "There are few things that make a man less attractive to women than financial instability," writes one contributor. "We can deal with men in therapy, we can deal with men crying, but I don't think gender equality will ever reach the point where we can deal with men broke."

Fathers who voluntarily choose the househusband role are challenging that sensibility. Last month three Chicago men gathered for breakfast at a suburban strip mall. Each has a wife with a lucrative job—two in finance, one in market research—and each man had achieved enough workplace success that he felt able to ease off the throttle. Ron Susser, 43, was chief financial officer for a consulting firm; today he practices the 4 O'Clock Shuffle, his name for his frantic afternoon cleaning binge. "When my wife comes home, she expects the pantry to be stocked, the

Richer or Poorer, Sickness and Health

Women have always worked, of course. But as economic conditions and social expectations have evolved over the millenniums, so have gender roles in marriage. Here's a brief look at some of the ways couples have shared the load.

Hunter-Gatherers
15,000 years ago: Prehistoric women forage for plants while their cavemen husbands hunt. In many climates, it is the gathering that keeps them alive.

Adam and Eve
Literature's first couple adheres to conventional sex roles: God creates Eve, the first woman, as the "help meet" for a lonely Adam.

The Middle Ages
Fifth century to 1300: Although women often work, they are prevented by law from controlling their own money.

The Renaissance
1300–1600: What's love got to do with it? This 15th-century wedding portrait by Jan van Eyck is a visual marriage contract. Matrimony is used to build capital, amass land and consolidate power.

The Age of Austen
Marriage is the sole option for upper- and middle-class women. In 1916, Jane Austen writes: "Single women have a dreadful propensity for being poor, which is one argument in favour of matrimony."

The Victorians
In the 19th century, middle- and upper-class women aspire to a life of purity, submissiveness, piety and domesticity.

Turn of the Century
With both men and women working and earning money, it becomes possible to choose a mate based on attraction and compatibility.

'The Man in the Gray Flannel Suit'
This 1956 film, starring Gregory Peck (left), reflects the dissatisfaction of a husband and commuter who is the sole breadwinner.

The Birth-Control Pill
1960s: For the first time, reliable birth control becomes available to all American women, kicking off the sexual revolution. It also allows women to time their pregnancies in order to pursue career and family as they wish.

Gloria Steinem
In the early 1970s, the feminist movement ignites a generation of women who demand equal pay for equal work. Says Steinem: "We have become the husbands we wanted to marry."Thirty years later women's wages still lag behind men's.

'Kramer vs. Kramer'
This 1979 movie explores a generation's uneasiness with traditional gender roles in marriage. The movie wins five Academy Awards.

Margaret and Denis Thatcher
In office from 1979 to 1990, the first female British P.M. is one of the most powerful politicians of her time. She lives at 10 Downing Street with her househusband, Denis.

Monica and Chandler
Recently Chandler quit work to be with his chef wife, Monica. But getting a new job isn't a high priority.

Bill and Hillary
She's a senator now, but back in 2000 Bill made news when he announced he would support his wife's political career after he left the White House.

Jennifer Sey and Winslow Warren, San Francisco, Calif.

SHE
Earns more than 100,000 a year at Levi Strauss. She planned to take time off to help raise the kids, but her salary was too good. She just had a second baby.

HE
Was laid off from a failed dot-com two years ago and has been raising their son Virgil, now 2 1/2, ever since. He loves looking after Virgil, "but it can be a little lonely."

house to be in order and dinner cooked—I consider that my job," Susser says. David Burns, 49, was a computer consultant; today he's a Brownie leader. Scott Keeve, 52, oversaw 150 employees for a food distributor. When the nanny told his two kids she'd quit if they didn't behave, Keeve took the job himself. Like so many women before them, these guys are learning to adapt to a job without paychecks, business lunches or "attaboys." You get the sense that if the Lifetime cable channel installed cameras in their homes, there's a ready-made reality show to be found in their bouts of ambivalence.

For Bill Laut, a former real-estate appraiser, those moments come frequently. While his wife, Sheila, racks up frequent-flier miles as a business-development executive, Bill hauls their 6-year-old triplets to the grocery store, where strangers gawk. "Your poor wife," they say, to which Laut has a standard reply: "I look around very dramatically and then ask them, 'Do you see her here?'" When his kids were younger, he'd be watching football with friends, and talk would inevitably turn to work. "I changed 27 diapers today," Bill would interject, only to be heckled: "Get a job!" "At parties I feel like an outcast," Bill says. "I tell people what I do and some of them are thinking, 'What a freeloader.' Everyone pats you on the back, but I wonder, are they patronizing me or being sincere?"

But on good days, many househusband-by-choice families are so jubilant about their lifestyle they sound like the "after" example in an ad for antidepressants. Dan and Lynn Murray were both Chicago lawyers when Lynn became pregnant with *their* triplets. Assessing their lives, they decided Lynn was happier in the office. "I'm sort of a type-A personality who likes to control my environment, and there's more of that at work than at home," she says. Today Dan cares for their five children; Lynn hopes he never returns to work. Brian and Maria Sullivan of Highland Park, Ill., saw their income drop 40 percent when Brian quit his sales job to care for their two kids, now 5 and 3 (Maria's a VP with a big computer company). Brian had resisted quitting, but now he sees the upside. "How many dads get to potty-train their kids?" he says. When they're teenagers, Brian would like to spend some afternoons on the golf course. "That's fine as long as he's chaperoning every field trip and is there at every sports practice," Maria says.

25%
of respondents to the NEWSWEEK Poll think it is generally 'not acceptable' for a wife to be the major wage earner

Many such couples have simply decided that no matter how much lip service companies pay to "family friendly" policies, it's simply not possible to integrate two fast-track careers and kids without huge sacrifices. So they do a cold-eyed calculation, measuring the size and upside potential of each parent's paycheck, and opting to keep whoever's is larger. For the highest-achieving women, the trend is striking. Last fall Fortune reported that more than one third of its "50 Most Powerful Women in Business" have a stay-at-home man (it dubbed them "trophy husbands"). But this trend reaches women far below the executive-vice-president rank. Patty Lewis, 42, is a video producer and meeting planner in east Dallas; her husband, Spencer Prokop, 45, is an actor. When son Chase arrived, her income was steadier, so Prokop stayed home. Dad feels isolated, and he's given up on lugging Chase along to occasional auditions. "This notion that I would have this time to work on myself—well, that goes right out the window," says Prokop, who misses the lux-

ury of uninterrupted bathroom time. After Lewis's 12-hour work-days, she's often too beat for spousal conversation. Sometimes Prokop thinks he's nagging his wife the same way his stay-at-home mom nagged his father. While they've no regrets that Chase enjoyed a full-time dad for 3 1/2 years, Prokop is ready for a change. Their son started day care two weeks ago.

The wives of these househusbands have one universal regret: they spend too little time with their children. Of course, two-career couples with kids in day care express similar sentiments. Still, becoming the family's only revenue stream can add a dose of anxiety, even to a job you love. "I feel an intense pressure being the sole wage earner," says Sally Williams, 28, a Philadelphia lawyer with a 4-year-old daughter and a stay-at-home husband. "The house, the car—everything is riding on my shoulders." Some Alpha Earners say colleagues assume that their husbands are deadbeats who can't hold jobs. They also complain about the other extreme: how the novelty of Dad's dialing back can lead people to lavish him with too much praise. Says Beth Burkstrand-Reid, a lawyer in Washington, D.C.: "I'm doing a good job of supporting the family, [but] no one is giving *me* a pat on the back."

Feminists see the emerging era—when it's no longer the default choice that the kids will be watched by Mom, the nanny or a day-care center—as a necessary evolution. "The first half [of the feminist vision] was to liberate women from domestic servitude," says Suzanne Levine, a founding editor of Ms. Magazine and author of "Father Courage: What Happens When Men Put Family First." "The second half was to integrate the men back into the family." But while many dads now help with 3 a.m. feedings, it hasn't led to wholesale acceptance of wives as breadwinners. In the NEWSWEEK Poll, 41 percent of Americans agreed that "it is much better for everyone involved if the man is the achiever outside the home and the woman takes care of the home and family." One in four said it was "generally not acceptable" for a woman to be the major wage earner in a marriage.

34%
of men say that if their wife earned more money, they'd consider quitting their job or reducing their hours

While those attitudes may fester, the data suggest women's economic power will only grow. And as you plot out those trend lines a few decades, it's easy to imagine more-dramatic implications. For example, conventional wisdom is that once a man earns a certain income, whether his wife works becomes optional. Does that

Hoping for the Best, Ready for the Worst

Thanks to recession and divorce, today's college kids are determined to break the rules about sex roles

BY BARBARA KANTROWITZ

A few years ago, when the University of Connecticut women's basketball team first captured the NCAA title, a popular bumper sticker declared the Storrs campus a place where the men are men and the women are champions. And with the Lady Huskies still stars, UConn students aren't afraid to break stereotypes. So last week senior Christopher Kyne, 22, was confident about heading to South Carolina after graduation because his girlfriend has a good job at the Medical University of South Carolina. "We're going on her money," he says. He hopes to enter grad school and become a teacher, partly because it's a family-friendly career. In the future, he says, "I'd be 100 percent satisfied if my wife made enough money so I could be a stay-at-home dad."

50%
of women say that when it came time to choose a mate, they considered his earning potential 'not at all important'

Openness to flexible roles in marriage and family distinguishes this generation of college students from their parents, say researchers who've studied their progress. The battle over whether mothers should work is moot now; families need the money. Young women are more ready to pick up the slack and the men feel less of a stigma if they stay home. Everyone is desperate to avoid his parents' mistakes. In the early 1980s, these kids' baby-boomer mothers swarmed into the work force without any of the supports common today—maternity leave, part-time career paths, flexible schedules. The children saw marriages crumble under the strain. They also watched the economy ricochet. In the current downturn, many of their forty-something fathers are out of work with little chance of getting rehired. In this context, rigid roles seem quaint,

says Kathleen Gerson, a sociologist at New York University who is writing a book called "The Children of the Gender Revolution." "If the economic opportunities are there for the woman, fine. As long as they are there for *somebody*."

They're hopeful but pragmatic, and understand that the real world can crush ideals. Many of these young women hope for a close family life, but with nearly half of all marriages eventually ending in divorce, they're prepared to be breadwinners. "That's a big thing for our age group," says Lucy Swetland, a 21-year-old junior who watched friends' mothers struggle. Even though her parents are married, she's learned that "you can't depend on someone else to carry you through." Women still want to have it all—although maybe not all at the same time. Jennifer Carosella, a 21-year-old senior, is going to law school so she can earn six-figure income. But at some point, she also wants to be home with her children—as her own mother was.

How comfortably the men adapt depends largely on the examples their fathers set, says University of Chicago sociologist Barbara Schneider, coauthor of "The Ambitious Generation." UConn junior Alfred Guante, 21, whose parents are divorced, was the main male figure in his household for much of his childhood—and being responsible for his family is important to him: "I think it's a man's role to get a job." But unlike many men in earlier generations, he would have no objections to his wife's working as well. Drama student Jeremy Andrews was inspired by his father, an engineer who trained as a nurse. It was a backup when his company left town so he could avoid dislocating his family. His father found another engineering job, but rarely missed his four sons' games, while his mother, a nurse, worked long hours. That gives Andrews the confidence to try acting—even if it doesn't bring in a steady paycheck.

Rather than bemoan a legacy of social upheaval, his generation seems determined to embrace possibilities. "You're not stuck in what you do," says UConn sophomore Caitlin Fitzpatrick. "People have four or five careers. There are so many opportunities." Maybe this time, the balancing act will work.

mean work will become equally optional for men whose wives bring home big paychecks? For many families, it appears so: in the NEWSWEEK Poll, 34 percent of men said that in their relationship, if the wife landed a big pay raise, the husband would consider not working or reducing his hours.

Steve and Kim Taylor: Ft. Thomas, Ky.

SHE
For 10 years Kim has been the steady earner, rising from the mailroom to a management position at Cincinnati Bell. She's supportive of her husband: "I have more than I hoped for."

HE
Steve left a steady factory job for a sales gig, but his career in sales never took off. For the past two years his professional life has been a series of dashed hopes and disappointments. After looking in vain for a new career, he recently took a job as a local courier and is caring for their son, Ben.

Here's a related twist: we know many women consider a man's earning potential when choosing spouses. (Why do you think they're hiding the bachelors' occupations on "Mr. Personality"?) But as women's earnings rise, are more men paying attention to women's earning potential when they choose a mate? Yes, says University of Wisconsin economist Maria Cancian, who believes high-earning women are starting to be seen by men as a "good catch." As for high-powered women, Cancian wonders if their view may be changing, too. "Are we now in a situation where very career-oriented women might look for husbands that are less career oriented" and better equipped to nurture the kids full time?

Those questions will take years to answer. In the short term, there are aspects of this role reversal that are less cheery. By all accounts, the shift to wife as breadwinner is far more difficult when it's forced on couples because of Hubby's layoff. Predicting which families will suffer most is largely intuitive. Men who identify closely with their jobs or believe in traditional gender roles are hit hardest. Younger couples—the ones who grew up listing to "Free to Be... You and Me" while their moms were at work—tend to take the turnabout more in stride (sidebar).

But there are also wrinkles that aren't obvious. Working-class families may suffer less psychic whiplash because lesser-skilled workers have always been more susceptible to layoffs. As layoffs have crept up into white-collar ranks, they've taken more families by surprise. "When transitions are unexpected, then people are more likely to think it's somehow your fault, and that compounds the problems," says University of California, Berkeley, marriage researcher Philip Cowan.

Sherie Zebrowski was so unprepared for her husband Sean's layoff that she thought he was kidding when he came home with the news. The $80,000-plus-commissions he'd earned as an Austin, Texas, software salesman had allowed Sherie to care for their two children, train for triathlons and teach Sunday school. After his layoff two years ago, Sean spent months unsuccessfully looking for a similar job. For a while, the couple just hung on. "I tried not to fault him—he was good at what he did," Sherie says. "But after a while, you can't help but question: Is he looking in the right places? Could he be doing more?" To pay the bills, Sherie began turning her hobby—decorative painting—into a business. Soon she was working 10-hour days—and doing most of the housework while Sean surfed the Web. When their parish priest asked how they were doing, Sherie burst into tears. She told the priest: "I understand how the stress of being unemployed can break up a marriage."

So the Zebrowskis sat down for what they recall as The Talk. "I said, 'Either get a job at a checkout counter or you have to help me," Sherie says. So Sean created a marketing plan for her painting business. He began estimating jobs and boosting prices. They began hiring subcontractors. They're surviving, but it's far from ideal. "I'm still looking for a job," Sean says. "When I get it, Sherie can go back to sleeping in. This is not what I want to do, but I like to eat. I will get back to selling software. It's just a matter of when."

One element of the Zebrowskis' experience is near universal; among these couples, who does the housework becomes a battlefield. Some men claim wives develop bionic eyesight once the husband is home all day. "I don't tend to see dirt, but she can spot a single molecule," says Brian Reid, a former reporter who now cares for daughter Clio while his wife practices law. Sociologists speculate that some men actually do *less* housework when they stop working. Why? Being out of work already threatens their manhood, and taking on "feminine" tasks like cleaning the toilet might only make them feel worse.

Bill and Sheila Laut: Hudson, Ohio

SHE
Six weeks after the triplets were born, Sheila went back to her corporate job and Bill quit working. Now she makes more than their two previous incomes combined.

HE
Bill does the child care, cooking, cleaning and laundry. He says: "I don't get a paycheck, but I make that paycheck happen. Sheila couldn't excel if I didn't do what I do."

For families of laid-off househusbands, there's a more obvious source of marital tension: money. During the Internet boom, Gregg Wetterman prospered by organizing networking parties for Dallas techies. His wife, Jennie, remembers those days fondly. "The summer of 2001, I was at the pool every day," Jennie says. "I went scuba diving, sky diving—I must have read 30 books that summer." But when the tech bubble burst, Gregg bounced through a series of unstable jobs. As his career outlook became bleaker, an old boss of Jennie's called and asked if she wanted a management job at Old Navy. Says Gregg: "When she got the opportunity, I said, 'You don't have to,' but inside I was saying, 'Please, please, please…'"

32%
of those polled are worried about their family's major wage earner losing his or her job, compared with 44% in 1991

While Jennie works 50 hours a week, Gregg carts their kids to school and works on documentary films (he hasn't sold anything yet). Their two cars have a combined 286,000 miles; they've ditched their cell phones to cut expenses. At the kitchen table, the tension is palpable. Gregg argues it's smarter for him to keep pursuing nonpaying opportunities related to his aspirations—filmmaking and technology marketing—than to take an unpleasant job just to pay the bills. When the economy picks up, he figures he'll find something that pays well in his field. But he realizes the family can't wait forever. "I'm not pulling my weight financially," he says. Jennie is sometimes resentful. "I would just like for everybody to do their part," she says. "I don't want to be in this situation two years down the road. I'll have to put my foot down." Gregg says it may not come to that. "There's no telling," he says "Jennie could get a better job."

For many couples, switching in and out of roles may become a routine part of life. Counselors say that 21st-century careers will involve more jumps between industries and more time out of work for retraining or as a result of downsizing. Ted and Jenny Cater, 40 and 43, already have that routine down pat. In 1999 Ted, a salesman, relocated to San Francisco with his company. When his employer went bankrupt, Jenny, who works in marketing, immediately received a call about a $100,000-a-year job in Atlanta. So they moved her career to the front burner; Ted stayed home with daughter Megan. Then two months ago Jenny was laid off. They're expecting a baby next month, but by July they'll both be job hunting. "Whoever wins the best position wins a ticket back to coffee breaks and time to check e-mail," Jenny says. "Not that we don't want to say at home with the kids, but we are both geared for working."

Some younger couples are talking about these issues long before kids or joblessness enters their lives. Jennifer McCaskill is a 33-year-old Washington, D.C., lawyer; Ryan Schock, 28, is an accountant. As they look ahead to their September wedding, they're already talking about who might care for their future children. "Quite honestly, I don't want to stay at home," McCaskill says. "I won't make partner if I'm not working full time—and my earnings potential is higher." Schock's response: he'd love to be a full-time father. "He has a lot more patience than I do," McCaskill says. "I think he would be a better parent for our kids." With his master's degree and experience, Schock doesn't think a few years off would kill his career. "She would lose more than I would," Schock says. As more Alpha Earners roam the earth, that kind of outlook may be worth a premium. Forget doctors or lawyers. For a certain kind of woman, a laid-back guy like Ryan Schock may become the ultimate good catch.

With KAREN SPRINGEN, PAT WINGERT, ELLISE PIERCE, NADINE JOSEPH, VANESSA JUAREZ, DANIEL I. DORFMAN, JULIE SCELFO, TARA WEINGARTEN and HILARY SHENFELD

Where Everyone's a MINORITY

Welcome to SACRAMENTO, America's most integrated city. What's life like in this melting pot, and why is there still racial tension?

By RON STODGHILL and AMANDA BOWER

SACRAMENTO

Sequoia way is easy for travelers to overlook. Nestled in the middle-class neighborhood of Village Park on the south side of Sacramento, Calif., it is an unremarkable stretch of single-story frame houses. But if you stroll a bit along the winding road and visit Sequoia Way's residents, you will quickly realize there's something extraordinary about this street.

You will meet Tom and Debra Burruss, who moved onto the street a couple of years ago. He's black and she's white, but on Sequoia the interracial union doesn't stand out. The Burrusses' next-door neighbors are also minorities, a Vietnamese couple named Ken Wong and Binh Lam. Living directly across are the Cardonas, a Hispanic-and-white couple. And nearby are the Farrys, a Japanese- and-white pair. In fact, sprinkled throughout the street are more flavors than you can get at Baskin-Robbins—Mexicans, African Americans, East Indians, Asians, you name it.

Now head downtown to William Land Elementary School. Here the classrooms are so ethnically diverse that teachers are considering switching from celebrating individual cultural holidays, like Black History Month, Cinco de Mayo and Chinese New Year, to holding a multiethnic festival. Of Land's 347 kids, 189 speak a language other than English at home. Immigrant parents are so common in Sacramento's public schools that one child volunteered that her father is also a foreigner—he's from New York.

Or go over to Downtown Plaza mall and chat with teenage couples like Kayla, 17, and Gerald, 18. Kayla's mother is white, and her father is black; Gerald's mother is Japanese, and his dad is black. As they munch pizza in a bustling food court as diverse as a U.N. cafeteria, Kayla shrugs her shoulders at the notion of same-race friendships. "Personally, it doesn't matter what color you are," she says. "I am mixed, he is mixed, and most everybody is mixed."

So it goes in America's most integrated city, as determined in research for TIME by the Civil Rights Project at Harvard University (*see box on next page*). In Sacramento everyone's a minority—including whites. Of the city's inhabitants, 41% are non-Hispanic white, 15.5% are black, 22% are Hispanic and 17.5% are Asian/Pacific Islander. Although many cities are diverse (think New York City or Los Angeles), in Sacramento people seem to live side by side more successfully. The city got that way thanks in part to affordable real estate for middle-class households (the black population has dropped in the Bay Area but increased in Sacramento over the past 10 years) as well as innovative housing programs for low-income families. In addition, state-government agencies and college campuses are sprinkled throughout the city, providing stable, well-paid, equal-opportunity employment.

But while Sacramento approaches an ideal for integration, it certainly isn't paradise. Beneath the multicolored surface, the city's 407,018 inhabitants vacillate between racial harmony and ethnic tension. You see a Sikh casually strolling into a Mexican restaurant for takeout, an Eskimo and a white punk hanging out together downtown. But you also see black and Hispanic parents outraged because their kids' test scores lag behind those of whites and Asians in integrated schools. And you hear Anne Gayles-White, the N.A.A.C.P. chapter president, saying "There's still too much hatred and racism in a city like this."

Sacramento's Crayola culture is no statistical anomaly. Indeed, it may well be a sign of the times. Non-Hispanic whites still account for 69% of the U.S. population and maintain a predominant share of the nation's fiscal and political power. But by 2059 at the latest, according to U.S. Census figures, there will no longer be a white majority in America. Sacramento, then, provides perhaps the clearest view into the nation's future—a glimpse into what our neighborhoods, schools, churches and police forces may look like just a few decades from now.

70 LANGUAGES, ONE SYSTEM

THREE WEEKS AGO, YUN QIAN (CINDY) Zhong, a sixth-grader assigned to Randy Helms' homeroom, walked into William Land Elementary School for the first time. She had all the gifts of a model student—intelligence, friendliness and an eagerness to learn. There was just one problem: Zhong, an immigrant from Canton, China, didn't speak a word of English.

Helms didn't panic. His students and their parents hail from as far away as Vietnam, Mexico, Germany, Portugal, Panama and, fortunately, China. By the end of Zhong's second week,

Helms, with help from the Cantonese-speaking students in his class, had taught Zhong to count past 10 as well as to answer yes and no to questions translated for her.

A William Land education doesn't come easy. The school is located in a poor community downtown (90% of Land's kids qualify for free lunch), the classes are big (Helms alone teaches 32 students) and language barriers are routine (many kids' parents speak no English). Kids are tested for English proficiency within 30 days of enrolling; most score from 1 to 5 out of a maximum of 10. Across Sacramento, educators face similar challenges. How does a school district of 53,400 students communicate with a parent group that speaks more than 70 languages? And perhaps even more pressing, how much do cultural differences contribute to the fact that Latino and African-American children do not perform as well on standardized tests as white and Asian kids in the city's integrated schools?

Take John F. Kennedy High School, which at first blush is a picture of integration, with 21% white students, 22% black, 35% Asian and 16% Latino (the remainder are primarily Pacific Islanders, Filipinos and American Indians). J.F.K. routinely ships top graduates to Ivy League schools. But while the typical Asian kid has a 3.01 grade-point average, African-American kids score 1.85. What's going on? School district superintendent Jim Sweeney attributes the gap to class differences. J.F.K. students come from two neighborhoods—a middle-class area known as the Pocket, and a low-income, predominantly black and Hispanic part of town called Meadowview. Lower-income parents, he says, are often less able to spend time helping their kids with homework and encouraging them to learn. "Some surveys say poor children actually hear a million less words a year in the formative years," he says.

That explanation is too simplistic for Patricia Gándara, a University of California at Davis professor of education and Sacramento resident. She believes that teachers and administrators stereotype students on the basis of race. There are plenty of examples—from the teacher who asked a Latino boy if his parents had jobs (his mother was a school principal) to the Mexican child in an advanced-placement class who was asked whether she was Asian (her classmates couldn't imagine that a Latina could perform so well). "The schools make assumptions along class lines about which parents care and which don't, and parents and children begin to read those signs very early," Gándara says.

The district is making some progress in closing the gap. One effective method: home visits, which foster a relationship between teachers and parents and encourage working together to meet a child's needs. Suggested by a parent in 1998, the program helped boost reading scores in the district's elementary schools 36% and math scores 73% (reading and math scores are still only at the 46th and 59th national percentile, respectively).

THE MOST SEGREGATED HOUR

IT IS SUNDAY MORNING IN SACRAMENTO'S Meadowview community, and hundreds of Russian-speaking immigrants—men in dark suits, women in traditional head scarves, children excited about the latest X-box game—are thronging into the First Slavic Evangelical Baptist Church. A couple of blocks away, African

WHY SACRAMENTO?

In determining Sacramento to be the most integrated major U.S. city, the Civil Rights Project at Harvard University, using raw data from the U.S. Census Bureau. focused on metropolitan areas that have at least half the national population share of the three main minority groups (not less than 6.3% African American, 2.1% Asian, 6.2% Hispanic). Using a measure known as the "dissimilarity index," researchers looked at the integration of those three groups with each other and with whites, then weighted the scores to account for specific minorities' varied histories. Black-white integration, in this analysis, is assigned more value than Asian-white. Places where the military is a major employer were eliminated, because barracks and military housing skew results. Last, experts compared the ethnic makeup of local public schools with that of the overall school-age population (a close match suggests that integration is stable).

Americans fill the sanctuary at Twenty-Fourth Street Baptist Church to listen to the Rev. Samuel Mullinax preach the same Gospel. An hour later, Latinos begin filing into the pews of nearby St. Anne's Catholic Church for a Spanish-language Mass. Meadowview residents live together, but many pray separately.

More than 30 years ago, Martin Luther King Jr. famously said that "the 11 o'clock hour on Sunday is the most segregated hour in American life." It's an indictment that still carries weight today, as an estimated 90% of Americans worship primarily with members of their race or ethnicity. Yet Sacramento's complex social tapestry challenges conventional notions that racial segregation in worship is a failure of America's national ideal of equality. Sometimes segregation is driven not by bigotry but by language barriers and cultural heritage.

When Ukrainian immigrant Tamila Demyanik says, through an interpreter, that "the church is the major part of my life," it is no understatement. To the Demyaniks, First Slavic is a lifeline in a foreign land. Her husband buys bread at First Slavic and checks its bulletin board and a Russian phone book for community information. Longtime church members accustomed to America provide emotional support to newcomers and help them negotiate thickets of red tape in health care, housing and more.

Kevin Armstrong, a United Methodist pastor and director of the Religion and Public Teaching Project, based in Indianapolis, Ind., concedes that segregation, whether voluntary or compulsory, seems at odds with religious ideals. But he argues that the outcome often justifies the practice, particularly in immigrant communities. "They preserve their tradition," Armstrong explains, "sing in their native language, eat the food of their own culture, [and are] with people who remember what their land looks like and who their people are."

SHADES OF BLUE

CRUISING DEL PASO HEIGHTS in an unmarked police car, Chou Vang, 33, gestures toward a section of tired apartment houses

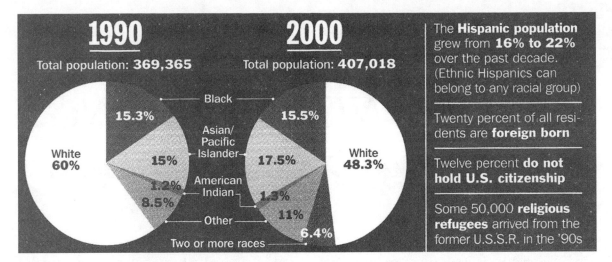

1990
Total population: **369,365**

White 60%

15.3% Black

15% Asian/Pacific Islander

1.2% American Indian

8.5% Other

2000
Total population: **407,018**

15.5%

17.5%

1.3%

11%

6.4% Two or more races

White 48.3%

The **Hispanic population** grew from **16% to 22%** over the past decade. (Ethnic Hispanics can belong to any racial group)

Twenty percent of all residents are **foreign born**

Twelve percent **do not hold U.S. citizenship**

Some 50,000 **religious refugees** arrived from the former U.S.S.R. in the '90s

and talks about gang violence. "Back in Laos, the Hmong are a minority ethnic group," he explains, "and the ethnic Lao ruled and ran the country. They have carried their old tensions to this country."

Vang is a police officer with the Sacramento police department, assigned to the problem-oriented policing unit. He is also a Laos-born member of the Hmong. The combination—his cop instincts and Hmong sensibility—enables Vang to be an effective negotiator in Hmong cases, including recurring episodes of gang violence between north-side teens and another Hmong gang in the southern part of town. Vang works on cases of all types, and frequently they involve drugs. In Del Paso Heights methamphetamines are the drug of choice. In Sacramento just last week federal authorities indicted 10 people on charges of importing *yaba*, a candy-flavored amphetamine.

The Sacramento police department has had difficulty attracting immigrant officers and people of color. White men still make up 46% of the department's staff; women swell the Caucasian ranks to 70%. Hispanics of any race account for 12%, blacks 8% and Asians 8%. Concern about racial profiling led the department to launch a study of its practices in 2000, and its first report found that 27% of drivers stopped by police were African American although African Americans make up only 15.5% of the local population. Despite such controversies, Vang feels he made the right move in signing up. "Occasionally someone will tell me to go back to my own country," he says. "But for the most part, I don't think they see me as an Asian. They just see me as a police officer."

ALL OF ME

WHEN MARIKO FERRONATO WAS 3 YEARS OLD, she would regularly quiz her mother about which half of her was white and which was Japanese. "I thought there was a physical line that divided the Japanese me from the Caucasian me," says Ferronato,

now 18 and a high school senior. A soccer goalie who plays the violin and has her eye on pre-med studies, Ferronato says her racial identity developed in stages. At her mostly white elementary school, she considered herself a white person "who happened to eat a lot of sticky rice." But in the ninth grade at her diverse high school, another student, who is white, called her a "cheating Jap." It hit hard. "I then tried to focus primarily on my Japanese side, completely ignoring my white side, as if to make up for all those years," she says.

In the 2000 U.S. Census, 24 in 1,000 people said they were multiracial (it's the first time Census pollers asked the question). It's often said with pride. While people of mixed race were once portrayed as tragic figures in movies, such as 1934's *Imitation of Life*, its 1959 remake and 1960's *I Passed for White*, today's pop-culture scene is bursting with mixed-race heroes, from movie tough guys Vin Diesel and The Rock to golfer Tiger Woods and rising tennis star James Blake to singers like Alicia Keys and Norah Jones. Sacramento is ahead of the curve; 2 of every 10 babies born here are multiracial. When those babies grow up and start marrying—a national survey shows more than 90% of today's teens approve of interracial marriage—the numbers will climb even higher.

It took time—and a feeling of not quite belonging at an Asian students' club—for Ferronato to finally realize that she is neither Japanese nor white. She is both. "Now I believe in the theory of hybrid vigor," she says. "A specimen derived from two different species has the strongest traits of both sides."

BUT PEOPLE ARE NOT PLANTS, AND THEORIES are not proofs. Sacramento, as a city, is still searching to find its best self, its strongest traits. Single-race parents of mixed-race children can offer guidance to their kids but not always full understanding. Sacramento is on a similar, unchaperoned journey. Will hybrid theory hold? Who can tell? But the blossoms will be something to see.

From *Time*, September 2, 2002, pp. 26-30. © 2002 by Time Inc. Reprinted by permission.

COMMUNITY BUILDING
STEPS TOWARD A GOOD SOCIETY

AMITAI ETZIONI

Well-formed national societies are not composed of millions of individuals but are constituted as communities of communities. These societies provide a framework within which diverse social groups as well as various subcultures find shared bonds and values. When this framework falls apart, we find communities at each other's throats or even in vicious civil war, as we sadly see in many parts of the world. (Arthur Schlesinger Jr. provides an alarming picture of such a future for our society in his book, *The Disuniting of America*.)

Our community of communities is particularly threatened in two ways that ought to command more of our attention in the next years. First, our society has been growing more diverse by leaps and bounds over recent decades, as immigration has increased and Americans have become more aware of their social and cultural differences. Many on the left celebrate diversity because they see it as ending white European hegemony in our society. Many on the right call for "bleaching out" ethnic differences to ensure a united, homogenous America.

A second challenge to the community of communities emanates from the fact that economic and social inequality has long been rising. Some see a whole new divide caused by the new digital technologies, although others believe that the Internet will bridge these differences. It is time to ask how much inequality the community of communities can tolerate while still flourishing. If we are exceeding these limits, what centrist corrections are available to us?

DIVERSITY WITHIN UNITY

As a multiethnic society, America has long debated the merit of unity versus pluralism, of national identity versus identity politics, of assimilation of immigrants into mainstream culture versus maintaining their national heritages. All of these choices are incompatible with a centrist, communitarian approach to a good society. Assimilation is unnecessarily homogenizing, forcing people to give up important parts of their selves; unbounded ra-

cial, ethnic, and cultural diversity is too conflict-prone for a society in which all are fully respected. The concept of a community of communities provides a third model.

The community of communities builds on the observation that loyalty to one's group, to its particular culture and heritage, is compatible with sustaining national unity as long as the society is perceived not as an arena of conflict but as a society that has some community-like features. (Some refer to a community of communities as an imagined community.) Members of such a society maintain layered loyalties. "Lower" commitments are to one's immediate community, often an ethnic group; "higher" ones are to the community of communities, to the nation as a whole. These include a commitment to a democratic way of life, to a constitution and more generally to a government by law, and above all to treating others—not merely the members of one's group—as ends in themselves and not merely as instruments. Approached this way, one realizes that up to a point, *diversity can avoid being the opposite of unity and can exist within it.*

Moreover, sustaining a particular community of communities does not contradict the gradual development of still more encompassing communities, such as the European Union, a North American community including Canada and Mexico, or, one day, a world community.

During the last decades of the 20th century, the U.S. was racked by identity politics that, in part, have served to partially correct past injustices committed against women and minorities, but have also divided the nation along group lines. Other sharp divisions have appeared between the religious right and much of the rest of the country. One of the merits of the centrist, communitarian approach has been that it has combined efforts to expand the common ground and to cool intergroup rhetoric. Thus communitarians helped call off the "war" between the genders, as Betty Friedan—who was one of the original endorsers of the Communitarian Platform—did in 1997.

New flexibility in involving faith-based groups in the provision of welfare, health care, and other social services, and even allowing some forms of religious activities in public schools, has defused some of the tension between the religious right and the rest of society. The national guidelines on religious expression in public schools, first released by the U.S. Department of Education on the directive of President Clinton in August of 1995, worked to this end. For example, in July of 1996, these guidelines spurred the St. Louis School Board to implement a clearly defined, districtwide policy on school prayer. This policy helped allay the confusion—and litigation—that had previously plagued the role of religion in this school district.

The tendency of blacks and whites not to dialogue openly about racial issues, highlighted by Andrew Hacker, has to some degree been overcome. The main, albeit far from successful, effort in this direction has been made by President Clinton's Advisory Board on Race. And for the first time in U.S. history, a Jew was nominated by a major political party for the post of vice president.

In the next years, intensified efforts are called for to balance the legitimate concerns and needs of various communities that constitute the American society on one hand, and the need to shore up our society as a community of communities on the other. Prayers truly initiated by students might be allowed in public schools as long as sufficient arrangements are made for students who do not wish to participate to spend time in other organized activities. There are no compelling reasons to oppose "after hours" religious clubs establishing themselves in the midst of numerous secular programs. Renewed efforts for honest dialogues among the races are particularly difficult and needed. None of these steps will cause the differences among various communities—many of which serve to enrich our culture and social life—to disappear. But they may go a long way toward reinforcing the framework that keeps American society together while it is being recast.

UNIFYING INEQUALITY

Society cannot long sustain its status as a community of communities if general increases in well-being, even including those that trickle down to the poorest segments of the society, keep increasing the economic distance between the elites and the common people. Fortunately, it seems that at least by some measures, economic inequality has not increased in the United States between 1996 and 2000. And by several measures, the federal income tax has grown surprisingly progressive. (The opposite must be said about rising payroll taxes.) About a third of those who filed income tax returns in 2000 paid no taxes or even got a net refund from the Internal Revenue Service (IRS). However, the level of inequality in income at the end of the 20th century was substantially higher than it was in earlier periods. Between 1977 and 1999, the after-tax income of the top 1 percent of the U.S. population increased by 115 percent, whereas the after-tax income of the U.S. population's lowest fifth decreased by 9 per-

cent. There is little reason to expect that this trend will not continue.

SOCIAL JUSTICE

We may debate what social justice calls for; however, there is little doubt about what community requires. If some members of a community are increasingly distanced from the standard of living of most other members, they will lose contact with the rest of the community. The more those in charge of private and public institutions lead lives of hyper-affluence—replete with gated communities and estates, chauffeured limousines, servants and personal trainers—the less in touch they are with other community members. Such isolation not only frays social bonds and insulates privileged people from the moral cultures of the community, but it also blinds them to the realities of the lives of their fellow citizens. This, in turn, tends to cause them to favor unrealistic policies ("let them eat cake") that backfire and undermine the trust of the members of the society in those who lead and in the institutions they head.

The argument has been made that for the state to provide equality of outcomes undermines the motivation to achieve and to work, stymies creativity and excellence, and is unfair to those who do apply themselves. It is also said that equality of outcomes would raise labor costs so high that a society would be rendered uncompetitive in the new age of global competition. Equality of opportunity has been extolled as a substitute. However, to ensure equality of opportunity, some equality of outcome must be provided. As has often been pointed out, for all to have similar opportunities, they must have similar starting points. These can be reached only if all are accorded certain basics. Special education efforts such as Head Start, created to bring children from disadvantaged backgrounds up to par, and training for workers released from obsolescent industries are examples of programs that provide some equality of results to make equality of opportunity possible.

Additional policies to further curb inequality can be made to work at both ends of the scale. Policies that ensure a rich basic minimum serve this goal by lifting those at the lower levels of the economic pyramid. Reference is often made to education and training programs that focus on those most in need of catching up. However, these work very slowly. Therefore, in the short run more effects will be achieved by raising the Earned Income Tax Credit and the minimum wage, and by implementing new inter-community sharing initiatives.

The poor will remain poor no matter how much they work as long as they own no assets. This is especially damaging because people who own assets, especially a place of residence (even if only an apartment), are most likely to "buy" into a society—to feel and be part of a community. By numerous measures, homeowners are more involved in the life of their communities, and their children are less likely to drop out of school. Roughly one-third of Americans do not own their residence; 73 percent of whites do, compared to 47 percent of African Americans and Hispanics.

MORTGAGES

Various provisions allowing those with limited resources to get mortgages through federally chartered corporations like Fannie Mae, which helps finance mortgages for many lower-income people, have been helpful in increasing ownership. More needs to be done on this front, especially for those of little means. This might be achieved by following the same model used in the Earned Income Tax Credit in the U.S. and the Working Families Tax Credit in the United Kingdom: providing people who earn below a defined income level with "earned interest on mortgages," effectively granting them two dollars for every dollar set aside to provide seed money for a mortgage. And sweat equity might be used as the future owner's contribution—for instance, if they work on their own housing site. (Those who benefit from the houses that Habitat for Humanity builds are required to either make some kind of a financial contribution themselves or help in the construction of their homes.) Far from implausible, various ideas along these lines were offered by both George W. Bush and Al Gore during the 2000 election campaign, as well as by various policy researchers.

Reducing hard core unemployment by trying to bring jobs to poor neighborhoods (through "enterprise zones") or by training the long-unemployed in entrepreneurial skills is often expensive and slow, and is frequently unsuccessful. The opposite approach, moving people from poor areas to places where jobs are, often encounters objections by the neighborhoods into which they are moved, as well as by those poor who feel more comfortable living in their home communities. A third approach should be tried much more extensively: providing ready transportation to and from places of employment.

Measures to cap the higher levels of wealth include progressive income taxes, some forms of inheritance tax, closing numerous loopholes in the tax codes, and ensuring that tax on capital is paid as it is on labor. Given that several of these inequality curbing measures cannot be adopted on a significant scale if they seriously endanger the competitive state of a country, steps to introduce many of them should be undertaken jointly with other Organization for Economic Cooperation and Development (OECD) countries, or better yet, among all the nations that are our major competitors and trade partners.

One need not be a liberal—one can be a solid communitarian—and still be quite dismayed to learn that the IRS audits the poor (defined as income below $25,000) more than the rich (defined as income above $100,000). In 1999, the IRS audited 1.36 percent of poor taxpayers, compared to 1.15 percent of rich taxpayers. In 1988, the percentage for the rich was 11.4. In one decade, there was thus a decline of about 90 percent in auditing the rich. This occurred because Congress did not authorize the necessary funds, despite the General Accounting Office's finding that the rich are more likely to evade taxes than are the poor. This change in audit patterns also reflects the concern of Republican members of Congress that the poor will abuse the Earned Income Tax Credit that the Clinton administration has introduced. It should not take a decade to correct this imbalance.

Ultimately, this matter and many others will not be properly attended to until there is a basic change in the moral culture of the society and in the purposes that animate it. Without such a change, a major reallocation of wealth can be achieved only by force, which is incompatible with a democratic society and will cause a wealth flight and other damage to the economy. In contrast, history from early Christianity to Fabian socialism teaches us that people who share progressive values will be inclined to share their wealth voluntarily. A good society seeks to promote such values through a grand dialogue rather than by dictates.

THE NEW GRAND DIALOGUE

The great success of the economy in the 1990s made Americans pay more attention to the fact that there are numerous moral and social questions of concern to the good society that capitalism has never aspired to answer and that the state should not promote. These include moral questions such as what we owe our children, our parents, our friends, and our neighbors, as well as people from other communities, including those in far away places. Most important, we must address this question: What is the ultimate purpose our personal and collective endeavors? Is ever greater material affluence our ultimate goal and the source of meaning? When is enough— enough? What are we considering the good life? *Can a good society be built on ever increasing levels of affluence? Or should we strive to center it around other values, those of mutuality and spirituality?*

The journey to the good society can benefit greatly from the observation, supported by a great deal of social science data, that ever increasing levels of material goods are not a reliable source of human well-being or contentment—let alone the basis for a morally sound society. To cite but a few studies of a large body of findings: Frank M. Andrews and Stephen B. Withey found that the level of one's socioeconomic status had meager effects on one's "sense of well-being" and no significant effect on "satisfaction with life-as-a-whole." Jonathan L. Freedman discovered that levels of reported happiness did not vary greatly among the members of different economic classes, with the exception of the very poor, who tended to be less happy than others. David G. Myers reported that although per capita disposable (after-tax) income in inflation-adjusted dollars almost exactly doubled between 1960 and 1990, 32 percent of Americans reported that they were "very happy" in 1993, almost the same proportion as did in 1957 (35 percent). Although economic growth slowed after the mid-1970s, Americans' reported happiness was remarkably stable (nearly always between 30 and 35 percent) across both high-growth and low-growth periods.

HAPPINESS

These and other such data help us realize that the pursuit of well-being through ever higher levels of consumption is Sisyphean. When it comes to material goods, enough is never enough. This is not an argument in favor of a life of sackcloth and ashes, of poverty and self-denial. The argument is that once basic material needs (what Abraham Maslow called "creature comforts") are well sated and securely provided for, additional income does not add to happiness. On the contrary, hard evidence—not some hippie, touchy-feely, LSD-induced hallucination—shows that profound contentment is found in nourishing ends-based relationships, in bonding with others, in community building and public service, and in cultural and spiritual pursuits. Capitalism, the engine of affluence, has never aspired to address the whole person; typically it treats the person as *Homo economicus.* And of course, statist socialism subjugated rather than inspired. It is left to the evolving values and cultures of centrist societies to fill the void.

Nobel laureate Robert Fogel showed that periods of great affluence are regularly followed by what he calls Great Awakenings, and that we are due for one in the near future. Although it is quite evident that there is a growing thirst for a purpose deeper than conspicuous consumption, we may not have the ability to predict which specific form this yearning for spiritual fulfillment will take.

There are some who hold firmly that the form must be a religious one because no other speaks to the most profound matters that trouble the human soul, nor do others provide sound moral guidance. These believers find good support in numerous indicators that there was a considerable measure of religious revival in practically all forms of American religion over the last decades of the 20th century. The revival is said to be evident not merely in the number of people who participate in religious activities and the frequency of their participation in these activities, but also in the stronger, more involving, and stricter kinds of commitments many are making to religion. (Margaret Talbot has argued effectively that conservative Christians, especially fundamentalists, constitute the true counterculture of our age; they know and live a life rich in fulfillment, not centered around consumer goods.) Others see the spiritual revival as taking more secular forms, ranging from New Age cults to a growing interest in applied ethics.

PRIORITIES

Aside from making people more profoundly and truly content individuals, a major and broadly based upward shift on the Maslovian scale is a prerequisite for being able to better address some of the most tantalizing problems plaguing modern societies, whatever form such a shift may take. That is what is required before we can come into harmony with our environment, because these higher priorities put much less demand on scarce resources than do lower ones. And such a new set of priorities may well be the only conditions under which those who are well endowed would be willing to support serious reallocation of wealth and power, as their personal fortunes would no longer be based on amassing ever larger amounts of consumer goods. In addition, transitioning to a knowledge-based economy would free millions of people (one hopes all of them, gradually) to relate to each other mainly as members of families and communities, thus laying the social foundations for a society in which ends-based relationships dominate while instrumental ones are well contained.

The upward shift in priorities, a return to a sort of moderate counterculture, a turn toward voluntary simplicity—these require a grand dialogue about our personal and shared goals. (A return to a counterculture is not a recommendation for more abuse of controlled substances, promiscuity, and self-indulgence—which is about the last thing America needs—but the realization that one can find profound contentment in reflection, friendship, love, sunsets, and walks on the beach rather than in the pursuit of ever more control over ever more goods.) Intellectuals and the media can help launch such a dialogue and model the new forms of behavior. Public leaders can nurse the recognition of these values by moderating consumption at public events and ceremonies, and by celebrating those whose achievements are compatible with a good society rather than with a merely affluent one.

But ultimately, such a shift lies in changes in our hearts and minds, in our values and conduct—what Robert Bellah called the "habits of the heart." We shall not travel far toward a good society unless such a dialogue is soon launched and advanced to a good, spiritually uplifting conclusion.

Mr. Etzioni is editor of The Responsive Community. *From "Next: Three Steps Towards A Good Society," by Amitai Etzioni,* The Responsive Community, *Winter 2000–01, pages 49–58.*

Reprinted from *Current,* January 2001, pp. 29-33. Originally printed in *The Responsive Community,* Vol. II, No. 1, Winter 2000/01, pp. 49-58, which was adapted from the author's book *Next: The Road to the Good Society* (New York: Basic Books, 2001).

UNIT 4

Stratification and Social Inequalities

Unit Selections

Key Points to Consider

- Explain why you believe that technology could reduce or increase social inequalities.

- What inequalities do you find unacceptable and what inequalities do you find acceptable?

- Why is stratification such an important theme in sociology?

- Which social groups are likely to rise in the stratification system in the next decade? Which groups will fall? Why?

- How does stratification along income lines differ from stratification along racial or gender lines?

- Do you think women and blacks are treated fairly in America? Are changes needed in the policies that deal with discrimination? Why or why not?

 **Links: www.dushkin.com/online/**
These sites are annotated in the World Wide Web pages.

Americans With Disabilities Act Document Center
http://www.jan.wvu.edu/links/adalinks.htm

American Scientist
http://www.amsci.org/amsci/amsci.html

Give Five
http://www.independentsector.org/give5/givefive.html

Joint Center for Poverty Research
http://www.jcpr.org

NAACP Online: National Association for the Advancement of Colored People
http://www.naacp.org

People are ranked in many different ways-by physical strength, education, wealth, or other characteristics. Those who are rated highly often have power over others, special status, and prestige. The differences among people constitute their life chances, the probability that an individual or group will be able to obtain the valued and desired goods in a society. These differences are referred to as stratification, the system of structured inequalities in social relationships.

In most industrialized societies, income is one of the most important divisions among people. Karl Marx described stratification in terms of class rather than income. For him social class referred mainly to two distinct groups: those who control the means of production and those who do not. This section examines the life chances of the rich and the poor and of various disadvantaged groups, which best demonstrates the crucial features of the stratification system in the United States.

The first subsection of this unit deals with income inequality and the hardship of the poor. In his article, "For Richer," Paul Krugman describes the great increase in the inequality of income in the past three decades and explains its causes. He also discusses some rather unpleasant political and social consequences of these inequalities. In the next article, Joel Stein shows some of the underside of the inequality that Krugman describes. He discusses homelessness but not the homelessness that is imaged in our minds by the drunk sleeping on the park bench. Increasingly the homeless are mothers with children and Joel Stein tells some of their stories. He also points out why this is the case.

The American welfare system is addressed in the second subsection of unit 4. The first article describes the generous welfare system for the rich, and the next describes the effects of the 1996 welfare reform on the poor. First, Donald Barlett and James Steele explain how corporations milk federal, state, and local governments of billions of dollars. It comes as no surprise to a student of society that the political economy is set up to ben-

efit the upper class and the powerful but the extent of that bias, when pointed out, can shock us anyway. The next article evaluates the results of the 1996 welfare reform. It begins by providing facts which show that it was not as bad as it was made out to be. For example, it was not very costly, being less than 5% of the costs of social security. Nevertheless, it needed to be reformed and the reform lowered caseloads 57 percent through 2001, and the majority of leavers are working (much of this change was due to the good economy). On the negative side, the jobs generally are bad jobs that pay little and are unsteady. Finally, on several counts the new welfare system is more punitive.

The most poignant inequality in America is the gap between blacks and whites. Recently there has been considerable good news that the gap has been closing and many indicators that quality of life has improved for blacks. In the next article Barbara Kantrowitz and Pat Wingert clarify where affirmative action is today. It had a glorious history when it pushed the nation toward fairness. However, what is its proper role today? Is it needed now and is it unfair now? This article clarifies what affirmative action is, where it stands legally today, and how universities should handle the issue.

In the next article, the authors demonstrate the prevalence of prejudice and hatred in America and how quickly hatred toward a group can evolve. Since September 11, 2001, hatred toward Muslims has erupted despite calls for tolerance from President George W. Bush and other public leaders. One explanation of hatred and prejudice against entire groups is social identity theory. People have a powerful drive to divide people into groups, identify with one group, and develop negative views of some of the out groups. Fortunately, "people who are concerned about their prejudices have the power to correct them."

The last subsection of unit 4 deals with sex inequalities. In the first article of the section, Judy Olian documents the many forms of sex inequality. She also explains why the inequality persists. Besides discrimination, she blames quite different formative experiences for boys and girls and the different attitudes that result from them, as well as several factors that operate in adult life. In the next article, Alice Leuchtag describes one of the great evils that is haunting the world today which is sex slavery. The sex trade system grows out of poverty and profits. Extreme poverty forces parents to sell their daughters into servitude often not knowing that they will become sex slaves. Considerable profits drive the system and the exploitation involved is horrendous. This is a worldwide human rights issue. In the last article, Michelle Conlin examines a very different sex inequality issue,

boys not being equal to girls. The new gender gap is the educational superiority of females over males. Conlin shows that from kindergarten to grad school girls outperform boys and have higher graduation rates. How can this be explained and what should be done about it if anything?

The articles in this unit portray tremendous differences in wealth and life chances among people. Systems of inequality affect what a person does and how he or she does it. An important purpose of this unit is to help you become more aware of how stratification operates in social life.

For Richer

How the permissive capitalism of the boom destroyed American equality.

By Paul Krugman

I. The Disappearing Middle

When I was a teenager growing up on Long Island, one of my favorite excursions was a trip to see the great Gilded Age mansions of the North Shore. Those mansions weren't just pieces of architectural history. They were monuments to a bygone social era, one in which the rich could afford the armies of servants needed to maintain a house the size of a European palace. By the time I saw them, of course, that era was long past. Almost none of the Long Island mansions were still private residences. Those that hadn't been turned into museums were occupied by nursing homes or private schools.

For the America I grew up in—the America of the 1950's and 1960's—was a middle-class society, both in reality and in feel. The vast income and wealth inequalities of the Gilded Age had disappeared. Yes, of course, there was the poverty of the underclass—but the conventional wisdom of the time viewed that as a social rather than an economic problem. Yes, of course, some wealthy businessmen and heirs to large fortunes lived far better than the average American. But they weren't rich the way the robber barons who built the mansions had been rich, and there weren't that many of them. The days when plutocrats were a force to be reckoned with in American society, economically or politically, seemed long past.

Daily experience confirmed the sense of a fairly equal society. The economic disparities you were conscious of were quite muted. Highly educated professionals—middle managers, college teachers, even lawyers—often claimed that they earned less than unionized blue-collar workers. Those considered very well off lived in split-levels, had a housecleaner come in once a week and took summer vacations in Europe. But they sent their kids to public schools and drove themselves to work, just like everyone else.

But that was long ago. The middle-class America of my youth was another country.

We are now living in a new Gilded Age, as extravagant as the original. Mansions have made a comeback. Back in 1999 this magazine profiled Thierry Despont, the "eminence of excess," an architect who specializes in designing houses for the super-rich. His creations typically range from 20,000 to 60,000 square feet; houses at the upper end of his range are not much smaller than the White House. Needless to say, the armies of servants are back, too. So are the yachts. Still, even J.P. Morgan didn't have a Gulfstream.

As the story about Despont suggests, it's not fair to say that the fact of widening inequality in America has gone unreported. Yet glimpses of the lifestyles of the rich and tasteless don't necessarily add up in people's minds to a clear picture of the tectonic shifts that have taken place in the distribution of income and wealth in this country. My sense is that few people are aware of just how much the gap between the very rich and the rest has widened over a relatively short period of time. In fact, even bringing up the subject exposes you to charges of "class warfare," the "politics of envy" and so on. And very few people indeed are willing to talk about the profound effects—economic, social and political—of that widening gap.

Yet you can't understand what's happening in America today without understanding the extent, causes and consequences of the vast increase in inequality that has taken place over the last three decades, and in particular the astonishing concentration of income and wealth in just a few hands. To make sense of the current wave of corporate scandal, you need to understand how the man in the gray flannel suit has been replaced by the imperial C.E.O. The concentration of income at the top is a key reason that the United States, for all its economic achievements, has more poverty and lower life expectancy than any other major advanced nation. Above all, the growing concentration of wealth has reshaped our political system: it is at the root both of a general shift to the right and of an extreme polarization of our politics.

But before we get to all that, let's take a look at who gets what.

II. The New Gilded Age

The Securities and Exchange Commission hath no fury like a woman scorned. The messy divorce proceedings of Jack Welch, the legendary former C.E.O. of General Electric, have had one unintended benefit: they have given us a peek at the perks of the corporate elite, which are normally hidden from public view. For it turns out that when Welch retired, he was granted for life the use of a Manhattan apartment (including food, wine and laundry), access to corporate jets and a variety of other in-kind benefits, worth at least $2 million a year. The perks were revealing: they illustrated the extent to which corporate leaders now expect to be treated like *ancien régime* royalty. In monetary terms, however, the perks must have meant little to Welch. In 2000, his last full year running G.E., Welch was paid $123 million, mainly in stock and stock options.

The 13,000 richest families in America now have almost as much income as the 20 million poorest. And those 13,000 families have incomes 300 times that of average families.

Is it news that C.E.O.'s of large American corporations make a lot of money? Actually, it is. They were always well paid compared with the average worker, but there is simply no comparison between what executives got a generation ago and what they are paid today.

Over the past 30 years most people have seen only modest salary increases: the average annual salary in America, expressed in 1998 dollars (that is, adjusted for inflation), rose from $32,522 in 1970 to $35,864 in 1999. That's about a 10 percent increase over 29 years—progress, but not much. Over the same period, however, according to Fortune magazine, the average real annual compensation of the top 100 C.E.O.'s went from $1.3 million—39 times the pay of an average worker—to $37.5 million, more than 1,000 times the pay of ordinary workers.

The explosion in C.E.O. pay over the past 30 years is an amazing story in its own right, and an important one. But it is only the most spectacular indicator of a broader story, the reconcentration of income and wealth in the U.S. The rich have always been different from you and me, but they are far more different now than they were not long ago—indeed, they are as different now as they were when F. Scott Fitzgerald made his famous remark.

That's a controversial statement, though it shouldn't be. For at least the past 15 years it has been hard to deny the evidence for growing inequality in the United States. Census data clearly show a rising share of income going to the top 20 percent of families, and within that top 20 percent to the top 5 percent, with a declining share going to families in the middle. Nonetheless, denial of that evidence is a sizable, well-financed industry. Conservative think tanks have produced scores of studies that try to discredit the data, the methodology and, not least, the motives of those who report the obvious. Studies that appear to refute claims of increasing inequality receive prominent endorsements on editorial pages and are eagerly cited by right-leaning government officials. Four years ago Alan Greenspan (why did anyone ever think that he was nonpartisan?) gave a keynote speech at the Federal Reserve's annual Jackson Hole conference that amounted to an attempt to deny that there has been any real increase in inequality in America.

The concerted effort to deny that inequality is increasing is itself a symptom of the growing influence of our emerging plutocracy (more on this later). So is the fierce defense of the backup position, that inequality doesn't matter—or maybe even that, to use Martha Stewart's signature phrase, it's a good thing. Meanwhile, politically motivated smoke screens aside, the reality of increasing inequality is not in doubt. In fact, the census data understate the case, because for technical reasons those data tend to undercount very high incomes—for example, it's unlikely that they reflect the explosion in C.E.O. compensation. And other evidence makes it clear not only that inequality is increasing but that the action gets bigger the closer you get to the top. That is, it's not simply that the top 20 percent of families have had bigger percentage gains than families near the middle: the top 5 percent have done better than the next 15, the top 1 percent better than the next 4, and so on up to Bill Gates.

Studies that try to do a better job of tracking high incomes have found startling results. For example, a recent study by the nonpartisan Congressional Budget Office used income tax data and other sources to improve on the census estimates. The C.B.O. study found that between 1979 and 1997, the after-tax incomes of the top 1 percent of families rose 157 percent, compared with only a 10 percent gain for families near the middle of the income distribution. Even more startling results come from a new study by Thomas Piketty, at the French research institute Cepremap, and Emmanuel Saez, who is now at the University of California at Berkeley. Using income tax data, Piketty and Saez have produced estimates of the incomes of the well-to-do, the rich and the very rich back to 1913.

The first point you learn from these new estimates is that the middle-class America of my youth is best thought of not as the normal state of our society, but as an interregnum between Gilded Ages. America before 1930 was a society in which a small number of very rich people controlled a large share of the nation's wealth. We became a middle-class society only after the concentration of income at the top dropped sharply during the New Deal, and especially during World War II. The economic historians Claudia Goldin and Robert Margo have dubbed the narrowing of income gaps during those years the Great Compression. Incomes then stayed fairly equally distributed until the 1970's: the rapid rise in incomes during the first postwar generation was very evenly spread across the population.

Since the 1970's, however, income gaps have been rapidly widening. Piketty and Saez confirm what I suspected: by most measures we are, in fact, back to the days of "The Great Gatsby." After 30 years in which the income shares of the top 10 percent of taxpayers, the top 1 percent and so on were far below their levels in the 1920's, all are very nearly back where they were.

And the big winners are the very, very rich. One ploy often used to play down growing inequality is to rely on rather coarse statistical breakdowns—dividing the population into five "quintiles," each containing 20 percent of families, or at most 10 "deciles." Indeed, Greenspan's speech at Jackson Hole relied mainly on decile data. From there it's a short step to denying that we're really talking about the rich at all. For example, a conservative commentator might concede, grudgingly, that there has been some increase in the share of national income going to the top 10 percent of taxpayers, but then point out that anyone with an income over $81,000 is in that top 10 percent. So we're just talking about shifts within the middle class, right?

Wrong: the top 10 percent contains a lot of people whom we would still consider middle class, but they weren't the big winners. Most of the gains in the share of the top 10 percent of taxpayers over the past 30 years were actually gains to the top 1 percent, rather than the next 9 percent. In 1998 the top 1 percent started at $230,000. In turn, 60 percent of the gains of that top 1 percent went to the top 0.1 percent, those with incomes of more than $790,000. And almost half of those gains went to a mere 13,000 taxpayers, the top 0.01 percent, who had an income of at least $3.6 million and an average income of $17 million.

A stickler for detail might point out that the Piketty-Saez estimates end in 1998 and that the C.B.O. numbers end a year earlier. Have the trends shown in the data reversed? Almost surely not. In fact, all indications are that the explosion of incomes at the top continued through 2000. Since then the plunge in stock prices must have put some crimp in high incomes—but census data show inequality continuing to increase in 2001, mainly because of the severe effects of the recession on the working poor and near poor. When the recession ends, we can be sure that we will find ourselves a society in which income inequality is even higher than it was in the late 90's.

So claims that we've entered a second Gilded Age aren't exaggerated. In America's middle-class era, the mansion-building, yacht-owning classes had pretty much disappeared. According to Piketty and Saez, in 1970 the top 0.01 percent of taxpayers had 0.7 percent of total income—that is, they earned "only" 70 times as much as the average, not enough to buy or maintain a mega-residence. But in 1998 the top 0.01 percent received more than 3 percent of all income. That meant that the 13,000 richest families in America had almost as much income as the 20 million poorest households; those 13,000 families had incomes 300 times that of average families.

And let me repeat: this transformation has happened very quickly, and it is still going on. You might think that 1987, the year Tom Wolfe published his novel "The Bonfire of the Vani-ties" and Oliver Stone released his movie "Wall Street," marked the high tide of America's new money culture. But in 1987 the top 0.01 percent earned only about 40 percent of what they do today, and top executives less than a fifth as much. The America of "Wall Street" and "The Bonfire of the Vanities" was positively egalitarian compared with the country we live in today.

III. Undoing the New Deal

IN the middle of the 1980's, as economists became aware that something important was happening to the distribution of income in America, they formulated three main hypotheses about its causes.

The "globalization" hypothesis tied America's changing income distribution to the growth of world trade, and especially the growing imports of manufactured goods from the third world. Its basic message was that blue-collar workers—the sort of people who in my youth often made as much money as college-educated middle managers—were losing ground in the face of competition from low-wage workers in Asia. A result was stagnation or decline in the wages of ordinary people, with a growing share of national income going to the highly educated.

A second hypothesis, "skill-biased technological change," situated the cause of growing inequality not in foreign trade but in domestic innovation. The torrid pace of progress in information technology, so the story went, had increased the demand for the highly skilled and educated. And so the income distribution increasingly favored brains rather than brawn.

> Some economists think the New Deal imposed norms of relative equality in pay that persisted for more than 30 years, creating a broadly middle-class society. Those norms have unraveled.

Finally, the "superstar" hypothesis—named by the Chicago economist Sherwin Rosen—offered a variant on the technological story. It argued that modern technologies of communication often turn competition into a tournament in which the winner is richly rewarded, while the runners-up get far less. The classic example—which gives the theory its name—is the entertainment business. As Rosen pointed out, in bygone days there were hundreds of comedians making a modest living at live shows in the borscht belt and other places. Now they are mostly gone; what is left is a handful of superstar TV comedians.

The debates among these hypotheses—particularly the debate between those who attributed growing inequality to globalization and those who attributed it to technology—were many and bitter. I was a participant in those debates myself. But I won't dwell on them, because in the last few years there has been a growing sense among economists that none of these hypotheses work.

I don't mean to say that there was nothing to these stories. Yet as more evidence has accumulated, each of the hypotheses has seemed increasingly inadequate. Globalization can explain part of the relative decline in blue-collar wages, but it can't explain the 2,500 percent rise in C.E.O. incomes. Technology may explain why the salary premium associated with a college education has risen, but it's hard to match up with the huge increase in inequality among the college-educated, with little progress for many but gigantic gains at the top. The superstar theory works for Jay Leno, but not for the thousands of people who have become awesomely rich without going on TV.

The Great Compression—the substantial reduction in inequality during the New Deal and the Second World War—also seems hard to understand in terms of the usual theories. During World War II Franklin Roosevelt used government control over wages to compress wage gaps. But if the middle-class society that emerged from the war was an artificial creation, why did it persist for another 30 years?

Some—by no means all—economists trying to understand growing inequality have begun to take seriously a hypothesis that would have been considered irredeemably fuzzy-minded not long ago. This view stresses the role of social norms in setting limits to inequality. According to this view, the New Deal had a more profound impact on American society than even its most ardent admirers have suggested: it imposed norms of relative equality in pay that persisted for more than 30 years, creating the broadly middle-class society we came to take for granted. But those norms began to unravel in the 1970's and have done so at an accelerating pace.

Exhibit A for this view is the story of executive compensation. In the 1960's, America's great corporations behaved more like socialist republics than like cutthroat capitalist enterprises, and top executives behaved more like public-spirited bureaucrats than like captains of industry. I'm not exaggerating. Consider the description of executive behavior offered by John Kenneth Galbraith in his 1967 book, "The New Industrial State": "Management does not go out ruthlessly to reward itself—a sound management is expected to exercise restraint." Managerial self-dealing was a thing of the past: "With the power of decision goes opportunity for making money.... Were everyone to seek to do so... the corporation would be a chaos of competitive avarice. But these are not the sort of thing that a good company man does; a remarkably effective code bans such behavior. Group decision-making insures, moreover, that almost everyone's actions and even thoughts are known to others. This acts to enforce the code and, more than incidentally, a high standard of personal honesty as well."

Thirty-five years on, a cover article in *Fortune* is titled "You Bought. They Sold." "All over corporate America," reads the blurb, "top execs were cashing in stocks even as their companies were tanking. Who was left holding the bag? You." As I said, we've become a different country.

Let's leave actual malfeasance on one side for a moment, and ask how the relatively modest salaries of top executives 30 years ago became the gigantic pay packages of today. There are two main stories, both of which emphasize changing norms rather than pure economics. The more optimistic story draws an

analogy between the explosion of C.E.O. pay and the explosion of baseball salaries with the introduction of free agency. According to this story, highly paid C.E.O.'s really are worth it, because having the right man in that job makes a huge difference. The more pessimistic view—which I find more plausible—is that competition for talent is a minor factor. Yes, a great executive can make a big difference—but those huge pay packages have been going as often as not to executives whose performance is mediocre at best. The key reason executives are paid so much now is that they appoint the members of the corporate board that determines their compensation and control many of the perks that board members count on. So it's not the invisible hand of the market that leads to those monumental executive incomes; it's the invisible handshake in the boardroom.

But then why weren't executives paid lavishly 30 years ago? Again, it's a matter of corporate culture. For a generation after World War II, fear of outrage kept executive salaries in check. Now the outrage is gone. That is, the explosion of executive pay represents a social change rather than the purely economic forces of supply and demand. We should think of it not as a market trend like the rising value of waterfront property, but as something more like the sexual revolution of the 1960's—a relaxation of old strictures, a new permissiveness, but in this case the permissiveness is financial rather than sexual. Sure enough, John Kenneth Galbraith described the honest executive of 1967 as being one who "eschews the lovely, available and even naked woman by whom he is intimately surrounded." By the end of the 1990's, the executive motto might as well have been "If it feels good, do it."

How did this change in corporate culture happen? Economists and management theorists are only beginning to explore that question, but it's easy to suggest a few factors. One was the changing structure of financial markets. In his new book, "Searching for a Corporate Savior," Rakesh Khurana of Harvard Business School suggests that during the 1980's and 1990's, "managerial capitalism"—the world of the man in the gray flannel suit—was replaced by "investor capitalism." Institutional investors weren't willing to let a C.E.O. choose his own successor from inside the corporation; they wanted heroic leaders, often outsiders, and were willing to pay immense sums to get them. The subtitle of Khurana's book, by the way, is "The Irrational Quest for Charismatic C.E.O.'s."

But fashionable management theorists didn't think it was irrational. Since the 1980's there has been ever more emphasis on the importance of "leadership"—meaning personal, charismatic leadership. When Lee Iacocca of Chrysler became a business celebrity in the early 1980's, he was practically alone: Khurana reports that in 1980 only one issue of Business Week featured a C.E.O. on its cover. By 1999 the number was up to 19. And once it was considered normal, even necessary, for a C.E.O. to be famous, it also became easier to make him rich.

Economists also did their bit to legitimize previously unthinkable levels of executive pay. During the 1980's and 1990's a torrent of academic papers—popularized in business magazines and incorporated into consultants' recommendations—argued that Gordon Gekko was right: greed is good; greed works. In order to get the best performance out of executives, these papers argued, it was necessary to align their interests with those of stockholders. And the way to do that was with large grants of stock or stock options.

It's hard to escape the suspicion that these new intellectual justifications for soaring executive pay were as much effect as cause. I'm not suggesting that management theorists and economists were personally corrupt. It would have been a subtle, unconscious process: the ideas that were taken up by business schools, that led to nice speaking and consulting fees, tended to be the ones that ratified an existing trend, and thereby gave it legitimacy.

What economists like Piketty and Saez are now suggesting is that the story of executive compensation is representative of a broader story. Much more than economists and free-market advocates like to imagine, wages—particularly at the top—are determined by social norms. What happened during the 1930's and 1940's was that new norms of equality were established, largely through the political process. What happened in the 1980's and 1990's was that those norms unraveled, replaced by an ethos of "anything goes." And a result was an explosion of income at the top of the scale.

IV. The Price of Inequality

It was one of those revealing moments. Responding to an e-mail message from a Canadian viewer, Robert Novak of "Crossfire" delivered a little speech: "Marg, like most Canadians, you're ill informed and wrong. The U.S. has the longest standard of living—longest life expectancy of any country in the world, including Canada. That's the truth."

But it was Novak who had his facts wrong. Canadians can expect to live about two years longer than Americans. In fact, life expectancy in the U.S. is well below that in Canada, Japan and every major nation in Western Europe. On average, we can expect lives a bit shorter than those of Greeks, a bit longer than those of Portuguese. Male life expectancy is lower in the U.S. than it is in Costa Rica.

Still, you can understand why Novak assumed that we were No. 1. After all, we really are the richest major nation, with real G.D.P. per capita about 20 percent higher than Canada's. And it has been an article of faith in this country that a rising tide lifts all boats. Doesn't our high and rising national wealth translate into a high standard of living—including good medical care—for all Americans?

Well, no. Although America has higher per capita income than other advanced countries, it turns out that that's mainly because our rich are much richer. And here's a radical thought: if the rich get more, that leaves less for everyone else.

That statement—which is simply a matter of arithmetic—is guaranteed to bring accusations of "class warfare." If the accuser gets more specific, he'll probably offer two reasons that it's foolish to make a fuss over the high incomes of a few people at the top of the income distribution. First, he'll tell you that what the elite get may look like a lot of money, but it's still a small share of the total—that is, when all is said and done the rich aren't getting that big a piece of the pie. Second, he'll tell you that trying to do anything to reduce incomes at the top will hurt, not help, people further down the distribution, because attempts to redistribute income damage incentives.

These arguments for lack of concern are plausible. And they were entirely correct, once upon a time—namely, back when we had a middle-class society. But there's a lot less truth to them now.

First, the share of the rich in total income is no longer trivial. These days 1 percent of families receive about 16 percent of total pretax income, and have about 14 percent of after-tax income. That share has roughly doubled over the past 30 years, and is now about as large as the share of the bottom 40 percent of the population. That's a big shift of income to the top; as a matter of pure arithmetic, it must mean that the incomes of less well off families grew considerably more slowly than average income. And they did. Adjusting for inflation, average family income—total income divided by the number of families—grew 28 percent from 1979 to 1997. But median family income—the income of a family in the middle of the distribution, a better indicator of how typical American families are doing—grew only 10 percent. And the incomes of the bottom fifth of families actually fell slightly.

Let me belabor this point for a bit. We pride ourselves, with considerable justification, on our record of economic growth. But over the last few decades it's remarkable how little of that growth has trickled down to ordinary families. Median family income has risen only about 0.5 percent per year—and as far as we can tell from somewhat unreliable data, just about all of that increase was due to wives working longer hours, with little or no gain in real wages. Furthermore, numbers about income don't reflect the growing riskiness of life for ordinary workers. In the days when General Motors was known in-house as Generous Motors, many workers felt that they had considerable job security—the company wouldn't fire them except in extremis. Many had contracts that guaranteed health insurance, even if they were laid off; they had pension benefits that did not depend on the stock market. Now mass firings from long-established companies are commonplace; losing your job means losing your insurance; and as millions of people have been learning, a 401(k) plan is no guarantee of a comfortable retirement.

Still, many people will say that while the U.S. economic system may generate a lot of inequality, it also generates much higher incomes than any alternative, so that everyone is better off. That was the moral Business Week tried to convey in its recent special issue with "25 Ideas for a Changing World." One of those ideas was "the rich get richer, and that's O.K." High incomes at the top, the conventional wisdom declares, are the result of a free-market system that provides huge incentives for performance. And the system delivers that performance, which means that wealth at the top doesn't come at the expense of the rest of us.

A skeptic might point out that the explosion in executive compensation seems at best loosely related to actual performance. Jack Welch was one of the 10 highest-paid executives in the United States in 2000, and you could argue that he earned it. But did Dennis Kozlowski of Tyco, or Gerald Levin of Time Warner, who were also in the top 10? A skeptic might also point out that even during the economic boom of the late

1990's, U.S. productivity growth was no better than it was during the great postwar expansion, which corresponds to the era when America was truly middle class and C.E.O.'s were modestly paid technocrats.

But can we produce any direct evidence about the effects of inequality? We can't rerun our own history and ask what would have happened if the social norms of middle-class America had continued to limit incomes at the top, and if government policy had leaned against rising inequality instead of reinforcing it, which is what actually happened. But we can compare ourselves with other advanced countries. And the results are somewhat surprising.

Many Americans assume that because we are the richest country in the world, with real G.D.P. per capita higher than that of other major advanced countries, Americans must be better off across the board—that it's not just our rich who are richer than their counterparts abroad, but that the typical American family is much better off than the typical family elsewhere, and that even our poor are well off by foreign standards.

But it's not true. Let me use the example of Sweden, that great conservative *bête noire*.

A few months ago the conservative cyberpundit Glenn Reynolds made a splash when he pointed out that Sweden's G.D.P. per capita is roughly comparable with that of Mississippi—see, those foolish believers in the welfare state have impoverished themselves! Presumably he assumed that this means that the typical Swede is as poor as the typical resident of Mississippi, and therefore much worse off than the typical American.

As the rich get richer, they can buy a lot besides goods and services. Money buys political influence; used cleverly, it also buys intellectual influence.

But life expectancy in Sweden is about three years higher than that of the U.S. Infant mortality is half the U.S. level, and less than a third the rate in Mississippi. Functional illiteracy is much less common than in the U.S.

How is this possible? One answer is that G.D.P. per capita is in some ways a misleading measure. Swedes take longer vacations than Americans, so they work fewer hours per year. That's a choice, not a failure of economic performance. Real G.D.P. per hour worked is 16 percent lower than in the United States, which makes Swedish productivity about the same as Canada's.

But the main point is that though Sweden may have lower average income than the United States, that's mainly because our rich are so much richer. The median Swedish family has a standard of living roughly comparable with that of the median U.S. family: wages are if anything higher in Sweden, and a higher tax burden is offset by public provision of health care and generally better public services. And as you move further down the income distribution, Swedish living standards are way ahead of those in the U.S. Swedish families with children that are at the 10th percentile—poorer than 90 percent of the population—

have incomes 60 percent higher than their U.S. counterparts. And very few people in Sweden experience the deep poverty that is all too common in the United States. One measure: in 1994 only 6 percent of Swedes lived on less than $11 per day, compared with 14 percent in the U.S.

The moral of this comparison is that even if you think that America's high levels of inequality are the price of our high level of national income, it's not at all clear that this price is worth paying. The reason conservatives engage in bouts of Sweden-bashing is that they want to convince us that there is no tradeoff between economic efficiency and equity—that if you try to take from the rich and give to the poor, you actually make everyone worse off. But the comparison between the U.S. and other advanced countries doesn't support this conclusion at all. Yes, we are the richest major nation. But because so much of our national income is concentrated in relatively few hands, large numbers of Americans are worse off economically than their counterparts in other advanced countries.

And we might even offer a challenge from the other side: inequality in the United States has arguably reached levels where it is counterproductive. That is, you can make a case that our society would be richer if its richest members didn't get quite so much.

I could make this argument on historical grounds. The most impressive economic growth in U.S. history coincided with the middle-class interregnum, the post-World War II generation, when incomes were most evenly distributed. But let's focus on a specific case, the extraordinary pay packages of today's top executives. Are these good for the economy?

Until recently it was almost unchallenged conventional wisdom that, whatever else you might say, the new imperial C.E.O.'s had delivered results that dwarfed the expense of their compensation. But now that the stock bubble has burst, it has become increasingly clear that there was a price to those big pay packages, after all. In fact, the price paid by shareholders and society at large may have been many times larger than the amount actually paid to the executives.

It's easy to get boggled by the details of corporate scandal—insider loans, stock options, special-purpose entities, mark-to-market, round-tripping. But there's a simple reason that the details are so complicated. All of these schemes were designed to benefit corporate insiders—to inflate the pay of the C.E.O. and his inner circle. That is, they were all about the "chaos of competitive avarice" that, according to John Kenneth Galbraith, had been ruled out in the corporation of the 1960's. But while all restraint has vanished within the American corporation, the outside world—including stockholders—is still prudish, and open looting by executives is still not acceptable. So the looting has to be camouflaged, taking place through complicated schemes that can be rationalized to outsiders as clever corporate strategies.

Economists who study crime tell us that crime is inefficient—that is, the costs of crime to the economy are much larger than the amount stolen. Crime, and the fear of crime, divert resources away from productive uses: criminals spend their time stealing rather than producing, and potential victims spend time and money trying to protect their property. Also, the things people do to avoid becoming victims—like avoiding dangerous districts—have a cost even if they succeed in averting an actual crime.

The same holds true of corporate malfeasance, whether or not it actually involves breaking the law. Executives who devote their time to creating innovative ways to divert shareholder money into their own pockets probably aren't running the real business very well (think Enron, WorldCom, Tyco, Global Crossing, Adelphia...). Investments chosen because they create the illusion of profitability while insiders cash in their stock options are a waste of scarce resources. And if the supply of funds from lenders and shareholders dries up because of a lack of trust, the economy as a whole suffers. Just ask Indonesia.

The argument for a system in which some people get very rich has always been that the lure of wealth provides powerful incentives. But the question is, incentives to do what? As we learn more about what has actually been going on in corporate America, it's becoming less and less clear whether those incentives have actually made executives work on behalf of the rest of us.

V. Inequality and Politics

In September the Senate debated a proposed measure that would impose a one-time capital gains tax on Americans who renounce their citizenship in order to avoid paying U.S. taxes. Senator Phil Gramm was not pleased, declaring that the proposal was "right out of Nazi Germany." Pretty strong language, but no stronger than the metaphor Daniel Mitchell of the Heritage Foundation used, in an op-ed article in The Washington Times, to describe a bill designed to prevent corporations from rechartering abroad for tax purposes: Mitchell described this legislation as the "Dred Scott tax bill," referring to the infamous 1857 Supreme Court ruling that required free states to return escaped slaves.

Twenty years ago, would a prominent senator have likened those who want wealthy people to pay taxes to Nazis? Would a member of a think tank with close ties to the administration have drawn a parallel between corporate taxation and slavery? I don't think so. The remarks by Gramm and Mitchell, while stronger than usual, were indicators of two huge changes in American politics. One is the growing polarization of our politics—our politicians are less and less inclined to offer even the appearance of moderation. The other is the growing tendency of policy and policy makers to cater to the interests of the wealthy. And I mean the wealthy, not the merely well-off: only someone with a net worth of at least several million dollars is likely to find it worthwhile to become a tax exile.

You don't need a political scientist to tell you that modern American politics is bitterly polarized. But wasn't it always thus? No, it wasn't. From World War II until the 1970's—the same era during which income inequality was historically low—political partisanship was much more muted than it is today. That's not just a subjective assessment. My Princeton political science colleagues Nolan McCarty and Howard Rosenthal, together with Keith Poole at the University of Houston, have done a statistical analysis showing that the

voting behavior of a congressman is much better predicted by his party affiliation today than it was twenty-five years ago. In fact, the division between the parties is sharper now than it has been since the 1920's.

What are the parties divided about? The answer is simple: economics. McCarty, Rosenthal and Poole write that "voting in Congress is highly ideological—one-dimensional left/right, liberal versus conservative." It may sound simplistic to describe Democrats as the party that wants to tax the rich and help the poor, and Republicans as the party that wants to keep taxes and social spending as low as possible. And during the era of middle-class America that would indeed have been simplistic: politics wasn't defined by economic issues. But that was a different country; as McCarty, Rosenthal and Poole put it, "If income and wealth are distributed in a fairly equitable way, little is to be gained for politicians to organize politics around nonexistent conflicts." Now the conflicts are real, and our politics is organized around them. In other words, the growing inequality of our incomes probably lies behind the growing divisiveness of our politics.

But the politics of rich and poor hasn't played out the way you might think. Since the incomes of America's wealthy have soared while ordinary families have seen at best small gains, you might have expected politicians to seek votes by proposing to soak the rich. In fact, however, the polarization of politics has occurred because the Republicans have moved to the right, not because the Democrats have moved to the left. And actual economic policy has moved steadily in favor of the wealthy. The major tax cuts of the past twenty-five years, the Reagan cuts in the 1980's and the recent Bush cuts, were both heavily tilted toward the very well off. (Despite obfuscations, it remains true that more than half the Bush tax cut will eventually go to the top 1 percent of families.) The major tax increase over that period, the increase in payroll taxes in the 1980's, fell most heavily on working-class families.

The most remarkable example of how politics has shifted in favor of the wealthy—an example that helps us understand why economic policy has reinforced, not countered, the movement toward greater inequality—is the drive to repeal the estate tax. The estate tax is, overwhelmingly, a tax on the wealthy. In 1999, only the top 2 percent of estates paid any tax at all, and half the estate tax was paid by only 3,300 estates, 0.16 percent of the total, with a minimum value of $5 million and an average value of $17 million. A quarter of the tax was paid by just 467 estates worth more than $20 million. Tales of family farms and businesses broken up to pay the estate tax are basically rural legends; hardly any real examples have been found, despite diligent searching.

You might have thought that a tax that falls on so few people yet yields a significant amount of revenue would be politically popular; you certainly wouldn't expect widespread opposition. Moreover, there has long been an argument that the estate tax promotes democratic values, precisely because it limits the ability of the wealthy to form dynasties. So why has there been a powerful political drive to repeal the estate tax, and why was such a repeal a centerpiece of the Bush tax cut?

There is an economic argument for repealing the estate tax, but it's hard to believe that many people take it seriously. More significant for members of Congress, surely, is the question of who would benefit from repeal: while those who will actually benefit from estate tax repeal are few in number, they have a lot of money and control even more (corporate C.E.O.'s can now count on leaving taxable estates behind). That is, they are the sort of people who command the attention of politicians in search of campaign funds.

But it's not just about campaign contributions: much of the general public has been convinced that the estate tax is a bad thing. If you try talking about the tax to a group of moderately prosperous retirees, you get some interesting reactions. They refer to it as the "death tax"; many of them believe that their estates will face punitive taxation, even though most of them will pay little or nothing; they are convinced that small businesses and family farms bear the brunt of the tax.

These misconceptions don't arise by accident. They have, instead, been deliberately promoted. For example, a Heritage Foundation document titled "Time to Repeal Federal Death Taxes: The Nightmare of the American Dream" emphasizes stories that rarely, if ever, happen in real life: "Small-business owners, particularly minority owners, suffer anxious moments wondering whether the businesses they hope to hand down to their children will be destroyed by the death tax bill,… Women whose children are grown struggle to find ways to re-enter the work force without upsetting the family's estate tax avoidance plan." And who finances the Heritage Foundation? Why, foundations created by wealthy families, of course.

The point is that it is no accident that strongly conservative views, views that militate against taxes on the rich, have spread even as the rich get richer compared with the rest of us: in addition to directly buying influence, money can be used to shape public perceptions. The liberal group People for the American Way's report on how conservative foundations have deployed vast sums to support think tanks, friendly media and other institutions that promote right-wing causes is titled "Buying a Movement."

Not to put too fine a point on it: as the rich get richer, they can buy a lot of things besides goods and services. Money buys political influence; used cleverly, it also buys intellectual influence. A result is that growing income disparities in the United States, far from leading to demands to soak the rich, have been accompanied by a growing movement to let them keep more of their earnings and to pass their wealth on to their children.

This obviously raises the possibility of a self-reinforcing process. As the gap between the rich and the rest of the population grows, economic policy increasingly caters to the interests of the elite, while public services for the population at large—above all, public education—are starved of resources. As policy increasingly favors the interests of the rich and neglects the interests of the general population, income disparities grow even wider.

VI. Plutocracy?

In 1924, the mansions of Long Island's North Shore were still in their full glory, as was the political power of the class that owned them. When Gov. Al Smith of New York proposed building a system of parks on Long Island, the mansion owners were bitterly opposed. One baron—Horace Havemeyer, the "sultan of sugar"—warned that North Shore towns would be "overrun with rabble from the city." "Rabble?" Smith said. "That's me you're talking about." In the end New Yorkers got their parks, but it was close: the interests of a few hundred wealthy families nearly prevailed over those of New York City's middle class.

America in the 1920's wasn't a feudal society. But it was a nation in which vast privilege—often inherited privilege—stood in contrast to vast misery. It was also a nation in which the government, more often than not, served the interests of the privileged and ignored the aspirations of ordinary people.

Those days are past—or are they? Income inequality in America has now returned to the levels of the 1920's. Inherited wealth doesn't yet play a big part in our society, but given time—and the repeal of the estate tax—we will grow ourselves a hereditary elite just as set apart from the concerns of ordinary Americans as old Horace Havemeyer. And the new elite, like the old, will have enormous political power.

Kevin Phillips concludes his book "Wealth and Democracy" with a grim warning: "Either democracy must be renewed, with politics brought back to life, or wealth is likely to cement a new and less democratic regime—plutocracy by some other name." It's a pretty extreme line, but we live in extreme times. Even if the forms of democracy remain, they may become meaningless. It's all too easy to see how we may become a country in which the big rewards are reserved for people with the right connections; in which ordinary people see little hope of advancement; in which political involvement seems pointless, because in the end the interests of the elite always get served.

Am I being too pessimistic? Even my liberal friends tell me not to worry, that our system has great resilience, that the center will hold. I hope they're right, but they may be looking in the rearview mirror. Our optimism about America, our belief that in the end our nation always finds its way, comes from the past—a past in which we were a middle-class society. But that was another country.

Paul Krugman is a Times columnist and a professor at Princeton.

THE REAL FACE OF Homelessness

More than ever, it is mothers with kids who are ending up on the streets. Bush has a plan, but will it help?

By JOEL STEIN

THE LIBERALS TRIED. THEY gave money. They watched boring news specials. They held hands all the way across America. They even pretended to laugh at sketches with Robin Williams, Billy Crystal and Whoopi Goldberg. But at some point in every one-way relationship, pity turns to resentment, and now even the liberals are turning on the homeless: San Francisco has voted to reduce their benefits 85%; Santa Monica, Calif., passed laws preventing them from sleeping in the doors of shops or receiving food from unlicensed providers; Madison, Wis., is handing them a record number of tickets; Seattle banned the sale of malt liquor and Thunderbird in Pioneer Square as its initiative to shoo away the alcoholics.

THE YOUNG MOM

LOCATION Falls Church, Va.

NAMES Jessica Lampman, 22; Destinee, 2

HOW THEY BECAME HOMELESS

After dropping out of ninth grade, Jessica fled her mom's home because her brother was using drugs. Looking for stability for her daughter, she pitched a tent at a campground. She got into a shelter and found a job, but a low salary and bad credit kept her from getting an apartment

Sensing an opening, the Bush Administration has decided to make the homeless problem a target of compassionate conservatism, which got pushed back after Sept. 11, when conservatism was everywhere but compassion was available only for the attack victims. And it's putting its central domestic doctrine to the test on an issue on which the Democrats have been unable to show much progress. It's a good choice, not only because the expectations are so low after decades of failure but also because it is unassailable in its immediate need.

With a freak-show economy in which unemployment has reached 60%—a 50% increase since November 2000—but housing prices have stayed at or near historic highs, the number of homeless appears to be at its highest in at least a decade in a wide range of places across the U.S., according to Bush's own

homelessness czar. "It's embarrassing to say that they're up," says czar Philip Mangano of the number, "but it's better to face the truth than to try to obfuscate."

THE PRICED-OUT

LOCATION Harlem, N.Y.

NAMES Kim Berrios, 26; Julius Cabrera, 22; Jonathan, 8; Sunsarei, 5; Jerimiah, 2

HOW THEY BECAME HOMELESS

Kim and Julius had to leave their Staten Island apartment when the landlord renovated and raised the rent. Kim's family is in Florida, and Julius' mother has five other kids in a three-bedroom apartment. "We couldn't go stay with anybody," says Kim, who is pregnant. After moving to a Harlem shelter, she quit work to take care of Jonathan, who has attention-deficit disorder; Julius had to quit a nighttime supermarket job owing to the shelter's curfew. They are waiting for an apartment in the projects

You don't see homeless people as much as you did in the '80s because the one great policy initiative of the past 20 years has been to move them from grates into the newest form of the poorhouse, the shelter. Even though cities are building shelters as fast as they can, the homeless are pouring out of them again, returning to the grates. Homeless numbers are notoriously unreliable (many people may be counted twice or not at all, and some homeless advocates include people who move in with family members), but a TIME survey of the eight jurisdictions that have good statistics shows that this population has grown significantly and that its fastest-growing segment is composed of families. Homeless parents and their kids made up roughly 15% of the case load in 1999—or, if you count every head, about 35% of all homeless people, according to the Urban Institute, a liberal D.C. think tank. The TIME survey suggests that population has since increased—registering year-over-year jumps in either 2001 or 2002 (*see graphic for individual cities*). These families mainly consist of single women with kids, whose greater housing needs, compared with those of single people, make them more vulnerable to rental increases than are single people.

Even as the problem worsens, there's little appetite in Washington for the large-scale solutions the Democrats have been advocating for 40 years: creating affordable housing and strengthening programs that attack the causes of poverty by finding people jobs, teaching them skills, giving them transportation to jobs, getting them off drugs, providing medical care—essentially trying to fix entire lives. Some homeless experts are beginning to wonder whether building shelters only exaggerates the numbers: they argue that poor people who wouldn't otherwise be homeless are attracted to shelters as a way of quickly tapping into government assistance. "It didn't take long for people to figure out that this was a way to scam the system," admits Andrew Cuomo, the Secretary of Housing and Urban Development (HUD) under President Bill Clinton. Given all this failure and disgust, Republicans could deal with this problem however they wanted.

The first G.O.P. member to pick up on this was Susan Baker, who had the ability to get the White House's attention because she's the wife of James Baker, chief of staff to Ronald Reagan, Secretary of State to Bush's father and, more important, the guy who ran W.'s election-after-the-election campaign in Florida. Baker is co-chairwoman of the National Alliance to End Homelessness, a cause in which she became interested in the early '80s, when she got involved in organizing D.C. food banks.

Baker read a 1998 study by University of Pennsylvania professor of social work Dennis Culhane that suggested that the most efficient solution to homelessness was to provide permanent housing to the "chronic homeless"—those helpless cases, usually the mentally ill, substance abusers or very sick—who will probably be homeless for life. The study found the chronic homeless make temporary shelters their long-term home; they take up 50% of the beds each year, even though they make up 10% of the homeless population. Culhane's idea appeals to conservatives: it has had proved results in 20-year-old projects across the country; it gets the really hard-to-look-at people off the street; and it saves money, because administrative costs make it more expensive to put up people at a shelter than to give them their own apartment (sheltering a homeless person on a cot in a New York City shelter, for example, costs on average $1,800 a month). It's similar to the problem faced by hospitals, where the uninsured use ambulances and emergency rooms as a very expensive version of primary care. Culhane's finding is also attractive in its simple if unspoken logic: because the mentally ill were put out into the street after the public discovered the abuses in mental hospitals and J.F.K. passed the 1963 Community Health Center Act, which deinstitutionalized 430,000 people, the plan really amounts to building much nicer, voluntary mental hospitals.

Three weeks after Bush named Mel Martinez his HUD Secretary, Baker landed a meeting with him. She sold him Culhane's research, arguing that with just 200,000 apartments, the Administration could end chronic homelessness in 10 years. The meeting went so well that the plan became Bush's official stance on homelessness: the 2003 budget has four paragraphs promising to end chronic homelessness in a decade.

THE LARGE FAMILY

LOCATION Dallas

NAMES Gina Christian, 36; David, 34; Alex, 14; Martin, 11; Thalia, 6; Tatiana, 4

HOW THEY BECAME HOMELESS

David worked as a mechanic in Austin, Texas, for a company that fixed Hertz cars. When the business went under, Gina's income as a nursing-home temp wasn't enough to cover rent and food for six. They hocked their belongings, and Gina resorted to begging. David still wasn't able to find work, so they moved to Dallas' Interfaith House, a private shelter for needy families. "We went from doing fine to one day being homeless," says Gina

Bush reinstated last spring the office of homeless czar, a position that had been dormant for six years, tapping Mangano to be head of the Interagency Council on Homelessness. He is liked by members of both parties and fits Bush's theme of faith-based compassion. A former rock manager who represented members of Buffalo Springfield and Peter, Paul and Mary, Mangano says his life changed in 1972 when he saw Franco Zeffirelli's *Brother Sun, Sister Moon,* a movie about the life of St. Francis. For Mangano, who calls himself a homeless abolitionist, ending chronic homeless is a moral call. "Is there any manifestation of homelessness more tragic or more visible than chronic homelessness experienced by those who are suffering from mental illness, addiction or physical disability?" he asks.

Building permanent housing for the chronically ill is in fact a long-standing Democratic initiative. In 1990 New York Governor Mario Cuomo began building "supportive housing" projects with attached mental-health services; there are now more than 60,000 such units across the country, funded by a combination of government and private organizations. While the buildings are not licensed like mental hospitals, nurses, social workers and psychologists keep office hours. In midtown Manhattan's Prince George Hotel, which has a ballroom, a restored lobby and salon, former street dwellers bake cookies, use the computer lab and take Pilates and yoga classes. Director Nancy Porcaro says the surroundings give the homeless enough help and pride to better themselves. "People do rise to the occasion, despite what the mainstream may think. They want more," she says.

That's the compassionate part. Here's the conservatives side: Bush isn't spending any money on this. While HUD already spends 30% of its homeless dollars on permanent housing, all the administration has added so far for its new push is $35 million, scraped together from within the existing budgets of three departments. To give a sense of how much that means in Washington budgetary terms, $35 million is equal to the money set aside to help keep insects from crossing the border. Although last month HUD touted the $1.1 billion in the budget for homeless services as the largest amount of homeless assistance in history, it's about the same as the amount set aside before Newt Gingrich's Congress made major cuts. And the Administration, more quietly, also announced a 30% cut in operating funds for public housing last week.

Congressman Barney Frank, ranking Democrat on the House Financial Services Committee (which oversees government housing agencies), is not kind about the Bush Administration's intentions. "They are just lying when they say they have a housing program," he says. And of the additional $35 million pledged to end chronic homelessness, Frank says, "it's not only peanuts; it's taking the peanuts from one dish and putting them in another." In fact, in October the House Appropriations Committee approved a bill that, if it becomes law, will cut $938 million from the President's budget for rental vouchers, one of the government's main methods of paying to house the homeless.

THE WANDERER

LOCATION Los Angeles

NAMES Debra Rollins, 35; two daughters, 11 and 16

HOW THEY BECAME HOMELESS

Having lived in 19 places in the past 30 years, including a stint as a teen-age runaway, Rollins spent the past five years in a one-bedroom flat with her two daughters, two friends and one of their kids. She moved to a hotel after falling out with her roommates. "I didn't have family or any friends around, so I didn't have anybody to help," she says. When her money ran out, she landed in a shelter. A high school dropout, Rollins is trying to obtain a GED and is working part time as a cashier so she can get a place of her own.

The old-school Democrats are also upset at the philosophy behind Bush's plan, which they argue is more interested in getting the homeless out of view than in solving their problems. "The largest-growing sector is actually women and children," says Donald Whitehead, the executive director of the National Coalition for the Homeless, the oldest and largest advocacy group on this issue. "A true strategy needs to include the entire population."

Andrew Cuomo, founder of HELP USA, a national, non-profit shelter provider, says the Administration is merely redefining the issue so as to appear to be doing something. "What makes you say that a guy who has been on the street for five years and is a heroin addict is any more needy than a woman who is being beaten nightly in front of her children?" he asks. For his part, Senator John Kerry, a Democrat running for President, has proposed legislation that would add 1.5 million units of affordable housing to address the fact that America's population has grown 11% in the past decade while rental stock has shrunk. According to the National Low Income Housing Coalition, which lobbies for government housing, for the fourth year in a row there isn't a single jurisdiction in the U.S., with the exception of places in Puerto Rico, where a person working full time for minimum wage can afford to rent a one-bedroom home at fair-market value.

Without a federal plan that has worked, cities have lost patience, concentrating on getting the homeless out of sight. In New York City, where shelter space can't be created fast enough, Mayor Mike Bloomberg has proposed using old cruise ships for housing. New Orleans removed park benches in Jackson Square to discourage the homeless; Philadelphia launched an ad campaign asking people not to give to panhandlers; and in Orlando, Fla., a new law makes it a jailable offense to lie down on the sidewalk.

THE LAID-OFF WORKER

LOCATION Dallas

NAME Gary Jones, 36

HOW HE BECAME HOMELESS

Jones was pulling in $12 an hour as a welder who often dangled from skyscrapers. Then he got laid off and started drinking heavily and doing drugs. "My self-esteem kind of left me," he says. "I've thought about trying to get back out there and find work, get myself off these here mean streets, but you have to be in the right frame of mind to do that."

Polls in San Francisco, where the streets are clogged with the homeless who lose the nightly lottery for limited shelter beds, indicate that homelessness is a major concern. Billboards show resident holding cardboard signs that read, I DON'T WANT TO HOLD MY BREATH PAST EVERY ALLEY. Voters last November overwhelmingly passed Proposition N, which cuts handouts from $395 a month to $59, providing food and shelter instead. The proposition was proposed by Gavin Newsom, 35, a member of the city's Board of Supervisors who describes himself as a liberal. Newsom's proposal was supported by a $1 million campaign and was so controversial that Newsom felt compelled to travel with police protection as Election Day approached. To his critics who contend that Proposition N doesn't do much to help the people whose assistance he's taking away, Newsom says, "We never said N is going to solve homelessness." Two weeks after the proposal became law, Newsom announced a mayoral bid.

Even in Miami, where homelessness has been reduced because of a 1997 court settlement that forced the city to decriminalize it and develop an elaborate system for dealing with it, citizens are demanding that the streets be cleared. New laws prevent sleeping on the beach and building shelters too close to one another. "They want to hide us with all kind of zoning tricks and such," says Steve Silva, 50, who makes $7 and a 5% commission selling Miami Heat tickets and lives in a shelter. "But it's a Band-Aid on a sucking chest wound, man."

Likewise in Dallas, where the problem continues to worsen, the homeless complain of cops delivering wake-up calls from their car loudspeakers by blaring "Wake up, crackheads!" and handing out vagrancy tickets. "It doesn't make you want to go and rejoin society," says Gary Jones, 36, a laid-off welder. "What's lower than writing a man a ticket for sleeping on the street? If he had somewhere else to go, don't you think he'd be there?"

Neither cracking down on vagrancy nor Bush's plan to end chronic homelessness is going to help the growing number of families without housing. David and Gina Christian and their four children have avoided the streets by staying in a 600-sq.-ft. apartment

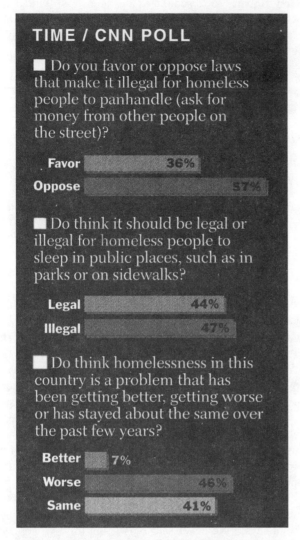

TIME / CNN POLL

■ Do you favor or oppose laws that make it illegal for homeless people to panhandle (ask for money from other people on the street)?

Favor	36%
Oppose	57%

■ Do think it should be legal or illegal for homeless people to sleep in public places, such as in parks or on sidewalks?

Legal	44%
Illegal	47%

■ Do think homelessness in this country is a problem that has been getting better, getting worse or has stayed about the same over the past few years?

Better	7%
Worse	46%
Same	41%

From a telephone poll of 1,006 adult Americans taken for TIME/CNN on Nov. 13-14 by Harris Interactive. Margin of error is ±3.1%. "Not sures" omitted

at the Interfaith House in Dallas, which provides three months' housing to 100 needy families each year. David, 34, lost his job fixing rental cars in Austin after Sept. 11 when the tourism industry fell apart. Gina, 36, wasn't making enough as a nursing-home temp to cover the family's expenses. The Christians hocked everything they owned—their TV, the kids' PlayStation, Dad's tools—to follow David's old boss to a new job in Dallas. When that business fell apart too, David sold the tires from their two cars to pay for their nightly meals of rice and beans. "I was reduced to begging. I felt degraded, like I was less than human," Gina says. "When I was a child growing up in Watts, there was a 10-month period where we were homeless. I didn't want that for my family." Interfaith has

found David an $8-an-hour job as a mechanic at a Texaco station, and now that the Christians are not paying rent, they are able to save a little money. But time at Interfaith is running out. The program already broke its own rule by letting the family back for a second stay.

Given that so many are without a home but have temporary shelter, the real policy debate is no longer about whether society is responsible for keeping people out of the cold—we have agreed it is—but whether it is obligated to give them somewhere permanent to live. By fighting to end chronic homelessness, the Bush Administration argues that we need to give houses to those who are incapable of providing for themselves. The others will have to weather the storm in a shelter, if it can be built fast enough.

RHODE ISLAND
Number of families, 700, topped singles for the first time, up 17% over '01

COLUMBUS, OHIO
Families jumped 11% in '02 to 340. The number has grown 20% in two years

ANCHORAGE
Families accounted for 1,700 people seeking shelter, up 17% from '00 to '01

PHILADELPHIA
After a decline in '01, the number of families rose 5% last year to 400

SPOKANE, WASH.
It sheltered 1,500 families in '01, up 35%, and numbers still grow

BOSTON
A city report in '01 found 1,692 family members, up 9%, as singles rose just 1%

KANSAS CITY, MO.
It counted 960 families in '01 in the area, up 18% from '00

NEW YORK CITY
Its system now harbors 9,000 families, up 40% in the past year

—Reported by Simon Crittle and Jyoti Thottam/New York, Laura A. Locke/San Francisco, Deborah Edler Brown and Margot Roosevelt/Los Angles, Tim Padgett/Miami, Melissa August/Washington, Adam Pitluk/Dallas, Greg Land/Atlanta and Matt Baron/Chicago

CORPORATE WELFARE

A TIME investigation uncovers how hundreds of companies get on the dole—and why it costs every working American the equivalent of two weeks' pay every year

By Donald L. Barlett and James B. Steele

How would you like to pay only a quarter of the real estate taxes you owe on your home? And buy everything for the next 10 years without spending a single penny in sales tax? Keep a chunk of your paycheck free of income taxes? Have the city in which you live lend you money at rates cheaper than any bank charges? Then have the same city install free water and sewer lines to your house, offer you a perpetual discount on utility bills—and top it all off by landscaping your front yard at no charge?

Fat chance. You can't get any of that, of course. But if you live almost anywhere in America, all around you are taxpayers getting deals like this. These taxpayers are called corporations, and their deals are usually trumpeted as "economic development" or "public-private partnerships." But a better name is corporate welfare. It's a game in which governments large and small subsidize corporations large and small, usually at the expense of another state or town and almost always at the expense of individual and other corporate taxpayers.

Two years after Congress reduced welfare for individuals and families, this other kind of welfare continues to expand, penetrating every corner of the American economy. It has turned politicians into bribery specialists, and smart business people into con artists. And most surprising of all, it has rarely created any new jobs.

While corporate welfare has attracted critics from both the left and the right, there is no uniform definition. By TIME's definition, it is this: any action by local, state or federal government that gives a corporation or an entire industry a benefit not offered to others. It can be an outright subsidy, a grant, real estate, a low-interest loan or a government service. It can also be a tax break—a credit, exemption, deferral or deduction, or a tax rate lower than the one others pay.

The rationale to curtail traditional welfare programs, such as Aid to Families with Dependent Children and food stamps, and to impose a lifetime limit on the amount of aid received, was compelling: the old system didn't work. It was unfair, destroyed incentive, perpetuated dependence and distorted the economy. An 18-month TIME investigation has found that the same indictment, almost to the word, applies to corporate welfare. In some ways, it represents pork-barrel legislation of the worst order. The difference, of course, is that instead of rewarding the poor, it rewards the powerful.

And it rewards them handsomely. The Federal Government alone shells out $125 billion a year in corporate welfare, this in the midst of one of the more robust economic periods in the nation's history. Indeed, thus far in the 1990s, corporate profits have totaled $4.5 trillion—a sum equal to the cumulative paychecks of 50 million working Americans who earned less than $25,000 a year, for those eight years.

> **During one of the most robust economic periods in our nation's history, the Federal Government has shelled out $125 billion in corporate welfare, equivalent to all the income tax paid by 60 million individuals and families.**

That makes the Federal Government America's biggest sugar daddy, dispensing a range of giveaways from tax abatements to price supports for sugar itself. Companies get government money to advertise their products; to help build new plants, offices and stores; and to train their workers. They sell their goods to foreign buyers that make the acquisitions with tax dollars supplied by the U.S. government; engage in foreign transactions that are insured by the government; and are excused from paying a portion of their income tax if they sell products overseas. They pocket lucrative government contracts to carry out ordinary business operations, and government grants to conduct research that will improve their profit margins. They are extended partial tax immunity if they locate in certain geographical areas, and they may write off as business expenses some of the perks enjoyed by their top executives.

The justification for much of this welfare is that the U.S. government is creating jobs. Over the past six years, Congress appropriated $5 billion to run the Export-Import Bank of the United States, which subsidizes companies that sell goods abroad. James A. Harmon, president and chairman, puts it this way: "American workers… have higher-quality, better-paying jobs, thanks to Eximbank's financing." But the numbers at the bank's five biggest beneficiaries—AT&T, Bechtel, Boeing, General Electric and McDonnell Douglas (now a part of Boeing)—tell another story. At these companies, which have accounted for about 40% of all loans, grants and long-term guarantees in this decade, overall employment has fallen 38%, as more than a third of a million jobs have disappeared.

The picture is much the same at the state and local level, where a different kind of feeding frenzy is taking place. Politicians stumble over one another in the rush to arrange special deals for select corporations, fueling a growing economic war among the states. The result is that states keep throwing money at companies that in many cases are not serious about moving anyway. The companies are certainly not reluctant to take the money, though, which is available if they simply utter the word relocation. And why not? Corporate executives, after all, have a fiduciary duty to squeeze every dollar they can from every locality waving blandishments in their face.

State and local governments now give corporations money to move from one city to another—even from one building to another—and tax credits for hiring new employees. They supply funds to train workers or pay part of their wages while they are in training, and provide scientific and engineering assistance to solve workplace technical problems. They repave existing roads and build new ones. They lend money at bargain-basement interest rates to erect plants or buy equipment. They excuse corporations from paying sales and property taxes and relieve them from taxes on investment income.

There are no reasonably accurate estimates on the amount of money states shovel out. That's because few want you to know. Some say they maintain no records. Some say they don't know where the files are. Some say the information is not public. All that's certain is that the figure is in the many billions of dollars each year—and it is growing, when measured against the subsidy per job.

In 1989 Illinois gave $240 million in economic incentives to Sears, Roebuck & Co. to keep its corporate headquarters and 5,400 workers in the state by moving from Chicago to suburban Hoffman Estates. That amounted to a subsidy of $44,000 for each job.

In 1991 Indiana gave $451 million in economic incentives to United Airlines to build an aircraft-maintenance facility that would employ as many as 6,300 people. Subsidy: $72,000 for each job.

In 1993 Alabama gave $253 million in economic incentives to Mercedes-Benz to build an automobile-assembly plant near Tuscaloosa and employ 1,500 workers. Subsidy: $169,000 for each job.

And in 1997 Pennsylvania gave $307 million in economic incentives to Kvaerner ASA, a Norwegian global engineering and construction company, to open a shipyard at the former Philadelphia Naval Shipyard and employ 950 people. Subsidy: $323,000 for each job.

This kind of arithmetic seldom adds up. Let's say the Philadelphia job pays $50,000. And each new worker pays $6,700 in local and state taxes. That means it will take nearly a half-century of tax collections from each individual to earn back the money granted to create his or her job. And that assumes all 950 workers will be recruited from outside Philadelphia and will relocate in the city, rather than move from existing jobs within the city, where they are already paying taxes.

All this is in service of a system that may produce jobs in one city or state, thus fostering the illusion of an uptick in employment. But it does not create more jobs in the nation as a whole. Market forces do that, and that's why 10 million jobs have been created since 1990. But most of those jobs have been created by small- and medium-size companies, from high-tech start-ups to franchised cleaning services. FORTUNE 500 companies, on the other hand, have erased more jobs than they have created this past decade, and yet they are the biggest beneficiaries of corporate welfare.

To be sure, some economic incentives are handed out for a seemingly worthwhile public purpose. The tax breaks that companies receive to locate in inner cities come to mind. Without them, companies might not invest in those neighborhoods. However well intended, these subsidies rarely produce lasting results. They may provide short-term jobs but not long-term employment. And in the end, the costs outweigh any benefits.

And what are those costs? The equivalent of nearly two weekly paychecks from every working man and woman in America—extra money that would stay in their pockets if it didn't go to support some business venture or another.

If corporate welfare is an unproductive end game, why does it keep growing in a period of intensive government cost cutting? For starters, it has good p.r. and an army of bureaucrats working to expand it. A corporate-welfare bureaucracy of an estimated 11,000 organizations and agencies has grown up, with access to city halls, statehouses, the Capitol and the White House. They conduct seminars, conferences and training sessions. They have their own trade associations. They publish their own journals and newsletters. They create attractive websites on the Internet. And they never call it "welfare." They call it "economic incentives" or "empowerment zones" or "enterprise zones."

Whatever the name, the result is the same. Some companies receive public services at reduced rates, while all others pay the full cost. Some companies are excused from paying all or a portion of their taxes due, while all others must pay the full amount imposed by law. Some companies receive grants, low-interest loans and other subsidies, while all others must fend for themselves.

In the end, that's corporate welfare's greatest flaw. It's unfair. One role of government is to help ensure a level playing field for people and businesses. Corporate welfare does just the opposite. It tilts the playing field in favor of the largest or the most politically influential or most aggressive businesses….

Requiem for Welfare

Evelyn Z. Brodkin

THERE WERE few mourners at welfare's funeral. In fact, its demise was widely celebrated when congressional Republicans teamed up with a majority of their Democratic colleagues and then-president Bill Clinton to enact a new welfare law in 1996. The law ended the sixty-one-year old federal commitment to aid poor families and ushered in a commitment to lower welfare rolls and put recipients to work.

To many politicians and the public, anything seemed preferable to the widely discredited program known as Aid to Families with Dependent Children (AFDC). Conservatives were sure that the new welfare would pull up the poor by their bootstraps and redeem them through the virtues of work. Liberals set aside their misgivings, hoping that work would redeem the poor politically and open opportunities to advance economic equality.

More than six years later, the demise of the old welfare remains largely unlamented. But what to make of the changes that have occurred in the name of reform? Often, laws produce more smoke than fire, intimating big change, but producing little. Not this time. In ways both apparent and not fully appreciated, welfare reform has reconfigured both the policy and political landscape. Some of these changes can evoke nostalgia for the bad old days of welfare unreformed.

Reconsidering Welfare's Fate

An immediate consequence of the new law was to defuse welfare as a hot political issue. There's little attention to it these days—apart from some five million parents and children who rely on welfare to alleviate their poverty (and the policy analysts who pore over mountains of data to calculate how it "works"). Legislators have shown no appetite for restarting the welfare wars of prior years. And is it any wonder? The news about welfare has looked good—at least, superficially. Caseloads have plummeted since implementation of the new welfare, dropping 57 percent between 1997 and 2001. Some smaller states essentially cleared their caseloads, with Wyoming and Idaho proudly announcing reductions of 88.9 percent and 85.1 percent, respectively. Even states with large, urban populations have cut caseloads by one-half to three-quarters.

As an issue, welfare ranked among the top five items of interest to the public in 1995 and 1996. But in recent years, it has almost dropped off the Gallup charts. Other polls show that, among respondents who are aware of welfare reform, more than 60 percent think it's working well. Meanwhile, the nation has moved on to other concerns: terrorism, Iraq, the economy. Why reopen the welfare issue now?

In part, the 1996 law itself spurred reassessment. The law was designed to expire in 2002 unless reauthorized by Congress. With Congress unable to reach agreement before the 2002 election, welfare's reauthorization became one of the many measures to get a temporary extension and a handoff to the 108th Congress.

Beyond reauthorization, welfare merits a close look because battles over welfare policy have often been a bellwether of broader political developments. Welfare policy was near the forefront of sixties social activism, one of the banners under which the urban poor, minorities, and other disaffected groups successfully pressed for greater government intervention on behalf of social and economic equality. For the national Democratic Party, the politics of poverty fit an electoral strategy aimed at mobilizing urban and minority voters. Although the expansion of welfare proved to be temporary and limited, the politics of poverty produced federal initiatives that had broad and lasting impact, among them Medicaid, food stamps, earned income tax credits, and programs to aid schools in poor communities.

Attacks on welfare marked the beginning of a conservative mobilization against the welfare state in the late 1970s. Lurid accounts in George Gilder's *Wealth and Poverty* and Mickey Kaus's *The End of Equality* portrayed welfare and the poor as enemies of the democratic marketplace. President Ronald Reagan picked up these themes and contributed his own colorful anecdotes about welfare cheats and fraud, as he pushed forward cuts in taxes and social welfare programs. These forays into the politics of personal piety fit a Republican electoral strategy aimed at mobilizing the religious right and bringing the white working class into the party fold.

Out with the "Old" Welfare

Reforming welfare assumed new urgency in the 1990s, an urgency grounded less in policy realities than in electoral politics. Alarms were sounded about a crisis of cost, although for three decades, spending on AFDC amounted to less than 2 percent of the federal budget. The $16 billion the federal government allocated to AFDC was dwarfed by spending on Social Security and defense, each costing more than $300 billion per year. Public opinion polls, however, indicated a different perception. Forty percent of respondents believed that welfare was one of the most expensive national programs, even larger than Social Security or defense.

Polls also indicated that much of the public believed welfare recipients had it too easy, although few knew what welfare really provided. In fact, AFDC gave only meager support to poor families. In 1996, the median monthly benefit for a family of three was $366. Even when combined with food stamps, welfare lifted few poor families above the federal poverty line. Even the much-touted crisis of dependency ("dependent" being a term loosely applied to anyone receiving welfare) was not reflected in the evidence. The share of families receiving welfare for extended periods declined between 1970 and 1985 and leveled off after that. Families that received welfare for more than six years constituted only a small minority of the welfare caseload at any point in time.

Although the hue and cry over a supposed welfare crisis was greatly overblown, Bill Clinton clearly appreciated welfare's potent political symbolism. As a presidential candidate, he famously pledged to "end welfare as we know it," a turn of phrase useful in demonstrating that he was a "new Democrat" unburdened by the liberalism of his predecessors. His proposals for reform emphasized neoliberal themes of work and individual responsibility, but coupled demands for work with provision of social services intended to improve individual employment prospects. The Clinton administration's plans also assumed the enactment of universal health insurance that would help underwrite the well-being of the working poor. But that did not happen.

After the Republicans took over Congress in 1994, and Clinton began his fateful descent into personal irresponsibility, the initiative shifted decidedly toward the right. House Majority Leader Newt Gingrich seized the opportunity to turn Clinton's pledge against him, sending the president two welfare measures then thought to be so harsh that they almost begged for a veto. The measures ended the federal guarantee of income support, imposed strict work rules, and set time limits on the provision of benefits. Clinton vetoed them.

But on the eve of his renomination at the 1996 Democratic convention, Clinton signed a measure much like those he had vetoed. There followed a few highly public resignations among indignant staff and a rebuke from the Congressional Black Caucus. But Clinton's decision (advocated by strategist Dick Morris and running mate Al Gore, among others) effectively took the welfare issue away from the Republicans and highlighted Clinton's "new Democratic" appeal to critical swing suburban and blue-collar, crossover voters.

Clinton became the first elected Democratic President since Franklin Roosevelt to win a second term. But Clinton was no Roosevelt. In fact, he redeemed his pledge to "end welfare" by presiding over the destruction of a pillar of the New Deal welfare state.

Enter the "New" Welfare

The Personal Responsibility and Work Opportunity Reconciliation Act of 1996 replaced AFDC with a program aptly named Temporary Assistance to Needy Families (TANF). AFDC had provided an open-ended entitlement of federal funds to states based on the amount of benefits they distributed to poor families. TANF ended that entitlement, establishing a five-year block grant fixed at $16.5 billion annually (based on the amount allocated to AFDC in its last year) that states could draw down to subsidize welfare and related expenditures.

Mistrusting the states' willingness to be tough enough on work, Congress incorporated detailed and coercive provisions. First, it set time limits for assistance, restricting federal aid to a lifetime maximum of sixty months. If states wanted to exceed those limits, they would have to pay for most of it themselves. Second, parents were required to work or participate in socalled work activities after a maximum of two years of welfare receipt. Third, TANF established escalating work quotas. States that wanted to collect their full portion of federal dollars would have to show, by 2002, that 50 percent of adults heading single-parent households were working thirty hours per week. Fourth, it meticulously specified those work "activities" that would enable states to meet their quotas, among them paid work, job search, and unpaid workfare (in which recipients "worked off" their welfare benefits at minimum wage or provided child care for other welfare recipients). It limited the use of education and vocational training as countable activities.

Although the "work" side of TANF was clearly pre-eminent, there were some modest provisions on the "opportunity" side, with Congress providing $2.3 billion to help subsidize child care for working mothers and $3 billion in a block grant for welfare-to-work programs.

Beyond these prominent features, the new welfare also packed some hidden punches. It rewarded states for cutting welfare caseloads, largely without regard to how they did it. States that reduced their caseloads (whether those losing welfare found work or not) received credit against officially mandated quotas. If Congress was worried about states' slacking off from its tough work demands, the law indicated no concern that they might go too far in restricting access to benefits or pushing people off the welfare rolls. Only caseload reductions counted.

Under the banner of devolution, the law also gave states new authority to design their own welfare programs. While the welfare debate highlighted the professed virtues of innovation, less obvious was the license it gave states to craft policies even tougher and more restrictive than those allowed by federal law.

Pushing welfare decision making to the state and local level has never been good for the poor. In many states, poor families and their allies have little political influence. Moreover, constitutional balanced-budget requirements make states structurally unsuited to the task of protecting vulnerable residents against economic slumps. When unemployment goes up and state tax revenue goes down, the downward pressure on social spending intensifies.

The secret triumph of devolution lay, not in the opportunities for innovation, but in the opportunity for a quiet unraveling of the safety net.

The Unfolding Story of Welfare Transformed[1]

What has happened since 1996? For one thing, the new welfare changed a national program of income assistance to an array of state programs, each with its own assortment of benefits, services, restrictions, and requirements. There has always been wide variation in the amount of cash aid states provided, and federal waivers allowed states to deviate from some national rules. But devolution spurred far greater policy inconsistency by allowing states, essentially, to make their own rules. Consequently, what you get (or whether you get anything at all) depends on where you live.

In addition, devolution set off a state "race to the bottom," not by reducing benefit levels as some had predicted, but by imposing new restrictions that limited access to benefits. States across the nation have taken advantage of devolution to impose restrictions tougher than those required by federal law.

For example, although federal law required recipients to work within two years, most states require work within one year, some require immediate work, and others demand a month of job search before they even begin to process an application for assistance. No longer required to exempt mothers with children under three years old from work requirements, most states permit an exemption only for mothers with babies under one year old, and some have eliminated exemptions altogether. In nineteen states, lifetime limits for welfare receipt are set below the federal maximum of sixty months. Other states have imposed so-called family caps that preclude benefits for babies born to mothers already receiving welfare. If federal policymakers secretly hoped that states would do part of the dirty work of cutting welfare for them, they must be pleased with these results.

However, the picture from the states is anything but consistent or uniformly punitive. Many help those recipients accepting low-wage jobs by subsidizing the costs of transportation, child care, and medical insurance (although often only for one year). Twenty-two states try to keep low-wage workers afloat by using welfare benefits to supplement their incomes, "stopping the clock" on time limits for working parents. Significantly, the federal clock keeps ticking, and states adopting this strategy must use their own funds to support working families reaching the five-year lifetime limit. With state budgets increasingly squeezed by recession, it is hard to predict how strong the state commitment to preserve these supports will be.

Many state and local agencies have already cut back work preparation and placement programs funded under a $3 billion federal welfare-to-work block grant. Those funds spurred a short-term boom in contracting to private agencies. But the block grant expired leaving little evidence that states were able to build new systems for supporting work over the long term. In fact, no one knows exactly what all of this contracting produced, as state and local agencies kept limited records and conducted few careful evaluations. A close look at contracting in Illinois, for example, revealed the creation of a diffuse array of short-term programs operating under contract requirements that left many agencies unable to build anything of lasting value.

There is another strange twist to the convoluted welfare story: in their zest for services over support, states actually shifted government funds from the pockets of poor families to the pockets of private service providers. They distributed 76 percent of their AFDC funds in cash aid to the poor in 1996, but gave poor families only 41 percent of their TANF funds in 2000. Substantial portions of the TANF budget were consumed by child care costs, although it is difficult to say exactly how all the TANF funds were used. The General Accounting Office suggests that there is a fair amount of "supplantation" of services previously funded from other budget lines but now paid for by TANF.

Beyond the Caseload Count

The picture becomes still more complicated when one attempts to peer behind the head count in order to assess what actually happened in the purge of welfare caseloads. Exactly how did states push those caseloads down? What has happened to poor families that no longer have recourse to welfare? What kind of opportunities does the lower wage labor market really offer? Research has only begun to illuminate these crucial questions, but the evidence is disheartening.

Finding Good Jobs: There are three ways to lower welfare caseloads. One is by successfully moving recipients into good jobs with stable employment where they can earn enough to maintain their families above poverty (or, at least, above what they could get on welfare). Recipients may find jobs on their own, which many do, or with connections facilitated by welfare agencies and service providers.

Financial supports provided by TANF have allowed some recipients to take jobs where they earn too little to make ends meet on their own. Child-care and transportation subsidies make a difference for those workers. They also benefit from federally funded food stamps that stretch the grocery budget. But food stamp use fell off 40 percent after 1994, although fewer families were receiving welfare and more had joined the ranks of the working poor. Absent external pressures, most states made no effort to assure access to food stamps for those losing welfare. In fact, government studies indicate that administrative hassles and misinformation discouraged low-income families from obtaining benefits.

Taking Bad Jobs: A second way to lower welfare caseloads is to pressure recipients into taking bad jobs. Not all lower wage jobs are bad, but many of those most readily available to former recipients undermine their best efforts to make it as working parents. These jobs are characterized by unstable schedules, limited access to health insurance or pensions, no sick leave, and job insecurity. Because high turnover is a feature of these jobs, at any given moment, many are apt to be available. Indeed, employers seeking to fill these undesirable "high-velocity" jobs, where there is continuous churning of the workforce, are all too eager to use welfare agencies as a hiring hall.

This may partially explain why more than a fifth of those leaving welfare for work return within a year or two. Proponents of the new welfare conveniently blame individual work behavior or attitudes for job churning, but ignore the role of employers who structure jobs in ways that make job loss inevitable. What's a supermarket clerk to do when her manager makes frequent schedule changes, periodically shortens her hours, or asks her to work in a store across town? What happens is that carefully constructed child care arrangements break down, lost pay days break the family budget, and the hours it takes to commute on public transportation become unmanageable. The family-friendly workplace that more sought-after workers demand couldn't be farther from the hard reality of lower wage jobs.

One of the little appreciated virtues of the old welfare is that it served as a sort of unemployment insurance for these lower wage workers excluded from regular unemployment insurance by their irregular jobs. Welfare cushioned the layoffs, turnover, and contingencies that go with the territory. Under the new welfare, these workers face a hard landing because welfare is more difficult to get and offers little leeway to acquire either the time or skills that might yield a job with a future. Over the longer term, low-wage workers may find their access to welfare blocked by time limits. Although the five-year lifetime limit ostensibly targets sustained reliance on welfare, this limit could come back to bite those who cycle in and out of the lower wage labor force. At this point, no one knows how this will play out.

Creating Barriers to Access: A third way to reduce welfare caseloads is by reducing access—making benefits harder to acquire and keep. Some states explicitly try to divert applicants by imposing advance job-search requirements, demanding multiple trips to the welfare office in order to complete the application process, or informally advising applicants that it may not be worth the hassle. In some welfare offices, caseworkers routinely encourage applicants to forgo cash aid and apply only for Medicaid and food stamps.

Benefits are also harder to keep, as caseworkers require recipients to attend frequent meetings either to discuss seemingly endless demands for documentation or to press them on issues involving work. Everyday life in an urban welfare office is difficult to describe and, for many, even harder to believe. There are the hours of waiting in rows of plastic chairs, the repeated requests for paperwork, the ritualized weekly job club lectures about how to smile, shake hands, and show a good attitude to employers. As inspiration, caseworkers leading job club sessions often tell stories from their own lives of rising from poverty to become welfare workers (positions likely to be cut back as caseloads decline). When clients tell their own tales of cycling from bad jobs to worse and ask for help getting a good job, caseworkers are apt to admonish them for indulging in a "pity party."

Access to welfare may also be constrained through a profoundly mundane array of administrative barriers that simply make benefits harder to keep. A missed appointment, misplaced documents (often lost by the agency), delayed entry of personal data—these common and otherwise trivial mishaps can result in a loss of benefits for "non-cooperation."

The Public Benefits Hotline, a call-in center that provides both advice and intervention for Chicago residents, received some ten thousand calls in the four years after welfare reform, most of them involving hassles of this sort.[2] In other parts of the country, these types of problems show up in administrative hearing records and court cases, where judges have criticized welfare agencies for making "excessive" demands for verification documents, conducting "sham assessments" leading to inappropriate imposition of work requirements, and sanctioning clients for missing appointments when they should have helped them deal with child care or medical difficulties.

Is There a Bottom Line?

The new welfare has produced neither the immediate cataclysm its opponents threatened nor the economic and social redemption its proponents anticipated. Opponents had warned that welfare reform would plunge one million children into poverty. In the midst of an unprecedented economic boom, that didn't happen. But, even in the best of times, prospects were not auspicious for those leaving welfare.

According to the Urban Institute, about half of those leaving welfare for work between 1997 and 1999 obtained jobs where they earned a median hourly wage of only $7.15. If the jobs offered a steady forty hours of work a week (which lower wage jobs usually don't), that would provide a gross annual income of $14,872. That places a mother with two children a precarious $1,000 above the formal poverty line for the year 2000 and a two-parent family with two children nearly $3,000 *below* that line. But more than one-fifth of those leaving welfare for work didn't make it through the year—either because they lost their jobs, got sick, or just couldn't make ends meet. The only thing surprising about these figures is that the numbers weren't higher. Others left or lost welfare, but did not find work, with one in seven adults losing welfare reporting no alternative means of support. Their specific fate is unknown, but most big cities have been reporting worrisome increases in homelessness and hunger.

If there is any bottom line, it is that caseloads have been purged. But neither the market for lower wage workers nor the policies put into practice in the name of welfare reform have purged poverty from the lives of the poor. Even in the last years of the economic boom, between 1996 and 1998, the Urban Institute found that three hundred thousand more individuals in single-parent families slipped into extreme poverty. Although they qualified for food stamps that might have stretched their resources a bit further, many did not get them. Government figures indicate that families leaving welfare for work often lose access to other benefits, which states do not automatically continue irrespective of eligibility.

More recently, census figures have begun to show the effects of recession coupled with an eroded safety net. The nation's poverty rate rose to 11.7 percent in 2001, up from 11.3 percent the prior year. More troubling still, inequality is growing and poverty is deepening. In 2001, the "poverty gap," the gap between the official poverty line and the income of poor individuals, reached its highest level since measurements were first taken in 1979. In California, often a harbinger of larger social trends, a startling two in three poor children now live in families where at least one adult is employed. Can the families of lower wage workers live without access to welfare and other government supports? Apparently, they can live, but not very well.

Slouching Toward Reauthorization

"We have to remember that the goal of the reform program was not to get people out of poverty, but to achieve financial independence, to get off welfare." This statement by a senior Connecticut welfare official quoted in the *New York Times* is more candid than most. But it illustrates the kind of political rationale that policymakers use to inoculate themselves against factual evidence of the new welfare's failure to relieve poverty.

With TANF facing reauthorization in the fall of 2002, it was clear that reconsideration of welfare policy would take place on a new playing field. Tough work rules, time limits, and devolution were just the starting point. The Bush administration advanced a reauthorization plan that increased work requirements, cut opportunities for education and training, added new doses of moralism, and extended devolution.

The Republican-controlled House passed a TANF reauthorization bill (later deferred by the Senate) requiring recipients to work forty hours a week and demanding that states enforce these requirements for 70 percent of families receiving welfare by 2007. The bill also created incentives for states to require work within a month of granting welfare benefits and continued to credit states for caseload reductions, regardless of whether families losing welfare had jobs that could sustain them.

Families would face harsh new penalties, simply for running afoul of administrative rules. The House-passed measure required states to impose full family sanctions if caseworkers find a recipient in violation of those rules for sixty days. This makes entire families vulnerable to losing aid if a parent misses a couple of appointments or gets tangled in demands to supply documents verifying eligibility, just the type of problem that crops up routinely in states with complicated rules and outdated record-keeping systems.

One of the least mentioned but most dangerous features of the House bill was a "superwaiver" that would allow the executive branch to release states from social welfare obligations contained in more than a dozen federal poverty programs, including not only TANF, but also food stamps and Medicaid. This stealth provision would allow the Bush administration to override existing legislation by fiat. The nominal justification for the superwaiver is that it would ease the path of state innovation and experimentation. It would also ease the path for state cuts in social programs beyond all previous experience.

A more visibly contentious feature of the House bill was a provision to spend $300 million dollars per year on programs to induce welfare recipients to marry. This provision is one of the favorites of the religious right, along with the administration's funding for faith-based social services. These moral redemption provisions may be more important for what they signify to the Republican Party's conservative base than for what they do, as many states have resisted these types of things in the past. However, on this point, it is irresistible to quote America's favorite president, the fictional President Josiah Bartlet of the television series *West Wing*, who quipped: "When did the government get into the yenta business?"

Of Poverty, Democracy, and Welfare

The demise of the old welfare marked more than an end to a policy that many believed had outlived its usefulness. It also marked the end of welfare *politics* as we knew it. In the tepid debate over reauthorization in the fall of 2002, the bitter conflicts of earlier years over government's role in addressing poverty were replaced by half-hearted tinkering. Even provisions with the potential to induce hand-to-hand combat—such as those on marriage or the superwaiver—elicited relatively low-intensity challenges.

Is this because the new welfare yielded the benefits that liberals had hoped for, removing a contentious issue from the table and conferring legitimation on the poor, not as recipients, but as workers? Did it satisfy conservatives by clearing caseloads and demanding work? That does not seem to be the case.

If the poor have benefited from a new legitimacy, it is hard to see the rewards. Congress has not rushed to offer extensive new work supports. In fact, the House bill contained $8 to $10 billion less for work supports than the Congressional Budget Office estimated would be needed. In 2002, Congress couldn't even agree to extend unemployment insurance for those outside the welfare system who were felled by recession, corporate collapses, and the high-tech slide. While conservatives celebrated the caseload count, they also savored the opportunity to raise the ante with more onerous work requirements and marriage inducements, and even made a bid to eliminate other social protections through the superwaiver.

In the aftermath of the November 2002 election, a conservative consolidation of power was in the air. In a televised interview with Jim Lehrer, Republican spokesman Grover Norquist dared Democrats to take on the welfare issue. "If the Democrats want to stand up against welfare reform, let them! Two years from now, they'll be in even worse shape in the Senate elections."

Some congressional Democrats did take tentative steps against the tide, suggesting provisions that would fund new welfare-to-work services, provide additional job subsidies, increase the child care allotment, provide alternatives to work for recipients categorized as having work "barriers," and restore benefits to legal immigrants who were cut from welfare in 1996. Maryland Representative Benjamin Cardin was chief sponsor of a bill suggesting that states should be held accountable, not only for caseload reduction, but for poverty reduction. This notion had little traction in the 107th Congress and is likely to have even less in the next. Without the foundation of a politics of poverty to build on, such laudable ideas seem strangely irrelevant, even to the Democrats' agenda.

If welfare is a bellwether of broader political developments, there's little mistaking which way the wind is blowing. It has a decidedly Dickensian chill. The politics of poverty that gave birth to the old welfare has been supplanted by the politics of personal piety that gave birth to the new. This reflects a convergence between a neoliberal agenda of market dominance and a neoconservative agenda of middle-class moralism. In this reconfigured politics, personal responsibility is code for enforcement of the market. The new Calvinism advanced by welfare policy treats inequality as a natural consequence of personal behavior and attitude in an impartial marketplace. It is consistent with a shift in the role of the state from defender of the vulnerable and buffer against the market to one of protector-in-chief of both market and morals. This shift does not favor a small state, but a different state, one capable of enforcing market demands on workers, responding to corporate demands for capital (through public subsidies, bailouts, and tax breaks), and, perhaps more symbolically, regulating morality.

Welfare policy neither created, nor could prevent, these developments. Nor is it a foregone conclusion that government will shirk its social responsibilities. After all, America's growing economic inequality is fundamentally at odds with its commitment to political equality.

In contrast to the United States, the policies of Western European countries suggest that there need not be an absolute conflict between the welfare state and the market. Despite their allegiance to the latter, other nations continue to offer greater social protection to their citizens and worry about the democratic consequences of excluding the disadvantaged from the economy and the polity. U.S. policymakers need to move past stale debates pitting work against welfare and the poor against the nonpoor, if they are to advance policies that promote both social inclusion and economic opportunity.

Welfare, though small in scope, is large in relevance because it is a place where economic, social, and political issues converge. The old welfare acknowledged, in principle, a political commitment to relieve poverty and lessen inequality, even if, in practice, that commitment was limited, benefits were ungenerous, and access uneven. The new welfare dramatically changed the terms of the relationship between disadvantaged citizens and their state. It devolved choices about social protection from the State to the states, and it placed the value of work over the values of family well-being and social equity. As bad as the old welfare may have been, there is reason to lament its demise after all.

Notes

1. The discussion in this section draws, in part, on research conducted for the Project on the Public Economy of Work at the University of Chicago, supported by the Ford Foundation, the National Science Foundation, and the Open Society Institute. The author and Susan Lambert are co-directors.

2. The Hotline is a collaborative effort of the Legal Assistance Foundation of Chicago and community antipoverty advocates.

EVELYN Z. BRODKIN is associate professor at the School of Social Service Administration and lecturer in the Law School of the University of Chicago. She writes widely on poverty and politics.

What's At Stake

In the competitive world of college admissions, 'fairness' is often in the eye of the beholder. Here are the facts about affirmative action.

BY BARBARA KANTROWITZ AND PAT WINGERT

IN 1978, THE SUPREME COURT opened the doors of America's elite campuses to a generation of minority students when it ruled that universities' admissions policies could take applicants' race into account. But the decision, by a narrowly divided court drawing a hairsplitting distinction between race as a "plus factor" (allowed) and numerical quotas (forbidden), did not end an often bitter and emotional debate. A quarter of a century after the ruling in *Regents of the University of California v. Bakke,* affirmative action is still being challenged by disappointed applicants to selective colleges and graduate schools, and still hotly defended by civil-rights groups. Now that two such cases, both involving the University of Michigan, have reached the Supreme Court, the issue can no longer be evaded: when, if ever, should schools give preferential treatment to minorities, based solely on their race?

4.3%
THE PERCENTAGE OF BLACK PLAYERS ON THE UNIVERSITY OF MICHIGAN FOOTBALL TEAM, 1941

45%
THE PERCENTAGE OF BLACK PLAYERS ON THE UNIVERSITY OF MICHIGAN FOOTBALL TEAM, 2002

7%
THE PERCENTAGE OF YALE UNIVERSITY STUDENTS WHOM ARE BLACK

It's a measure of how far we've come that the desirability of improving opportunities for black and Hispanic students is a given in the debate. But the fundamental question of where "fairness" lies hasn't changed, and the competition keeps growing. Each year, more students apply to the top universities, which by and large have not increased the sizes of their classes in the past 50 years. The court will have to decide who deserves first crack at those scarce resources. (Right now, about one sixth of blacks get college degrees, compared with 30 percent of whites and 40 percent of Asians.) And if the court allows affirmative action to continue in some form, it will only set the stage for future debate over even more perplexing questions. Do all minorities deserve an edge or just those from disadvantaged backgrounds? What about white students from poor families? And how do you balance the academic records of students from the suburbs and the inner cities? As the controversy heats up, here's a 10-step guide to sorting out the issues at stake:

1 What is affirmative action?

When President Kennedy first used the term in the early 1960s, "affirmative action" simply meant taking extra measures to ensure integration in federally funded jobs. Forty years later, a wide range of programs fall under this rubric, although all are meant to encourage enrollment of underrepresented minorities—generally blacks, Hispanics and Native Americans. Schools vary in how much weight they assign to the student's race. For some, it's a decisive consideration; for others, it's jut one among a number of factors such as test scores, grades, family background, talents and extracurricular activities. After the *Bakke* decision emphasized the importance of campus diversity as a "compelling" benefit to society, colleges quickly responded with efforts not just to attract minorities but to create a broader geographic and socioeconomic mix, along with a range of academic, athletic or artistic talent.

In 2003, the debate over the merits of affirmative action essentially boils down to questions of fairness for both black and white applicants. Critics say it results in "reverse discrimination" against white applicants who are passed over in favor of less well-qualified black students, some of whom suffer when they attend schools they're not prepared for. But Gary Orfield, director of Harvard University's Civil Rights Project, argues that emphasizing diversity has not meant admitting unqualified students. "I have been on the admissions committees of five different

Diversity Is Essential...
He knew he was in for a fight. But it's a battle the former University of Michigan president believes must be won.

BY LEE C. BOLLINGER

When I became president of the University of Michigan in 1997, affirmative action in higher education was under siege from the right. Buoyed by a successful lawsuit against the University of Texas Law School's admissions policy and by ballot initiatives such as California's Proposition 209, which outlawed race as a factor in college admissions, the opponents set their sights on affirmative-action programs at colleges across the country.

The rumor that Michigan would be the next target in this campaign turned out to be correct. I believed strongly that we had no choice but to mount the best legal defense ever for diversity in higher education and take special efforts to explain this complex issue, in simple and direct language, to the American public. There are many misperceptions about how race and ethnicity are considered in college admissions. Competitive colleges and universities are always looking for a mix of students with different experiences and backgrounds—academic, geographic, international, socioeconomic, athletic, public-service oriented and, yes, racial and ethnic.

It is true that in sorting the initial rush of applications, large universities will give "points" for various factors in the selection process in order to ensure fairness as various officers review applicants. Opponents of Michigan's undergraduate system complain that an applicant is assigned more points for being black, Hispanic or Native American than for having a perfect SAT score. This is true, but it trivializes the real issue: whether, in principle, race and ethnicity are appropriate considerations.

The simple fact about the Michigan undergraduate policy is that it gives overwhelming weight to traditional academic factors—some 110 out of a total of 150 points. After that, there are some 40 points left for other factors, of which 20 can be allocated for race or socioeconomic status.

Race has been a defining element of the American experience. The historic *Brown v. Board of Education* decision is almost 50 years old, yet metropolitan Detroit is more segregated now than it was in 1960. The majority of students who each year arrive on a campus like Michigan's graduated from virtually all-white or all-black high schools. The campus is their first experience living in an integrated environment.

This is vital. Diversity is not merely a desirable addition to a well-rounded education. It is as essential as the study of the Middle Ages, of international politics and of Shakespeare. For our students to better understand the diverse country and world they inhabit, they must be immersed in a campus culture that allows them to study with, argue with and become friends with students who may be different from them. It broadens the mind, and the intellect—essential goals of education.

Reasonable people can disagree about affirmative action. But it is important that we do not lose the sense of history, the compassion and the largeness of vision that defined the best of the civil-rights era, which has given rise to so much of what is good about America today.

BOLLINGER is president of Columbia University.

... But Not at This Cost
Admissions policies like Michigan's focus not on who, but what, you are—perpetuating a culture of victimhood

BY ARMSTRONG WILLIAMS

Back in 1977, when I was a senior in high school, I received scholarship offers to attend prestigious colleges. The schools wanted me in part because of my good academic record—but also because affirmative action mandates required them to encourage more black students to enroll. My father wouldn't let me take any of the enticements. His reasoning was straightforward: scholarship money should go to the economically deprived. And since he could pay for my schooling, he would. In the end, I chose a historically black college—South Carolina State.

What I think my father meant, but was perhaps too stern to say, was that one should always rely on hard work and personal achievement to carry the day—every day. Sadly, this rousing point seems lost on the admissions board at the University of Michigan, which wrongly and unapologetically discriminates on the basis of skin color. The university ranks applicants on a scale that awards points for SAT scores, highschool grades and race. For example, a perfect SAT score is worth 12 points. Being black gets you 20 points. Is there anyone who can look at those two numbers and think they are fair?

Supporters maintain that the quota system is essential to creating a diverse student body. And, indeed, there is some validity to this sort of thinking. A shared history of slavery and discrimination has ingrained racial hierarchies into our national identity, divisions that need to be erased. There is, however, a very real danger that we are merely reinforcing the idea that minorities are first and foremost victims. Because of this victim status, the logic goes, they are owed special treatment. But that isn't progress, it's inertia.

If the goal of affirmative action is to create a more equitable society, it should be need-based. Instead, affirmative action is defined by its tendency to reduce people to fixed categories: at many universities, it seems, admissions officers look less at who you are than *what* you are. As a result, affirmative-action programs rarely help the least among us. Instead, they often benefit the children of middle- and upper-class black Americans who have been conditioned to feel they are owed something.

This is alarming. We have finally, after far too long, reached a point where black Americans have pushed into the mainstream—and not just in entertainment and sports. From politics to corporate finance, blacks succeed. Yet many of us still feel entitled to special benefits—in school, in jobs, in government contracts.

It is time to stop. We must reach a point where we expect to rise or fall on our own merits. We just can't continue to base opportunities on race while the needs of the poor fall by the wayside. As a child growing up on a farm, I was taught that personal responsibility was the lever that moved the world. That is why it pains me to see my peers rest their heads upon the warm pillow of victim status.

WILLIAMS is a syndicated columnist.

universities," he says, "and I have never seen a student admitted just on the basis of race. [Committees] think about what the class will be like, what kind of educational experience the class will provide." Opponents also say that with the expansion of the black middle class in the past 20 years, these programs should be refocused on kids from low-income homes. "It just doesn't make sense to give preference to the children of a wealthy black businessman, but not to the child of a Vietnamese boat person or an Arab-American who is suffering discrimination," says Curt Levey, director of legal affairs at the Center for Individual Rights, which is representing the white applicants who were turned down by the University of Michigan.

Despite the public perception that affirmative action is rampant on campuses, these programs really only affect a very small number of minority students. It's a legal issue mainly on highly selective public campuses, such as Michigan, Berkeley or Texas. Even at these schools, the actual numbers of minority students are still small—which is why supporters of affirmative action say race should still matter. Blacks account for 11 percent of undergraduates nationally; at the most elite schools the percentage is often smaller. For example, fewer than 7 percent of Harvard's current freshman class is black, compared with 12.9 percent of the overall population.

2 How did the University of Michigan become the test case?

Both sides say it was really a matter of chance more than anything else. "It's not like we studied 1,000 schools and picked them out," says Levey. To have the makings of a test case, the suit had to involve a public university whose admissions information could be obtained under the Freedom of Information Act. It also had to be a very large school that relied on some kind of numerical admissions formula—unlike the more individualized approach generally used by private colleges with large admissions staffs.

In fact, Michigan is just one of a number of public universities that have faced legal challenges in recent years. In 1996, the U.S. Court of Appeals for the Fifth Circuit banned the use of race in admissions at the University of Texas Law School. The Supreme Court declined to hear the law school's appeal, but by that time, the university had changed its admissions procedures anyway. The University of Georgia dropped race as a factor after a similar suit. But when Michigan's admissions policy came under challenge in the mid-1990s, university officials decided to fight back—all the way to the Supreme Court.

3 How does the Michigan system work?

Although President George W. Bush reduced Michigan's complex admissions process to a single sound bite—comparing the relative values given to SAT scores and race—a student's academic record is actually the most important factor. For undergraduate applicants, decisions are made on a point system. Out of a total of 150 possible points, a student can get up to 110 for academics. That includes a possible 80 points for grades and 12 points for standardized test scores. Admissions counselors then add or subtract points for the rigor of the high school (up to 10) and the difficulty of the curriculum (up to 8 for students who take the toughest courses). Applicants can get up to 40 more points for such factors as residency in underrepresented states (2 points) or Michigan residency (10 points, with a 6-point bonus for living in an underrepresented county). Being from an underrepresented minority group or from a predominantly minority high school is worth 20 points. So is being from a low-income family—even for white students. The same 20 points are awarded to athletes. Students also earn points for being related to an alumnus (up to 4 points), writing a good personal essay (up to 3 points) and participating in extracurricular activities (up to 5 points). Admissions officials say the scale is only a guide; there's no target number that automatically determines whether a student is admitted or rejected. Michigan also has a "rolling" admissions policy, which means that students hear a few months after they apply. The number of spaces available depends on when in this cycle a student applies.

At the law school, there's no point system, but the admissions officers say higher grades and standardized test scores do increase an applicant's chances. Those factors are considered along with the rigor of an applicant's courses, recommendations and essays. The school also says that race "sometimes makes the difference in whether or not a student is admitted."

4 Does the Michigan system create quotas?

This is an issue the court will probably have to decide. Awarding points could amount to a quota if it resulted in routinely filling a fixed number of places. Levey claims that the fact that the number of minority students admitted is relatively stable from year to year proves there is a target Michigan tries to hit. Michigan's president, Mary Sue Coleman, is adamant that that's not the case. "We do not have, and never have had, quotas or numerical targets in either the undergraduate or Law School admissions programs," she said in a statement issued after Bush's speech last week. At the law school, the most recent entering class of 352 students included 21 African-Americans, 24 Latinos and 8 Native Americans. The year before, there were 26 African-Americans, 16 Latinos and 3 Native Americans. The university says that over the past nine years, the number of blacks in the entering class has ranged from 21 to 37. On the undergraduate level, the university says that blacks generally make up between 7 and 9 percent of the entering class.

In general, few outright quota systems exist anymore. "The only legal way to have quotas today is to address a proven constitutional violation," says Orfield. "For instance, if you can prove that a police or fire department intentionally did not hire any blacks for 25 years, and you can prove discrimination, a judge can rule that there can be a quota for the next five years."

Affirmative Action, 25 Years Later

Lawsuits are prompting the Supreme Court to revisit a landmark 1978 decision in favor of race-based college admissions. Affirmative action's legacy, and its uncertain future.

SAT Scores

SAT1: 2002 NAT'L AVERAGE	
White	1060
Black	857
Hispanic	910
Asian/Pac. Islander	1070
Native American	962
SAT1: 2002 UNIV. AVERAGE	
UC Berkeley	1180–1440*
Univ. of Florida (2001)	1229
Univ. of Michigan	1180–1390*
UT Austin	1222

The Case Against Michigan

Plaintiff Barbara Grutter claims she lost her spot at Michigan Law School to less qualified minorities; 100% of blacks with Grutter's ranking were accepted the year she applied, but only 9% of whites.

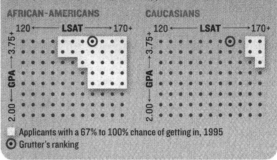

□ Applicants with a 67% to 100% chance of getting in, 1995
◉ Grutter's ranking

Univ. of Mich. Point System

The university uses a point scale to rate prospective students. Its policy of awarding minorities an extra 20 has stirred protest. Here's how a fictional applicant would score a promising 130:

GPA Score	Points
2.0	40
2.1	42
2.2	44
2.3	46
2.4	48
2.5	50
2.6	52
2.7	54
2.8	56
2.9	58
3.0	60
3.1	62
3.2	64
3.3	66
3.4	68
3.5	(70)
3.6	72
3.7	74
3.8	76
3.9	78
4.0	80

HIGH-SCHOOL QUALITY

Score	Points
0	0
1	2
2	4
3	(6)
4	8
5	10

DIFFICULTY OF CURRICULUM

Score	Points
-2	-4
-1	-2
0	0
1	2
2	(4)
3	6
4	8

TEST SCORES

ACT	SAT1	Points
1–19	400–920	0
20–21	930–1000	6
22–26	1010–1190	(10)
27–30	1200–1350	11
31–36	1360–1600	12

Points (maximum of 40)

GEOGRAPHY
- (10) Michigan resident
- 6 Underrepresented Michigan county
- 2 Underrepresented state

ALUMNI
- 4 Legacy (parents, stepparents)
- 1 Other (grandparents, siblings)

ESSAY
- 1 Very good
- (2) Excellent
- 3 Outstanding

PERSONAL ACHIEVEMENT
- 1 State
- (3) Regional
- 5 National

LEADERSHIP AND SERVICE
- 1 State
- 2 Regional
- (5) National

MISCELLANEOUS (choose one)
- 20 Socioeconomic disadvantage
- (20) Underrepresented racial/ ethnic minority identification or education
- 5 Men in nursing
- 20 Scholarship athlete
- 20 Provost's discretion

Race and Higher Education

The number of minorities attending four-year colleges has risen about 85% since the Supreme Court OK'd affirmative action in admissions.

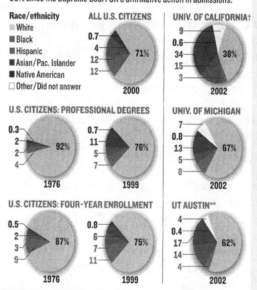

Race/ethnicity
- White
- Black
- Hispanic
- Asian/Pac. Islander
- Native American
- Other/Did not answer

ALL RACES ARE NON-HISPANIC EXCEPT "HISPANIC." NUMBERS DO NOT ADD TO 100 DUE TO ROUNDING. *25TH TO 75TH PERCENTILES. †FRESHMAN ADMITS ONLY. **UNDERGRADUATES. SOURCES: U.S. CENSUS BUREAU, UC BERKELEY, UNIV. OF MICHIGAN, UT AUSTIN, UNIV. OF FLORIDA, THE CENTER FOR INDIVIDUAL RIGHTS, THE COLLEGE BOARD. RESEARCH AND TEXT BY JOSH ULICK. GRAPHIC BY BONNIE SCRANTON.

New Options for Diversity?

Several states have enacted the alternatives to affirmative action that Bush favors. But do they reach an equal number of minorities?

• **CALIFORNIA**: Voters passed Proposition 209 in **1996.** It bans affirmative action in university admissions. The plan promises a state-university spot for the top **4%** of students from every high school, including the most disadvantaged ones. Other factors may be involved, but Berkeley's black undergraduate enrollment has dropped **33%** from **1996** to **2001.**

• **TEXAS:** A **1997** plan ended affirmative action in admissions. High-school students in the top **10%** of their class are guaranteed slots at state schools. Since then, black enrollment has remained relatively stable at UT Austin.

• **FLORIDA:** As of **2000,** state universities no longer consider race in admissions, but promise slots for students in the top **20%** of classes.

AFFIRMATIVE ACCESS

Making the Grade
Bush wants admissions policies to look like his home state's. But in Texas, his plan gets middling marks.

BY LEIF STRICKLAND

Natalie Fogiel, an 18-year-old high-school senior in Dallas, has SAT scores higher than the Ivy League's collective average—she scored 1490 out of 1600. She's a National Merit Scholar semifinalist, and she's active in Student Congress. Fogiel doesn't want to go to Harvard or Yale. She wants to go to the business school at her state university's flagship campus, the University of Texas at Austin. But under Texas's five-year-old "affirmative access" policy—which guarantees admission to any state university for all seniors graduating in the top 10 percent of their classes—Fogiel isn't sure she'll get in. Because she goes to Highland Park High School in Dallas—one of the most competitive public schools in the country—she's only in the top 15 percent.

As the Supreme Court prepares to review the constitutionality of affirmative-action programs, President Bush has been championing programs such as Texas's, which passed when he was governor. But at some of the state's best schools, the policy has been attacked with the same words—"unfair" and "divisive"—that Bush uses to describe affirmative action. "If I had gone anywhere else, I probably would be in the top 1 percent," Fogiel says. While Texas's program prohibits using race as a factor, Texas's many segregated high schools mean the result is much the same. Since the 10 percent plan was implemented, minority enrollment at UT Austin has returned to roughly the same levels as when affirmative action was in effect.

The problem with the 10 percent policy, some Highland Park students say, is that it assumes all high schools are alike. And Highland Park High—with its 97 percent white student population—is clearly unique. Even a student who scores all A's in regular classes for four straight years wouldn't be guaranteed a place in the top quarter of his class. (You'd need to add honors classes to the mix.)

But elsewhere, the policy is playing well. Israel Hernandez is in the top 10 percent of W. H. Adamson High School, which is overwhelmingly Hispanic. He's the first member of his family to go to college; he'll be attending Texas A&M in the fall. "It's like everyone has their hopes and dreams on me," he says. Texas A&M has been to Adamson (average SAT score: 838) more than a dozen times this year touting its Century Scholars program, which specifically targets promising inner-city students like Hernandez.

Texas's plan doesn't just help traditional minorities. "The 10 percent diversifies economically," says Harvard Law professor Lani Guinier. "It benefits rural west Texas, which is primarily white but also very poor."

The policy isn't causing Highland Park students too much hardship—98 percent of its graduates went to college last year. Most of those who applied to UT and didn't get into their preferred programs were admitted to the university nonetheless—either into another school or to a provisional program. For her part, Fogiel says she probably won't go to UT if she isn't accepted to Austin's business program. She'll opt for one of her safeties: Georgetown or Boston College.

With MARK MILLER in Dallas

On campuses, some education experts say that what appear to be quotas may actually just reflect a relatively steady number of minority applicants within a certain state. "I don't know of a public or private institution that uses quotas," says Alexander Astin, director of the Higher Education Research Institute at UCLA. "That's a red herring. There is always a consideration of merit given." Nonetheless, admissions officers at public and private universities admit that they are always very conscious of demography—and work hard to make sure that the number of minority students does not decline precipitously from one year to the next.

5 How can the court rule?

The short answer is: the Supreme Court can do whatever it wants. The options range from leaving the *Bakke* decision intact to barring any use of race in college admissions. Or the court could issue a narrowly tailored opinion, one that would affect only Michigan's point system and perhaps only the number of points the university assigns to race. "I think it's a good guess that they may say that they cannot give minorities a specific number of points, or say points are fine, but they can only award 10," says Levey.

The experts agree that the key vote will belong to Justice Sandra Day O'Connor. Some court watchers predict that she will try to find a very specific solution that will leave affirmative action largely intact. "She probably won't buy anything that's open-ended," says Sheldon Steinbach, general counsel of the American Council on Education, a consortium of the nation's leading research universities. "Maybe she will say that it can be done in some narrowly defined way." Steinbach doesn't think the court will order schools to disregard everything but the supposedly objective criteria of grades and test scores. Such a ruling "would tie the hands of admissions officers from shaping the kind of class they want to fulfill the academic mission of the institution," Steinbach says. Another possibility is that the court will order schools to give preference to students who are economically disadvantaged, which would cover many minority applicants.

6 Will the decision affect private universities and colleges?

The answer really depends on what the justices rule, but legal experts generally agree that private institutions would have to follow the court's guidelines because virtually all receive some federal funding. However, the ruling would have a noticeable impact only at elite institutions since most colleges in this country accept the vast majority of applicants. And the elite schools—no more than several dozen around the country—generally employ multistep admissions procedures that leave plenty of room for subjective judgments. Unlike the numerical formulas used by large public universities, these would be difficult to challenge in court.

Already, several landmark state cases have pushed private schools to make changes. In the wake of the Texas decision, officials at highly selective Rice University in Houston, on the advice of the state attorney general, banned the use of race in all admissions decisions. Clerks were told to strip any reference to a student's race or ethnicity from admissions and financial-aid applications before they were forwarded to the admission committee. Although the proportion of minorities dropped right after the change, it's now back up to the levels before the ruling, officials say—about 7 percent black and 10.5 percent Hispanic. That was accomplished through "significant" recruiting, a Rice spokesman said.

7 How would an anti-affirmative-action ruling affect other preferences for legacies and athletes?

Some educators think legacies (the children or grandchildren of alumni) could become unintended victims of an anti-affirmative-action ruling. On the face of it, providing preferential treatment to these applicants does not violate the Constitution, but as a matter of fairness—and politics—legacies would be hard to defend, since they are usually white and middle class. However, many colleges would probably resist the change because legacies bring a sense of tradition and continuity to the school. (They also are a powerful inducement to alumni donations.) Athletic preferences are a different story. They don't disproportionately favor whites so they're probably not as vulnerable.

8 Whom does affirmative action hurt and whom does it help?

Opponents of affirmative action claim it actually hurts some minority students, particularly those who end up struggling to compete in schools they're not prepared for. And, they say, it unfairly tars well-qualified minority students with the suspicion that they were admitted because of their race. Supporters say that's a spurious argument because race may sometimes be the deciding factor between qualified applicants, but it is never the only reason a student is admitted.

The more obvious potential victims, of course, are white students who have been denied admission—like the plaintiffs in the Michigan suit. But there's no guarantee that these students would have been admitted even if there were no black applicants. In their 1998 book "The Shape of the River," William Bowen and Derek Bok (former presidents of Princeton and Harvard, respectively) analyzed the records of 45,000 students at elite universities and found that without race-sensitive admissions, white applicants' chances of being admitted to selective universities would have increased only slightly, from 25 to 26.2 percent. But Bowen and Bok also found that black applicants' chances were greatly enhanced by affirmative action, and the vast majority of black students went on to graduate within six years—even at the most selective institutions. The black graduates were more likely to go to graduate or professional school than their white counterparts and more likely to be leaders of community, social service or professional organizations after college.

Supporters of affirmative action say both white and black students benefit from living in a diverse academic environment, one that closely resembles the increasingly diverse workplace. Opponents say schools don't need affirmative action to create a diverse campus; instead they say that other admissions strategies, such as "affirmative access," can accomplish the same goals.

9 What is "affirmative access"?

In the wake of lawsuits, several states have adopted alternative ways to bring minority students to campus. Modern political marketing seems to require a label for everything, and "affirmative access" has emerged as the label for these plans. Each operates differently. In California, the top 4 percent of students at each in-state high school is guaranteed admission to the University of California (although not necessarily to the most prestigious campuses, Berkeley and UCLA). For the University of Texas, it's the top 10 percent, and in Florida, the top 20 percent. The success of these new initiatives varies. California's plan was enacted after the passage of Proposition 209, which forbids using race in admissions. In 1997, the last year before the use of race was banned, 18.8 percent of the class consisted of underrepresented minorities. Last year that number was 19.1 percent systemwide. But some individual campuses, like Berkeley and UCLA, have not returned to pre-1997 levels. At the University of Texas, the percentage of black and Hispanic entering freshmen has remained fairly steady, but officials say the 10 percent law alone isn't enough. "You have to add some targeted procedures that work in tandem with the law," says University of Texas president Larry Faulkner. "And for us that's been pretty aggressive recruiting programs aimed at top 10 percent students in areas where minority students live, and carefully tailored scholarship programs aimed at students in areas or schools that have not historically attended UT."

Opponents of affirmative access like lawyer Martin Michaelson, who specializes in higher-education cases, say these programs rest on the dubious premise that "residential segregation patterns are a better method for choosing a college class than the judgment of educators" and create, in effect, a built-in constituency for continued segregation. Critics also worry that a program that mixes schools of widely different qualities may reward less-

What Merit Really Means

JONATHAN ALTER

ANYONE WITH HALF A BRAIN KNOWS THAT GRADES AND TEST scores aren't the only way to define "merit" in college admissions. Sometimes a good jump shot or batting average is "merit." Or a commitment to a soup kitchen. Or the ability to overcome an obstacle in life. Conscientious admissions officers take a wide variety of factors into account and make rounded, subtle judgments about the composition of the incoming class. The debate over affirmative action in education boils down to whether universities should be free to make that judgment or be told by the government how to choose.

The problem with affirmative action is not, as some conservatives suggest, that it has eroded standards and dumbed down elite institutions. The level of academic achievement among freshmen at, say, Yale is far higher than it was when George W. Bush entered in 1964. With his highschool record, he probably wouldn't be admitted today, even if he were black. No, what's wrong with affirmative action is that it has too often been routinized and mechanized, and has thus begun to resemble the very thinking it was supposed to replace.

Conservatives, trying to stand on principle, argue that affirmative action is simply reverse discrimination. In certain realms, like the awarding of federal contracts, that may be true. But college is different. The college experience is partly about preparing students for adult life, which increasingly means learning to deal with people of many different backgrounds. To hear the Bill Bennetts of the world, whites and Asian-Americans rejected by the colleges of their choice are like blacks rejected by the lunch counters of their choice in the Jim Crow South. It's a lame analogy. Lunch counters (and other public facilities) have no right to discriminate; neither do nonselective colleges, about 80 percent of the total. But exclusive institutions, by definition, must exclude.

The basis on which they do so should at least be consistent. You either favor weighing immutable nonacademic "preferences" or you don't. Some conservatives want to continue preferences for alumni children and end those for minorities. Some liberals want the reverse—to keep affirmative action but end legacies. Both sides ace their hypocrisy boards. Personally, I go for preferences, within limits, because I want the smart alumni kid from Pacific Palisades to sit in the dining hall and get to know the smart poor kid from Camden. Neither the University of Michigan policy nor the Bush administration challenge to it are likely to take us closer to that end.

The larger problem is that exclusive colleges too often use that worn-out crutch of a word—"diversity"—to cover for their lack of genuine integration (in dorms, for instance), and a lack of progress on socioeconomic affirmative action. Only 3 percent of students in top universities come from the poorest quarter of the American population. A Harvard study last year found that colleges are too often "recyclers of privilege" instead of "engines of upward mobility." Harvard itself falls short on this score, with fewer than 9 percent of its students coming from families eligible for Pell grants (i.e., the modest means). Princeton and Notre Dame are among those that don't do discernibly better.

Ironically, colleges like these with nice-sounding "needs-blind admission" policies consistently admit fewer poorer kids because, as a James Irvine Foundation report discovered, "they feel like they're off the hook." They're so proud of themselves for not calculating students' ability to pay in making admissions decisions that they do less than they could to recruit poorer students—and thus fail to take enough "affirmative action" (in its original, beating-the-bushes sense) to redress socioeconomic disparities. It's easier to go with familiar, relatively affluent high schools they know will produce kids more likely to succeed.

Recently, Berkeley, UCLA and USC have done twice or three times better than every other elite school in enrolling economically disadvantaged students. Why? Because California has abolished racial preferences, which forced these schools to adopt economic affirmative action. Richard Kahlenberg of The Century Foundation says that's the only way to get more poor kids admitted. A forthcoming study from that foundation will show that substituting economic preferences for race at the top 146 schools would lessen the black and Hispanic representation only two percentage points (from 12 percent currently to 10 percent).

But I still think it makes sense to allow both class and race to be considered—and to let 1,000 other factors bloom, as good colleges do. Just don't make it mechanical. The anti-affirmative-action forces have to abandon the notion that GPAs and SATs add up to some numerical right to admission; the advocates for the status quo have to give up the numerical awarding of points for things like race, because sometimes being African American or Hispanic or Native American should be a big plus, and sometimes it shouldn't. It depends on the kid. All of which means that no matter what happens in the Supreme Court, the University of Michigan and other large schools should spend the money needed for a more subtle and subjective quest for true merit.

---

qualified students than more-traditional programs. At the University of Texas, Faulkner says no; he believes that class rank is a better predictor of collegiate success than test scores, even at high schools with large numbers of disadvantaged students. But Orfield, who is in the final stages of completing a formal study of these programs, disagrees; he says that less-qualified students are being admitted under the percentage programs. Often, Orfield says, 60 percent of kids at suburban high schools have better credentials than the top 10 percent of kids at inner-city schools (sidebar). The affirmative-access approach would also be hard to apply in nonstate colleges and graduate schools that draw students from all over the country.

Another approach would be to target students from low-income homes, regardless of race. That would eliminate the problem of giving middle-class blacks an edge. But Orfield says that being middle class does not protect black students from the effects of racism, and they are still often at a disadvantage in the admissions process. "Race still matters," he says. "It's fine with me if we apply affirmative action to poor people, but I think we need it for middle-class blacks as well."

10 So what is the most equitable way to select the best-qualified applicants?

In judging admissions policies, it's important to remember that schools aren't just looking to reward past achievement. They want to attract students who will create the richest academic and social communities, and who have the best odds of success in college and later life. As a result, admissions officers say, what they really look for are signs of intellectual energy and personal enthusiasm—qualities that can show up in grades, scores, essays, recommendations, extracurricular activities, or a mix of all these. "Merit" has become particularly difficult to define in an era when elite colleges are getting many more well-qualified applicants than they can possibly accept, and when distrust of standardized admissions tests is growing. And making hard and fast distinctions based on race isn't going to get any easier as the growing trend toward racial mixing increases over the next century and people choose to identify with more than one group. The only thing educators who have struggled with these issues agree on is that there is no magic formula, not even for the Supreme Court.

With VANESSA JUAREZ
and ANA FIGUEROA

WHY WE HATE

We may not admit it, but we are plagued with xenophobic tendencies. Our hidden prejudices run so deep, we are quick to judge, fear and even hate the unknown.

By Margo Monteith, Ph.D. and Jeffrey Winters

BALBIR SINGH SODHI WAS SHOT TO DEATH ON September 15 in Mesa, Arizona. His killer claimed to be exacting revenge for the terrorist attacks of September 11. Upon his arrest, the murderer shouted, "I stand for America all the way." Though Sodhi wore a turban and could trace his ancestry to South Asia, he shared neither ethnicity nor religion with the suicide hijackers. Sodhi—who was killed at the gas station where he worked—died just for being different in a nation gripped with fear.

For Arab and Muslim Americans, the months after the terrorist attacks have been trying. They have been harassed at work and their property has been vandalized. An Arab San Francisco shop owner recalled with anger that his five-year-old daughter was taunted by name-callers. Classmates would yell "terrorist" as she walked by.

Public leaders from President George W. Bush on down have called for tolerance. But the Center for American-Islamic Relations in Washington, D.C., has tallied some 1,700 incidents of abuse against Muslims in the five months following September 11. Despite our better nature, it seems, fear of foreigners or other strange-seeming people comes out when we are under stress. That fear, known as xenophobia, seems almost hardwired into the human psyche.

Researchers are discovering the extent to which xenophobia can be easily—even arbitrarily—turned on. In just hours, we can be conditioned to fear or discriminate against those who differ from ourselves by characteristics as superficial as eye color. Even ideas we believe are just common sense can have deep xenophobic underpinnings. Research conducted this winter at Harvard reveals that even among people who claim to have no bias, the more strongly one supports the ethnic profiling of Arabs

at airport-security checkpoints, the more hidden prejudice one has against Muslims.

But other research shows that when it comes to whom we fear and how we react, we do have a choice. We can, it seems, choose not to give in to our xenophobic tendencies.

THE MELTING POT

America prides itself on being a melting pot of cultures, but how we react to newcomers is often at odds with that self-image. A few years ago, psychologist Markus Kemmelmeier, Ph.D., now at the University of Nevada at Reno, stuck stamped letters under the windshield wipers of parked cars in a suburb of Detroit. Half were addressed to a fictitious Christian organization, half to a made-up Muslim group. Of all the letters, half had little stickers of the American flag.

Would the addresses and stickers affect the rate at which the letters would be mailed? Kemmelmeier wondered. Without the flag stickers, both sets of letters were mailed at the same rate, about 75 percent of the time. With the stickers, however, the rates changed: Almost all the Christian letters were forwarded, but only half of the Muslim letters were mailed. "The flag is seen as a sacred object," Kemmelmeier says. "And it made people think about what it means to be a good American."

In short, the Muslims didn't make the cut.

Not mailing a letter seems like a small slight. Yet in the last century, there have been shocking examples of xenophobia in our own back yard. Perhaps the most famous in American history was the fear of the Japanese during World War II. This particular wave of hysteria lead to the rise of slurs and bigoted depictions in the media, and more alarmingly, the mass internment of 120,000 people of Japanese ancestry beginning in 1942. The internments have become a national embarrassment: Most of the Japanese held were American citizens, and there is little evidence that the imprisonments had any real strategic impact.

Today the targets of xenophobia—derived from the Greek word for *stranger*—aren't the Japanese. Instead, they are Muslim immigrants. Or Mexicans. Or Chinese. Or whichever group we have come to fear.

Just how arbitrary are these xenophobic feelings? Two famous public-school experiments show how easy it is to turn one "group" against another. In the late 1960s, California high school history teacher Ron Jones recruited students to participate in an exclusive new cultural program called "the Wave." Within weeks, these students were separating themselves from others and aggressively intimidating critics. Eventually, Jones confronted the students with the reality that they were unwitting participants in an experiment demonstrating the power of nationalist movements.

Sonam Wangmo:
"Am I fearful of Arab men in turbans? No, I am not. I was born and raised in India, and I am familiar with other races. I have learned to be attuned to different cultures. I find that there are always new, positive things to be learned from other people; it brings out the best in us."

A few years later, a teacher in Iowa discovered how quickly group distinctions are made. The teacher, Jane Elliott, divided her class into two groups—those with blue eyes and those with brown or green eyes. The brown-eyed group received privileges and treats, while the blue-eyed students were denied rewards and told they were inferior. Within hours, the once-harmonious classroom became two camps, full of mutual fear and resentment. Yet, what is especially shocking is that the students were only in the third grade.

SOCIAL IDENTITY

The drive to completely and quickly divide the world into "us" and "them" is so powerful that it must surely come from some deep-seated need. The exact identity of that need, however, has been subject to debate. In the 1970s, the late Henri Tajfel, Ph.D., of the University of Bristol in England, and John Turner, Ph.D., now of the Australian National University, devised a theory to explain the psy-chology behind a range of prejudices and biases, not just xenophobia. Their theory was based, in part, on the desire to think highly of oneself. One way to lift your self-esteem is to be part of a distinctive group, like a winning team; another is to play up the qualities of your own group and denigrate the attributes of others so that you feel your group is better.

Terry Kalish:
"I am planning a trip to Florida, and I'm nervous about flying with my kids; I'm scared. If an Arab man sat next to me, I would feel nervous. I would wonder, 'Does he have explosives?' But then I feel ashamed to think this way. These poor people must get so scrutinized. It's wrong."

Tajfel and Turner called their insight "social identity theory," which has proved valuable for understanding how prejudices develop. Given even the slenderest of criteria, we naturally split people into two groups—an "in-group" and an "out-group." The categories can be of geopolitical importance—nationality, religion, race, language—or they can be as seemingly inconsequential as handedness, hair color or even height.

Once the division is made, the inferences and projections begin to occur. For one, we tend to think more highly of people in the in-group than those in the out-group, a belief based only on group identity. Also, a person tends to feel that others in the in-group are similar to one's self in ways that—although stereotypical—may have little to do with the original criteria used to split the groups. Someone with glasses may believe that other people who wear glasses are more voracious readers—even more intelligent—than those who don't, in spite of the fact that all he really knows is that they don't see very well. On the other hand, people in the out-group are believed to be less distinct and less complex than are cohorts in the in-group.

Although Tajfel and Turner found that identity and categorization were the root cause of social bias, other researchers have tried to find evolutionary explanations for discrimination. After all, in the distant past, people who shared cultural similarities were found to be more genetically related than those who did not. Therefore, favoring the in-group was a way of helping perpetuate one's genes. Evolutionary explanations seem appealing, since they rely on the simplest biological urges to drive complicated behavior. But this fact also makes them hard to prove. Ironically, there is ample evidence backing up the "softer" science behind social identity theory.

HIDDEN BIAS

Not many of us will admit to having strong racist or xenophobic biases. Even in cases where bias becomes public debate—such as the profiling of Arab Muslims at airport-security screenings—proponents of prejudice claim that they are merely promoting common sense. That reluctance to admit to bias makes the issue tricky to study.

To get around this problem, psychologists Anthony Greenwald, Ph.D., of the University of Washington in Seattle, and Mahzarin Banaji, Ph.D., of Harvard, developed the Implicit Association Test. The IAT is a simple test that measures reaction time: The subject sees various words or images projected on a screen, then classifies the images into one of two groups by pressing buttons. The words and images need not be racial or ethnic in nature—one group of researchers tested attitudes toward presidential candidates. The string of images is interspersed with words having either pleasant or unpleasant connotations, then the participant must group the words and images in various ways—Democrats are placed with unpleasant words, for instance.

Rangr:

"For the months following 9/11, I had to endure my daily walk to work along New York City's Sixth Avenue. It seemed that half the people stared at me with accusation. It became unbearable. Yet others showed tremendous empathy. Friends, co-workers and neighbors, even people I had never met, stopped to say, 'I hope your turban has not caused you any trouble.' At heart, this is a great country."

The differences in reaction time are small but telling. Again and again, researchers found that subjects readily tie in-group images with pleasant words and out-group images with unpleasant words. One study compares such groups as whites and blacks, Jews and Christians, and young people and old people. And researchers found that if you identify yourself in one group, it's easier to pair images of that group with pleasant words—and easier to pair the opposite group with unpleasant imagery. This reveals the underlying biases and enables us to study how quickly they can form.

Really though, we need to know very little about a person to discriminate against him. One of the authors of this story, psychologist Margo Monteith, Ph.D., performed an IAT experiment comparing attitudes toward two sets of made-up names; one set was supposedly "American,"

the other from the fictitious country of Marisat. Even though the subjects knew nothing about Marisat, they showed a consistent bias against it.

While this type of research may seem out in left field, other work may have more "real-world" applications. The Southern Poverty Law Center runs a Web version of the IAT that measures biases based on race, age and gender. Its survey has, for instance, found that respondents are far more likely to associate European faces, rather than Asian faces, with so-called American images. The implication being that Asians are seen as less "American" than Caucasians.

Similarly, Harvard's Banaji has studied the attitudes of people who favor the racial profiling of Arab Muslims to deter terrorism, and her results run contrary to the belief that such profiling is not driven by xenophobic fears. "We show that those who endorse racial profiling also score high on both explicit and implicit measures of prejudice toward Arab Muslims," Banaji says. "Endorsement of profiling is an indicator of level of prejudice."

BEYOND XENOPHOBIA

If categorization and bias come so easily, are people doomed to xenophobia and racism? It's pretty clear that we are susceptible to prejudice and that there is an unconscious desire to divide the world into "us" and "them." Fortunately, however, new research also shows that prejudices are fluid and that when we become conscious of our biases we can take active—and successful—steps to combat them.

Researchers have long known that when observing racially mixed groups, people are more likely to confuse the identity of two black individuals or two white ones, rather than a white with a black. But Leda Cosmides, Ph.D., and John Tooby, Ph.D., of the Center for Evolutionary Psychology at the University of California at Santa Barbara, and anthropologist Robert Kurzban, Ph.D., of the University of California at Los Angeles, wanted to test whether this was innate or whether it was just an artifact of how society groups individuals by race.

To do this, Cosmides and her colleagues made a video of two racially integrated basketball teams locked in conversation, then they showed it to study participants. As reported in the *Proceedings of the National Academy of Sciences*, the researchers discovered that subjects were more likely to confuse two players on the same team, regardless of race, rather than two players of the same race on opposite teams.

Cosmides says that this points to one way of attacking racism and xenophobia: changing the way society imposes group labels. American society divides people by race and by ethnicity; that's how lines of prejudice form. But simple steps, such as integrating the basketball teams, can reset mental divisions, rendering race and ethnicity less important.

This finding supports earlier research by psychologists Samuel Gaertner, Ph.D., of the University of Delaware in Newark, and John Dovidio, Ph.D., of Colgate University in Hamilton, New York. Gaertner and Dovidio have studied how bias changes when members of racially mixed groups must cooperate to accomplish shared goals. In situations where team members had to work together, bias could be reduced by significant amounts.

Monteith has also found that people who are concerned about their prejudices have the power to correct them. In experiments, she told subjects that they had performed poorly on tests that measured belief in stereotypes. She discovered that the worse a subject felt about her performance, the better she scored on subsequent tests. The guilt behind learning about their own prejudices made the subjects try harder not to be biased.

This suggests that the guilt of mistaking individuals for their group stereotype—such as falsely believing an Arab is a terrorist—can lead to the breakdown of the belief in that stereotype. Unfortunately, such stereotypes are reinforced so often that they can become ingrained. It is difficult to escape conventional wisdom and treat all people as individuals, rather than members of a group. But that seems to be the best way to avoid the trap of dividing the world in two—and discriminating against one part of humanity.

READ MORE ABOUT IT:

Nobody Left to Hate: Teaching Compassion After Columbine, Elliot Aronson (W.H. Freeman and Company, 2000)
The Racist Mind: Portraits of American Neo-Nazis and Klansmen, Madonna Kolbenschlag (Penguin Books, 1996)

Margo Monteith, Ph.D., is an associate professor of psychology at the University of Kentucky. Jeffrey Winters is a New York-based science writer.

The Past and Prologue

FEMALE EXECUTIVES AND PROFESSIONALS

Address by JUDY OLIAN, *Dean of Penn State's Smeal College of Business Administration*
Delivered to the Penn State Professional Women's Network, New York city, New York, February 7, 2001

Thanks so much for this warm invitation to this terrific group of women. It's not a topic I talk much about. I usually contemplate the future of business, networked organizations, or the Smeal College, and I haven't taken much time to collect the information or to introspect about women's professional or executive careers. If I were to do that, I probably would have been tempted to reflect on female professional experiences by extrapolating from my own, and from my friends' and acquaintances' personal work histories. And, if I were to generalize from the power concentrated in this room, all is well among female professional America! There are many extraordinarily successful women here tonight whose expertise and professionalism have propelled them to the senior ranks of public and private organizations. Is that the whole story? I'm not sure.

This invitation prompted me to dig a little, so if you'll forgive me, I'll present a lot of numbers, I'll probably flood you with numbers and survey results as ingredients in shaping this story. Each of us will stir this pot of ingredients and see probably a slightly different picture or taste a slightly different dish, to use the metaphor. I'd be especially interested in hearing these differences in perception as we open the floor up for discussion. Let me start with a few factoids about the state of women in business in the year 2000.

In the year 2000:

46.5% of the workforce is female
29.5% of the managerial and professional specialty positions are held by women
12.5% of corporate officers are women among Fortune 500
11.7% of Fortune 500 members of the Board of Directors are women
That's 419 of the Fortune 500 who have female Board members, slightly down from the prior year
6.2% of the highest titled in the Fortune 500 are women

4.1% of the top earners are women, and I remind you that as a baseline, 46.5% of the workforce is female
2 of the Fortune 500 CEOs are women, 1 less than in the prior year

The only indicator that seems to go up consistently in the Fortune 500 is the number of companies with more than 3 female directors (it's now 45, up from 34 companies the prior year). I'll talk later about tokenism issues, and whether there's a minimum threshold, a small critical mass of people before one can break a dominant pattern. Interestingly, there seem to be more successes among the Fortune 500 than among the Fortune 501–1,000, perhaps because of the concerted public efforts and visibility of the Fortune 500.

If I compare the Fortune 500 to the Fortune 501–1000:

11.7% of the Fortune 500 versus 8.5% of the Fortune 501–1000 Board seats are held by women
16% of the Fortune 500 versus 38% of the Fortune 501 to 1000 companies have zero women on the Board, that is, the Fortune 500 are more than twice as likely to have female board members
84% of the Fortune 500 have at least one woman on the Board, compared to 62% among Fortune 501–1000. So, the numbers are far less attractive in the Fortune 501 to 1000.

Those are just the raw numbers on the "state of the world"—for professional women in the U.S. What accounts for this story in the year 2001—37 years after passage of Title VII of the Civil Rights Act of 1964 which assured equal opportunity for both men and women? My hypothesis, is that three areas account for the critical path differences between men and women:

Formative experiences
Career take-off experiences

Career experiences

1. Let's start with formative experiences. What happens pre-entry into business school careers is not equal between the genders:

Looking at pre-career experiences, boys choose computer sciences or computer engineering 5 times more frequently than girls, even though both agree on the importance of computer skills. That's from an Arthur Anderson survey of 650, 15–18 year olds, [C] 2000.

Boys are twice as likely to want to be CEO of tech company, versus girls aspiring to a career in health services, to be CEO of a clothing company, teacher, or small business owner (Anderson survey).

92% of girls report the need for female role models, but don't see enough of them (Anderson survey).

Today, overall, 48% of business students are women at the undergraduate level, and at the MBA level in top Business Schools that declines to 30% who are women.

From a Catalyst survey of 888 women and 796 males who are MBA alumni of top Business Schools (© 2000), the biggest reported reason for the relative scarcity of women in MBA programs is the absence of female role models. We saw that in the statistics presented earlier among business corporations, boards and CEO's. That is true also for Business Schools—22% of faculty across all B Schools are women, 7% of deans across all B Schools are women and certainly fewer among the major business schools.

Female MBAs report lower confidence in their math abilities.

Male freshmen report double the confidence in their computer skills than women, even though there is virtually identical computer use (from a UCLA survey of 400,000 incoming freshmen in 2000).

Women are less likely to be in feeder careers for MBAs— 25% of males getting MBAs have engineering backgrounds vs. 9% of female MBAs; conversely, 23% of females getting MBAs are from the arts and humanities compared to 14% of males.

Both males and females see business careers as incompatible with work and life balance. But, women MBAs rate free time and relaxation as very important, more so than do men (60% women vs. 47% men who rate this as very important).

Few women view wealth accumulation as very important to them, 15% women vs. 22% men (GMAC).

These pre-business differences in self-confidence factors, aspirations, and feeder entry points into MBA programs account for some differences in the likelihood of getting an MBA, and the expectations about pay-offs from a business career. Undoubtedly that affects the extent to which women pursue MBAs, and what they aspire to do afterwards.

My second hypothesis is that the difference in the population of male and female professional demographics is attributable to early career take-off experiences.

When women accept jobs post-business education, they are more likely to be affected by location preferences (50% of women versus 35% of men indicate location as key), perhaps because women have more mobility constraints.

Women's choices after their business education are much more likely to be affected by their perception of jobs' contribution to society (14% of women say that's very important vs. 7% for men—GMAC).

Women are much more likely to be affected by the availability of family friendly benefits in their first job (8% vs. 2% for men—GMAC survey).

Among B School graduates, men are much more likely to start in management positions (36% vs. 27% of women—GMAC survey).

More men are in line positions post MBA (45% vs. 37% among women); more women are in staff positions post MBA (40% women vs. 30% men).

Men are more likely to work in Finance and General management; women are more likely to work in consulting.

Men are generally more satisfied with their career advancement.

Even when women take global assignments which is critical for their subsequent career progression, they appear to make their decision with more constraints. They are more likely to be single than are men, and if they are married, they are twice as likely than men to have a fully employed working spouse. So, there is a greater likelihood of making this choice because they are single rather than married, or if they are married they are more constrained than men because of a less movable spouse.

The third conjecture for why the world looks different for professional women is that they experience different career outcomes, and make different career decisions based on their career experiences.

When men change employers during the course of their career, their average salary increase is $25,000 compared to an average salary increase for women of $10,000. This figure controls for job tenure and any other job differences between the men and women. Why? The authors of this study just recently published by the Academy of Management suggest it has to do with more extensive social net works that men have, and pure discrimination.

Women report significantly more time out of their careers over the course of their first ten years post-MBA—an average of 22 months out of the workforce versus 10 months for men. The reasons for women are much more likely to be family related—birth/adoption, childcare, versus for men it's attributed to company mergers, company dissolutions, or reorganizations.

Women MBA graduates are much more likely to work part-time than male MBA graduates (27% vs. 5%), mainly again for childcare and birth/adoption reasons.

Among graduates of MBA programs, women are more likely than men to cite flexibility, lifestyle issues as reasons to start their own business, compared to male entrepreneurs who cite market, financial, and personality reasons such as independence to start their own businesses.

Women entrepreneurs are more likely to own small businesses (71% of female entrepreneurs have businesses of less than $250,000 in revenues a year, compared to 22% of male entrepreneurs); however bigger entrepreneurs with more than $1M in revenues a year are much more likely to be men (62% vs. 17% among women).

Men are much more likely to work continuously post MBAs (61% vs. 29% among women), and the differences are more extreme among MBA grads with children, where women are more likely to disrupt their career.

Interestingly, men and women are dissatisfied with their work/life balance (25% of men and 33% of women). The dissatisfaction with work/life balance goes up linearly, the more hours the person works.

Males and females use flex-time and telecommuting similarly, but again, women are much more likely to resort to part-time work, leave, or compressed work weeks in response to these difficulties.

Among MBA graduates from the Catalyst survey, the top three reasons cited by female executives as barriers to their advancement at work are:

Stereotyping and preconceptions (partially a function of whom they report to, and who reports to them)

Exclusion from informal networks—whether it's golf, sports, spectator events or late night drinking

Inhospitable corporate environments. In fact, just last week, in the Chronicle of Higher Education, I was looking at a statement coming out of the top eight universities in the country. The statement acknowledged mistreatment of female faculty in the sciences and engineering and described various steps that they are going to take to remedy that mistreatment—a public acknowledgement of the in-hospitality of those corporate environments.

Based on this factual "dump" of survey and demographic data, what overarching conclusions can we reach regarding women professionals as a group? Any generalized conclusions, of course, overlook huge individual differences, as is evident in this room.

There are similarities between male and female career experiences.

There are very few differences between men and women regarding their satisfaction with career and job opportunities post MBA.

There are few differences between men and women regarding risk preferences and personal investment decisions.

More women than men are "CEOs at home"—62% of women vs. 38% of men manage their home checking account, 53% women vs. 38% men create the family budget, 46% of women vs. 42% of men make the family's savings and investment decisions (WingspanBank.com survey)

Both are dissatisfied with work/home imbalances

But there are also some real differences:

The cultures of our upbringing, preparatory experiences and self concepts create differences in confidence factors that are critical to choice of business careers especially true of men and women's self concepts true of their math and computer skills and aspirations.

Women make, or are channeled into, initial career choices that are not natural feeders into graduate business education or business careers.

Once into a career women choose, or are assigned, non-line positions or functional areas which are not as visible or natural springboards for promotion.

If in global positions, they're either single, or have less flexibility because of the complexity of a working spouse.

Women appear to respond (by choice or situation) in different ways than men to the extreme stresses associated with work/home imbalances. They respond by reducing or withdrawing entirely from their work involvement.

As entrepreneurs, they go for more modest ventures than men.

The low numbers in female enrollment in MBA Programs (and actually that's a modest decline relative to more recent years), is not due to their entrepreneurial ventures. It's more due to perceived lack of role models, lack of hospitality of the work environment, and balance challenges.

Knowing what we know about female executive styles, how do women fit with the changing workplace, merged global markets and the transformation to a technology based economy? In a nutshell, today's and tomorrow's organizations are going to be global, churning and changing, flat, relying very heavily on networked technologies that empower through knowledge sharing and through various options for work arrangements. Tomorrow's organizations offer opportunities for entrepreneurship in yet to be founded industries, with rewards for creativity and risk taking.

Is that good news or bad news for women? I think it's both.

The bad news is that organizations without boundaries, that are so porous between work and non-work, pose huge challenges for personal balance. The absence of boundaries between work and non-work means that people are tethered all the time, and if they're tethered, that exacerbates the challenges of balance between work and personal lives. Women may suffer even more given their unequal burden regarding family care, at least to date.

Women are also more prone to make choices to avoid competition and conflict. That's based on the work of Deborah Tannen and Judy Rosener and various developmental psychologists. Fighting for scarce resources in competitive situations creates conflict, often inevitable in leadership positions. Women have to make those choices, and sometimes play those roles, despite their disposition against such behaviors (again, ignoring individual differences).

We know, also from developmental psychologists, that women are less likely to be self-promoting and are more deferential, not a recipe for leadership and visibility enhancement. Women may not network as well, especially when they're in predominantly male corporations and functions. Churning organizations that repeatedly change configurations through mergers, acquisitions, and reorganizations place an even greater premium on networking, and whom you know.

Women may not be as good as men at creating a network around them that supports their leadership, that is, others who handle conflict and deliver the bad news on their behalf, and therefore protect their leadership position.

And, women still cite as barriers the stereotypes and attributions made by others—colleagues, superiors and subordinates—that reflect others' discomfort with their power and leadership, which may lead to disadvantage. This may not be intentional discrimination, but merely discomfort with their role as leaders, resulting in exactly the same kind of disadvantage in promotion or placement.

The good news, and I think it's very good news, is that knowledge organizations do place a premium on functioning without a formal power base. Women do that better, according again to developmental psychologists, Deborah Tannen, Judy Rosener and others. Women tend to be more interactive and transformational leaders, and tend not to lead through command, control, reward, and punishment. Women tend to derive their power from their personal charisma, from their work record and accomplishments, and from personal relationships, not from hierarchy, title, and position. In today's flat, organizations that really fits well.

Women tend also to be more comfortable with sharing power and inviting participation, perfect for today's flat, knowledge-based organization. And they tend to recognize and enhance the self-worth of others, again suited to today's flat, knowledge-based organization.

The fiber optically networked workplace does create more options on how to work—when, where, how much—so that it may, over time, reduce the disadvantaged choices that women are making. Over time, virtual workplace structures may alleviate the juggling played between work and non-work and the difficulties both men and women confront because of the balance challenges. But women will especially benefit because, at this point, the data demonstrate that they assume the disproportionate burden.

The other piece of good news is that once women become more than a token, and the threshold of "the first one" is crossed, it seems to get a little easier (e.g., Boards of Directors with 3 or more women).

In sum, this is a mixed view and a set of conjectures that I propose to you. I presented a mind boggling set of numbers and survey data and I'm interested in your reactions on the basis of experience, or your insights into survey data. Thank you for your patience. I genuinely appreciated the opportunity to introspect, through you, more than you can imagine.

From *Vital Speeches of the Day*, April 15, 2001, pp. 398-401. © 2001 by City News Publishing Company, Inc.

Human Rights, Sex Trafficking, and Prostitution

by Alice Leuchtag

Despite laws against slavery in practically every country, an estimated twenty-seven million people live as slaves. Kevin Bales, in his book *Disposable People: New Slavery in the Global Economy* (University of California Press, Berkeley, 1999), describes those who endure modern forms of slavery. These include indentured servants, persons held in hereditary bondage, child slaves who pick plantation crops, child soldiers, and adults and children trafficked and sold into sex slavery.

A Life Narrative

Of all forms of slavery, sex slavery is one of the most exploitative and lucrative with some 200,000 sex slaves worldwide bringing their slaveholders an annual profit of $10.5 billion. Although the great preponderance of sex slaves are women and girls, a smaller but significant number of males—both adult and children—are enslaved for homosexual prostitution.

The life narrative of a Thai girl named Siri, as told to Bales, illustrates how sex slavery happens to vulnerable girls and women. Siri is born in northeastern Thailand to a poor family that farms a small plot of land, barely eking out a living. Economic policies of structural adjustment pursued by the Thai government under the aegis of the World Bank and the International Monetary Fund have taken former government subsidies away from rice farmers, leaving them to compete against imported, subsidized rice that keeps the market price artificially depressed.

Siri attends four years of school, then is kept at home to help care for her three younger siblings. When Siri is fourteen, a well-dressed woman visits her village. She offers to find Siri a "good job," advancing her parents $2,000 against future earnings. This represents at least a year's income for the family. In a town in another province the woman, a trafficker, "sells" Siri to a brothel for $4,000. Owned by an "investment club" whose members are business and professional men—government bureaucrats and local politicians—the brothel is extremely profitable. In a typical thirty-day period it nets its investors $88,000.

To maintain the appearance that their hands are clean, members of the club's board of directors leave the management of the brothel to a pimp and a bookkeeper. Siri is initiated into prostitution by the pimp who rapes her. After being abused by her first "customer," Siri escapes, but a policeman—who gets a percentage of the brothel profits—brings her back, whereupon the pimp beats her up. As further punishment, her "debt" is doubled from $4,000 to $8,000. She must now repay this, along with her monthly rent and food, all from her earnings of $4 per customer. She will have to have sex with three hundred men a month just to pay her rent. Realizing she will never be able to get out of debt, Siri tries to build a relationship with the pimp simply in order to survive.

The pimp uses culture and religion to reinforce his control over Siri. He tells her she must have committed terrible sins in a past life to have been born a female; she must have accumulated a karmic debt to deserve the enslavement and abuse to which she must reconcile herself. Gradually Siri begins to see herself from the point of view of the slaveholder—as someone unworthy and deserving of punishment. By age fifteen she no longer protests or runs away. Her physical enslavement has become psychological as well, a common occurrence in chronic abuse.

Siri is administered regular injections of the contraceptive drug Depo-Provera for which she is charged. As the same needle is used for all the girls, there is a high risk of HIV and other sexual diseases from the injections. Siri knows that a serious illness threatens her and she prays to Buddha at the little shrine in her room, hoping to earn merit so he will protect her from dreaded disease. Once a month she and the others, at their own expense, are tested for HIV. So far Siri's tests have been negative. When Siri tries to get the male customers to wear condoms—distributed free to brothels by the Thai Ministry of Health—some resist wearing them and she can't make them do so.

As one of an estimated 35,000 women working as brothel slaves in Thailand—a country where 500,000 to one million prostituted women and girls work in conditions of degradation and exploitation short of brothel slavery—Siri faces at least a 40 percent chance of contracting the HIV virus. If she is lucky, she can look forward to live more years before she becomes too ill to work and is pushed out into the street.

Thailand's Sex Tourism

Though the Thai government denies it, the World Health Organization finds that HIV is epidemic in Thailand, with the largest segment of new cases among wives and girlfriends of men who buy prostitute sex. Viewing its women as a cash crop to be exploited, and depending on sex tourism for foreign exchange dollars to help pay interest on the foreign debt, the Thai government can't acknowledge the epidemic without contradicting the continued promotion of sex tourism and prostitution.

By encouraging investment in the sex industry, sex tourism creates a business climate conducive to the trafficking and enslavement of vulnerable girls such as Siri. In 1996 nearly five million sex tourists from the United States, Western Europe, Australia, and Japan visited Thailand. These transactions brought in about $26.2 billion—thirteen times more than Thailand earned by building and exporting computers.

In her 1999 report *Pimps and Predators on the Internet: Globalizing the Sexual Exploitation of Women and Children,* published by the Coalition Against Trafficking in Women (CATW), Donna Hughes quotes from postings on an Internet site where sex tourists share experiences and advise one another. The following is one man's description of having sex with a fourteen-year-old prostituted girl in Bangkok:

> "Even though I've had a lot of better massages... after fifteen minutes, I was much more relaxed... Then I asked for a condom and I fucked her for another thirty minutes. Her face looked like she was feeling a lot of pain.... She blocked my way when I wanted to leave the room and she asked for a tip. I gave her 600 bath. Altogether, not a good experience."

Hughes says, "To the men who buy sex, a 'bad experience' evidently means not getting their money's worth, or that the prostituted woman or girl didn't keep up the act of enjoying

what she had to do... one glimpses the humiliation and physical pain most girls and women in prostitution endure."

Nor are the men oblivious to the existence of sexual slavery. One customer states, "Girls in Bangkok virtually get sold by their families into the industry; they work against their will." His knowledge of their sexual slavery and lack of sensitivity thereof is evident in that he then names the hotels in which girls are kept and describes how much they cost!

As Hughes observes, sex tourists apparently feel they have a right to prostitute sex, perceiving prostitution only from a self-interested perspective in which they commodify and objectify women of other cultures, nationalities, and ethnic groups. Their awareness of racism, colonialism, global economic inequalities, and sexism seems limited to the way these realities benefit them as sex consumers.

Sex Traffickers Cast Their Nets

According to the *Guide to the New UN Trafficking Protocol* by Janice Raymond, published by the CATW in 2001, the United Nations estimates that sex trafficking in human beings is a $5 billion to $7 billion operation annually. Four million persons are moved illegally from one country to another and within countries each year, a large proportion of them women and girls being trafficked into prostitution. The United Nations International Children's Emergency Fund (UNICEF) estimates that some 30 percent of women being trafficked are minors, many under age thirteen. The International Organization on Migration estimates that some 500,000 women per year are trafficked into Western Europe from poorer regions of the world. According to *Sex Trafficking of Women in the United States: International and Domestic Trends,* also published by the CATW in 2001, some 50,000 women and children are trafficked into the United States each year, mainly from Asia and Latin America.

Because prostitution as a system of organized sexual exploitation depends on a continuous supply of new "recruits," trafficking is essential to its continued existence. When the pool of available women and girls dries up, new women must be procured. Traffickers cast their nets ever wide and become ever more sophisticated. The Italian Camorra, Chinese Triads, Russian Mafia, and Japanese Yakuza are powerful criminal syndicates consisting of traffickers, pimps, brothel keepers, forced labor lords, and gangs which operate globally.

After the breakdown of the Soviet Union, an estimated five thousand criminal groups formed the Russian Mafia, which operates in thirty countries. The Russian Mafia traffics women from African countries, the Ukraine, the Russian Federation, and Eastern Europe into Western Europe, the United States, and Israel. The Triads traffic women from China, Korea, Thailand, and other Southeast Asian countries into the United States and Europe. The Camorra traffics women from Latin America into Europe. The Yakuza traffics women from the Philipines, Thailand, Burma, Cambodia, Korea, Nepal, and Laos into Japan.

A Global Problem Meets a Global Response

Despite these appalling facts, until recently no generally agreed upon definition of trafficking in human beings was written into international law. In Vienna, Austria, during 1999 and 2000, 120 countries participated in debates over a definition of trafficking. A few nongovernmental organizations (NGOs) and a minority of governments—including Australia, Canada, Denmark, Germany, Ireland, Japan, the Netherlands, Spain, Switzerland, Thailand, and the United Kingdom—wanted to separate issues of trafficking from issues of prostitution. They argued that persons being trafficked should be divided into those who are forced and those who give their consent, with the burden of proof being placed on persons being trafficked. They also urged that the less explicit means of control over trafficked persons—such as abuse of a victim's vulnerability—not be included in the definition of trafficking and that the word *exploitation* not be used. Generally supporters of this position were wealthier countries where large numbers of women were being trafficked and countries in which prostitution was legalized or sex tourism encouraged.

People being trafficked shouldn't be divided into those who are forced and those who give their consent because trafficked persons are in no position to give meaningful consent.

The CATW—140 other NGOs that make up the International Human Rights Network plus many governments (including those of Algeria, Bangladesh, Belgium, China, Columbia, Cuba, Egypt, Finland, France, India, Mexico, Norway, Pakistan, the Philippines, Sweden, Syria, Venezuela, and Vietnam)—maintains that trafficking can't be separated from prostitution. Persons being trafficked shouldn't be divided into those who are forced and those who give their consent because trafficked persons are in no position to give meaningful consent. The subtler methods used by traffickers, such as abuse of a victim's vulnerability, should be included in the definition of trafficking and the word *exploitation* be an essential part of the definition. Generally supporters of this majority view were poorer countries from which large numbers of women were being trafficked or countries in which strong feminist, anti-colonialist, or socialist influences existed. The United States, though initially critical of the majority position, agreed to support a definition of trafficking that would be agreed upon by consensus.

The struggle—led by the CATW to create a definition of trafficking that would penalize traffickers while ensuring that all victims of trafficking would be protected—succeeded when a compromise proposal by Sweden was agreed to. A strongly worded and inclusive *UN Protocol to Prevent, Suppress, and Punish Trafficking in Persons*—especially women and children—was drafted by an ad hoc committee of the UN as a supplement to the Convention Against Transnational Organized Crime. The UN protocol specifically addresses the trade in human beings for purposes of prostitution and other forms of sexual exploitation, forced labor or services, slavery or practices similar to slavery, servitude, and the removal of organs. The protocol defines trafficking as:

> The recruitment, transportation, transfer, harboring or receipt of persons, by means of the threat or use of force or other forms of coercion, of abduction, of fraud, of deception, of the abuse of power or of a position of vulnerability or of the giving or receiving of payments or benefits to achieve the consent of a person having control over another person, for the purpose of exploitation.

While recognizing that the largest amount of trafficking involves women and children, the wording of the UN protocol clearly is gender and age neutral, inclusive of trafficking in both males and females, adults and children.

In 2000 the UN General Assembly adopted this convention and its supplementary protocol; 121 countries signed the convention and eighty countries signed the protocol. For the convention and protocol to become international law, forty countries must ratify them.

Highlights

Some highlights of the new convention and protocol are:

For the first time there is an accepted international definition of trafficking and an agreed-upon set of prosecution, protection, and prevention mechanisms on which countries can base their national legislation.

- The various criminal means by which trafficking takes place, including indirect and subtle forms of coercion, are covered.
- Trafficked persons, especially women in prostitution and child laborers, are no longer viewed as illegal migrants but as victims of a crime.

For the first time there is an accepted international definition of trafficking and an agreed-upon set of prosecution, protection, and prevention mechanisms on which countries can base their national legislation.

- The convention doesn't limit its scope to criminal syndicates but defines an organized criminal group as "any structured group of three or more persons which engages in criminal activities such as trafficking and pimping."

- All victims of trafficking in persons are protected, not just those who can prove that force was used against them.
- The consent of a victim of trafficking is meaningless and irrelevant.
- Victims of trafficking won't have to bear the burden of proof.
- Trafficking and sexual exploitation are intrinsically connected and not to be separated.
- Because women trafficked domestically into local sex industries suffer harmful effects similar to those experienced by women trafficked transnationally, these women also come under the protections of the protocol.
- The key element in trafficking is the exploitative purpose rather than the movement across a border.

The protocol is the first UN instrument to address the demand for prostitution sex, a demand that results in the human rights abuses of women and children being trafficked. The protocol recognizes an urgent need for governments to put the buyers of prostitution sex on their policy and legislative agendas, and it calls upon countries to take or strengthen legislative or other measures to discourage demand, which fosters all the forms of sexual exploitation of women and children.

As Raymond says in the *Guide to the New UN Trafficking Protocol:*

"The least discussed part of the prostitution and trafficking chain has been the men who buy women for sexual exploitation in prostitution.... If we are to find a permanent path to ending these human rights abuses, then we cannot just shrug our shoulders and say, "men are like this," or "boys will be boys," or "prostitution has always been around." Or tell women and girls in prostitution that they must continue to do what they do because prostitution is inevitable. Rather, our responsibility is to make men change their behavior, by all means available—educational, cultural and legal."

Two U.S. feminist, human rights organizations—Captive Daughters and Equality Now—have been working toward that goal. Surita Sandosham of Equality Now says that when her organization asked women's groups in Thailand and the Philippines how it could assist them, the answer came back, "Do something about the demand." Since then the two organizations have legally challenged sex tours originating in the United States and have succeeded in closing down at least one operation.

Refugees, Not Illegal Aliens

In October 2000 the U.S. Congress passed a bill, the Victims of Trafficking and Violence Protection Act of 2000, introduced by New Jersey republican representative Chris Smith. Under this law penalties for traffickers are raised and protections for victims increased. Reasoning that desperate women are unable to give meaningful consent to their own sexual exploitation, the law adopts a broad definition of sex trafficking so as not to exclude so-called consensual prostitution or trafficking that occurs solely within the United States. In these respects the new federal law conforms to the UN protocol.

Two features of the law are particularly noteworthy:

- In order to pressure other countries to end sex trafficking, the U.S. State Department is to make a yearly assessment of other countries' anti-trafficking efforts and to rank them according to how well they discourage trafficking. After two years of failing to meet even minimal standards, countries are subject to sanctions, although not sanctions on humanitarian aid. "Tier 3" countries—those failing to meet even minimal standards—include Greece, Indonesia, Israel, Pakistan, Russia, Saudi Arabia, South Korea, and Thailand.
- Among persons being trafficked into the United States, special T-visas will be provided to those who meet the criteria for having suffered the most serious trafficking abuses. These visas will protect them from deportation so they can testify against their traffickers. T-non immigrant status allows eligible aliens to remain in the United States temporarily and grants specific non-immigrant benefits. Those acquiring T-1 non-immigrant status will be able to remain for a period of three years and will be eligible to receive certain kinds of public assistance—to the same extent as refugees. They will also be issued employment authorization to "assist them in finding safe, legal employment while they attempt to retake control of their lives."

A Debate Rages

A worldwide debate rages about legalization of prostitution fueled by a 1998 International Labor Organization (ILO) report entitled *The Sex Sector: The Economic and Social Bases of Prostitution in Southeast Asia.* The report follows years of lobbying by the sex industry for recognition of prostitution as "sex work." Citing the sex industry's unrecognized contribution to the gross domestic product of four countries in Southeast Asia, the ILO urges governments to officially recognize the "sex sector" and "extend taxation nets to cover many of the lucrative activities connected with it." Though the ILO report says it stops short of calling for legalization of prostitution, official recognition of the sex industry would be impossible without it.

Raymond points out that the ILO's push to redefine prostitution as sex work ignores legislation demonstrating that countries can reduce organized sexual exploitation rather than capitulate to it. For example, Sweden prohibits the purchase of sexual services with punishments of still fines or imprisonment, thus declaring that prostitution isn't a desirable economic and labor sector. The government also helps women getting out of prostitution to rebuild their lives. Venezuela's Ministry of Labor has ruled that prostitution can't be considered work because it lacks the basic elements of dignity and social justice. The Socialist Republic of Vietnam punishes pimps, traffickers, brothel owners, and buyers—sometimes publishing buyer's names in the mass media. For women in prostitution, the government finances medical, educational, and economic rehabilitation.

Instead of transforming the male buyer into a legitmate customer, the ILO should give thought to innovative programs that make the buyer accountable for his sexual exploitation.

Raymond suggests that instead of transforming the male buyer into a legitimate customer, the ILO should give thought to innovative programs that make the buyer accountable for his sexual exploitation. She cites the Sage Project, Inc. (SAGE) program in San Francisco, California, which educates men arrested for soliciting women in prostitution about the risks and impacts of their behavior.

Legalization advocates argue that the violence, exploitation, and health effects suffered by women in prostitution aren't inherent to prostitution but simply result from the random behaviors of bad pimps or buyers, and that if prostitution were regulated by the state these harms would diminish. But examples show these arguments to be false.

Prostituted women are even more marginalized and tightly locked into the system of organized sexual exploitation while the state, now an official party to the exploitation, has become the biggest pimp of all.

In the pamphlet entitled *Legalizing Prostitution Is Not the Answer: The Example of Victoria, Australia,* published by the CATW in 2001, Mary Sullivan and Sheila Jeffreys describe the way legalization in Australia has perpetuated and strengthened the culture of violence and exploitation inherent in prostitution. Under legalization, legal and illegal brothels have proliferated, and trafficking in women has accelerated to meet the increased demand. Pimps, having even more power, continue threatening and brutalizing the women they control. Buyers continue to abuse women, refuse to wear condoms, and spread the HIV virus—and other sexually transmitted diseases—to their wives and girlfriends. Stigmatized by identity cards and medial inspections, prostituted women are even more marginalized and tightly locked into the system of organized sexual exploitation while the state, now an official party to the exploitation, has become the biggest pimp of all.

The government of the Netherlands has legalized prostitution, doesn't enforce laws against pimping, and virtually lives off taxes from the earnings of prostituted women. In the book *Making the Harm Visible* (published by the CATW in 1999), Marie-Victoire Louis describes the effects on prostituted

women of municipal regulation of brothels in Amsterdam and other Dutch cities. Her article entitled "Legalizing Pimping, Dutch Style" explains the way immigration policies in the Netherlands are shaped to fit the needs of the prostitution industry so that traffickers are seldom prosecuted and a continuous supply of women is guaranteed. In Amsterdam's 250 officially listed brothels, 80 percent of the prostitutes have been trafficked in from other countries and 70 percent possess no legal papers. Without money, papers, or contact with the outside world, these immigrant women live in terror instead of being protected by the regulations governing brothels, prostituted women are frequently beaten up and raped by pimps. These "prostitution managers" have practically been given a free hand by the state and by buyers who, as "consumers of prostitution," feel themselves entitled to abuse the women they buy. Sadly and ironically the "Amsterdam model" of legalization and regulation is touted by the Netherlands and Germany as "self-determination and empowerment for women." In reality it simply legitimizes the "right" to buy, sexually use, and profit from the sexual exploitation of someone else's body.

A Human Rights Approach

As part of a system of organized sexual exploitation, prostitution can be visualized along a continuum of abuse with brothel slavery at the furthest extreme. All along the continuum, fine lines divide the degrees of harm done to those caught up in the system. At the core lies a great social injustice no cosmetic reforms can right: the setting aside of a segment of people whose bodies can be purchased for sexual use by others. When this basic injustice is legitimized and regulated by the state and when the state profits from it, that injustice is compounded.

In her book *The Prostitution of Sexuality* (New York University Press, 1995), Kathleen Barry details a feminist human rights approach to prostitution that points the way to the future. Ethically it recognizes prostitution, sex trafficking, and the globalized industrialization of sex as massive violations of women's human rights. Sociologically it considers how and to what extent prostitution promotes sex discrimination against individual women, against different racial categories of women, and against women as a group. Politically it calls for decriminalizing prostitutes while penalizing pimps, traffickers, brothel owners, and buyers.

Understanding that human rights and restorative justice go hand in hand, the feminist human rights approach to prostitution addresses the harm and the need to repair the damage. As Barry says:

> "Legal proposals to criminalize customers, based on the recognition that prostitution violates and harms women, must... include social-service, health and counseling and job retraining programs. Where states would be closing down brothels if customers were criminalized, the economic resources poured into the

former prostitution areas could be turned toward producing gainful employment for women."

With the help of women's projects in many countries—such as Buklod in the Philippines and the Council for Prostitution Alternatives in the United States—some women have begun to confront their condition by leaving prostitution, speaking out against it, revealing their experiences, and helping other women leave the sex industry.

Ending the sexual exploitation of trafficking and prostitution will mean the beginning of a new chapter in building, a hu-

manist future—a more peaceful and just future in which men and women can join together in love and respect, recognizing one another's essential dignity and humanity. Humanity's sexuality then will no longer be hijacked and distorted.

Freelance writer Alice Leuchtag has worked as a social worker, counselor, college instructor, and researcher. Active in the civil rights, peace, socialist, feminist, and humanist movements, she has helped organize women in Houston to oppose sex trafficking.

THE NEW GENDER GAP

From kindergarten to grad school, boys are becoming the second sex.

BY MICHELLE CONLIN

Lawrence High is the usual fortress of manila-brick blandness and boxy 1960s architecture. At lunch, the metalheads saunter out to the smokers' park, while the AP types get pizzas at Marinara's, where they talk about—what else?—other people. The hallways are filled with lip-glossed divas in designer clothes and packs of girls in midriff-baring track tops. The guys run the gamut, too: skate punks, rich boys in Armani, and saggy-panted crews with their Eminem swaggers. In other words, they look pretty much as you'd expect.

But when the leaders of the Class of 2003 assemble in the Long Island high school's fluorescent-lit meeting rooms, most of these boys are nowhere to be seen. The senior class president? A girl. The vice-president? Girl. Head of student government? Girl. Captain of the math team, chief of the yearbook, and editor of the newspaper? Girls.

It's not that the girls of the Class of 2003 aren't willing to give the guys a chance. Last year, the juniors elected a boy as class president. But after taking office, he swiftly instructed his all-female slate that they were his cabinet and that he was going to be calling all the shots. The girls looked around and realized they had the votes, says Tufts University-bound Casey Vaughn, an Intel finalist and one of the alpha femmes of the graduating class. "So they impeached him and took over."

The female lock on power at Lawrence is emblematic of a stunning gender reversal in American education. From kindergarten to graduate school, boys are fast becoming the second sex. "Girls are on a tear through the educational system," says Thomas G. Mortenson, a senior scholar at the Pell Institute for the Study of Opportunity in Higher Education in Washington. "In the past 30 years, nearly every inch of educational progress has gone to them."

Just a century ago, the president of Harvard University, Charles W. Eliot, refused to admit women because he feared they would waste the precious resources of his school. Today, across the country, it seems as if girls have built a kind of scholastic Roman Empire alongside boys' languishing Greece. Although Lawrence High has its share of boy superstars—like this year's valedictorian—the gender takeover at some schools is nearly complete. "Every time I turn around, if something good is happening, there's a female in charge," says Terrill O. Stammler, principal of Rising Sun High School in Rising Sun, Md. Boys are missing from nearly every leadership position, academic honors slot, and student-activity post at the school. Even Rising Sun's girls' sports teams do better than the boys'.

At one exclusive private day school in the Midwest, administrators have even gone so far as to mandate that all awards and student-government positions be divvied equally between the sexes. "It's not just that boys are falling behind girls," says William S. Pollock, author of *Real Boys: Rescuing Our Sons from the Myths of Boyhood* and a professor of psychiatry at Harvard Medical School. "It's that boys themselves are falling behind their own functioning and doing worse than they did before."

It may still be a man's world. But it is no longer, in any way, a boy's. From his first days in school, an average boy is already developmentally two years behind the girls in reading and writing. Yet he's often expected to learn the same things in the same way in the same amount of time.

While every nerve in his body tells him to run, he has to sit still and listen for almost eight hours a day. Biologically, he needs about four recesses a day, but he's lucky if he gets one, since some lawsuit-leery schools have banned them altogether. Hug a girl, and he could be labeled a "toucher" and swiftly suspended—a result of what some say is an increasingly anti-boy culture that pathologizes their behavior.

If he falls behind, he's apt to be shipped off to special ed, where he'll find that more than 70% of his classmates are also boys. Squirm, clown, or interrupt, and he is four times as likely to be diagnosed with attention deficit hyperactivity disorder. That often leads to being forced to take Ritalin or risk being expelled, sent to special ed, or having parents accused of negligence. One study of public schools in Fairfax County, Va., found that more than 20% of upper-middle-class white boys were taking Ritalin-like drugs by fifth grade.

Once a boy makes it to freshman year of high school, he's at greater risk of falling even further behind in grades, extracurricular activities, and advanced placement. Not even science and math remain his bastions. And while the girls are busy working on sweeping the honor roll at graduation, a boy is more likely to be bulking up in the weight room to enhance his steroid-fed Adonis complex, playing Grand Theft Auto: Vice City on his PlayStation2, or downloading rapper 50 Cent on his iPod. All the while, he's 30% more likely to drop out, 85% more likely to commit murder, and four to six times more likely to kill himself, with boy suicides tripling since 1970. "We get a bad rap," says Steven Covington, a sophomore at Ottumwa High School in Ottumwa, Iowa. "Society says we can't be trusted."

As for college—well, let's just say this: At least it's easier for the guys who get there to find a date. For 350 years, men outnumbered women on college campuses. Now, in every state, every income bracket, every racial and ethnic group, and most industrialized Western nations, women reign, earning an average 57% of all BAs and 58% of all master's degrees in the U.S. alone. There are 133 girls getting BAs for every 100 guys—a number that's projected to grow to 142 women per 100 men by 2010, according to the U.S. Education Dept. If current trends continue, demographers say, there will be 156 women per 100 men earning degrees by 2020.

Overall, more boys and girls are in college than a generation ago. But when adjusted for population growth, the percentage of boys entering college, master's programs, and most doctoral programs—except for PhDs in fields like engineering and computer science—has mostly stalled out, whereas for women it has continued to rise across the board. The trend is most pronounced among Hispanics, African Americans, and those from low-income families.

The female-to-male ratio is already 60–40 at the University of North Carolina, Boston University, and New York University. To keep their gender ratios 50–50, many Ivy League and other elite schools are secretly employing a kind of stealth affirmative action for boys. "Girls present better qualifications in the application process—better grades, tougher classes, and more thought in their essays," says Michael S. McPherson, president of Macalester College in St. Paul, Minn., where 57% of enrollees are women. "Boys get off to a slower start."

The trouble isn't limited to school. Once a young man is out of the house, he's more likely than his sister to boomerang back home and sponge off his mom and dad. It all adds up to the fact that before he reaches adulthood, a young man is more likely than he was 30 years ago to end up in the new and growing class of underachiever—what the British call the "sink group."

For a decade, British educators have waged successful classroom programs to ameliorate "laddism" (boys turning off to school) by focusing on teaching techniques that re-engage them. But in the U.S., boys' fall from alpha to omega status doesn't even have a name, let alone the public's attention. "No one wants to speak out on behalf of boys," says Andrew Sum, director of the Northeastern University Center for Labor Market Studies. As a social-policy or educational issue, "it's near nonexistent."

Women are rapidly closing the M.D. and PhD gap and make up almost half of law students.

On the one hand, the education grab by girls is amazing news, which could make the 21st the first female century. Already, women are rapidly closing the M.D. and PhD gap and are on the verge of making up the majority of law students, according to the American Bar Assn. MBA programs, with just 29% females, remain among the few old-boy domains.

Still, it's hardly as if the world has been equalized: Ninety percent of the world's billionaires are men. Among the super rich, only one woman, Gap Inc. co-founder Doris F. Fisher, made, rather than inherited, her wealth. Men continue to dominate in the highest-paying jobs in such leading-edge industries as engineering, investment banking, and high tech—the sectors that still power the economy and build the biggest fortunes. And women still face sizable obstacles in the pay gap, the glass ceiling, and the still-Sisyphean struggle to juggle work and child-rearing.

But attaining a decisive educational edge may finally enable females to narrow the earnings gap, punch through more of the glass ceiling, and gain an equal hand in rewriting the rules of corporations, government, and society. "Girls are better able to deliver in terms of what modern society requires of people—paying attention, abiding by rules, being verbally competent, and dealing with interpersonal relationships in offices," says James Garbarino, a professor of human development at Cornell

University and author of *Lost Boys: Why Our Sons Turn Violent and How We Can Save Them*.

Righting boys' problems needn't end up leading to reversals for girls. But some feminists say the danger in exploring what's happening to boys would be to mistakenly see any expansion of opportunities for women as inherently disadvantageous to boys. "It isn't a zero-sum game," says Susan M. Bailey, executive director of the Wellesley Centers for Women. Adds Macalester's McPherson: "It would be dangerous to even out the gender ratio by treating women worse. I don't think we've reached a point in this country where we are fully providing equal opportunities to women."

Men could become losers in a global economy that values mental powers over might.

Still, if the creeping pattern of male disengagement and economic dependency continues, more men could end up becoming losers in a global economy that values mental powers over might—not to mention the loss of their talent and potential. The growing educational and economic imbalances could also create societal upheavals, altering family finances, social policies, and work-family practices. Men are already dropping out of the labor force, walking out on fatherhood, and disconnecting from civic life in greater numbers. Since 1964, for example, the voting rate in Presidential elections among men has fallen from 72% to 53%—twice the rate of decline among women, according to Pell's Mortenson. In a turnaround from the 1960s, more women now vote than men.

Boys' slide also threatens to erode male earnings, spark labor shortages for skilled workers, and create the same kind of marriage squeeze among white women that already exists for blacks. Among African Americans, 30% of 40- to 44-year-old women have never married, owing in part to the lack of men with the same academic credentials and earning potential. Currently, the never-married rate is 9% for white women of the same age. "Women are going to pull further and further ahead of men, and at some point, when they want to form families, they are going to look around and say, 'Where are the guys?'" says Mortenson.

Corporations should worry, too. During the boom, the most acute labor shortages occurred among educated workers—a problem companies often solved by hiring immigrants. When the economy reenergizes, a skills shortage in the U.S. could undermine employers' productivity and growth.

Better-educated men are also, on average, a much happier lot. They are more likely to marry, stick by their children, and pay more in taxes. From the ages of 18 to 65, the average male college grad earns $2.5 million over his lifetime, 90% more than his high school counterpart. That's

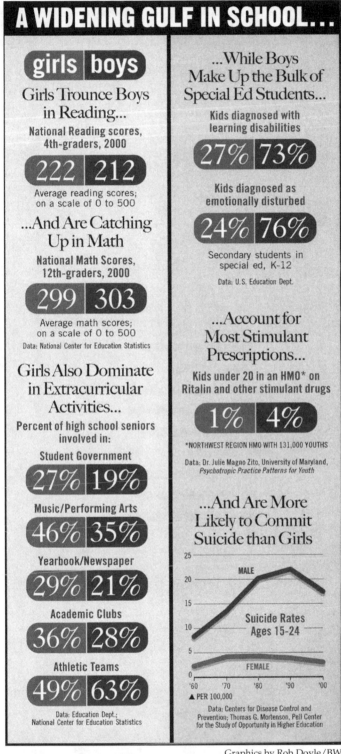

Graphics by Rob Doyle/BW

up from 40% more in 1979, the peak year for U.S. manufacturing. The average college diploma holder also contributes four times more in net taxes over his career than a high school grad, according to Northeastern's Sum. Meanwhile, the typical high school dropout will usually get $40,000 more from the government than he pays in, a net drain on society.

Certainly, many boys continue to conquer scholastic summits, especially boys from high-income families with

...LEADS MORE AND MORE TO A GIRLS' CLUB IN COLLEGE

The Gender Gap Spans Every Racial and Ethnic Group...

Bachelor's degrees awarded to students by race/ethnicity, as a percent of total

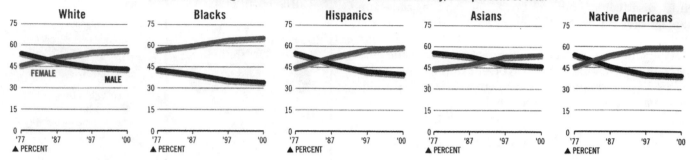

...And Most of the Industrialized World...

Ages 25 to 34, with at least a college education, plus advanced degrees

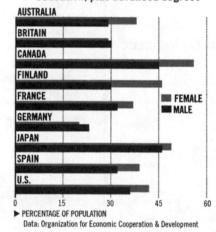

▶ PERCENTAGE OF POPULATION
Data: Organization for Economic Cooperation & Development

...And Is Projected to Get Worse...

Number of U.S. women awarded degrees per 100 men

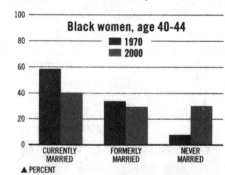

Data: Andrew Sum, Northeastern University Center for Labor Market Studies

...Threatening the Marriage Squeeze Among Whites That Blacks Already Face

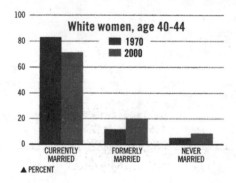

Data: *Mismatch*, by Andrew Hacker; National Center for Education Statistics; Bureau of Labor Statistics; Census Bureau

Graphics by Rob Doyle/BW

educated parents. Overall, boys continue to do better on standardized tests such as the scholastic aptitude test, though more low-income girls than low-income boys take it, thus depressing girls' scores. Many educators also believe that standardized testing's multiple-choice format favors boys because girls tend to think in broader,

more complex terms. But that advantage is eroding as many colleges now weigh grades—where girls excel— more heavily than test scores.

Still, it's not as if girls don't face a slew of vexing issues, which are often harder to detect because girls are likelier to internalize low self-esteem through depression or the

THE NEW SHAPE OF THE WORKFORCE

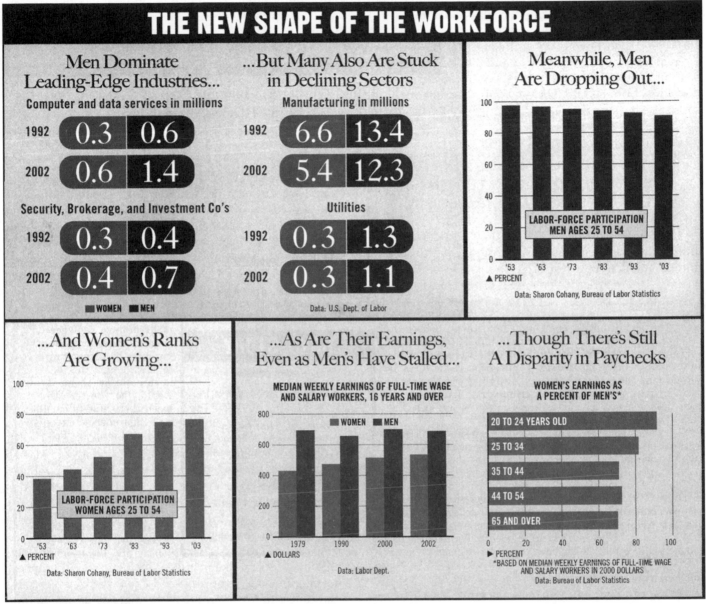

Men Dominate Leading-Edge Industries...

Computer and data services in millions

	WOMEN	MEN
1992	0.3	0.6
2002	0.6	1.4

Security, Brokerage, and Investment Co's

	WOMEN	MEN
1992	0.3	0.4
2002	0.4	0.7

■ WOMEN ■ MEN

...But Many Also Are Stuck in Declining Sectors

Manufacturing in millions

	WOMEN	MEN
1992	6.6	13.4
2002	5.4	12.3

Utilities

	WOMEN	MEN
1992	0.3	1.3
2002	0.3	1.1

Data: U.S. Dept. of Labor

Meanwhile, Men Are Dropping Out...

LABOR-FORCE PARTICIPATION MEN AGES 25 TO 54

▲ PERCENT

Data: Sharon Cohany, Bureau of Labor Statistics

...And Women's Ranks Are Growing...

LABOR-FORCE PARTICIPATION WOMEN AGES 25 TO 54

▲ PERCENT

Data: Sharon Cohany, Bureau of Labor Statistics

...As Are Their Earnings, Even as Men's Have Stalled...

MEDIAN WEEKLY EARNINGS OF FULL-TIME WAGE AND SALARY WORKERS, 16 YEARS AND OVER

■ WOMEN ■ MEN

▲ DOLLARS

Data: Labor Dept.

...Though There's Still A Disparity in Paychecks

WOMEN'S EARNINGS AS A PERCENT OF MEN'S*

20 TO 24 YEARS OLD
25 TO 34
35 TO 44
44 TO 54
65 AND OVER

▶ PERCENT

*BASED ON MEDIAN WEEKLY EARNINGS OF FULL-TIME WAGE AND SALARY WORKERS IN 2000 DOLLARS

Data: Bureau of Labor Statistics

Graphics by Rob Doyle/BW

---

desire to starve themselves into perfection. And while boys may act out with their fists, girls, given their superior verbal skills, often do so with their mouths in the form of vicious gossip and female bullying. "They yell and cuss," says 15-year-old Keith Gates, an Ottumwa student. "But we always get in trouble. They never do."

Before educators, corporations, and policymakers can narrow the new gender gap, they will have to understand its myriad causes. Everything from absentee parenting to the lack of male teachers to corporate takeovers of lunch rooms with sugar-and-fat-filled food, which can make kids hyperactive and distractable, plays a role. So can TV violence, which hundreds of studies—including recent ones by Stanford University and the University of Michigan—have linked to aggressive behavior in kids. Some believe boys are responding to cultural signals—downsized dads cast adrift in the New Economy, a dumb-and-

dumber dude culture that demeans academic achievement, and the glamorization of all things gangster that makes school seem so uncool. What can compare with the allure of a gun-wielding, model-dating hip hopper? Boys, who mature more slowly than girls, are also often less able to delay gratification or take a long-range view.

Schools have inadvertently played a big role, too, losing sight of boys—taking for granted that they were doing well, even though data began to show the opposite. Some educators believed it was a blip that would change or feared takebacks on girls' gains. Others were just in denial. Indeed, many administrators saw boys, rather than the way schools were treating them, as the problem.

Thirty years ago, educational experts launched what's known as the "Girl Project." The movement's noble objective was to help girls wipe out their weaknesses in math and science, build self-esteem, and give them the undisputed message: The opportunities are yours; take them. Schools focused on making the classroom more girl-friendly by including teaching styles that catered to them. Girls were also powerfully influenced by the women's movement, as well as by Title IX and the Gender & Equity Act, all of which created a legal environment in which discrimination against girls—from classrooms to the sports field—carried heavy penalties. Once the chains were off, girls soared.

For 30 years, the focus at schools has been to empower girls, in and out of the classroom.

Yet even as boys' educational development was flat-lining in the 1990s—with boys dropping out in greater numbers and failing to bridge the gap in reading and writing—the spotlight remained firmly fixed on girls. Part of the reason was that the issue had become politically charged and girls had powerful advocates. The American Association of University Women, for example, published research cementing into pedagogy the idea that girls had deep problems with self-esteem in school as a result of teachers' patterns, which included calling on girls less and lavishing attention on boys. Newspapers and TV newsmagazines lapped up the news, decrying a new confidence crisis among American girls. Universities and research centers sponsored scores of teacher symposiums centered on girls. "All the focus was on girls, all the grant monies, all the university programs—to get girls interested in science and math," says Steve Hanson, principal of Ottumwa High School in Iowa. "There wasn't a similar thing for reading and writing for boys."

Some boy champions go so far as to contend that schools have become boy-bashing laboratories. Christina Hoff Sommers, author of The War Against Boys, says the AAUW report, coupled with zero-tolerance sexual harassment laws, have hijacked schools by overly feminizing classrooms and attempting to engineer androgyny.

The "earliness" push, in which schools are pressured to show kids achieving the same standards by the same age or risk losing funding, is also far more damaging to boys, according to Lilian G. Katz, co-director of ERIC Clearinghouse on Elementary and Early Childhood Education. Even the nerves on boys' fingers develop later than girls', making it difficult to hold a pencil and push out perfect cursive. These developmental differences often unfairly sideline boys as slow or dumb, planting a distaste for school as early as the first grade.

Instead of catering to boys' learning styles, Pollock and others argue, many schools are force-fitting them into an unnatural mold. The reigning sit-still-and-listen paradigm isn't ideal for either sex. But it's one girls often tolerate better than boys. Girls have more intricate sensory capacities and biosocial aptitudes to decipher exactly what the teacher wants, whereas boys tend to be more

anti-authoritarian, competitive, and risk-taking. They often don't bother with such details as writing their names in the exact place instructed by the teacher.

Experts say educators also haven't done nearly enough to keep up with the recent findings in brain research about developmental differences. "Ninety-nine-point-nine percent of teachers are not trained in this," says Michael Gurian, author of Boys and Girls Learn Differently. "They were taught 20 years ago that gender is just a social function."

In fact, brain research over the past decade has revealed how differently boys' and girls' brains can function. Early on, boys are usually superior spatial thinkers and possess the ability to see things in three dimensions. They are often drawn to play that involves intense movement and an element of make-believe violence. Instead of straitjacketing boys by attempting to restructure this behavior out of them, it would be better to teach them how to harness this energy effectively and healthily, Pollock says.

As it stands, the result is that too many boys are diagnosed with attention-deficit disorder or its companion, attention-deficit hyperactivity disorder. The U.S.—mostly its boys—now consumes 80% of the world's supply of methylphenidate (the generic name for Ritalin). That use has increased 500% over the past decade, leading some to call it the new K–12 management tool. There are school districts where 20% to 25% of the boys are on the drug, says Paul R. Wolpe, a psychiatry professor at the University of Pennsylvania and the senior fellow at the school's Center for Bioethics: "Ritalin is a response to an artificial social context that we've created for children."

Instead of recommending medication—something four states have recently banned school administrators from doing—experts say educators should focus on helping boys feel less like misfits. Experts are designing new developmentally appropriate, child-initiated learning that concentrates on problem-solving, not just test-taking. This approach benefits both sexes but especially boys, given that they tend to learn best through action, not just talk. Activities are geared toward the child's interest level and temperament. Boys, for example, can learn math through counting pinecones, biology through mucking around in a pond. They can read Harry Potter instead of Little House on the Prairie, and write about aliens attacking a hospital rather than about how to care for people in the hospital. If they get antsy, they can leave a teacher's lecture and go to an activity center replete with computers and manipulable objects that support the lesson plan.

Paying attention to boys' emotional lives also delivers dividends. Over the course of her longitudinal research project in Washington (D.C.) schools, University of Northern Florida researcher Rebecca Marcon found that boys who attend kindergartens that focus on social and emotional skills—as opposed to only academic learning—perform better, across the board, by the time they reach junior high.

Indeed, brain research shows that boys are actually more empathic, expressive, and emotive at birth than girls. But Pollock says the boy code, which bathes them in a culture of stoicism and reticence, often socializes those aptitudes out of them by the second grade. "We now have executives paying $10,000 a week to learn emotional intelligence," says Pollock. "These are actually the skills boys are born with."

The gender gap also has roots in the expectation gap. In the 1970s, boys were far more likely to anticipate getting a college degree—with girls firmly entrenched in the cheerleader role. Today, girls' expectations are ballooning, while boys' are plummeting. There's even a sense, including among the most privileged families, that today's boys are a sort of payback generation—the one that has to compensate for the advantages given to males in the past. In fact, the new equality is often perceived as a loss by many boys who expected to be on top. "My friends in high school, they just didn't see the value of college, they just didn't care enough," says New York University sophomore Joe Clabby. Only half his friends from his high school group in New Jersey went on to college.

They will face a far different world than their dads did. Without college diplomas, it will be harder for them to find good-paying jobs. And more and more, the positions available to them will be in industries long thought of as female. The services sector, where women make up 60% of employees, has ballooned by 260% since the 1970s. During the same period, manufacturing, where men hold 70% of jobs, has shrunk by 14%.

These men will also be more likely to marry women who outearn them. Even in this jobless recovery, women's wages have continued to grow, with the pay gap the smallest on record, while men's earnings haven't managed to keep up with the low rate of inflation. Given that the recession hit male-centric industries such as technology and manufacturing the hardest, native-born men experienced more than twice as much job loss as native-born women between 2000 and 2002.

Some feminists who fought hard for girl equality in schools in the early 1980s and '90s say this: So what if girls have gotten 10, 20 years of attention—does that make up for centuries of subjugation? Moreover, what's wrong with women gliding into first place, especially if they deserve it? "Just because girls aren't shooting 7-Eleven clerks doesn't mean they should be ignored," says Cornell's Garbarino. "Once you stop oppressing girls, it stands to reason they will thrive up to their potential."

Moreover, girls say much of their drive stems from parents and teachers pushing them to get a college degree because they have to be better to be equal—to make the same money and get the same respect as a guy. "Girls are more willing to take the initiative… they're not afraid to do the work," says Tara Prout, the Georgetown-bound senior class president at Lawrence High. "A lot of boys in my school are looking for credit to get into college to look good, but they don't really want to do the grunt work."

A new world has opened up for girls, but unless a symmetrical effort is made to help boys find their footing, it may turn out that it's a lonely place to be. After all, it takes more than one gender to have a gender revolution.

BOYS' STORY

For further reading:

- *Lost Boys* by James Garbarino
- *Boys and Girls Learn Differently* by Michael Gurian
- *Mismatch* by Andrew Hacker
- *Raising Cain* by Dan Kindlon and Michael Thompson
- *Real Boys* by William Pollack
- *The War Against Boys* by Christina Hoff Sommers

UNIT 5

Social Institutions: Issues, Crises, and Changes

Unit Selections

Key Points to Consider

- Discuss whether or not it is important to preserve some continuity in institutions.

- How can institutions outlive their usefulness?

- Why are institutions so difficult to change? Cite examples where changes are instituted from the top down and others where they are instituted from the bottom up. Do you see a similar pattern of development for these types of changes?

- Is it possible to reform the political system to greatly reduce the corrupting role of money in politics? Why or why not?

- What basic changes in the economic system are evident in the things that you observe daily?

- How should issues like abortion and genetic engineering be decided?

 **Links: www.dushkin.com/online/**
These sites are annotated in the World Wide Web pages.

Center for the Study of Group Processes
http://www.uiowa.edu/~grpproc/
International Labour Organization (ILO)
http://www.ilo.org
IRIS Center
http://www.iris.umd.edu
National Center for Policy Analysis
http://www.ncpa.org
National Institutes of Health (NIH)
http://www.nih.gov

Social institutions are the building blocks of social structure. They accomplish the important tasks of society—for example, regulation of reproduction, socialization of children, production and distribution of economic goods, law enforcement and social control, and organization of religion and other value systems.

Social institutions are not rigid arrangements; they reflect changing social conditions. Institutions generally change slowly. At the present time, however, many of the social institutions in the United States and many other parts of the world are in crisis and are undergoing rapid change. Eastern European countries are literally transforming their political and economic institutions. Economic institutions, such as stock markets, are becoming truly international, and when a major country experiences a recession, many other countries feel the effects. In the United States, major reform movements are active in political, economic, family, medical, and educational institutions.

The first subsection of unit 5 examines American political institutions. In the first article, G. William Domhoff examines the power structure of the American political system and finds it dominated by the corporate community. But how does his view account for democracy and the power that it gives the average person? What about the evident influence of workers, liberals, environmentalists, and challenge groups? Domhoff argues that these forces may get media coverage, but they cannot prevent the corporate community from controlling the federal government on basic issues of income, wealth, and economic power. Moreover, he shows how this community exercises its power.

The following subsection deals with major issues and problems of the economy. The first issue is the big question of how "good" is the U.S. economy. W. Michael Cox and Richard Alm provide an assessment which includes but goes beyond economic statistics. They say that we are the world's wealthiest nation with the highest consumption (e.g., home ownership) but also have a balanced life. This includes more leisure, more pleasant work, greater safety, more convenience, a cleaner environment, and more variety. All this supports the authors' thesis that our type of free enterprise system is one of the best in the world.

The next two issues deal with the work-world. First, John A. Challenger describes the transition to new rules for the workplace which involve almost no commitment of the corporation to its workers or of the workers toward the corporation. The increased control of investors over basic corporate policies forces corporations to emphasize cost cutting, and therefore, heartless personnel policies. International competition requires rapid adaptations and constantly changing size of the workforce. The second work-world issue is the migration of American jobs to

overseas as described by Jyoti Thottam in the next article. The loss of blue-collar jobs is ancient history. Now increasingly white-collar jobs are migrating overseas. The numbers are small today but increasing very rapidly.

The social sphere is also in turmoil, as illustrated by the articles in the last subsection. A key issue for many parents and children is the quality of education, and the public's perception is rather negative. James Comer reviews many suggested solutions to the failure of American schools and finds them deficient because they are not based on sound principles of child development. The real solution requires powerful positive social interactions between students and teachers. The medical sphere is also in turmoil and plagued with problems. The particular problem discussed in the next article is the soaring costs of malpractice insurance which are driving many doctors out of business.

Who Rules America?

G. William Domhoff

Power and Class in the United States

Power and *class* are terms that make Americans a little uneasy, and concepts like *power elite* and *dominant class* immediately put people on guard. The idea that a relatively fixed group of privileged people might shape the economy and government for their own benefit goes against the American grain. Nevertheless,... the owners and top-level managers in large income-producing properties are far and away the dominant power figures in the United States. Their corporations, banks, and agribusinesses come together as a *corporate community* that dominates the federal government in Washington. Their real estate, construction, and land development companies form *growth coalitions* that dominate most local governments. Granted, there is competition within both the corporate community and the local growth coalitions for profits and investment opportunities, and there are sometimes tensions between national corporations and local growth coalitions, but both are cohesive on policy issues affecting their general welfare, and in the face of demands by organized workers, liberals, environmentalists, and neighborhoods.

As a result of their ability to organize and defend their interests, the owners and managers of large income-producing properties have a very great share of all income and wealth in the United States, greater than in any other industrial democracy. Making up at best 1 percent of the total population, by the early 1990s they earned 15.7 percent of the nation's yearly income and owned 37.2 percent of all privately held wealth, including 49.6 percent of all corporate stocks and 62.4 percent of all bonds. Due to their wealth and the lifestyle it makes possible, these owners and managers draw closer as a common social group. They belong to the same exclusive social clubs, frequent the same summer and winter resorts, and send their children to a relative handful of private schools. Members of the corporate community thereby become a *corporate rich* who create a nationwide *social upper class* through their social interaction.... Members of the growth coalitions, on the other hand, are *place entrepreneurs,* people who sell locations and buildings. They come together as local upper classes in their respective cities and sometimes mingle with the corporate rich in educational or resort settings.

The corporate rich and the growth entrepreneurs supplement their small numbers by developing and directing a wide variety of nonprofit organizations, the most important of which are a set of tax-free charitable foundations, think tanks, and policy-discussion groups. These specialized nonprofit groups constitute a *policy-formation network* at the national level. Chambers of commerce and policy groups affiliated with them form similar policy-formation networks at the local level, aided by a few national-level city development organizations that are available for local consulting.

Those corporate owners who have the interest and ability to take part in general governance join with top-level executives in the corporate community and the policy-formation network to form the *power elite,* which is the leadership group for the corporate rich as a whole. The concept of a power elite makes clear that not all members of the upper class are involved in governance; some of them simply enjoy the lifestyle that their great wealth affords them. At the same time, the focus on a leadership group allows for the fact that not all those in the power elite are members of the upper class; many of them are high-level employees in profit and nonprofit organizations controlled by the corporate rich....

The power elite is not united on all issues because it includes both moderate conservatives and ultraconservatives. Although both factions favor minimal reliance on government on all domestic issues, the moderate conservatives sometimes agree to legislation advocated by liberal elements of the society, especially in times of social upheaval like the Great Depression of the 1930s and the Civil Rights Movement of the early 1960s. Except on defense spending, ultraconservatives are characterized by a complete distaste for any kind of government programs under any circumstances—even to the point of opposing government support for corporations on some issues. Moderate conservatives often favor foreign aid, working through the United Nations, and making attempts to win over foreign enemies through patient diplomacy, treaties, and trade agreements. Historically, ultraconservatives have opposed most forms of foreign involvement, although they have become more tolerant of foreign trade agreements over the past thirty or forty years. At the same time, their hostility to the United Nations continues unabated.

Members of the power elite enter into the electoral arena as the leaders within a *corporate-conservative coalition,* where they are aided by a wide variety of patriotic, antitax, and other single-issue organizations. These conservative advocacy organizations are funded in varying degrees by the corporate rich, direct-mail appeals, and middle-class conservatives. This coalition has played a large role in both political parties at the presidential level and usually succeeds in electing a conservative majority to both houses of Congress. Historically, the conservative majority in Congress was made up of most Northern Republicans and most Southern Democrats, but that arrangement has been changing gradually since the 1960s as the conservative Democrats of the South are replaced by even more conservative Southern Republicans. The corporate-conservative coalition also has access to the federal government in Washington through lobbying and the appointment of its members to top positions in the executive branch....

Despite their preponderant power within the federal government and the many useful policies it carries out for them, members of the power elite are constantly critical of government as an alleged enemy of freedom and economic growth. Although their wariness toward government is expressed in terms of a dislike for taxes and government regulations, I believe their underlying concern is that government could change the power relations in the private sphere by aiding average Americans through a number of different avenues: (1) creating government jobs for the unemployed; (2) making health, unemployment, and welfare benefits more generous; (3) helping employees gain greater workplace rights and protections; and (4) helping workers organize unions. All of these initiatives are opposed by members of the power elite because they would increase wages and taxes, but the deepest opposition is toward any government support for unions because unions are a potential organizational base for advocating the whole range of issues opposed by the corporate rich....

Where Does Democracy Fit In?

...[T]o claim that the corporate rich have enough power to be considered a dominant class does not imply that lower social classes are totally powerless. *Domination* means the power to set the terms under which other groups and classes must operate, not total control. Highly trained professionals with an interest in environmental and consumer issues have been able to couple their technical information and their understanding of the legislative and judicial processes with well-timed publicity, lobbying, and lawsuits to win governmental restrictions on some corporate practices. Wage and salary employees, when they are organized into unions and have the right to strike, have been able to gain pay increases, shorter hours, better working conditions, and social benefits such as health insurance. Even the most powerless of people—the very poor and those discrim-

inated against—sometimes develop the capacity to influence the power structure through sit-ins, demonstrations, social movements, and other forms of social disruption, and there is evidence that such activities do bring about some redress of grievances, at least for a short time.

More generally, the various challengers to the power elite sometimes work together on policy issues as a *liberal-labor coalition* that is based in unions, local environmental organizations, some minority group communities, university and arts communities, liberal churches, and small newspapers and magazines. Despite a decline in membership over the past twenty years, unions are the largest and best-financed part of the coalition, and the largest organized social force in the country (aside from churches). They also cut across racial and ethnic lines more than any other institutionalized sector of American society....

The policy conflicts between the corporate-conservative and liberal-labor coalitions are best described as *class conflicts* because they primarily concern the distribution of profits and wages, the rate and progressivity of taxation, the usefulness of labor unions, and the degree to which business should be regulated by government. The liberal-labor coalition wants corporations to pay higher wages to employees and higher taxes to government. It wants government to regulate a wide range of business practices, including many that are related to the environment, and help employees to organize unions. The corporate-conservative coalition resists all these policy objectives to a greater or lesser degree, claiming they endanger the freedom of individuals and the efficient workings of the economic marketplace. The conflicts these disagreements generate can manifest themselves in many different ways: workplace protests, industrywide boycotts, massive demonstrations in cities, pressure on Congress, and the outcome of elections.

Neither the corporate-conservative nor the liberal-labor coalition includes a very large percentage of the American population, although each has the regular support of about 25–30 percent of the voters. Both coalitions are made up primarily of financial donors, policy experts, political consultants, and party activists....

Pluralism. The main alternative theory [I] address.... claims that power is more widely dispersed among groups and classes than a class-dominance theory allows. This general perspective is usually called *pluralism,* meaning there is no one dominant power group. It is the theory most favored by social scientists. In its strongest version, pluralism holds that power is held by the general public through the pressure that public opinion and voting put on elected officials. According to this version, citizens form voluntary groups and pressure groups that shape public opinion, lobby elected officials, and back sympathetic political candidates in the electoral process....

The second version of pluralism sees power as rooted in a wide range of well-organized "interest groups" that are often based in economic interests (e.g., industrialists, bankers, labor unions), but also in other interests as well (e.g., environmental, consumer, and civil rights groups). These interest groups join together in different coalitions depending on the specific issues. Proponents of this version of pluralism sometimes concede that public opinion and voting have only a minimal or indirect influence, but they see business groups as too fragmented and antagonistic to form a cohesive dominant class. They also claim that some business interest groups occasionally join coalitions with liberal or labor groups on specific issues, and that business-dominated coalitions sometimes lose. Furthermore, some proponents of this version of pluralism believe that the Democratic Party is responsive to the wishes of liberal and labor interest groups.

In contrast, I argue that the business interest groups are part of a tightly knit corporate community that is able to develop classwide cohesion on the issues of greatest concern to it: opposition to unions, high taxes, and government regulation. When a business group loses on a specific issue, it is often because other business groups have been opposed; in other words, there are arguments within the corporate community, and these arguments are usually settled within the governmental arena. I also claim that liberal and labor groups are rarely part of coalitions with business groups and that for most of its history the Democratic Party has been dominated by corporate and agribusiness interests in the Southern states, in partnership with the growth coalitions in large urban areas outside the South. Finally, I show that business interests rarely lose on labor and regulatory issues except in times of extreme social disruption like the 1930s and 1960s, when differences of opinion between Northern and Southern corporate leaders made victories for the liberal-labor coalition possible....

How the Power Elite Dominates Government

This [section] shows how the power elite builds on the ideas developed in the policy-formation process and its success in the electoral arena to dominate the federal government. Lobbyists from corporations, law firms, and trade associations play a key role in shaping government on narrow issues of concern to specific corporations or business sectors, but their importance should not be overestimated because a majority of those elected to Congress are predisposed to agree with them. The corporate community and the policy-formation network supply top-level governmental appointees and new policy directions on major issues.

Once again, as seen in the battles for public opinion and electoral success, the power elite faces opposition from a minority of elected officials and their supporters in labor unions and liberal advocacy groups. These opponents are sometimes successful in blocking ultra-conservative initiatives, but most of the victories for the liberal-labor coalition are the result of support from moderate conservatives....

Appointees to Government

The first way to test a class-dominance view of the federal government is to study the social and occupational backgrounds of the people who are appointed to manage the major departments of the executive branch, such as state, treasury, defense,

and justice. If pluralists are correct, these appointees should come from a wide range of interest groups. If the state autonomy theorists are correct, they should be disproportionately former elected officials or longtime government employees. If the class-dominance view is correct, they should come disproportionately from the upper class, the corporate community, and the policy-formation network.

There have been numerous studies over the years of major governmental appointees under both Republican and Democratic administrations, usually focusing on the top appointees in the departments that are represented in the president's cabinet. These studies are unanimous in their conclusion that most top appointees in both Republican and Democratic administrations are corporate executives and corporate lawyers—and hence members of the power elite....

Conclusion

This [section] has demonstrated the power elite's wide-ranging access to government through the interest-group and policy-formation processes, as well as through its ability to influence appointments to major government positions. When coupled with the several different kinds of power discussed in earlier [sections] this access and involvement add up to power elite domination of the federal government.

By *domination,* as stated in the first [section], social scientists mean the ability of a class or group to set the terms under which other classes or groups within a social system must operate. By this definition, domination does not mean control on each and every issue, and it does not rest solely on involvement in government. Influence over government is only the final and most visible aspect of power elite domination, which has its roots in the class structure, the corporate control of the investment function, and the operation of the policy-formation network. If government officials did not have to wait for corporate leaders to decide where and when they will invest, and if government officials were not further limited by the general public's acceptance of policy recommendations from the policy-formation network, then power elite involvement in elections and government would count for a lot less than they do under present conditions.

Domination by the power elite does not negate the reality of continuing conflict over government policies, but few conflicts, it has been shown, involve challenges to the rules that create privileges for the upper class and domination by the power elite. Most of the numerous battles within the interest-group process, for example, are only over specific spoils and favors; they often involve disagreements among competing business interests.

Similarly, conflicts within the policy-making process of government often involve differences between the moderate conservative and ultraconservative segments of the dominant class. At other times they involve issues in which the needs of the corporate community as a whole come into conflict with the needs of specific industries, which is what happens to some extent on tariff policies and also on some environmental legislation. In neither case does the nature of the conflict call into question the domination of government by the power elite.

…Contrary to what pluralists claim, there is not a single case study on any issue of any significance that shows a liberal-labor victory over a united corporate-conservative coalition, which is strong evidence for a class-domination theory on the "Who wins?" power indicator. The classic case studies frequently cited by pluralists have been shown to be gravely deficient as evidence for their views. Most of these studies reveal either conflicts among rival groups within the power elite or situations in which the moderate conservatives have decided for their own reasons to side with the liberal-labor coalition.…

More generally, it now can be concluded that all four indicators of power introduced in [the first section] point to the corporate rich and their power elite as the dominant organizational structure in American society. First, the wealth and income distributions are skewed in their favor more than in any other industrialized democracy. They are clearly the most powerful group in American society in terms of "Who benefits?" Second, the appointees to government come overwhelmingly from the corporate community and its associated policy-formation network. Thus, the power elite is clearly the most powerful in terms of "Who sits?"

Third, the power elite wins far more often than it loses on policy issues resolved in the federal government. Thus, it is the most powerful in terms of "Who wins?" Finally, as shown in reputational studies in the 1950s and 1970s,… corporate leaders are the most powerful group in terms of "Who shines?" By the usual rules of evidence in a social science investigation using multiple indicators, the owners and managers of large income-producing properties are the dominant class in the United States.

Still, as noted at the end of the first [section], power structures are not immutable. Societies change and power structures evolve or crumble from time to unpredictable time, especially in the face of challenge. When it is added that the liberal-labor coalition persists in the face of its numerous defeats, and that free speech and free elections are not at risk, there remains the possibility that class domination could be replaced by a greater sharing of power in the future.

Off the Books

The benefits of free enterprise that economic statistics miss

W. Michael Cox and Richard Alm

AMERICA'S CONSUMER CULTURE is all around us. It's along our highways, studded with shopping malls, fast food joints, and flashy neon signs. It's in our homes, filled with gadgets, furnishings, toys, and closets of clothes. It permeates the media, where ads tell us happiness and sex appeal are as close as the nearest store. It's even within us, at least to the extent that we tie status and identity to the cars we drive, the clothes we wear, and the food we eat.

That's our reputation: a consumer-driven, somewhat crass, shop-'til-you-drop society. As the world's wealthiest nation, we *should* consume a lot, but the portrait of Americans as consumption crazed misses as much as it captures. We're not working just to acquire more goods and services. Most of us strive for something broader: a balanced life.

Consumption is part of that, of course. We buy myriad things: Chevrolet cars, Sony TV sets, Levi's jeans, Nike sneakers, McDonald's hamburgers, Dell computers. But our wish list doesn't stop there. We also want leisure time, a respite to enjoy life. We want pleasant working conditions and good jobs, so earning a living isn't too arduous. We want safety and Security, so we don't live in fear. We want variety, the spice of life. We want convenience, which makes everyday life a little easier. We want a cleaner environment, which enhances health and recreation.

A full description of a balanced life would entail much more, with considerations for family and friends, perhaps even spirituality. Here we want to focus on the components of happiness that clearly depend on the market but are not reflected in the gross domestic product (GDP). Our free enterprise system provides much more than the goods and services we consume; it furnishes ingredients of a balanced life that are often overlooked in discussions of economic performance.

Capitalism creates wealth. During the last two centuries, the United States became the world's richest nation as it embraced an economic system that promotes growth, efficiency, and innovation. Real GDP per capita tripled from 1900 to 1950; then it tripled again from 1950 to 2000, reaching $35,970.

The wealth didn't benefit just a few. It spread throughout society. For many people, owning a home defines the American Dream, and 68 percent of families now do—the highest percentage on record. Three-quarters of Americans drive their own cars. The vast majority of households possess color televisions (98 percent), videocassette recorders (94 percent), microwave ovens (90 percent), frost-free refrigerators (87 percent), washing machines (83 percent), and clothes dryers (75 percent). In the past decade or so, computers and cell phones have become commonplace.

As people become wealthier, they continue to consume more, but they also look to take care of other needs and wants. They typically choose to forgo at least some additional goods and services, taking a portion of their new wealth in other forms.

Compared to previous generations, today's Americans are starting work later in life, spending less time on chores at home, and living longer after retirement. All told, 70 percent of a typical American's waking life-time hours are available for leisure, up from 55 percent in 1950.

Consider a nation that rapidly increases its productive capacity with each passing generation. Workers could toil the same number of hours, taking all of the gains as consumption. They may choose to do so for a while, but eventually they will give up some potential material gains for better working conditions or additional leisure. Hours of work shrink. Workplaces become more comfortable. In the same way, we give up consumption in favor of safety, security, variety, convenience, and a cleaner environment.

Less Work, More Play

In the early years of the Industrial Revolution, most Americans were poor, and they wanted, above all, more goods and services. These factory workers sharply improved their lives as consumers, even though for most of them it meant long hours of toil in surroundings we'd consider abominable today. As America grew richer, what workers wanted began to change, and leisure became a higher priority.

Few of us want to dedicate every waking hour to earning money. Free time allows us to relax and enjoy ourselves, spend time with family and friends. Higher pay means that each hour of work yields more consumption—in essence, the price for an hour of leisure is going up—but we're still choosing to work less than ever before. According to economists' estimates and Department of Labor figures, the average workweek shrank from 59 hours in 1890 to 40 hours in 1950. Although today we hear stories about harried, overworked Americans who never seem to have enough time, the proportion of time spent on the job has continued to fall. Average weekly hours for production workers dropped from 39 in 1960 to 34 in 2001.

Since 1950 time off for holidays has doubled, to an average of 12 days a year. We've added an average of four vacation days a year. Compared to previous generations, today's Americans are starting work later in life, spending less time on chores at home, and living longer after retirement. All told, 70 percent of a typical American's waking lifetime hours are available for leisure, up from 55 percent in 1950.

Even at work, Americans aren't always doing the boss's bidding. According to University of Michigan time diary studies, the average worker spends more than an hour a day engaged in something other than assigned work while on the job. Employees run errands, socialize with colleagues, make personal telephone calls, send e-mail, and surf the Internet. More than a third of American workers, a total of 42 million, access the Internet during working hours. The peak hours for submitting bids on eBay, the popular online auction site, come between noon and 6 p.m., when most Americans are supposedly hard at work.

With added leisure, the United States has turned arts, entertainment, and recreation into a huge industry. Since 1970, attendance per 100,000 people has risen for symphonies, operas, and theaters as well as for national parks and big-league sporting events. The annual *Communications Industry Forecast*, compiled by New York-based Veronis, Suhler & Associates, indicates that we watch an average of 58 hours of movies at home each year. Yet Americans go out to an average of 5.4 movies a year, up from 4.5 three decades ago.

Adjusted for inflation, per capita spending on recreation nearly quadrupled in the last three decades. Leisure and recreation are even important enough to have become an academic subject: 350 colleges and universities offer degree programs in it.

The number of amusement parks has increased from 362 in 1970 to 1,164 today. The number of health and fitness facilities has more than doubled, to 11,241. Adjusted for inflation, per capita spending on recreation nearly quadrupled in the last three decades. Leisure and recreation are even important enough to

have become an academic subject: 350 colleges and universities offer degree programs in it.

The explosion of leisure spending and activities confirms the addition of more free time to our lives. If we hadn't reduced our hours of work, we couldn't spend as much time and money as we do on entertainment and recreation. Americans may find themselves pressed for time, but it's not because we're working harder than we used to. We're busy having fun.

Better Work Too

As the Industrial Revolution arrived in the 19th century, workers migrated from family farms to factories, from the Old World to the New World. They saw their paychecks rise but became, like Charlie Chaplin's character in *Modern Times*, mere cogs in a vast engine of mass production. Work was often brutal. Early factories were noisy, smelly, and dirty; they were cold in the winter and hot in the summer. The labor itself was repetitive, physically exhausting, and often dangerous. It was a time of mind-numbing repetition, standing on assembly lines, nose to the conveyor belt. To eke out a meager living, employees toiled an average of 10 hours a day, Monday through Friday, plus another half-day on the weekend. Breaks were few and far between. Work rules were draconian: no talking, no eating or drinking, not a minute late punching the time clock.

We've come a long way since then. For the most part, modern work takes place in a clean, well-lit, and air conditioned environment. A growing number of modern workplaces offer on-the-job amenities previous generations didn't even contemplate, such as on-site day care for children, exercise facilities, and concierge services. More and more employees are getting paternity leave, stock options, personal days off, and paid sabbaticals.

Jeans, sport shirts, and slacks are in. Ties and pantyhose are out. A July 2000 survey by the catalog retailer Land's End found that dress had become more casual in the previous five years at more than 80 percent of *Fortune* 500 firms.

More Americans than ever are free to choose the time and place for work, as long as the job gets done. In 1997, 28 percent of American workers were on flexible schedules, double the percentage in 1985. With laptop computers, cell phones, fax machines, electronic mail, and the Internet, fewer employees are tethered to the office. Telecommuting began with a handful of workers three decades ago. By 2001, 29 million Americans worked at least part of the time away from their companies' places of business.

Work isn't just more pleasant. It's also safer. Occupational injuries and illnesses, as tallied by the National Safety Council, are at an all-time low of 63 per 1,000 workers. The number of Americans killed on the job has fallen to a record low of 38 per million workers, down from 87 in 1990 and 214 in 1960.

Safer workplaces come in part from fewer accidents in such dangerous occupations as construction and manufacturing, At the same time, our economic base is shifting toward services, where jobs are less risky. The nature of the work we do is changing too. For most Americans in past generations, long days on the job involved tasks that were repetitive, physically exhausting, and often dangerous. Modern work is more likely to require analytical and interpersonal skills. Fewer employees make their livings with their backs and hands.

Jobs Rated Almanac 2001 provides a handy database of 300 occupations, ranked from best to worst. To focus on working conditions rather than pay, wages are taken out of the equation. Once that's done, it's clear our employment base is shifting in a positive direction. Since 1970 the 30 best jobs—including computer scientist, legal assistant, and engineer—have risen from 9 percent to 13 percent of total employment. At the same time, the 30 worst occupations—from logger to textile mill worker—have declined from 13 percent to 9 percent of all jobs. The trend toward better jobs is likely to continue. The Bureau of Labor Statistics estimates that the 10 best jobs will grow by 27 percent through 2008, while the 30 worst jobs will expand by just 7 percent.

Making workplaces more pleasant takes money. The added expense figures, along with wages, into the overall bill for labor. Companies pay it to attract new workers and retain those already on board. Employers shouldn't care whether the money goes for wages, time off, or working conditions. By their decisions on where to work, employees reveal their preferences.

Safer Lives

Although concerns about security have come to the fore since September 11, we shouldn't forget how far the United States has already come in making life safer. The toll of death and disease has been steadily reduced. Annual deaths per 1 million people are at an all-time low. The age-adjusted death rate has fallen by two-thirds since 1900. Fatalities from nearly all major diseases, tracked by the U.S. Centers for Disease Control and Prevention, have declined sharply from their peak rates. The rate of fatalities per 100,000 due to natural causes has fallen from 767 in 1950 to 422 in 1998, the most recent year for which data are available. The incidence of accidental deaths, both at home and on the job, is declining. So are fatalities associated with floods, tornadoes, and hurricanes.

Gains in transportation safety have been dramatic. In the five-year period ending in 2000, according to the Federal Highway Administration, annual deaths on American roads averaged 16 per billion miles driven, compared with 53 in the five years ending in 1970 and 83 for the post-World War II years. The Air Transportation Association reports that deaths per billion passenger miles flown fell from 16.7 a year in 1946–50 to 1.3 in 1966–70 to 0.14 in 1996–2000.

As a wealthy nation, we can afford to spend time and money to reduce life's risks. We can buy alarms for our homes and cars. We can buy insurance on our property and our lives. We can reduce the financial risks of illness and old age by taking part of our pay in health benefits and retirement savings.

We can also shift resources to the military to create an even more fearsome fighting force. During World War 11, defense spending per capita averaged $3,475 a year in today's dollars,

or 29 percent of total output. Today, each American's share of the defense budget comes to $1,079, just 3 percent of GDP.

Making America a safer place owes much to advances in engineering and technology. Divided highways, better roads, anti-lock brakes, radial tires, and air bags are reducing the highway death toll. More-sophisticated weather forecasting gear provides warnings of severe weather, so we can take refuge in time.

New medicines and treatments have reduced the incidence of fatal diseases. More are probably on the way. The stock market values the nation's 10 largest pharmaceutical companies at more than $1 trillion, an indication that we expect their sales to grow from future advances in health.

Greater safety and security didn't come about by accident. It's what we, as a people, wanted. We put a high value on our lives and physical well-being, and we're willing to pay the costs of protecting ourselves against the sometimes unpleasant facts of life.

Life is inherently risky, and protecting ourselves must be weighed against the considerations of cost and convenience. We'll never achieve a perfect safety record. In an uncertain world, we possess the wealth to afford more safety and security and the know-how to provide it, if that's what we decide we want.

A Safer, Healthier Life

	1970	The Latest *
Age-adjusted death rate per 100,000 people	1,222.6	872.4
Deaths per 100,000 people from 15 leading diseases	**731.6**	**605.3**
Accidental deaths in the home per 1 million people	132.0	107.0
Work-related deaths per 1 million workers	**178.0**	**38.0**
Deaths per billion miles driven	53.3	15.9
Deaths per billion miles flown	**1.3**	**0.14**
Homicide deaths per 1 million people	79.0	57.0
Deaths per 100 tornadoes per 100,000 people	**6.8**	**1.8**
Deaths per hurricane per 100,000 people	10.1	3.3
Life expectancy at birth	**70.8**	**77.1**
Median age of the population	28.1	35.3
Injuries per 100 full- time workers in manufacturing	**15.2**	**7.8**
Incidence per 100,000 people of 14 reportable diseases	659.0	184.0

* Years range from 1999 to 2000 depending on the original source.
Source: Federal Reserve Bank of Dallas

Convenience and Variety

By introducing industrial efficiency to his factories, Henry Ford brought the automobile within the reach of an emerging middle class. The miracle of mass production delivered the goods but didn't adapt easily, so all Model T's looked alike. Ford's attitude can be summed up in what he reputedly said about the car's paint: "The consumer can have any color he wants, as long as it's black." Ford's company still makes black cars for drivers who want them, but it now offers a rainbow of colors: red, green, aquamarine, white, silver, purple.

The U.S. marketplace teems with variety. Just since the early 1970s, there's been an explosion of choice: The number of car models is up from 140 to 239, soft drinks from 50 to more than 450, toothpaste brands from four to 35, over-the-counter pain relievers from two to 41.

The market offers 7,563 prescription drugs, 3,000 beers, 340 kinds of breakfast cereal, 50 brands of bottled water. Plain milk sits on the supermarket shelf beside skim milk, 0.5-percent-fat milk, 1-percent-fat milk, 2-percent-fat milk, lactose-reduced milk, hormone-free milk, chocolate milk, buttermilk, and milk with a shelf life of six months. Not long ago, the typical TV viewer had access to little more than NBC, CBS, ABC, and PBS. Today, more than 400 channels target virtually every consumer interest—science, history, women's issues, Congress, travel, animals, foreign news, and more.

Like variety, convenience has emerged as a hallmark of our times. Companies compete for business by putting their products and services within easy reach of their customers.

In 1970 the nation's lone automated teller machine was at the main office of the Chemical Bank in New York. Now ATMs are ubiquitous—not just at banks but at supermarkets, service stations, workplaces, sports facilities, and airports. All told, 273,000 machines offer access to cash 24 hours a day.

Remote controls are proliferating, the newest models incorporating voice-activated technology. Computers and digital devices go with us everywhere. A cell phone is no longer a pricey luxury: The average bill fell from $150 a month in 1988 to $45 in 2001 in constant dollars. No wonder 135 million Americans now own mobile telephones. The number will continue to rise as prices continue to decline and more of us seek the peace of mind and convenience that come with communications in the pocket or purse.

Convenience stores are in nearly every neighborhood. Just one firm, industry leader 7-Eleven, has increased its locations from 3,734, in 1970 to 21,142 today. The Internet may be the ultimate convenience store, bringing shopping into the home. We're buying music, clothing, software, shoes, toys, flowers, and other products with a click of the mouse. Last year, a third of all computers and a fifth of all peripherals were sold online. Thirty-three million buyers ordered books on the Internet, accounting for $1 of every $8 spent in that category.

Convenience and variety aren't trivial extravagances. They're a wealthy, sophisticated society's way of improving consumers' lot. The more choices, the easier access to goods and services, the better. A wide selection of goods and services increases the chance that each of us will find, somewhere among all the shelves, showrooms, and Web sites, products that meet our requirements. Convenience allows us to economize on the valuable commodity of time, getting what we want more quickly and easily.

A Cleaner Environment

The environment presents a textbook case for tradeoffs between consumption and other aspects of life. Traditionally, economists teach that markets undervalue clean air, fresh water, pristine vistas, and endangered species because they aren't owned, like factories, houses, or other private property. Without clear title and market prices, there's little economic incentive to reduce pollution or husband resources. The nation's natural assets end up underpriced and overexploited.

GDP may be accurate as a tally of how much our farms, factories, and offices produce, but it's increasingly inadequate as a measure of how well the economy provides us with what we want. Our ability to choose a balanced life is one of the market's most important success stories.

Our desire for a balanced life mitigates the classic dilemma of market failure and the environment. A wealthier nation possesses the time, money, and inclination to shift the balance from exploiting the environment to preserving it. We want clean air and water for reasons of health, recreation, and aesthetics. We've developed a sense of moral obligation toward lesser species. We find unspoiled nature pleasant—although we tend to want clean linens and good food along with it.

Our desires have had a dramatic effect in recent decades. Levels of such major air pollutants as particulate matter, sulfur oxides, volatile organic compounds, carbon monoxide, and lead were at their peaks in 1970 or earlier. Levels of nitrogen oxides peaked in 1980. Water quality has improved since the 1960s, when authorities banned fishing in Lake Erie. Through government and private foundations, we're spending billions of dollars every year to preserve natural areas from development and save threatened species from extinction.

Capitalism's penchant for innovation is helping us act on our concern for the environment. We've developed less polluting gases for air conditioning systems, so we can stay cool at a lower cost to air quality. Fish farms are creating another compromise, providing salmon for our dinner tables while reducing fishing for wild species.

Taking better care of the environment is a natural extension of economic progress. At one time, the air in Pittsburgh was very dirty. It was the price we were willing to pay for all those consumer goods the industrial age offered. It wasn't that we liked pollution; it was just that the price of cleaner air was too high. Today, having grown richer, we can afford the pollution controls that have made Pittsburgh's air sweeter than an ocean breeze. Exploitation of the environment is worst in poor countries, where the economic imperative lies in producing the food, goods, and services needed for daily life. Wealthier countries possess the means and motive for a balanced life, and they do a better job of taking care of their surroundings.

Beyond Statistics

The statistics that measure our economy are reasonably good at counting the value of the cars, clothing, food, sports gear, jewelry, and other goods and services we buy. When we choose an additional hour off over additional income, though, GDP shrinks with the loss of the hour's income and output. We don't count leisure as an economic benefit because we haven't assigned a dollar value to it, even though we opt for time off because it improves our lives.

When it comes to many aspects of a balanced life, our economic barometers come up short. Safety and security are all about preventing bad things from happening. Increased spending on highway safety registers in GDP, but we don't track how much better off we are because of the accidents, injuries, and deaths we avoid. If investing in prevention works, it can actually reduce total output, at least the way we measure it, because less money is spent treating the sick and injured, repairing damage, and replacing lost property.

Variety makes products more valuable by giving us the designs, colors, and features that fit our preferences, but the statistics count everything as plain vanilla. How conveniently our wants and needs are fulfilled doesn't matter to GDP. A cleaner environment makes for a better country, but it may come at the cost of economic growth.

Inflation-adjusted GDP figures indicate economic growth at an annual average of 3 percent during the last two decades. GDP may be entirely accurate as a tally of how much our farms, factories, and offices produce, but it's increasingly inadequate as a measure of how well the economy provides us with what we want. Our ability to choose a balanced life is one of the market's most important success stories.

Some may argue that it isn't the market that makes a balanced life possible. They might concede that our economy produces abundant goods and services, but they credit government agencies, with their regulations, and unions and pressure groups, with their advocacy, for everything else. History tells us government and advocates play their roles, but they aren't the ultimate source of progress. They don't foot the bill for the choices we make to gain a balanced life. Whatever we want must be paid for, and money ultimately comes from the economy.

Companies improve working conditions because they can afford to, not simply because workers, unions, or government agencies demand it. The dismal work environments in now-defunct socialist nations—all supposedly designed to benefit the worker and eradicate the capitalist—provide a powerful testament to the fact that good intentions are hollow without the ability to pay.

The main role of collective action has been to act as a voice for what we want. Environmental groups formed as the result of our desire for cleaner air and water. When we take our preferences for leisure and better working conditions to unions or elected officials, they help create consensus among employees and lower the cost of communicating these desires to employers.

In the long run, we cannot afford any component of a balanced life—be it consumption, leisure, easier workdays, safety and security, variety and convenience, or environmental cleanup—that we don't earn by becoming more productive. When counting our blessings, we should first thank the economic system. Not federal agencies, not advocacy groups, not unions.

Our quest for a balanced life will never end. The U.S. economy, now recovering from its first recession in a decade, will make our society wealthier in the years ahead. We'll take some of our gains in goods and services, but we will also continue to satisfy our desires for the less tangible aspects of life.

W. Michael Cox (wm.cox@dal.frb.org), senior vice president and chief economist at the Federal Reserve Bank of Dallas, and Richard Alm (rgalm@aol.com), a business writer for The Dallas Morning News, are the authors of Myths of Rich and Poor: Why We're Better Off Than We Think (Basic Books).

Establishing Rules for the NEW WORKPLACE

"The forces of technology, globalization, deregulation, shareholder power, and free agency have combined to change the social contract between the individual and the organization."

BY JOHN A. CHALLENGER

FOR AMERICAN BUSINESSES and their employees, the rules on such basic issues as hiring and layoffs, work schedules, and corporate structure are changing at a rapid pace. They are driven by macro forces such as globalization and the rise of shareholder power, as well as more-personal decisions, like the desire to balance work and family life or to keep on working past traditional retirement age.

For example, there is a fusion going on between home and work. We cannot get away from work when we are at home, and we cannot get away from home when we are at work. I recently visited the Northern Telecom headquarters in Toronto, Canada—an indoor city complete with a main street, cyber café, dry cleaners, video rental, exercise studio, museum, pharmacy, bank, kitchens, recreation rooms, and sleeping quarters.

In fact, childcare and eldercare centers in many offices today mean that your offspring and parents are there, too! The only home-oriented things missing from the millennium workplace are churches and synagogues, but I have been hearing more and more about spirituality in the workplace.

On the other hand, we cannot get away from work even when we are not there. Since the film "2001: A Space Odyssey" debuted more than three decades ago, we have been wondering when computers would become human or superhuman. What sneaked up behind us was the opposite: Human beings are becoming increasingly electronic. We carry our cell phones, beepers, fax machines, e-mail, portable CD players, and laptops—our office—with us at all times.

Our cell phones are ringing off the hook. Commuting to an office is not downtime because there are customers to be called. On the morning or evening commuter train, there used to be a subtle taboo about talking on a cell phone, but that has disappeared. We can look to Hong Kong for the future. When you go into some restaurants there, you aren't asked about smoking or nonsmoking, but whether you wish to be seated in the section where you can leave your cell phone on. Golf courses around the U.S. are banning the use of cell phones during play.

When you leave for vacation, the office wants to know where you are going to be. One woman executive recently told me that she sat on the beach in the Dominican Republic talking on her cell phone until 3 p.m. Satellite technology and global positioning mean there is no place to hide. The one place and time when you cannot be reached is on a plane during takeoff and landing, and that's only because of Federal regulations.

The global marketplace further erodes our personal time. Three major business zones are forming: the Americas, Europe/Africa, and Asia. If American businesses have customers who need servicing in Asia, it is essential that they work from 5 p.m. to 11 p.m.; for customers in Europe, they better be up at 3 a.m.

All of this technology makes workers highly mobile, and some companies never want them at a central office facility. Consultants today spend their workweeks on the road, in the air, and at the customer site. Four or five days of travel are not unusual. If they do need an office, they are often ho-teling, checking in with the receptionist in Dallas, being assigned an office, hooking into the network, and turning on the cell phone so that customers, clients, bosses, colleagues, direct reports, and copier and financial services salesmen can reach them 24 hours a day at any location in the country. Two days later, it may be Pittsburgh, where they greet a new receptionist who assigns a similar-looking office. Bringing their children's pictures in a briefcase to set on the desk helps to personalize the equipment.

The line between work and home, public and private, is increasingly blurry. Multiple e-mail addresses and phone numbers are one way to try to redraw those boundaries. I need an e-mail address that is my personal one for family and friends, a different one for work, and I would love still another one for all the junk e-mail that comes my way. I worry about what happens if too many junk mailers get my personal e-mail. Will I have to keep changing identities? I don't have the time to wade through all of the e-mails I get every day. Now, I have to check two different names several times a day. This change has happened so suddenly that we were not prepared.

The overburdened worker must reclaim some of those boundaries. Tell your employer: I do not want to be called on the weekend or on vacation (except in an emergency). Do not take your cell phone with you when you are in your car; you might get in an accident while concentrating on soothing an irate customer. Don't travel on Saturdays and Sundays.

The problem is, you might lose your job. One side effect of all these technological advances and the rise of a global economy is that no one's job is ever totally secure and no company can remain an industry leader without constant innovation and attention to the bottom line.

How did we get here? Let's take a look back at the ways life has changed for American companies and workers in the last few decades.

The former economic system in the U.S. was characterized by a variety of structures that restricted the flow of people. Lifetime employment was a goal that companies and individuals alike hoped to achieve. When individuals accepted employment offers, they expected, as long as they did not do anything too wrong—like coming in late constantly, embarrassing the boss, or embezzling funds—that their jobs would be safe. The cornerstone of the social contract between the organization and the individual was long-term—even lifetime—employment.

Individual identity was tied in with the company. IBM employees thought themselves privileged because of their identification with the organization. Big Blue hired the best and the brightest. People built their lives around the company. Often, a worker's closest friends came from within it. People closely integrated their working and personal lives. They bore witness to each other's lives, developing deep, solid, secure relationships over a lifetime. It was not unusual for coworkers to be godparents of each other's children.

After God and family, loyalty to the company was at the top of the value scale. The employee trusted the firm would provide job security; the employee returned that loyalty in kind, by pledging not to leave and certainly never thinking seriously about working for the competition. In fact, most workers cultivated an authentic dislike for rival companies. In the 1960s and 1970s, most of our outplacement clients, who had been terminated by their former employers, refused to even consider working for other companies in the same industry, willingly sacrificing organizations that had a special need for their industry knowledge.

There was a balance between shareholders and stakeholders. The latter—in this case meaning employees and communities—were once critical factors in long-term strategic decisions by companies. Moving plants and warehouses and jobs to another area of the country or world was unthinkable because of the damage it would do to the local community.

Hiring by big companies occurred mostly at the entry level. The Fortune 500 did not bring in many people over 40. The primary entry point into the organization occurred soon after graduation. New hires entered onto an upward, progressive career track until they plateaued or "Peter-principled."

CEO power and control were at their zenith, while a rubber-stamp advisory board of directors was not unusual. Often, CEOs handpicked the board members, who might be third- or fourth-generation family members, or the positions were sinecures for VIPs. Many did not serve even in an advisory role; the board membership was largely ceremonial.

The dominant cultural archetype was the Organization Man, who sacrificed his own goals for the good of the company. Refusing to take on an assignment meant the end of one's career growth. A firm could not trust an individual who did not put the organization first, ahead of more-personal and selfish needs like family and friends and roots.

Unions were predominant and effective. It was taken for granted that unions had won the battle for job security, so labor focused on other goals like better wages and working conditions. A company that sought to terminate the employment of a union member needed an ironclad case of wrongful behavior, and still could expect a battle from the union.

U.S. companies focused on domestic labor markets. They did not build plants overseas, especially to manufacture products for domestic markets. A large network of support companies spread out around a region—*e.g.,* in the Midwest, suppliers and original equipment manufacturers burgeoned and eventually surrounded the auto industry in Detroit. Shipping and logistics costs were prohibitive and effectively prevented companies from locating operations in other parts of the world.

The forces of change

Several primary forces brought about systemic change in the economy in the 1980s and 1990s. The American economic system, which had come of age after World War II and grew unchecked until the Vietnam War, was beset by economic and social crises.

Globalization forced the U.S. out of its isolation. Companies began to look for new markets overseas. Coca-Cola and McDonald's spread throughout the world. NAFTA, GATT, and free trade brought down barriers that had once prevented a more-open flow of goods and services and human resources around the world. Inevitably, the law of unintended consequences took effect on the American economy. Protected industries like automakers faced serious competition from overseas for the first time, with devastating consequences. Chrysler came within a hair's breadth of closing down, and General Motors announced it was cutting 74,000 jobs in December, 1991, the single-largest downsizing of the 1990s—and perhaps ever.

Technology and automation transformed the way companies operated. The PC revolution brought power to the desktop that was unimaginable a few decades before. Enterprise software programs, laptops, cell phones, e-mail and the Internet, e-commerce, business-to-business exchanges/alliances, and supply chain destruction and reformulation—these technological phenomena have emerged in rapid succession.

Big computer makers like IBM lost their dominant position because of an onslaught of competition from Apple and other companies making PC clones. IBM announced the second-largest downsizing of the 1990s, with 63,000 job cuts in July, 1993.

Diversity and antidiscrimination forces that flowered in the 1960s worked their way into the mainstream. There was a strong push from outsider segments of the population on the moral, legal, and legislative front to repair age, gender, race, and ethnicity discrimination damage. The fact that the dominant social group—white males—could expect to face discrimination once they reached their 50s contributed to a recognition of the fundamental unfairness and the eventual breakdown of the former caste system.

The deregulation of protected industries in the 1980s and 1990s created competition for companies where none had previously existed. The telecom, banking, energy, and aerospace industries were roiled by the change. The big bureaucratic corporations that had dominated these protected industries were forced to compete in an open market and started letting people go in sizable numbers in the early 1990s. It was not surprising that telecom, financial services, and aerospace dominated the list of those experiencing the heaviest downsizing in the early to mid 1990s.

Shareholder activism grew unchecked as more and more people started to invest their savings, IRAs, and 401(k)s. Today, shareholders seat members on boards of directors; they scrutinize and second-guess every decision of the CEO and have access to swaths of information about companies that were once hidden; and they dole out swift punishment to the share price of companies that underperform.

The forces outlined above combined to create a new set of "rules of the game" in the American workplace. In the 1990s, companies stopped thinking about holding onto steady workforce levels during periods of slowdown. Today, when orders and revenue increase, organizations hire more people; when business drops, they are quick to eliminate idle hands and downsize. Companies constantly scrutinize their operations, jettisoning products and services that are losing market share, becoming marginally profitable, or coming to the end of the product life cycle.

It is no wonder that the term "personnel" gave way in the 1990s to "human resources," which is not a far cry from "human capital," a phrase that is creeping into wider usage today. Companies such as Dell Computer led the movement toward "just-in-time inventory principles," taking the slack out of the supply chain. Now, those principles have filtered into the employment sphere. As leaders of companies began to think of their employees as resources and capital, they realized that people who "sat on the shelf" during periods of order slowdown were an economic liability. The problem was even more apparent to shareholders, who saw that employment costs were the heaviest expense on the balance sheet in a service economy.

In periods of recession, companies do not just shed the bottom performers. They slash and burn. In the recession of 2001, the first one in which the new rules of the game were fully in place, downsizing escalated to nearly 2,000,000 job cuts.

The large number of temporaries, contractors, and consultants at American companies today constitute a "flexible employment system." Not only is a segment of the blue-collar workforce permanently temporary and project-based, but we also have seen the creation and exponential growth of large-scale organizations of highly talented temporary business experts such as Deloitte & Touche, Accenture, and McKinsey. When a downturn hits, companies can immediately cut back on costs by eliminating temporaries, overtime, perks, and various other soft benefits put in place to attract the best workers in times of expansion.

When orders begin to mount, companies can cautiously add man-hours, output,

and productivity by hiring the growing army of people who work on a part-time, project basis. As the recovery gets legs, prospering businesses can convert these workers to full-time positions. Business owners can buy time to make sure that another dip is not in the offing as they wind up the recruiting machinery. In past recessions, unemployment continued to worsen as economic recovery began. Enhanced technological ability to detect new orders quickly, combined with flexible workforce options, should act to diminish this traditional unemployment lag.

Entrepreneurialism exploded in the 1990s as a generation of young people lost faith in the large Fortune 500 companies after witnessing the despair and outrage of their downsized parents. Most of the extraordinary job creation of the 1990s— more than 21,000,000 new ones—came from the small-business sector. Workers in the U.S. possess a risky, yet highly viable, option when they are asked to leave an organization. They can start their own business, buy a franchise, or hang out a shingle as a self-employed free agent. Entrepreneurialism thrives in the U.S. to a degree that is not found anywhere else in the world. Bright, highly educated, hardworking, newly discharged managers and non-big company types start up new businesses and avoid the politics and whims of large organizations.

The influence of the stakeholder and the shareholder in corporate decisions and governance that once was evenly balanced has tilted significantly over to the side of the shareholder. In 2002, the shareholder is king. In the bear market of 2001, 50% hits to the stock price were not unusual when a company failed to meet its quarterly numbers. Such organizations must swiftly install cost-cutting programs when problems arise or risk the wrath of Wall Street. They take little account of the concerns of employees or communities—*i.e.*, the stakeholders—when revenues start to fall.

As individual identity has become uncoupled from a particular company, people have focused on functional career areas (*e.g.*, law, human resources, financial operations, sales and marketing, and manufacturing professionals). We are returning to an age of guilds, where people organize themselves professionally. In the last decade, professional associations and functional groupings have seen explosive membership gains as more and more individuals seek community, safety, certification, and networking opportunities in the

company of likeminded career professionals.

Employers have instituted a wide array of training and development programs in order to equip employees with appropriate technology skills. When companies are unable to find enough skilled workers trained in state-of-the-art technology, they hire people and train them on the job, supplemented with e-learning. Workers are incentivized through tuition reimbursement programs to acquire more training and to view their education as a lifelong process, rather than one ending in their 20s.

Home and family are much more important as people seek out a work/life balance. Women in the workplace, especially, have forced changes in how companies manage the boundary between home and work. Job sharing, telecommuting, sabbaticals, reentry into the workplace after the childbearing years, and transplacement programs to help the trailing spouse find a new job are examples of new initiatives offered to accommodate work/life needs. The baby boom generation of fathers is no longer happy with long-distance relationships with their young children, turning down jobs and promotions that require too much time away from home.

Discriminatory barriers to entry into the job market are falling. Age, sex, race, religion, and ethnicity biases are slowly being rooted out of the system at the legal, social, and educational levels. During the red-hot job market of the 1990s, when unemployment reached the lowest rate since the Vietnam War, companies had no choice but to hire people who otherwise would have been ignored. Biased managers took chances on individuals they normally would have avoided and were shocked to find that many of these former outsiders became the hardest-working employees in their respective departments. Meritocracy made major gains as the most-productive people became recognized for their achievements in the ultracompetitive, profit-driven economic environment of recent years.

Technological innovation has opened up the potential for enormous changes in the job marketplace. In the early 1990s, the Clinton Administration proposed a national job bank where accessibility to job openings would be coordinated and widely disseminated. The plan was abandoned, but the emergence of the Internet created the beginnings of a national source on the Web.

The Internet job bank facilitates the flow of workers to areas of the country where demand is high. The job-seeker who used to purchase the *Boston Globe* and the *Wall Street Journal* can now easily check out the classified ad sections from virtually every city in the country from his or her desktop. Each of these innovations speeds up throughput of workers to hot industries or regions, giving job-seekers and employers more options in times of recession and drying up pockets of unemployment in periods of economic expansion.

Another major innovation transforming how organizations and people come together is through systems like Resumix. These are huge corporate databases of candidates, allowing companies to locate appropriate workers on a scale unimaginable a few years back.

Not just U.S. workers are affected by these changes. We are moving into an era when the labor supply is global. Mexican *mequilladoras*, American middle managers working in Japanese-owned companies and vice versa, and technology workers from India and New Zealand (sometimes referred to as software factories) attest to the shrinking of the world and the internationalization of an unskilled and highly skilled workforce.

The rules have changed

Over the last decade, people have come to realize that the "rules of the game" have changed and, like Curt Flood, the baseball player who pioneered free agency in Major League Baseball, they must view themselves as free agents, willing to offer their services where and when they want and to the highest bidder. In increasing numbers, people are open to the idea of leaving jobs voluntarily for better ones, rather than waiting passively and reactively for the company to offer them a promotion or a pink slip.

Job boards like Monster have opened up wide possibilities for expansion of worker free agency. The secret and anonymous posting of resumés allows currently employed workers to advertise their skills confidentially to interested employers. The statistics for growth in voluntary job movement are impressive.

The new environment of just-in-time employment policies and no-fault job loss is truly democratic in that everyone from the CEO to the assembler on the third shift is vulnerable. The boss who terminates 10% of his workforce knows that he or she could easily be next. No matter the position and level, all jobs are precarious.

The recognition on the part of all individuals of common and shared job security/insecurity has led to the development of programs aimed at helping people bridge to their next job, and to the tacit expectation that all companies must provide a secure safety net to terminated individuals. The safety net that each individual has come to expect and feel entitled to in the case of job loss includes three primary components: severance, health insurance continuation, and outplacement services—job-seeking support to reduce the duration of unemployment and improve the quality of the worker's next position. Most organizations used to throw their people out on the street with no help at all, assuming that the termination was entirely the worker's fault and not the firm's. Today, ethical companies realize that the blame must be shared.

Despite our current troubles, it seems the government and Federal Reserve have used monetary and fiscal tools to smooth out the highs and lows of the economic cycle. It is also possible that the economy itself is more resilient, better able to weather the economic storms because of deregulation domestically, free trade internationally, and the demise of other artificial constraints. If enhanced economic resiliency turns out to be true, then shorter, V-shaped recessions may be in our future—steep, short slowdowns with equally quick returns to periods of growth and long-term stability. Perhaps companies really are less flabby and more agile. Such freedom of movement may create an environment in which companies swiftly recognize upturns and invest in new areas of growth when the economy perks up.

For the moment, downsizing is still rampant. Companies must swiftly pare costs because of the profit recession. Shareholders insist that expenses fall in proportion to revenue declines to ensure that earnings remain steady. However, downsizing damages the organization in the long term as morale is irreparably harmed, corporate memory is lost, and continuity of decisionmaking is broken.

The forces of technology, globalization, deregulation, shareholder power, and free agency have combined to change the social contract between the individual and the organization. For workplace designers and suppliers, the new roles pose new challenges. How do you design space for a worker who is much more mobile?

Wireless technology is unchaining the worker from his or her desk or cubicle. In fact, it may have been the electrical and phone cables that tethered workers to their desks and offices in the first place. Fixed equipment is disappearing. Batteries are replacing cables and power supplies. Workers are carrying their offices on their backs and to their homes. For these "road warriors," the workplace is sometimes the car, airport, ballpark/golf course, or garden.

Employees who are telecommuting or constantly on the road can become isolated from the company and their fellow workers. In the free agent economy, people are changing jobs so often that it is hard really to get to know your coworkers over the long term. This creates more potential for isolation.

Corporate spending on training and development is up 25% in the last five years. Skills constantly need to be updated. The half-life of knowledge is decreasing. Companies are entering into more partnerships with community colleges and other educational institutions.

The workforce is aging. Each age group has its preferred method of working; young and old have different workstyles. At the same time, mentoring between young and old is very important to business continuity, corporate memory, and skills development. For women, the glass ceiling is breaking apart because young females are achieving many more advanced degrees than their male counterparts. These degrees are the keys to economic and social advancement. The new meritocracy of the educated elite is replacing the establishment that ruled in the U.S. through much of the 20th century.

The ultimate workplace tragedy—the terrorist attacks of Sept. 11—prompted concern about safety as well as a desire for more meaning from work and a stronger emphasis on community outside of the workplace, reinforcing many of the work/life issues already gaining prominence there.

Redesigning the workplace

Companies must take into account a separate, but related, set of issues in order to design a workplace that accommodates the new rules:

• Constantly changing size of the workforce

• Frequent strategic adjustments to maximize profit areas

• Unrelenting pressure to control fixed costs

• Customers, suppliers, and employees located around the world.

Given the issues racing workers and companies in this new era, the value of any workplace design will be measured by how well it addresses the needs of a business in four broad areas:

Flexibility. Companies are leasing less space and making greater use of it. Space and furniture must be multifunctional so that it can be used alternately for training, hoteling, conferencing, individualized offices, team projects, and big and small meetings. It must set up and dismantle quickly. Smart buildings will feature movable walls and adjustable lighting. Employees who are in the office only part time will share space, which can be converted easily into two or more private offices if circumstances change.

The global economy forces companies to be agile, building up and cutting back the workforce quickly in response to circumstances, altering products and services to meet changing demands. Office design and equipment must enable, not hinder, those moves if a company is to survive in the ultracompetitive economy.

Technology. Buildings must have the electronic infrastructure, including fiber-optic lines and routers, to support cutting-edge technology. Furniture must mold itself to the technology and increasingly smart buildings. Power is being "battery-ized" or wireless. How do you design space and furniture for people who carry their offices with them?

Again, flexibility is key because not all employees will be wireless road warriors. In fact, the multigenerational workplace means that technology comfort and adaptability run a wide spectrum. Each age group has a preferred method of working. You may need telephones and full-sized PCs in some offices, while other employees carry in and take home their cell phone and battery-powered flat-screen laptop.

If younger recruits don't see that the workplace is outfitted with the latest technology, or at least has the capability to "plug and play," they will assume the company is out of date. On the other hand, an aging workforce is not going to want to be overwhelmed by new technology. So, adaptable work stations that allow different age groups a way to connect become vital.

Community. Common and open or public areas are more important at companies increasingly populated by free agents and others who have little or no corporate loyalty or memory. The same technology that gives people the freedom to change jobs frequently and set their own schedules at work also leaves them isolated. Today, we see people coming together who have little mutual history individually or with the company. They have not developed the rapport that comes from working together for many years.

Spaces should be designed with common areas that force people together, such as war rooms to encourage strategic collaboration and teamwork, and areas that create water-cooler conversations, enhance productivity and make people want to stay. Post-Sept. 11, security-conscious companies will have less-conspicuous entrances and public areas for nonemployees, but public areas inside the workplace will be a vital design feature.

The changing rules of the workplace make the large corner office and its "aircraft-carrier" desk obsolete, an overt display of power and status within the workplace. Private offices will become smaller, accommodating hoteling salesmen, consultants, and temporary workers as well as those who spend hours in the office each day. Private space will be in the middle of the building and public rooms on the perimeter, with windows and lots of natural light. To maintain costs, some space could flip between public and private, with furniture that adapts to multiple purposes.

Work/life balance. Even if they share space with others or push a "personalized pedestal" with their files in it to a temporary office, workers need to express their identity with personal touches. Small shelves or other design features could make it easier to place family photos and other items that maintain a connection to home in the office. People want to feel they have their own identity within an organization. They do not want to be nameless or detached from their life outside of the workplace.

Flex-time, telecommuting, and the demands of the global, 24/7 economy stretch out the workweek, requiring that offices be functional at odd hours and weekends. For many companies, this means support staff cannot always be on hand, and supplies and tools must be readily available and us-able by employees at all levels. Firms might also invest in small satellite offices that are closer to some workers' homes and available for most functions.

A number of companies are bringing elements of the home into the workspace. The home-workplace fusion means sleeping quarters for a global workforce, living rooms, music, kitchen tables, couches, fishbowls, TVs, game rooms, fireplaces, coffeehouses, washing rooms, concierges, and cubbyholes. Many workers live in other areas of the country and may come to a city constantly or actually move there on a project basis for several months. Companies are providing the living and work-space for these people. Will organizations devote certain floors or areas to living space?

Finally, there is the issue of home offices. Are companies going to be forced at some point to start building home offices for their people? How will they manage the liability issues? What about personal design considerations?

Obviously, design makes a difference in how workers do their jobs and live their lives. Earlier, I mentioned that the telephone and its cable were important to the creation of office work. So were elevators and file cabinets. Technology will keep changing, and office design will evolve with it. More importantly, the structure of business organizations and the relationship between workers and companies has undergone a profound shift. A good deal of the future will be spent working on ways to improve the work environment to reflect this new reality.

There will be successes and failures. Think of the dot.com revolution and the changes it brought—open teaming, more color and edgy materials, and raw ceilings and floors. There was a backlash as well. Things became too loose. The time has come to bring back traditions and more professionalism.

No matter the era, the bottom line is always productivity. People need to come into an environment that is conducive to focusing and working hard, but also makes them comfortable. Like most good ideas, it sounds simple. The difficulty will be in the execution.

John A. Challenger is CEO of Challenger, Gray & Christmas, Inc., Chicago, Ill.

WHERE THE GOOD JOBS ARE GOING

Forget sweatshops. U.S. companies are now shifting high-wage work overseas, especially to India

By JYOTI THOTTAM

Little by little, Sab Maglione could feel his job slipping away. He worked for a large insurance firm in northern New Jersey, developing the software it uses to keep track of its agents. But in mid-2001, his employer introduced him to Tata Consultancy Services, India's largest software company. About 120 Tata employees were brought in to help on a platform-conversion project. Maglione, 44, trained and managed a five-person Tata team. When one of them was named manager, he started to worry. By the end of last year, 70% of the project had been shifted to India and nearly all 20 U.S. workers, including Maglione, were laid off.

Since then, Maglione has been able to find only temporary work in his field, taking a pay cut of nearly 30% from his former salary of $77,000. For a family and mortgage, he says, "that doesn't pay the bills." Worried about utility costs, he runs after his two children, 11 and 7, to turn off the lights. And he has considered a new career as a house painter. "It doesn't require that much skill, and I don't have to go to school for it," Maglione says. And houses, at least, can't be painted from overseas.

Jobs that stay put are becoming a lot harder to find these days. U.S. companies are expected to send 3.3 million jobs overseas in the next 12 years, primarily to India, according to a study by Forrester Research. If you've ever called Dell about a sick PC or American Express about an error on your bill, you have already bumped the tip of this "offshore outsourcing" iceberg. The friendly voice that answered your questions was probably a customer-service rep in Bangalore or New Delhi. Those relatively low-skilled jobs were the first to go, starting in 1997.

But more and more of the jobs that are moving abroad today are highly skilled and highly paid—the type that U.S. workers assumed would always remain at home. Instead Maglione is one of thousands of Americans adjusting to the unsettling new reality of work. "If I can get another three years in this industry, I'll be fortunate," he says. Businesses are embracing offshore outsourcing in their drive to stay competitive, and almost any company, whether in manufacturing or services, can find some part of its work that can be done off site. By taking advantage of lower wages overseas, U.S. managers believe they can cut their overall costs 25% to 40% while building a more secure, more focused work force in the U.S. Labor leaders—and nonunion workers, who make up most of those being displaced—aren't buying that rationale. "How can America be competitive in the long run sending over the very best jobs?" asks Marcus Courtney, president of the Seattle-based Washington Alliance of Technology Workers. "I don't see how that helps the middle class."

On the other side of the world, though, educated Indian workers are quickly adjusting to their new status as the world's most sought-after employees. They have never been more confident and optimistic—as Americans usually like to think of themselves. For now, at least, in ways both tangible and emotional, educated Americans and Indians are trading places.

INCOMING
Uma Satheesh
Bangalore, India

Satheesh, 32, manages 38 Wipro employees who work on networking software for Hewlett-Packard in Bangalore—in jobs that were once done mainly in the U.S.

Uma Satheesh, 32, an employee of Wipro, one of India's leading outsourcing companies, is among her country's new elite. She manages 38 people who work for Hewlett-Packard's enterprise-servers group doing maintenance, fixing defects and enhancing the networking software developed by HP for its clients. Her unit includes more than 300 people who work for HP, about 90 of whom were added last November when HP went through a round of cost-cutting.

"We've been associated with HP for a long time, so it was an emotional thing," Satheesh says. "It was kind of a mixed feeling. But that is happening at all the companies, and it's going to continue." Satheesh says that five years ago, computer-science graduates had one career option in India: routine, mind-numbing computer programming. Anything more rewarding required emigrating. "Until three years ago, the first preference was to go overseas," she says. Nowadays her colleagues are interested only in business trips to the U.S. "People are pretty comfortable with the

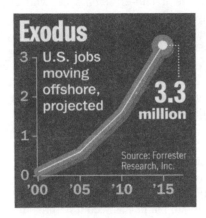

Exodus

U.S. jobs moving offshore, projected

3.3 million

Source: Forrester Research, Inc.

jobs here and the pay here"—not to mention the cars and houses that once seemed out of reach. Employees in her group earn from $5,200 a year to $36,000 for the most experienced managers.

And as American companies have grown more familiar with their Indian outsourcing partners, they have steadily increased the complexity of work they are willing to hand over. Rajeshwari Rangarajan, 28, leads a team of seven Wipro workers enhancing the intranet site on which Lehman Brothers employees manage personal benefits like their 401(k) accounts. "I see myself growing with every project that I do here," Rangarajan says. "I really don't have any doubts about the growth of my career."

Her experience with a leading brokerage will probably help. Financial-services companies in the U.S. are expected to move more than 500,000 jobs overseas in the next five years, according to a survey by management consultant A.T. Kearney, and India is by far the top destination. U.S. banks, insurance firms and mortgage companies have been using outsourcing to handle tech support for years. Now these firms are using Indian workers to handle the business operations—say, assessing loan applications and credit checks—that the technology supports. Kumar Mahadeva, CEO of the thriving outsourcing firm Cognizant, explains the appeal: "It becomes logical for them to say, 'Hey, you know everything about the way we do claims processing. Why not take a piece of it?'"

The next logical step, says Andrea Bierce, a co-author of the A.T. Kearney study, is jobs that require more complex financial skills such as equity research

and analysis or market research for developing new business. Evalueserve, a niche outsourcing company in Delhi, already performs research for patent attorneys and consulting firms in the U.S. In April, J.P. Morgan Chase said it would hire about 40 stock-research analysts in Bombay—about 5% of its total research staff. Novartis employs 40 statisticians in Bombay who process data from the drug company's clinical research.

OUTSOURCED
Bernie Lantz
Logan, Utah

Lantz, 58, says offshore hirings made his troubleshooting job with a Texas software firm obsolete. He left the tech business to teach computer science at Utah State University

But as educated workers in India are finding new opportunities, those in the U.S. feel the doors closing. Last week Bernie Lantz drove 1,400 miles from his home in Plano, Texas, to begin a new life in Utah. He is 58 years old, a bachelor, and had lived in the Dallas area for 24 years. "I'm leaving all my friends," he says with a sigh. "It's quite an upheaval." Lantz used to earn $80,000 a year as a troubleshooter for Sabre, a company based in Southlake, Texas, whose software powers airline-reservations systems. But over the past two years, Sabre has gradually standardized and has centralized its software service. As Sabre began to outsource its internal IT services, Lantz says, he became convinced that jobs like his were becoming endangered. He was laid off in December. (A company spokesman denies that Lantz's firing was related to outsourcing.)

Discouraged by a depressed job market in Dallas, Lantz realized he would have to do something else. In the fall he will begin teaching computer science at Utah State University in Logan, and in the meantime he has learned a lesson of his own: "Find a job that requires direct hands-on work on site," Lantz advises. "Anything that can be sent overseas is going to be sent overseas."

Pat Fluno, 53, of Orlando, Fla., says she, like Maglione, had to train her replacement—a common practice in the

Playing the Savings Game		
As these average-salary figures show, outsourcing lowers costs		
SOFTWARE PROGRAMMER U.S. $66,100 INDIA $10,000		
MECHANICAL ENGINEER U.S. $55,600 INDIA $5,900		
IT MANAGER U.S. $55,000 INDIA $8,500		
ACCOUNTANT U.S. $41,000 INDIA $5,000		
FINANCIAL OPERATIONS U.S. $37,625 INDIA $5,500		
Sources: PayScale Inc; the Paàras Group		

domestic outsourcing industry—when her data-processing unit at Germany-based Siemens was outsourced to India's Tata last year. "It's extremely insulting," she says. "The guy's sitting there doing my old job." After 10 months of looking, she is working again, but she had to take a $10,000 pay cut.

BYPASSED
Pat Fluno
Orlando, Fla.

Fluno's 12-person data-processing unit at the local Siemens operation was replaced by a team from Tata Consultancy Services in India. It took her 10 months—and a $10,000 cut in pay—to find a new job.

To protect domestic jobs, U.S. labor activists are pushing to limit the number of H-1B and L-1 visas granted to foreign workers. That would make it harder for offshore companies to have their employees working on site in the U.S. "Those programs were designed for a booming high-tech economy, not a busting high-tech economy," says Courtney of the Washington Alliance of Technology Workers. Courtney and his allies are starting to get the attention of lawmakers. Several congressional committees have held hearings on the impact of offshore outsourcing on the U.S. economy, and lawmakers in five states have introduced bills that would limit or forbid filling government contracts through offshore outsourcing.

Stephanie Moore, a vice president of Forrester Research, says companies are concerned about the backlash but mainly because of the negative publicity. "The retail industry is very hush-hush about its offshoring," she says. But within the boardroom, such outsourcing enjoys wide support. In a June survey of 1,000 firms by Gartner Research, 80% said the backlash would have no effect on their plans.

The advantages, businesses say, are just too great to ignore. They begin with cost but don't end there. Jennifer Cotteleer, vice president of Phase Forward, a Waltham, Mass., company that designs software for measuring clinical-trials data for drug companies, has for the past two years used offshore employees from Cognizant to customize the application for specific drug trials. Lately she has been relying on their expertise to develop even more-tailored programming. "I certainly couldn't have grown this fast without them," Cotteleer says. Her company is growing 30% annually, on track to reach $65 million in revenue this year. "What I've been able to do in very tough economic times is manage very directly to my margins," she says. "I'm providing job security for the workers I do have."

Creative use of offshore outsourcing, says Debashish Sinha of Gartner Research, offers benefits that outweigh the direct loss of jobs. In an economy that has shed 2 million jobs over two years, he contends, the 200,000 that have moved overseas are less significant than the potential for cost savings and strategic growth. But he concedes that "when you're a laid-off employee who can't find a job, that's hard to understand."

Perhaps some will follow the example of Dick Taggart, 41, of Old Greenwich, Conn. After 18 years in financial services, most recently at J.P. Morgan Chase, he now works for Progeon, an affiliate of the Indian outsourcing giant Infosys, as its man on Wall Street. One week out of every six or seven, he takes securities firms to India to show them the savings that are possible. He knows the transition is painful for the workers left behind, but he has seen it before. "It was the same thing when we moved from Wall Street to New Jersey and then to Dallas," he says. "Guess what? This is next."

—*With reporting by Sean Gregory/ New York City*

Schools That Develop Children

BY JAMES P. COMER

American schools are said to be failing. Like nineteenth-century medicine men, everybody is promoting everything, whether there is any evidence that it works or not. Over here we have vouchers, charters, privatization, longer school days, summer school, and merit pay. Over there we have the frequent testing of students, the testing of teachers, smaller class size, report cards on schools, and high-stakes accountability. And over here, a very special offer: student uniforms, flag-raising ceremonies every morning, the posting of the Ten Commandments on schoolhouse walls, and sophisticated diagnostic instruments to identify children at risk for acting violently—when many administrators and teachers can't even identify children who need glasses.

Most of these "cures"—traditional and reform—can't work or, at best, will have limited effectiveness. They all are based on flawed models. We will be able to create a successful system of education nationwide only when we base everything we do on what is known about how children and youths develop and learn. And this knowledge must be applied throughout the enterprise of education—in child rearing before school age, in schools and school districts, in schools of education, in state education departments, in legislatures, and everywhere else that personnel preparation takes place and school policy is made.

Given the purpose of education—to prepare students to become successful workers, family members, and citizens in a democratic society—even many "good" traditional schools, as measured by high test scores, are not doing their job adequately. But test scores alone are too narrow a measure. A good education should help students to solve problems encountered at work and in personal relationships, to take on the responsibility of caring for themselves and their families, to get along well in a variety of life settings, and to be motivated, contributing members of a democratic society. Such learning requires conditions that promote positive child-and-youth development.

Children begin to develop and learn through their first interactions with their consistent caretakers. And the eventual learning of basic academic skills—reading, writing, mathematics—and development are inextricably linked. Indeed, learning is an aspect of development and simultaneously facilitates it. Basic academic skills grow out of the fertile soil of overall development; they provide the platform for higher-order learning.

Through the early interactions, a bond is established that enables the child to imitate, identify with, and internalize the attitudes, values, and ways of their caretakers, and then those of other people around them. These people become important because they mediate (help make sense of and manage) a child's experiences and protect the child and help him or her to grow along the important developmental pathways—physical, social-interactive, psycho-emotional, ethical, linguistic, intellectual-cognitive, and eventually academic. The more mature thus help the less mature to channel potentially harmful aggressive energy into the energy of constructive learning, work, and play. But good early development is not a kind of inoculation that will protect a child for life. Future good development builds on the past and is mediated continuously by more mature people, step by step.

Understanding this process is no longer a matter of conjecture or the whining of "fuzzy-headed" social scientists or, as in my case, psychiatrists. Hard science—brain research—has confirmed the nature and critical importance of this interactive process. Without it children can lose the "sense"—the intelligence potential—they were born with. Children who have had positive developmental experiences before starting school acquire a set of beliefs, attitudes, and values—as well as social, verbal, and problem-solving skills, connections, and power—that they can use to succeed in school. They are the ones best able to elicit a positive response from people at school and to bond with them.

People at school can then influence children's development in ways similar to competent parents. To be successful, schools must create the conditions that make good development and learning possible: positive and powerful social and academic interactions between students and staff. When this happens, students gain social and academic competence, confidence, and comfort. Also, when parents and their social networks value school success and school experiences are positive and powerful, students are likely to acquire an internal desire to be successful in school and in life, and to gain and express the skills and behavior necessary to do so.

Vouchers do not address the challenge of child development. They simply change mechanisms of infrastructure, curriculum, and service delivery.

In order to realize the full potential of schools and students, we must create—and adequately support—a wide and deep pool of teachers and administrators who, in addition to having thorough knowledge of their disciplines, know how children develop generally and academically and how to support that development. They must be able to engage the families of students and the institutions and people in communities in a way that benefits student growth in school and society.

Vouchers and similar reforms currently being touted do not address these standards. They are simply changes in infrastructure, curriculum, and service delivery. They do not offer the potential for a nationwide transformation that a developmental focus does. And vouchers can reduce funds needed to improve the schools that must educate the majority of American children.

THE CHALLENGE OF CHANGE

The function of promoting good child-and-youth development and achievement was once served in our society through families and their social networks and through community life in small towns and rural areas. If students did not do well in school, they could leave, earn a living, still take care of themselves and their families, and become positive, contributing members of their communities. Despite massive and rapid scientific, technological, and social change, children have the same needs they always did: They must be protected and their development must be guided and supported by the people around them. They cannot rear themselves.

High mobility and modern communication created by technological change have undermined supports for child-and-youth development. Children experience many stimulating models of potentially troublesome behaviors—often in the absence of emotionally meaningful, influential adults. As a result, too many young people receive too little help in learning to manage feelings and act appropriately on the increased and more stimulating information they receive. This makes adequate social, psychological, and ethical development difficult.

Meanwhile, the new economy has made a high level of development and education a necessity for 90 percent of the population instead of the 20 percent we got by with half a century ago. Yet the rise of technology has led to an overvaluation of measured intelligence rather than an appreciation of overall development and the kind of intellectual growth that promotes strong problem-solving capacities.

Many successful people are inclined to attribute their situations to their own ability and effort—making them, in their minds, more deserving than less successful people. They ignore the support they received from families, networks of friends and kin, schools, and powerful others. They see no need for improved support of youth development. These misperceptions influence many education policies and practices.

Adequate support for development must be restored. And school is the first place this can happen. It is the common pathway for all children—the only place where a significant number of adults are working with young people in a way that enables them to call on family and community resources to support growth systematically and continually. And school is one of the few places where students, staff, and community can create environments in which to help young people achieve the necessary levels of maturity.

In the early 1980s, James Coleman, the late and respected University of Chicago sociologist, called what children gain from their parents and their networks "social capital." I do not like this term in discussing humans, but it is much used. Many poor children grow up in primary social networks that are marginal to mainstream institutions and transmit social capital that is different from that needed for school success. School requires mainstream social capital. In a January 2000 *New York Times Magazine* article, James Traub said that "Coleman consistently pointed out that we now expect the school to provide all the child's human and social capital—an impossibility."

I agree that the school can't do it alone. But schools can do much more than what they now do. Most students, even those from very difficult social conditions, enter school with the potential needed to gain mainstream social capital. But traditional schools—and most reforms—fail such students.

Not long ago I asked approximately 300 experienced teachers and administrators from across the country if they'd taken a child development course; about half had. But when I asked how many had taken a school-based, supervised course in applied child development, only seven hands remained up. This lack of training is why many educators can't discuss the underlying factors involved in a playground fight or how to create social and academic experiences that motivate learning by tapping into the developmental needs and information level of today's students.

Even fewer could construct environments conducive to overcoming racial, ethnic, income, and gender barriers.

But schools can succeed if they are prepared to embrace poor or marginalized families and to provide their children with conditions that promote mainstream skills. And when these conditions are continued throughout the school years, children from low-income backgrounds can do well in school; they will have better life chances. I was first convinced that this was the case for very personal reasons.

My mother was born into the family of a sharecropper in rural Mississippi in 1904. Her father was a good man, but he was killed by lightning when she was six years old. There were no family assistance programs, and a cruel, abusive stepfather came into their lives. He would not allow the children to go to school, and they lived under conditions of extreme poverty. At about eight years of age, as a barefoot child in the cotton fields, my mother realized that education was the way to a better life. When she was 16, she ran away to live with a sister in East Chicago, Indiana, with the hope of getting an education. But that was not possible.

When she had to leave school, my mother declared that if she ever had children, she would make certain they all got a good education. And then she set out—very, very, very carefully—to find my father, a person of like mind and purpose. Her caution paid off. My father, with six or seven years of education, worked as a steel mill laborer; and my mother, with no education, worked as a domestic. The two of them eventually sent the five of us to college, where we earned a total of 13 degrees.

Our family was enmeshed in an African-American church culture that provided the necessary social, ethical, and emotional context. My parents took us to everything educational they could afford; they talked and interacted with us in a way that encouraged learning and promoted overall development. Working for and respected by some of the most powerful people in our community, my mother observed and acquired mainstream success skills and made useful social contacts. Most of the summer jobs that helped us pay our way through college came from those contacts. And I enjoyed caviar brought home after parties before my working-class friends knew that it existed. Indeed, many European, black, and brown immigrants "made it" through similar experiences.

My three best friends were as intelligent as anybody in our family and in the predominantly white working- and middle-class school we attended. On the playground and the street corner, they could think as fast and as well as students who were more successful in school. But all three went on a downhill course: one died early from alcoholism, one spent time in jail, and one was in and out of mental institutions until he died recently. My parents had the same kind of jobs as their parents did, and we all attended the same school. Why the difference? It was the more useful developmental experience we were provided.

This notion was confirmed a few years ago when I visited my mother in the hospital. My spry, 80-plus-year-old first-grade teacher, Ms. Walsh, was a hospital volunteer.

When she saw me, she threw her arms around me and said, "Oh, my little James." I was 55 years old going on six. She stepped back and said, "We just loved the Comer children. You came to school with those bright, eager eyes, and you got along so well with the other children, and you all were so smart," and more. She was describing the outcome of a home and community experience that provided adequate development and school readiness—social capital, if I must use the term.

I acknowledge that my parents, perhaps even my community and school, were not and are not typical. And again, the community conditions that supported family functioning, child rearing, and development to a much greater degree in the past are weaker today. The positive connections that the poor previously had with the more privileged in American society have decreased.

A few scattered programs make good education and life opportunities possible for poor and working-class children. Prep for Prep lays the groundwork for students to attend elite private schools; A Better Chance places students in good suburban schools; the Summer Study Skills Program prepares students for challenging academic courses. These "pull-out" programs provide the social capital, knowledge, and skills needed for mainstream participation. But they do not serve that large body of able young people, like my childhood friends, who are lost in elementary schools. Prepared and supported differently, such children could succeed.

MODELS OF DEVELOPMENT

The Yale Child Study Center's School Development Program has been working with schools for the past 32 years. The outcomes suggest that by basing what we do in schools (and in the education enterprise beyond schools) on what we know about how children develop and learn, we can provide most children with what they need to succeed in school and in life.

I recently visited the Samuel Gompers Elementary School in one of the poorest neighborhoods in Detroit, a school with 97 percent student poverty. The Yale program has been used in this school for the past six years. The neighborhood was a disaster; the school was a pearl. The students were lively, spontaneous, and engaged in their work at appropriate times, yet quiet and attentive when they were supposed to be. They got along well with one another and were eager to demonstrate their skills to their parents and teachers. Eighty percent of the students passed the 1999 fourth-grade Michigan Educational Assessment Program (MEAP) test in reading and science, and 100 percent passed in mathematics. In 2000 they achieved the highest MEAP test scores among elementary schools in their size category in the state. Why here? It is not a mystery.

The Gompers School's success is related as much to the conditions that promote development and learning as it is to curriculum and instruction. How did it create these conditions and achieve good academic outcomes? The Yale program provided the conceptual and operational framework, child development–centered training for staff and parents, and very limited field support. The Skillman Foundation in Detroit, the Detroit Public Schools, Eastern Michigan University College of Education staff members, and parents (key members of the education enterprise) all came together to help the Gompers School and others provide the social capital the students need. The philosophy of the principal, Marilee Bylsma, is an important underpinning: "The school should be a safe haven for children, someplace that inspires learning." The staff, parents, and students did the work.

Committees, operations, and guidelines help schools create a culture of mutual respect and collaboration as well as social and academic programs that enable them to support students' development and learning. The transformation is gradual but frequent in schools that work to form good adult relationships. Good student relationships can follow.

At Gompers there is a 15-minute assembly every morning in which the students say the Pledge of Allegiance and make a school pledge. They sing a patriotic song and the school song. The custodian recognizes the "birthday boys and girls." (Message: It's everybody's school; we all play important roles.) The class with the best previous-day behavior gets "Gator points." Other recognitions take place. During the announcements, the students often discuss what's going on in their lives—the unexpected death of a teacher, problems in the neighborhood, and so on—and the adults help them learn to manage related feelings.

In traditional high schools, teachers are often much more anchored in subject matter than in student development.

When the school basketball team lost a tournament they had expected to win, the principal gave much thought to how to help the players manage their disappointment and grow from the experience. The next morning, she talked about how important it is to try to be number one in all you do. But the team members should celebrate their effort, she explained—they came in third in a large field—and look forward to the next opportunity. The students can tell you that they participate in extracurricular activities to create a good community, a condition that they value.

Activities and interactions like those at Gompers can't be carried out very long, if at all, in a school where the staff members don't like, trust, or respect one another or the parents. And you can't just mandate these conditions. Child

development–oriented structures and processes must operate in a way that brings about these conditions.

Initially, the Yale program's work was just in elementary schools, but it is now being carried out in many middle schools and high schools. Admittedly, middle school is difficult, and high school is even more so. That's when teens are "placing" themselves in the world and establishing their identity. Young people who place themselves and their futures in family and social networks that are dysfunctional are likely to perform in school in ways that lead to similar poor or marginal outcomes for themselves. Additionally, they are physically able to engage in adult behaviors. Only a half-century ago, many teens were married, working, and raising families; but in these more complex times, they often lack the experiences and resultant judgment, personal control, discipline, and problem solving skills needed to manage adult living.

In traditional high schools, teachers are often much more anchored in subject matter than in student development. Peer groups provide belonging and therefore become very powerful. They are sometimes positive, but too often are troublesome—it's the inexperienced and immature leading the inexperienced and immature. Aside from athletic coaches and teachers in the arts and other special areas, too few mature adults can interact with students in sustained and meaningful ways. These are powder keg conditions. And in communities where there are too few constructive supports for good development both inside and outside school, bad things happen—among staff, students, and parents.

In all schools—but particularly in low-income and nonmainstream communities—it is important for the staff to expose students to mainstream work as well as civic activities so that the connection between learning and later expectations is clear. School should help young people to learn what is needed for life success. Social and academic skills, attitudes, management of feelings, and other attributes needed to participate successfully in the mainstream can then be developed.

West Mecklenberg High School in Charlotte, North Carolina, received an additional 222 students in 1992 from a competing high school; its enrollment went from 1,144 to 1,366, precipitating a crisis. The school was almost evenly divided between whites and African Americans. Most of the students were children of blue-collar workers. Fourteen guns and many knives were confiscated during the first year, and parents, teachers, and students were concerned about their safety. Dennis Williams was assigned to the school as principal; Haywood Homsley, then the guidance counselor and coach, became the Yale-program facilitator. Williams and Homsley began to focus on reducing intergroup tensions and creating a climate that enabled staff members to consider and respond to the developmental needs of the students.

The transformation was dramatic. On April 28, 1995, *The Leader*, Charlotte's major newspaper, highlighted the gains seen at West Mecklenberg since the Yale program was introduced: Scholastic Assessment Test (SAT) scores rose by an average of 16 points; the number of students who made the honor roll jumped 75 percent; the number of students enrolled in advanced courses increased 25 percent; and the average daily attendance rate for the year went from 89 percent to almost 94 percent. The process of change at West Mecklenberg was essentially the same as in elementary schools like Gompers except that the students themselves were more involved in the thinking and planning of the programs.

In the 1994–1995 academic year, West Mecklenberg was designated a "school of excellence" by the state of North Carolina for the high level at which it reached its benchmark goals, and it was the only high school of 11 in its district to attain this status. Despite the fact that there have been three principals since 1992, the school has held the "excellence" rating for three of the past five years.

SUSTAINING GAINS

Are the academic gains large enough? Can they be sustained? What about the schools that do not improve? And what about middle- and upper-income young people, who face a more complex world? Even with developmentally based programs and other reform models, it's true that academic gains in schools serving students who are most in need do not quickly and routinely match those of more privileged students. Sometimes they can't be sustained; and sometimes there is no improvement at all. But when the process is well implemented, large gains have been achieved and sustained.

Frequent changes in administrators or teachers can undo in several months or less a school culture that took years to create.

For example, the Norman Weir K-8 school in Paterson, New Jersey, went from 34th to first in academic achievement among eighth-graders in 1995. They equaled or surpassed suburban schools for four consecutive years. A school in Virginia went from 24th to first but fell apart the next year because the principal and several key senior staff members were removed or left and were replaced by untrained staff. Weir escaped the same fate because a group of staff members went to the superintendent and asked for

and were assigned a good principal whose educational philosophy was grounded in child development.

Before a school can experience large, widespread, sustained achievement-test gains and adequately prepare students for adult life, it must be able to promote student development and manage its way to success, as Gompers, West Mecklenberg, and others have done. For this to be possible, we must produce large numbers of adequately prepared and supported staff. The policies and practices of the major players in the education enterprise nationwide—schools of education, legislators at all levels, state and federal departments of education, school districts, businesses—must be coherent by virtue of being based in child-and-youth development.

There are many obstacles to significant school improvement. Five in particular are very troublesome yet more accessible than the seemingly intransigent issues of race, class, and financial equity. These five are the ones that prevent the education enterprise as a whole from empowering school staffs, as in the case of the Gompers School. If these were addressed all at once, the United States could begin to foster widespread, sustained, high-level school improvement—and perhaps, eventually, could even address the most resistant issues.

First, frequent changes in personnel—particularly in districts and schools faced with great challenges—is a major problem. Child development–based strategies require continuity, training, and support of school staff. Frequent changes in administrators or governance at the district or building level, or in teachers—without careful selection and training of new people—can undo in several months or less a school culture that took three to five years to create. Understanding student and organization needs, developing resources and staff, and building community support isn't possible in the two-year tenure of most school superintendents.

Second, education policy is often fragmented rather than prioritized. This is because it is made everywhere—legislatures, state departments, districts, unions, city councils, businesses, and more. Many policy makers have no expertise in child development, teaching, and learning. And when crafting policy, most do not talk to one another, to students, or to school staff. Rarely are these policies guided by what we know about child growth and development and its relationship to learning.

And legislators, businesspeople, state departments, and others are—like school administrators—under great pressure to "Do something!" Because they widely believe that test scores alone can measure school effectiveness, that is what they focus on most. And without well-considered, evidence-based, coherent education policies, equitable funding will be impossible. In one city, eight of the 10 schools listed as "failing" had made the greatest gains in the system over the previous two years. The listing was demoralizing and led to harmful staff turnover and achievement setbacks, but it was the only way to get funds to help those schools.

Third, most schools of education do not provide future teachers or administrators with adequate knowledge or skills to promote a culture supportive of overall student development. Most focus—and in the college classroom, particularly—on curriculum, instruction, assessment, administration, and, sometimes, use of technology.

Sound knowledge of academic disciplines is important but not sufficient. Many schools of education provide courses in abnormal child development but no study of normal development. And the preparation to teach reading is often limited. Yet a child who has difficulty learning to read—the academic task that serves as a foundation for all future learning—is likely to experience feelings that limit emotional, psychological, ethical, and social developmental growth, or that promote troublesome growth.

Fourth, schools of education are seldom involved with other departments of the university in mutually enriching ways. Meaningful interaction between colleges of education and other university departments would be beneficial also to the institutions and the communities around them.

And fifth, there is no vehicle in universities or among research-and-development groups that will enable working educators to update their skills regularly and learn best practices. Also, there is no existing way to address these five most troublesome obstacles simultaneously so that synergy results.

Agricultural extension provides a useful model for educators. The Smith-Lever Act of 1914 created the Agricultural Extension Service to transmit knowledge to a large number of farmers through federal, state, and county partnerships. Farm agents, in addition to changing farmer practice, changed policy makers' and the public's understanding of best practice, as well as the policies needed to promote it. Improved agriculture enriched the economy and made America the breadbasket of the world.

Education is to the information-age economy of today what agriculture was to the economy at the turn of the twentieth century. Schools of education could create centers designed to overcome major obstacles in the education enterprise. Such centers would provide education agents. Schools of education will need to incorporate and institutionalize child development knowledge and expertise. But once this is done, education scholars and agents will be well positioned to share with and learn from colleagues at universities, to help future and current teachers and administrators become more effective practitioners, and to help policy makers and the public better understand and support good schooling.

Few schools of education or university programs are presently prepared to work in this way. We should not rush into such programs without sound pilot and infrastructure work. But knowledge, organization, and support can be acquired. The states—who are legally responsible for educating America's children—should support such efforts. Most, largely through their departments of education, have been involved in standard-setting as well as in regulatory and oversight activities. They are involved in takeovers of failing districts. Yet they have little experience in—and no mechanisms for—correcting the complex problems involved in school improvement.

The decisions we make in the next few years will involve significant amounts of money and will lock us into helpful or harmful directions. A miracle quick fix is not possible. But if we today begin to mount programs that connect to practice and to policy what we know about how children develop and learn, we could soon be well on our way to having better-functioning systems of education in five years and good ones in a decade. If we continue to be guided by tradition, ideology, and power, however, we will reach a point of no return—one where too many young people are undereducated, acting out, and gradually undermining our economy and our democracy.

JAMES P. COMER, M.D., is the Maurice Falk Professor of Child Psychiatry at the Yale University Child Study Center. He founded the Center's School Development Program in 1968.

THE DOCTOR WON'T SEE YOU NOW

THE SOARING COST OF MALPRACTICE insurance may seem a problem just for errant physicians. But it's becoming a worry for everyone, especially patients who see their doctors move away, change specialties—or quit medicine altogether

By DANIEL EISENBERG AND MAGGIE SIEGER JOLIET

Dr. ALEXANDER SOSENKO IS PROUD OF HIS SKILLS, BUT these days they don't seem to be the ones he needs to keep his medical practice going. A pulmonologist for 19 years, he knows just about everything there is to know about the lungs and is cherished by patients for his concerned, direct manner. But by his own admission, he's not great at lobbying. And, unfortunately, that's how Sosenko, 49, has lately been spending much of his time—circulating petitions at the local hospital, pleading with politicians for help. He has spent sleepless nights worrying that he may have to uproot his wife and three children from their home in Joliet, Ill., or else give up the profession he loves—all because he can't find affordable malpractice insurance.

An Abandoned Patient
Taking the Highway to Have a Baby

It wasn't morning sickness that made Vanessa Valdez's first trimester of pregnancy so hard—it was homesickness. So when the check-cashing company she worked for in Tucson, Ariz., offered her a transfer to her hometown of Douglas, she jumped at the chance. Four months pregnant at the time, Valdez, 24, was delighted to come home to her boyfriend, her parents and the 2-year-old son she left in their care when her job took her out of town. But now, as she prepares to give birth to a baby girl, she is dealing with a major drawback: there is no obstetrician within an hour's drive to deliver her child.

Valdez gave birth to her first child at Copper Queen Community Hospital in Bisbee, an old mining town just 26 miles northwest of Douglas. But when six family practitioners decided they couldn't afford the soaring malpractice premiums required for them to keep delivering babies, the hospital was forced to close its delivery room. Suddenly rural Cochise County, a 6,000-sq.-mi. expanse of mountains and desert along the Mexican border, had but one delivery room left for its 118,000 residents. It is in Sierra Vista, 50 miles northwest of Valdez's home. Which means that a week before her Aug. 4 due date, Valdez will pack her bags and camp out at a home of family friends near the hospital. "It sucks. It's not the same as being in your house, with your friends and your family," says Valdez, a petite woman who is otherwise quick to laugh.

As rising malpractice-insurance costs force a growing number of physicians to change states, drop certain procedures and even quit medicine, many patients like Valdez are finding themselves abandoned. In Las Vegas, where a number of obstetricians have stopped accepting patients, forcing some women to drive to Utah for prenatal care, a pregnant radio host took to the airwaves and begged her listeners to help her find an ob-gyn. (Her unorthodox method worked.)

In Pennsylvania, a particularly unlucky senior has lost his neurosurgeon and orthopedic surgeon to other states, and now his rheumatologist and urologist are threatening to move as well.

Valdez doesn't have it quite so bad—but don't try to tell her that. While she is busy looking for a new doctor in Sierra Vista for the big day in August, she is still commuting two hours to keep appointments with her current doctor in Tucson. The road to Sierra Vista winds through mountains and creosote flats. "It's going to be summer now, and it's getting hotter here," she says. "I'm afraid of the car breaking down again"—as it did recently while Valdez was driving alone on her way home from Tucson.

Some expectant couples rent motel rooms in Sierra Vista for when their babies are due. But some who can't afford a room or whose timing is off end up with the baby arriving in the middle of the night while they're racing along the highway, according to Copper Queen Hospital CEO James Dickson. The intersection of Highways 80 and 90 is listed as the place of birth on the certificate of a baby girl born in the front passenger seat of a car where those highways cross. Women lacking transportation, a common problem in this working-poor area, have given birth in ambulances. Others may be giving birth across the border in Mexico or at home, says Dr. Jennifer Ryan, CEO of the Elfrida-based Chiricahua Community Health Centers.

Health-care administrators in Cochise County plan to open a birthing center in Bisbee, which would be run by the federally qualified Chiricahua clinic and would be able to shelter doctors from high malpractice-insurance premiums. If all goes well, the center will be open next spring. But for Valdez and many other new mothers, that will be too late. Valdez doesn't know whom to blame—doctors, lawyers or insurance companies. She just knows that come late July, she will have to spend the final, awkward week of her pregnancy waddling around as a houseguest. That's enough to make anyone feel homesick.

—By Leslie Berestein

A Malpractice Victim
How the System Failed One Sufferer

Jim McDonough went into the hospital in 1997 to have a calcified growth, which the doctor said could be cancerous, removed from his neck. Two days later he awoke to find himself paralyzed from the chest down. Still in the intensive-care unit, he felt strangled by a noose of pain and needed three excruciating gasps of air to cry for help. "I was crushed," says McDonough, 69, a former weapons-plant inspector from Littleton, Colo. He once loved to fish and dreamed of restoring his ideal car: a 1965 Chrysler. But he soon realized that he could do neither and came to believe that his surgery had been unnecessary. A jury agreed. It found his neurosurgeon guilty of malpractice and in 2001 awarded McDonough $5.8 million. He has yet to see a dollar.

Jim McDonough feels he was mistreated by his doctor and by caps on his malpractice award

McDonough is a victim again, this time of the move to cap jury awards. Colorado is one of the few states that limit jury awards of both economic damages (say, for lost income) and noneconomic ones (for pain and suffering). Judge Warren Martin, now retired, cut McDonough's award to $1.33 million, concluding that although his injuries merited an exception to the $1 million cap, the jury had gone too far. (Colorado's caps limit economic damages to $750,000 and pain-and-suffering awards to $250,000. The former can be increased if a plaintiff shows future economic loss that exceeds that level.) McDonough appealed to the Colorado Supreme Court but was denied. He later tried to settle, but the defense argued that he had waited too long, and another judge ordered a new trial to determine damages. It will begin in August—a fresh chapter in McDonough's nightmare.

Proponents of damage caps say they simplify malpractice cases and weed out frivolous claims. But they can also entangle victims of heartbreaking tragedy like McDonough. No longer able to work, he spends his days doing crossword puzzles and preparing again for court. That was not the intention of the first jury, whose award was based not on mere sympathy but on calculations of McDonough's direct financial burden. According to foreman Joanne Kramer, in arriving at the $5.8 million in damages, the jury considered everything from home health-care aides to a van, a wheelchair, the loss of his home and the loss of income for his wife, who spends hours every day caring for him. Jurors also discussed whether McDonough's award would add to rising malpractice premiums but decided he should not be penalized for that. "We still had a responsibility to Mr. McDonough, who was a victim," says Kramer. "What's the point of having a jury if the judge can basically do what he wants?"

McDonough isn't giving up the fight. In February he wheeled himself into a state legislative hearing on damage caps. The Colorado Supreme Court ruled that "physical impairment and disfigurement" are exempt from limits on jury awards, but this spring the state's lawmakers limited the effect of the court's decision. "The doctor who performed this unnecessary operation has left the state and is continuing with his life elsewhere," McDonough testified. That neurosurgeon, Richard Branan, 59, declined to comment about McDonough. Branan practices in Los Angeles and faces two other trials this year in Colorado. His attorney in one case, in which the patient died, says, "We have a very defensible case." His attorney in the other trial, also a spinal-surgery case, says Branan "did not cause any injuries to the patient."

Despite Colorado's unusually strict damage cap, the state's largest insurer raised premiums 14% this year, the biggest jump in 15 years. So far at least, the cap law is failing to deliver the relief that it promised to doctors even as it blocks relief to acknowledged victims like Jim McDonough.

—*By Rita Healy/Denver*

An Uninsured Doctor
Alexander Sosenko, a pulmonologist in Joliet, Ill., can't find affordable malpractice coverage.

A few months ago, Sosenko and the five other doctors at the practice he founded, Midwest Pulmonary Consultants, learned that their malpractice insurer, American Physicians Capital, would not be renewing their policy when it expired at the end of March. They weren't exactly shocked. Over the past two years, insurers of doctors in Illinois, worried by a rise in malpractice awards by juries in the state, have dwindled in number from more than two dozen to six. But then it got personal. Sosenko and his partners discovered that their insurer was not leaving Illinois entirely but was limiting its exposure. Although Sosenko and his colleagues had not lost or settled a single lawsuit over the years—an impressive record in this litigious age—they are named in a couple of cases that have been grinding through the courts since the late 1990s. Sosenko and his colleagues have denied all the allegations and refuse to settle.

When the doctors started looking for an insurer to replace APC, none of the mainstream malpractice insurers offered coverage. One smaller firm came up with a package for nearly $100,000 a doctor (up from about $14,000 only two years earlier), plus $500,000 a year for "tail" coverage, to insure the practice for any suits that might arise from care provided before the new policy took effect. The doctors couldn't afford it. So after one of them left the practice to try to go it alone, the rest enlisted their state senator, who persuaded their original carrier to give them an extension—which expired at the end of last week. What next? Will they change specialties? Will they change addresses to a less litigious state? And what of their 6,000 patients, who would have to drive an hour to

A Chastened Insurer

He Sets Your Doctor's Bill

You don't have to feel sorry for the insurance industry to appreciate Donald Zuk's predicament. The CEO of SCPIE Holdings, California's second largest malpractice insurer, Zuk launched an ambitious plan in 1996 to expand into new states like Texas and Georgia and into new lines of business, such as insuring dentists and higher-risk doctors. It was a disaster.

Zuk, 66, a burly former football player, found himself fighting a multistate price war, cutting premiums to grab market share and badly underestimating how much his firm would pay out for claims against doctors. "The loss ratios were going through the roof," Zuk says. SCPIE raised premiums for policies outside California about 40% in 2001 and 30% in 2002. Yes, Zuk is one of the people responsible for the malpractice-insurance crisis that is disrupting the lives of so many doctors and patients. But he's not exactly profiteering. His firm has posted $96 million in losses over the past two years.

The Los Angeles-based company has retreated to California, pulling out of the malpractice business in other states. Says Zuk: "We knew that there was a risk when you go into a state without tort reform"—limits placed on personal-injury lawsuits and damages. "We thought the rates were sufficient, so we went with it. Today I know what's going on around the country. I won't go into Texas, Florida or any of the states I pulled back from until there's some semblance of tort reform."

As long as investment income held up, insurers could ignore rising claims.

Zuk has plenty of company in his malpractice losses and in his zeal for reform. In 2001 medical-malpractice insurers paid out $1.53 in claims and expenses for each $1 in premiums they collected. The industry has lost a combined $8 billion since 1995, and its reserves for estimated future claims are underfunded by about $4.6 billion. So if insurers aren't profiting from higher premiums, who is? Zuk and his peers point to trial lawyers and frivolous claimants. Insurers are lobbying alongside doctors for caps on noneconomic damages (for pain and suffering), like the ones in California and 18 other states. Rising awards, Zuk says, are bleeding money out of the system and forcing insurers to raise premiums. Cap the damages, and premiums will fall in line, he says.

Not everyone accepts that link. "In theory, tort reform would have an impact on premiums. In reality, that has not been the case," says Martin Weiss, chairman of Weiss Ratings, an independent insurance-rating agency in Palm Beach Gardens, Fla. In a study published this week, Weiss Ratings found that in states without caps on noneconomic damages, median annual premiums for standard medical-malpractice coverage rose 36% between 1991 and 2002. But in states with caps, premiums rose even more—48%. In the two groups of states, median 2002 premiums were about the same. Weiss found nine states with flat or declining premiums; two of them had caps, seven didn't. Weiss speculates that regulation of premium increases made the difference. In California, consumer groups argue that the state's tough oversight of the insurance industry, not its caps on damages, explains why rates have grown more slowly.

Caps on noneconomic damages may not hold down doctors' insurance costs, but they have boosted insurers' profits. In states with caps, the Weiss study found, claims payments grew only 38%, compared with 71% in states without them. By raising premiums, insurers have improved their ratio of claims to premiums, a key measure of profitability, from 110% in 2000 to 89% in 2002. "The caps are great for insurers," Weiss says. "Their payouts will be lower. In a perfect world, they would pass that savings on." But the industry's losses have been so large that lower claims will not reverse them; insurers are likely to keep raising premiums.

Raising rates is exactly what malpractice insurers failed to do in the 1990s, even as claims were rising. Zuk concedes that the industry has to accept some blame. "No one wanted to be the first guy to say, 'We've got to start charging the right premium,'" he says. The insurers feared losing market share, and as long as investment income held up, they could ignore rising claims.

The malpractice-insurance industry went through similar cycles of low rates, squeezed profits and price hikes in the mid-1970s and again in the mid-'80s. Zuk, who enrolled in law school in the '70s just to learn torts, says ballooning malpractice claims make the current crisis worse than previous ones. From 1997 to 2001, the median malpractice jury award doubled, to $1 million, but that counts results only in the 1% of lawsuits that are won by plaintiffs. The number of malpractice suits has remained stable, and although some states have seen sharp jumps, the average claim payment has grown about 8% a year, close to the rate of medical inflation.

Industry analysts say insurers' investment losses, not just jury awards, are behind the crisis. In bull markets, insurers count on investment income to offset underwriting losses; that ended when the 1990s' stock bubble burst. Although malpractice insurers make only about 20% of their investment income from stocks, the losses were steep and came in tandem with low bond yields.

Insurance firms, Zuk says, must stabilize the disruptive cycle of cutting rates and then raising them when losses grow too big. Regulators could stop an insurer from underpricing premiums and "protect it from its own stupidity," as Zuk puts it. "The industry has to say, 'Forget investment income. Let's just write to an underwriting profit.'"

Some industry experts suggest national standards for acceptable outcomes in medical procedures. Zuk says a separate malpractice torts system would be a better solution. New standards, he argues, would only put doctors on the defensive. He recalls his own knee replacement in 2001. His doctors, he says, focused on treating him, not providing disclaimers or ordering tests. Zuk is convinced he knows why: "They don't have to worry about me suing them."

—*By Jyoti Thottam*

the nearest lung specialist, in Chicago? "We doctors can move on," says Sosenko, tilting back in his office chair. "But our patients can't."

LIKE SOSENKO'S PATIENTS, MILLIONS across America might turn up for an appointment one day soon and find the doctor is out—for good. Thousands have already lost their doctors to a malpractice crisis that, while concentrated for now in certain states and specialties, is spreading. Doctors are being handed malpractice-insurance bills that are double those of a couple of years ago, forcing many of them to move from high-premium states—like Florida, Nevada and Pennsylvania—to more affordable venues like California and Indiana. The crisis is compelling some doctors and medical students to switch from lawsuit-magnet specialties like obstetrics, neurology and pulmonology to "safer" ones like dermatology and ophthalmology, or to refuse to perform high-risk procedures like delivering babies and operating on spines.

How They're Coping
DOCTORS DRIVEN AWAY

Smacked by big insurance bills, many physicians are moving, scaling back or quitting. Three M.D.s describe their tough choices.

I Had to Quit Medicine—
And Became a Lawyer

While most doctors and lawyers blame each other, Dr. Stephanie Rifkinson-Mann, 51, sees malpractice from both sides. Two years ago, after reimbursements fell as insurance premiums rose, the veteran pediatric neurosurgeon from Mount Kisco, N.Y., became a product-liability lawyer. She still does medical consultations one day a week. She quips, "Now that I'm a lawyer, I can afford to see patients."

I Had to Stop Delivering Babies

Dr. Mary-Emma Beres, a family practitioner in Sparta, N.C., has always loved delivering babies. But last year Beres, 35, concluded that she couldn't afford a tripling of her $17,000 malpractice premium and had to stop. With just one obstetrician left in town for high-risk cases, some women who need C-sections now must take a 40-minute ambulance ride.

I Had to Move My Practice

"I was happy taking care of my high school friends and their families," says neurosurgeon Brian Holmes, 42, who left his hometown of Scranton, Pa., last fall. Facing an estimated $200,000 annual malpractice premium, Holmes moved his wife and three children 190 miles southeast to Hagerstown, Md., where a policy cost just $30,000. "The move continues to be difficult."

WHILE THERE IS NO EVIDENCE that the total number of physicians in the U.S. has declined, some veteran practitioners in states with sky-high malpractice premiums are quitting medicine. Even in states where malpractice insurance remains relatively affordable, doctors are increasingly practicing more "defensive medicine," trying to gird themselves against possible lawsuits by ordering unnecessary tests and thereby driving up health-care costs.

In one 6,000-sq.-mi. expanse of Arizona, high malpractice premiums have prompted six obstetricians to stop delivering babies. Many women now have to drive an hour or more to reach a hospital with a delivery room, forcing several, like Melinda Sallard, 22, to give birth in

the car en route to the hospital. Seniors in parts of Pennsylvania travel an hour or two to see a neurosurgeon, and one orthopedic surgeon from Philadelphia commutes every week to see patients in the Midwest, where malpractice-insurance costs are lower. Emergency rooms from Orlando, Fla., to Belleville, Mo., report that rising insurance premiums are making it difficult for them to employ the trauma specialists needed to treat car-accident victims. In protest, doctors from New Jersey to Washington State are taking to the streets and engaging in work slowdowns and strikes. Nearly 100 physicians in and around Jacksonville, Fla., have stopped performing elective surgery, making the county activate an emergency response system that it typically uses to deal with natural disasters like hurricanes.

The system is clearly broken, and there is no quick fix in sight. To doctors like Sosenko, the main problems are frivolous lawsuits and multimillion-dollar judgments awarded for tragic but sometimes unavoidable outcomes. (A banner at a rally read SICK? CALL A LAWYER.) The waiting room at Sosenko's Midwest Pulmonary these days looks almost like a campaign headquarters. Banners declaring WE HAVE A CRISIS! hang alongside lists of politicians' names and phone numbers. Sosenko's patients have signed petitions calling on politicians to make malpractice reform a top priority.

It's easy to see why they want to help. Sosenko is a native and a favorite son of Joliet, a middle-class town about 45 miles southwest of Chicago. The child of Ukrainian immigrants who fled a displaced-persons camp in Germany after World War II, Sosenko grew up in Joliet watching his father, Roman, serve the town as a family doctor. He wanted to do the same for his friends and neighbors, treating people suffering from diseases such as asthma, bronchitis, emphysema and lung cancer.

Over the years, Sosenko and his colleagues at MPC have earned a reputation as not only capable but also unusually attentive. Phone calls are promptly returned, day or night, and doctors make house calls when necessary. "It's such a relief, just knowing he's here," says Pat Falkenberg, 48, a patient of Sosenko's who is battling pulmonary fibrosis and awaiting a lung transplant. During a stay in the hospital, Falkenberg says, Sosenko stopped by her room so many times that she "often wondered if he ever went home."

A math whiz with almost total recall, Sosenko is legendary around the office for remembering practically every one of the several thousand patients he has seen— and details of their conditions—even if it's been 15 years between visits. He personally coordinates most of his patients' care, calling other specialists for tests and appointments. "Any wheezing? How about panting?" Sosenko asks Richard Escherick, 61, during an office visit. In his blunt but friendly style, Sosenko quizzes the man about his nighttime cough. "Is it like this?" he asks, making a hacking sound. "Or like this?"—and he rattles his throat, sounding like a tom turkey. Sitting on a round

Where It's Spreading

The medical-malpractice crisis is concentrated mostly in litigious states
with generous juries and financially shaky insurers—but its contagious

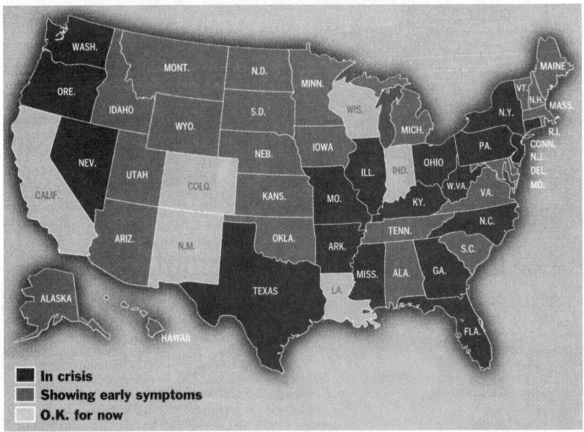

In crisis

Showing early symptoms

O.K. for now

Source: American Medical Association

WASHINGTON Nearly 1,000 doctors rallied last week to support medical-liability reforms. In May the state's largest neurosurgery group lost its insurance, leaving many hospitals without emergency-room coverage. Half of Tacoma's ob-gyns won't deliver babies

NEVADA More than 30 ob-gyns have closed their practices, and last summer the only first-rate trauma center in Las Vegas shut down for 10 days, prompting state legislators to pass a cap on noneconomic awards

ILLINOIS Thousands of physicians rallied in Chicago last month to protest skyrocketing medical-malpractice liability premiums. In Joliet last year three neurosurgeons stopped performing brain surgery. Head-trauma patients now need to be flown by helicopter to a center 45 miles away

MISSISSIPPI About 100 doctors have left or plan to leave the state. The only pediatric specialist in Rolling Fork has moved to North Dakota

PENNSYLVANIA Since 2001 some 900 doctors have closed practices, limited their services or left the state. The biggest loss: young doctors. Fewer than 5% of the state's M.D.s are younger than 35, down from 12% in 1989

NEW JERSEY Doctors have staged three rallies to urge state legislators to pass medical-liability reforms. A three-day walkout in February led to a 60% hike in the number of patients treated in emergency rooms

FLORIDA Seven hospital obstetric units have closed, and six medical centers no longer perform mammographies. Some South Florida women now must wait four months for the test

stool, with his legs crossed, and peering over the top of his reading glasses, Sosenko gives his patients as much time as they need to ask questions and voice concerns. These days, their worries often go beyond what medication to take. When Sosenko tells Richard Tea, 73, that he wants to see him again in three months, Tea's wife Mary Ellen nervously asks, "Are *you* going to be here in three months?"

Sosenko's petition drive generated more than 1,000 letters to Illinois' congressional delegation in Washington

and to state legislators in Springfield. It got the attention of state senator Larry Walsh, a Democrat from Joliet. Concerned about the availability of medical care in his hometown, Walsh persuaded Midwest Pulmonary's original carrier to give the practice a special two-month extension—albeit a pricey one, costing about $35,000. Walsh has reason to be worried. Sosenko's practice isn't the only one in Joliet that is perilously close to shutting down. The area's last remaining neurosurgeon, after learning he would have to pay $468,000 a year for insurance, up from

Who's Paying the Most

	NEUROSURGEON	OB-GYN	EMERGENCY PHYSICIAN	ORTHOPEDIC SURGEON	GENERAL SURGEON
Average annual cost of medical-liability premium	**$71,200**	**$56,546**	**$53,500**	**$38,000**	**$36,354**
Percentage increase	35.6% *from 2001 to 2002*	19.6% *from 2001 to 2002*	56.2% *from 2002 to 2003*	22.5% *from 2001 to 2002*	25% *from 2001 to 2002*
Cities with the highest premiums	**$283,000** *Chicago* **$267,000** *Philadelphia*	**$210,576** *Miami* **$152,496** *Cleveland*	**$150,000** *Miami* **$102,000** *Houston*	**$135,000** *Philadelphia* **$110,000** *Chicago*	**$174,268** *Miami* **$107,139** *Detroit*

SOURCES: American Academy of Orthopaedic Surgeons; American Association of Neurological Surgeons/Congress of Neurological Surgeons; American College of Emergency Physicians; American College of Obstetricians and Gynecologists; American Medical Association; Medical Liability Monitor

An Undisciplined Doctor
Why Wasn't He Stopped Sooner?

For years, Raymond Hilson thought the infection that left him disfigured was just a stroke of bad luck. Today he thinks it could have been worse. A school-bus driver from Colfax, Wis., Hilson, now 73, underwent heart-bypass surgery in 1994 at Luther Hospital in Eau Claire. At first the procedure seemed to have gone well. But Hilson contracted a severe staph infection. To treat it, doctors "kept cutting back the flesh and bone," he recalls, until his entire sternum was removed, leaving his beating heart visible just under the skin.

While there is no evidence that Hilson's surgeon was responsible for the infection, the hospital volunteered cash compensation to Hilson, which he accepted. And there are many things he knows today that he wishes he had known before his surgery. Only six months earlier, the physician operating on him, Dr. Michael McEnany, then 55, had resigned as chief of cardiovascular surgery at San Francisco Kaiser Permanente Medical Center after peers raised serious questions about his competency. He had been forbidden to operate without another surgeon assisting. Hilson had no way of knowing that background, or that the medial board of California would later accuse McEnany of incompetence and gross negligence in eight surgeries that went awry during his time at Kaiser, or that McEnany would experience other complications, including sternal wound infections, among his surgical patients in Wisconsin.

A small group of doctors causes the lion's share of malpractice payouts

You might think that McEnany would have had a hard time landing the Wisconsin job after his California experience. But as part of his resignation deal, according to California officials, Kaiser agreed to terminate McEnany's practice review and not file a report to the medical board of California, as the hospital was required to do. When officials at Luther Hospital ran a routine background check on McEnany, there were no red flags. Had a Kaiser whistle-blower not tipped off the medical board in 1996, sparking an investigation that led to McEnany's surrender of his licenses in California and Wisconsin, he could still be practicing. Instead, he is fighting off the remainder of 28 lawsuits filed against him between 1998 and 2000.

Although McEnany declined requests for interviews, one of his attorneys, Steven Sager of Fond du Lac, Wis., says, "I think that the doctor provided good care." He noted that several cases have been dismissed and McEnany has so far made no payments in Wisconsin.

For critics of doctor discipline, the McEnany case represents an extreme example of a familiar problem. While the vast majority of doctors perform with care and lose few, if any, legal judgments or settlements, a small number of negligent or incompetent doctors endanger patients and drive up malpractice-insurance costs for everyone. Since 1990, one-third of malpractice awards and settlements have resulted from just 5% of doctors making such payouts, according to the National Practitioner Data Bank (NPDB). Yet doctors and hospitals too often fail to discipline repeat offenders.

Hospitals are required to report to their state medical board and NPDB any revocation, suspension or restriction of a doctor's clinical privileges for more than 30 days. But hospitals don't always comply. By the end of 2001, 55% of all nonfederal hospitals registered with the NPDB had not reported a single disciplinary action against a doctor. (Two Kaiser administrators paid nearly $20,000 to settle with the state after failing to report McEnany, and the medical center says reporting procedures "are definitely different now.")

Hospitals face many incentives not to report a disciplined doctor—and not to discipline him at all. A hospital may want to limit its liability by not airing the problem. Or it may be afraid of a legal battle with the physician. And doctors are loath to report a colleague's bad behavior. Consumer advocates say that self-policing by doctors and hospitals is not sufficient and that patients need access to state medical board and NPDB records that are denied to them today.

That's why Raymond Hilson didn't know about the $200,000 settlement that Kaiser paid in 1992 to Richard Lord and his family for the loss of his wife Eleanor, who, according tho the California investigation, bled to death while in McEnany's care. If Hilson had known more, he says, he would have gone elsewhere. Learning the surgeon's history has made him see things in a different light. Strange as it may sound, he says, "I feel lucky to be a survivor."

—By Leslie Berestein/Los Angeles

$180,000, is considering moving to South Dakota or quitting for good. And a local group of 16 cardiologists—as well as 60 general practitioners—may lose their insurance at the end of this month.

A Medical Student
Today's Lesson: Switch Specialty

Martin Palmeri has changed his mind before. Until his fourth year of college, he was planning a career in investment banking. But one afternoon, while volunteering in a North Carolina medical clinic, Palmeri realized that he was much happier in the hospital than in economics class. Palmeri was drawn to obstetrics and gynecology, he says, for the "emotion and passion" involved in delivering babies. "It's tremendously rewarding."

Or so he thought. Last year, his third at the Brody School of Medicine at East Carolina University, Palmeri, 28, began investigating what he calls the "litigious juggernaut" of ob-gyn and decided the risks of the specialty were greater than its rewards. He's not alone. More than 10% of respondents to an informal poll on the American Medical Student Association website say they have switched their intended specialty because of the rising cost of malpractice insurance. An additional 36% are considering a change for the same reason. In the first round of the process that matches medical-school graduates to most residency programs, 30% of positions in ob-gyn and 20% in E.R. medicine went unfilled by this year's U.S. graduates. (Most spots were ultimately taken by foreign-school graduates and U.S. students who did not get their first choice.)

Palmeri did his homework before giving up on ob-gyn. He attended a workshop held by the American College of Obstetricians and Gynecologists, at which he heard alarming stories of physicians turning away high-risk patients for fear of litigation, or losing their practice because of skyrocketing insurance costs. Palmeri then observed the civil trial of a Wilson, N.C., obstetrician who was sued after the plaintiff's baby suffered neurological damage during birth. The doctor claimed that the plaintiff had refused to have a C-section despite his insistence that a vaginal birth would endanger both mother and baby. The plaintiff claimed she had received no such advice. Palmeri says he was disturbed to see that "the trial focused on the poor outcome and not on what the physician actually did." The jury was hung, and the doctor—who says he had to pay at least $30,000 in office overhead while he earned nothing sitting in court—settled the case. His insurance premiums jumped from $22,000 in 1998, the year he delivered the baby, to almost $70,000 this year. "I just couldn't imagine having to go through what he did every couple of years," Palmeri says. He's now considering radiology.

Professional groups for high-risk specialties are concerned about the loss of people like Palmeri and Peter Chien Jr., a New York University medical student who contemplated orthopedics but is opting for dermatology, a less litigious field. Perhaps even more troubling, a quarter of final-year medical students polled said they would not study medicine if they started their education over. Thankfully for his patients, that's a change of attitude Palmeri hasn't shared.

—By Amanda Bower

Soon after he got the two-month extension of his group's insurance, Sosenko thought he might have found a more permanent solution, courtesy of the local Provena Saint Joseph Hospital. Surgeons like to have a pulmonologist standing by when they perform a complicated procedure like open heart surgery. So the hospital offered to hire Sosenko and his colleagues as staff physicians and cover them under its liability insurance. However, Provena's insurance company wouldn't cover the doctors if they continued to see patients outside the hospital, even part time. "Maybe it was silly to take the two-month extension," says Dr. Gregg Cohan, 41, one of Sosenko's partners. "Maybe all we did was prolong the death."

The insurers blame rate hikes and policy cancellations on what they describe as a rising tide of lawsuits and $1 million–plus jury awards. Their solution (which many doctors, including Sosenko, support): caps of $250,000 on noneconomic damages awarded for pain and suffering. President Bush and other Republicans, whose campaigns are supported by doctors and insurance firms, endorse such legislation, and the House of Representatives has passed a bill along those lines. But plaintiffs' lawyers, who contribute heavily to the campaigns of Democrats, are lobbying their friends in the Senate, and national "tort reform" may remain more of a rallying cry than a real prospect.

The states could step in. Sosenko would love to see Illinois politicians ride to his rescue—and at the very least require a panel of qualified medical experts, rather than one hired gun, to sign off on a suit before it can go forward. But he doesn't hold out much hope. Twice in the past two decades, the state legislature has passed caps on noneconomic jury awards only to have them struck down as unconstitutional by the state supreme court. (Courts in other states, including California, have upheld similar caps.) Many state politicians are more than happy to hand the thorny issue off to Congress. State senator Walsh says some of his colleagues believe that the crisis eventually "will just work itself out." Sosenko says with disgust, "Talking to politicians is like hitting your head against a wall."

But the legal system is not the only culprit in the malpractice mess. Critics say soaring premiums are less the result of lawsuits than of insurers rushing to make up for their losses in underpriced premiums and poorly performing investments. An independent study by Weiss Ratings to be released this week shows that states with caps on malpractice damages have not enjoyed much relief in malpractice-insurance premiums but have instead seen insurers shore up profits. Sosenko's anger at the insurers moved him to join several hundred other Illinois physicians at a rally in the state capital earlier this year, calling on legislators to freeze malpractice premiums for six months and investigate the industry's pricing practices. "These companies pretty much have a free hand to do what they want," he says.

A Frustrated Lawmaker
Why Nothing Gets Fixed

The medical malpractice issue is a great one if you're a Republican looking out for the doctors and insurers who get sued. It's not so great if you're trying to find a compromise among these powerful, warring professions. But Senator Dianne Feinstein, a liberal Democrat from California, decided to give it a try, and her experience is a case study in how the politics of malpractice insurance works—or doesn't—in Washington.

Feinstein, 69, would seem well positioned to broker a deal. A member of the Senate Judiciary Committee, she has close ties with lawyers, who contributed almost $500,000 to her campaigns over the past five years, more than she received from any other group. Yet she sponsored a bill to protect high-tech firms from Y2K liability, which trial lawyers opposed. And she comes from a medical family. Her father was chairman of the department of surgery at the University of California Medical Center, and her second husband Dr. Bertram Feinstein, who died in 1978, was a neurosurgeon. He had eight malpractice suits filed against him but neurosurgeons get sued a lot because of their high-risk operations.

Late last year Senator Feinstein began meeting with California doctors in an effort to come up with a national version of her state's malpractice law. California allows unlimited amounts to be awarded for the economic damages a patient suffers as a result of a doctor's error, such as lost wages and medical bills, but caps noneconomic awards for pain and suffering at $250,000. The cap works, Feinstein believes. Nationwide, doctors' insurance premiums grew 420% from 1975 to 2001, while California's premiums, she says, are up only 168%. (Some experts credit the lower premiums to insurance reforms the state also adopted.)

After President Bush praised the California law in January, Feinstein said she would work with the White House. The next day she got a call from new Senate majority leader Bill Frist. A renowned surgeon, Frist desperately wanted the Senate to pass a bill curbing malpractice-insurance costs. And he just as desperately needed a Democrat to co-sponsor the measure. Feinstein agreed to help.

It was complicated from the start. Doctors and lawyers spend heavily to protect their interests on Capitol Hill. The American Medical Association contributed $2.7 million to candidates in the 2002 congressional elections (60% went to Republicans), and the Association of Trial Lawyers gave out $3.7 million (89% went to Democrats). Feinstein was hit from all sides. Senate Democrats, most of whom oppose curbs on jury awards, were angry with her for breaking ranks. Lawyers' groups and consumer activists complained that the caps discriminated against low-income victims of malpractice. Some said she couldn't be objective because her late husband had faced malpractice suits.

Feinstein and Frist drafted a compromise. Since California's $250,000 cap was set 28 years ago, says Feinstein, today it would be an inflation-adjusted $780,000. So she and Frist suggested doubling the cap to $500,000. For catastrophic cases that resulted in severe disfigurement, severe physical disability or death, says Feinstein, the cap would be the greater of $2 million or $50,000 times the number of years of life expectancy. The 25 states that have laws limiting damages could keep their caps if they did not want to adopt the Federal Government's.

When Feinstein floated the draft measure, she hit two walls. Trial lawyers hated caps. And doctors said the caps were too high and wouldn't stabilize their malpractice premiums. "There's just no way to proceed at this time," Feinstein says. The House, where Republicans have firmer control, has passed the $250,000 cap Bush wants. But for now, a bill like Feinstein's won't pass in the Senate. She blames the deadlock mostly on doctors who won't compromise. "There has to be a change of heart in the medical profession," she says, "for something to proceed."

—By Douglas Waller/Washington

However, physicians themselves deserve at least part of the blame. "Doctors," says Dr. John Walsh, 46, one of Sosenko's partners, "haven't sold themselves as a self-policing group." The vast majority of conscientious physicians have been forced to subsidize the higher insurance costs of a few incompetents. Consider this: between September 1990 and March 2003, just 5% of the doctors who have made medical malpractice payments accounted for a third of all the money paid out, according to the Federal Government's National Practitioner Data Bank.

SOSENKO'S CRASH COURSE IN LAW and politics is taking an emotional toll on him and his family. An avid windsurfer and science-fiction buff whose favorite books are *The Hobbitt* and *The Lord of the Rings*, Sosenko hasn't been able to enjoy himself much for the past several months. He hardly has the time or energy to play video games with his son Nick, 10. For the first time in recent memory, he has missed some of his 12-year-old daughter Teresa's afterschool volleyball games, though he still manages to take the kids to their classes at the Ukrainian cultural center on Saturdays. (The family speaks Ukrainian at home.) Sosenko has always been a bit moody. His office is littered with Tasmanian-devil toys given to him by his family, an inside joke alluding to his occasional temper. But nowadays he is regularly depressed and irritable. "Alex takes everything to heart," says his wife Maria, 46, a rheumatologist (whose malpractice premiums nearly doubled this year, from $8,592 to $15,472). "He's frantically searching for help."

With Medicare, Medicaid and HMO reimbursements falling and malpractice premiums steadily rising, Sosenko's income has dropped 40% over the past five years, to about $200,000 last year. That might sound like a lot, until you consider the 13 years he studied after high school, the debts he built up, the nights and weekends he works. As his colleague Cohan says, with only a little exaggeration, "Our income is completely controlled by the government, but we have no control on our expenses." Both men are bracing for a potentially bigger pay cut. Sosenko has put off indefinitely any major expenditures, including having the house repainted. But while his colleagues and even his wife have considered moving across Illinois' eastern border to Indiana, where malpractice premiums are lower, Sosenko can't imagine cutting his ties to his hometown. Not only would he have to take his kids away from their school and friends, but he would have to relocate his wife's elderly parents, whom he and his wife recently moved to Joliet. "I don't want to leave here. I'm too old to start from scratch," Sosenko says.

Early retirement is an equally unattractive prospect for Sosenko, a driven perfectionist who avidly reads medical journals to stay current with his specialty and holds his children to his exacting standards. If necessary, Sosenko says, he would "probably work without insurance," a dangerous gamble for any doctor these days but one that some physicians, particularly in Florida, are now taking. Another option he's exploring is work as a cardiopulmonary trainer and tester for fire fighters and others who must have good respiratory fitness for their job. As for the career plans of his children, Sosenko probably won't en-

courage his oldest son Alexander, 18, to follow in Dad's or his grandfather's footsteps. "I want him to be successful," Sosenko says. "I'm not sure [anymore] that the doctor has job security."

That has been painfully clear to Sosenko in recent weeks. After the collapse of their talks with Provena Hospital, the doctors of MPC, who had pledged to stick it out together, suddenly fractured. The three who haven't been named in either of the lawsuits pending against the practice—Drs. Walsh, Visvanatha Giri and Phillip Leung—created a separate partnership and secured malpractice insurance. Sosenko is planning to take the next couple of weeks off now that his policy has run out and then try to find a new medical group to join. Even so, he says, there are no hard feelings against his former colleagues. He's too busy for that. There are too many patients to treat. And too many people to lobby.

—With reporting by Dody Tsiantar/New York, Anne Berryman/Athens, Ga., Paul Cuadros/Sparta, N.C., and Michael Peltier/Tallahassee

---

UNIT 6

Social Change and the Future

Unit Selections

Key Points to Consider

- What are the advantages of slowing world population growth? How can it be done?

- What dangers does humankind's overexploitation of the environment create?

- What are some of the major problems that technology is creating?

- How bright is America's future? What are the main threats to it? What are some of its main challenges?

- Would you say that both democracy and capitalism are triumphant today? Explain your answer. What kind of problems can democracy and capitalism cause?

 **Links: www.dushkin.com/online/**
These sites are annotated in the World Wide Web pages.

Communications for a Sustainable Future
http://csf.colorado.edu

Human Rights and Humanitarian Assistance
http://www.etown.edu/vl/humrts.html

The Hunger Project
http://www.thp.org

National Immigrant Forum
http://www.immigrationforum.org/index.htm

Terrorism Research Center
http://www.terrorism.com/index.shtml

United Nations Environment Program (UNEP)
http://www.unep.ch

William Davidson Institute
http://www.wdi.bus.umich.edu

Fascination with the future is an enduring theme in literature, art, poetry, and religion. Human beings are anxious to know if tomorrow will be different from today and in what ways it might differ. Coping with change has become a top priority in the lives of many. One result of change is stress. When the future is uncertain and the individual appears to have little control over what happens, stress can be a serious problem. On the other hand, stress can have positive effects on people's lives if they can perceive changes as challenges and opportunities.

Any discussion of the future must begin with a look at the interface of population and the environment. Some scholars are very concerned about population's impact on the environment and others are confident that technological developments will solve most of the problems. Since the debate is about the future, neither view can be "proved." Nevertheless, it is important to understand the seriousness of the problem. In the first unit article, Lester Brown, Gary Gardner, and Brian Halweil discuss 16 impacts of population growth. The way societies are providing for the present 6 billion people is badly damaging Earth's ecosystems and crowding or overshooting environmental limits. Many changes are needed in the next few decades to achieve sustainability, including stabilizing world population.

The next article discusses current scientific thinking about global warming. The environment is in trouble in many ways from overplowing, overgrazing, overfishing, overtimbering, and species loss to resource depletion, toxic wastes, and water shortages, but the focal issue today is global warming. The predictions are scary. The low estimates of warmer world temperatures would cause considerable trouble, but the high estimates "could be disastrous." Michael Lemonick reviews many of the possible impacts and urges that the world take steps now to substantially reduce greenhouse gases to prevent these impacts.

The next subsection in unit 6 addresses the linkage between technological change and society. Both articles in this section raise concerns about the possible negative effects of supposedly beneficial technologies. The first article, by Eduardo Goncalves, evaluates another sophisticated technology-nuclear power. It can win wars and supply useful electrical energy, but it may have already killed 175 million people. Furthermore, the way scientists and governments have acted regarding nuclear energy shows that they cannot always be trusted to pursue the public good in their decisions regarding new technologies. One big technology story concerns genetic engineering, and one of its important areas of application is agriculture. The crucial question is whether it produces great agricultural advances or ecological nightmares. J. Madeleine Nash tells the story of the noble efforts to engineer beta-carotene into rice to make children in developing countries more resistant to diseases. Many lives would be saved or improved, but the haunting question is whether this new technology will have harmful unintended consequences.

The next section focuses on the new crisis of terrorism. It begins with an article by Steven Simon that discusses how terrorism has changed from limited violence as a tactic in political struggles to religiously motivated indiscriminate mass killings to inflict maximum harm on a hated people. How can the U.S. protect itself from such a foe? Not being land based, it is very hard to combat militarily. Its attacks will be surprises and defense is nearly impossible with so many potential targets to protect. The world faces a new kind of *terrorism* as described in this essay, by L. Paul Bremer, III, and it must devise a new strategy for *countering terrorism*. State support for terrorism must be ended, and an international consensus built against it. Fellow members of ethnic and religious groups to which the terrorists belong must condemn terrorism.

The final subsection looks at the future in terms of some of the most important trends and how to create a good future out of them. William Van Dusen Wishard, president of a firm that does research on trends, has authored the first of these articles. Armed with many interesting statistics on trends, he argues that the world is undergoing a great transition that is based on globalization, rapid technological development, and "a long-term spiritual and psychological reorientation that's increasingly generating uncertainty and instability." As a result, "the soul of America—indeed, of the world—is in a giant search for some deeper and greater expression of life." The last article by Fareed Zakaria provides a hopeful picture of world progress in the twentieth century in political development toward democracy and in economic development toward competitive capitalism. However, these processes can also be destructive and challenging to old orders that make it difficult to speculate about what these trends will bring about in the twentieth first century.

16 Impacts of Population Growth

Ongoing global population growth may be THE most critical issue of today.
Here are 16 ways it affects human prospects.

By Lester R. Brown, Gary Gardner, and Brian Halweil

The world's population has doubled during the last half century, climbing from 2.5 billion in 1950 to 5.9 billion in 1998. This unprecedented surge in population, combined with rising individual consumption, is pushing our claims on the planet beyond its natural limits.

The United Nations projects that human population in 2050 will range between 7.7 billion and 11.2 billion people. We use the United Nation's middle-level projection of 9.4 billion (from *World Population Prospects: The 1996 Revision*) to give an idea of the strain this "most likely" outcome would place on ecosystems and governments in the future and of the urgent need to break from the business-as-usual scenario.

Our study looks at 16 dimensions or effects of population growth in order to gain a better perspective on how future population trends are likely to affect human prospects:

Impacts on Food and Agriculture

1. Grain Production

From 1950 to 1984, growth in the world grain harvest easily exceeded that of population. But since then, the growth in the grain harvest has fallen behind that of population, so per-person output has dropped by 7% (0.5% a year), according to the U.S. Department of Agriculture.

The slower growth in the world grain harvest since 1984 is due to the lack of new land and to slower growth in irrigation and fertilizer use because of the diminishing returns of these inputs.

Now that the frontiers of agricultural settlement have disappeared, future growth in grain production must come almost entirely from raising land productivity. Unfortunately, this is becoming more difficult. The challenge for the world's farmers is to reverse this decline at a time when cropland area per person is shrinking, the amount of irrigation water per person is dropping, and the crop yield response to additional fertilizer use is falling.

2. Cropland

Since mid-century, grain area—which serves as a proxy for cropland in general—has increased by some 19%, but global population has grown by 132%. Population growth can degrade farmland, reducing its productivity or even eliminating it from production. As grain area per person falls, more and more nations risk losing the capacity to feed themselves.

The trend is illustrated starkly in the world's four fastest-growing

U.S. AID

Shanty town life in Bangladesh. Countries that fail to reduce population growth will endure the breakdown of their economic and social systems, according to the authors.

large countries. Having already seen per capita grain area shrink by 40%–50% between 1960 and 1998, Pakistan, Nigeria, Ethiopia, and Iran can expect a further 60%–70% loss by 2050—a conservative projection that assumes no further losses of agricultural land. The result will be four countries with a combined population of more than 1 billion whose grain area per person will be only 300–600 square meters—less than a quarter of the area in 1950.

3. Fresh Water

Spreading water scarcity may be the most underrated resource issue in the world today. Wherever population is growing, the supply of fresh water per person is declining.

Evidence of water stress can be seen as rivers are drained dry and water tables fall. Rivers such as the Nile, the Yellow, and the Colorado have little water left when they reach the sea. Water tables are now falling on every continent, including in major food-producing regions. Aquifers are being depleted in the U.S. southern Great Plains, the North China Plain, and most of India.

The International Water Management Institute projects that a billion people will be living in countries facing absolute water scarcity by 2025. These countries will have to reduce water use in agriculture in order to satisfy residential and industrial water needs. In both China and India, the two countries that together dominate world irrigated agriculture, substantial cutbacks in irrigation water supplies lie ahead.

4. Oceanic Fish Catch

A fivefold growth in the human appetite for seafood since 1950 has pushed the catch of most oceanic fisheries to their sustainable limits or beyond. Marine biologists believe that the oceans cannot sustain an annual catch of much more than 93 million tons, the current take.

As we near the end of the twentieth century, overfishing has become the rule, not the exception. Of the 15 major oceanic fisheries, 11 are in decline. The catch of Atlantic cod—long a dietary mainstay for western Europeans—has fallen by 70% since peaking in 1968. Since 1970, bluefin tuna stocks in the West Atlantic have dropped by 80%.

With the oceans now pushed to their limits, future growth in the demand for seafood can be satisfied only by fish farming. But as the world turns to aquaculture to satisfy its needs, fish begin to compete with livestock and poultry for feedstuffs such as grain, soybean meal, and fish meal.

The next half century is likely to be marked by the disappearance of some species from markets, a decline in the quality of seafood caught, higher prices, and more conflicts among countries over access to fisheries. Each year, the future oceanic catch per person will decline by roughly the amount of population growth, dropping to 9.9 kilograms (22 pounds) per person in 2050, compared with the 1988 peak of 17.2 kilograms (37.8 pounds).

5. Meat Production

When incomes begin to rise in traditional low-income societies, one of the first things people do is diversify their diets, consuming more livestock products.

World meat production since 1950 has increased almost twice as fast as population. Growth in meat

189

©PHOTODISC, INC.

The demand for energy will grow faster than population and create even more pollution as developing countries try to become as affluent as industrialized nations.

production was originally concentrated in western industrial countries and Japan, but over the last two decades it has increased rapidly in East Asia, the Middle East, and Latin America. Beef, pork, and poultry account for the bulk of world consumption.

Of the world grain harvest of 1.87 billion tons in 1998, an estimated 37% will be used to feed livestock and poultry, producing milk and eggs as well as meat, according to the U.S. Department of Agriculture. Grain fed to livestock and poultry is now the principal food reserve in the event of a world food emergency.

Total meat consumption will rise from 211 million tons in 1997 to 513 million tons in 2050, increasing pressures on the supply of grain.

Environment and Resources

6. Natural Recreation Areas

From Buenos Aires to Bangkok, dramatic population growth in the world's major cities—and the sprawl and pollution they bring—threaten natural recreation areas that lie beyond city limits. On every continent, human encroachment has reduced both the size and the quality of natural recreation areas.

In nations where rapid population growth has outstripped the carrying capacity of local resources, protected areas become especially vulnerable. Although in industrial nations these areas are synonymous with camping, hiking, and picnics in the country, in Asia, Africa, and Latin America most national parks, forests, and preserves are inhabited or used for natural resources by local populations.

Migration-driven population growth also endangers natural recreation areas in many industrial nations. Everglades National Park, for example, faces collapse as millions of newcomers move into southern Florida.

Longer waiting lists and higher user fees for fewer secluded spots are likely to be the tip of the iceberg, as population growth threatens to eliminate the diversity of habitats and cultures in addition to the peace and quiet that protected areas currently offer.

7. Forests

Global losses of forest area have marched in step with population growth for much of human history, but an estimated 75% of the loss in global forests has occurred in the twentieth century.

In Latin America, ranching is the single largest cause of deforestation. In addition, overgrazing and overcollection of firewood—which are often a function of growing population—are degrading 14% of the world's remaining large areas of virgin forest.

Deforestation created by the demand for forest products tracks closely with rising per capita consumption in recent decades. Global use of paper and paperboard per person has doubled (or nearly tripled) since 1961.

The loss of forest areas leads to a decline of forest services. These include habitat for wildlife; carbon storage, which is a key to regulating climate; and erosion control, provision of water across rainy and dry seasons, and regulation of rainfall.

8. Biodiversity

We live amid the greatest extinction of plant and animal life since the dinosaurs disappeared 65 million years ago, at the end of the Cretaceous period, with species losses at 100 to 1,000 times the natural rate. The principal cause of species extinction is habitat loss, which tends to accelerate with an increase in a country's population density.

A particularly productive but vulnerable habitat is found in coastal areas, home to 60% of the world's population. Coastal wetlands nurture two-thirds of all commercially caught fish, for example. And coral reefs have the second-highest concentration of biodiversity in the world, after tropical rain forests. But human encroachment and pollution are degrading these areas: Roughly half of the world's salt marshes and mangrove swamps have been eliminated or radically altered, and two-thirds of the world's coral reefs have been degraded, 10% of them "beyond recognition." As coastal migration continues—coastal dwellers could account for 75% of world population within 30 years—the pressures on these productive habitats will likely increase.

9. Climate Change

Over the last half century, carbon emissions from fossil-fuel burning expanded at nearly twice the rate of population, boosting atmospheric concentrations of carbon dioxide, the principal greenhouse gas, by 30% over preindustrial levels.

The 20 Largest Countries Ranked According to Population Size (in millions)

1998 Rank	Country	Population	2050 Country	Population
1	China	1,255	India	1,533
2	India	976	China	1,517
3	United States	274	Pakistan	357
4	Indonesia	207	United States	348
5	Brazil	165	Nigeria	339
6	Pakistan	148	Indonesia	318
7	Russia	147	Brazil	243
8	Japan	126	Bangladesh	218
9	Bangladesh	124	Ethiopia	213
10	Nigeria	122	Iran	170
11	Mexico	96	The Congo	165
12	Germany	82	Mexico	154
13	Vietnam	78	Philippines	131
14	Iran	73	Vietnam	130
15	Philippines	72	Egypt	115
16	Egypt	66	Russia	114
17	Turkey	64	Japan	110
18	Ethiopia	62	Turkey	98
19	Thailand	60	South Africa	91
20	France	59	Tanzania	89

SOURCE: UNITED NATIONS, WORLD POPULATION PROSPECTS: THE 1996 REVISION.

Fossil-fuel use accounts for roughly three-quarters of world carbon emissions. As a result, regional growth in carbon emissions tend to occur where economic activity and related energy use is projected to grow most rapidly. Emissions in China are projected to grow over three times faster than population in the next 50 years due to a booming economy that is heavily reliant on coal and other carbon-rich energy sources.

Emissions from developing countries will nearly quadruple over the next half century, while those from industrial nations will increase by 30%, according to the Intergovernmental Panel on Climate Change and the U.S. Department of Energy. Although annual emissions from industrial countries are currently twice as high as from developing ones, the latter are on target to eclipse the industrial world by 2020.

10. Energy

The global demand for energy grew twice as fast as population over the last 50 years. By 2050, developing countries will be consuming much more energy as their populations increase and become more affluent.

When per capita energy consumption is high, even a low rate of population growth can have signifi-cant effects on total energy demand. In the United States, for example, the 75 million people projected to be added to the population by 2050 will boost energy demand to roughly the present energy consumption of Africa and Latin America.

World oil production per person reached a high in 1979 and has since declined by 23%. Estimates of when global oil production will peak range from 2011 to 2025, signaling future price shocks as long as oil remains the world's dominant fuel.

In the next 50 years, the greatest growth in energy demands will come where economic activity is projected to be highest: in Asia, where consumption is expected to

Demographic Fatigue

To assess the likelihood that the U.N. population projections will actually occur, it is useful to bear in mind the concept of the demographic transition, formulated by Princeton demographer Frank Notestein in 1945. Its three stages help to explain widely disparate population-growth rates.

The first stage describes pre-industrial societies: Birthrates and death rates are both high, offsetting each other and leading to little or no population growth. In stage two, countries reach an unsustainable state as they begin to modernize: Death rates fall to low levels while birthrates remain high. In the third state, modernization continues: Birth and death rates are again in balance, but at lower levels, and populations are essentially stable. All countries today are in either stage two or stage three.

One key question now facing the world is whether the 150 or so countries that are still in stage two, with continuing population growth, can make it into stage three by quickly reducing births. Governments of countries that have been in stage two for several decades are typically worn down and drained of financial resources by the consequences of rapid population growth, in effect suffering from "demographic fatigue." Such countries are losing the struggle to educate their children, create jobs, and cope with environmental problems such as erosion, deforestation, and aquifer depletion.

Demographic fatigue is perhaps most evident in the inability of many governments to combat the resurgence of traditional diseases, such as malaria or tuberculosis, and new diseases, such as AIDS. If these threats are not dealt with, they can force countries back into stage one. For several African countries with high HIV infection levels, this is no longer a hypothetical prospect. Although most industrialized nations have held infection levels under 1%, governments overwhelmed by population pressures have not.

Zimbabwe, for example, has a 26% adult HIV infection rate and cannot pay for the costly drugs needed to treat the disease. Zimbabwe is expected to reach population stability in 2002 as death rates from the HIV/AIDS epidemic climb to offset birthrates, essentially falling back into stage one. Other African countries that are likely to follow include Botswana, Namibia, Zambia, and Swaziland.

—*Lester R. Brown, Gary Gardner, and Brian Halweil*

grow 361%, though population will grow by just 50%. Energy consumption is also expected to increase in Latin America (by 340%) and Africa (by 326%). In all three regions, local pressures on energy sources, ranging from forests to fossil fuel reserves to waterways, will be significant.

11. Waste

Local and global environmental effects of waste disposal will likely worsen as 3.4 billion people are added to the world's population over the next half century. Prospects for providing access to sanitation are dismal in the near to medium term.

A growing population increases society's disposal headaches—the garbage, sewage, and industrial waste that must be gotten rid of. Even where population is largely stable—the case in many industrialized countries—the flow of waste products into landfills and waterways generally continues to increase. Where high rates of economic and population growth coincide in

coming decades, as they will in many developing countries, mountains of waste will likely pose difficult disposal challenges for municipal and national authorities.

Economic Impacts and Quality of Life

12. Jobs

Since 1950, the world's labor force has more than doubled—from 1.2 billion people to 2.7 billion—outstripping the growth in job creation. Over the next half century, the world will need to create more than 1.9 billion jobs in the developing world just to maintain current levels of employment.

While population growth may boost labor demand (through economic activity and demand for goods), it will most definitely boost labor supply. As the balance between the demand and supply of labor is tipped by population growth, wages tend to decrease. And in a situation of labor surplus, the quality of

jobs may not improve as fast, for workers will settle for longer hours, fewer benefits, and less control over work activities.

As the children of today represent the workers of tomorrow, the interaction between population growth and jobs is most acute in nations with young populations. Nations with more than half their population below the age of 25 (e.g., Peru, Mexico, Indonesia, and Zambia) will feel the burden of this labor flood. Employment is the key to obtaining food, housing, health services, and education, in addition to providing self-respect and self-fulfillment.

13. Income

Incomes have risen most rapidly in developing countries where population has slowed the most, including South Korea, Taiwan, China, Indonesia, and Malaysia. African countries, largely ignoring family planning, have been overwhelmed by the sheer numbers of young people who need to be educated and employed.

Small families are the key to stabilizing population. Convincing couples everywhere to restrict their childbearing to replacement-level fertility is important enough to warrant a worldwide campaign, according to the authors.

If the world cannot simultaneously convert the economy to one that is environmentally sustainable and move to a lower population trajectory, economic decline will be hard to avoid.

14. Housing

The ultimate manifestation of population growth outstripping the supply of housing is homelessness. The United Nations estimates that at least 100 million of the world's people—roughly equal to the population of Mexico—have no home; the number tops 1 billion if squatters and others with insecure or temporary accommodations are included.

Unless population growth can be checked worldwide, the ranks of the homeless are likely to swell dramatically.

15. Education

In nations that have increasing child-age populations, the base pressures on the educational system will be severe. In the world's 10 fastest-growing countries, most of which are in Africa and the Middle East, the child-age population will increase an average of 93% over the next 50 years. Africa as a whole will see its school-age population grow by 75% through 2040.

If national education systems begin to stress lifelong learning for a rapidly changing world of the twenty-first century, then extensive provision for adult education will be necessary, affecting even those countries with shrinking child-age populations.

Such a development means that countries which started population-stabilization programs earliest will be in the best position to educate their entire citizenry.

16. Urbanization

Today's cities are growing faster: It took London 130 years to get from 1 million to 8 million inhabitants; Mexico City made this jump in just 30 years. The world's urban population as a whole is growing by just over 1 million people each week. This urban growth is fed by the natural increase of urban populations, by net migration from the country-side, and by villages or towns expanding to the point where they become cities or they are absorbed by the spread of existing cities.

If recent trends continue, 6.5 billion people will live in cities by 2050, more than the world's total population today.

Actions for Slowing Growth

As we look to the future, the challenge for world leaders is to help countries maximize the prospects for achieving sustainability by keeping both birth and death rates low. In a world where both grain output and fish catch per person are falling, a strong case can be made on humanitarian grounds to stabilize world population.

What is needed is an all-out effort to lower fertility, particularly in the high-fertility countries, while there is still time. We see four key steps in doing this:

Assess carrying capacity. Every national government needs a carefully articulated and adequately supported population policy, one that takes into account the country's carrying capacity at whatever consumption level citizens decide on.

Without long-term estimates of available cropland, water for irrigation, and likely yields, governments are simply flying blind into the future, allowing their nations to drift into a world in which population growth and environmental degradation can lead to social disintegration.

Fill the family-planning gap. This is a high-payoff area. In a world where population pressures are mounting, the inability of 120 million of the world's women to get family-planning services is inexcusable. A stumbling block: At the International Conference on Population and Development in Cairo in 1994, the industrialized countries agreed to pay one-third of the costs for reproductive-health services in devel-oping countries. So far they have failed to do so.

Educate young women. Educating girls is a key to accelerating the shift to smaller families. In every society for which data are available, the more education women have, the fewer children they have. Closely related to the need for education of young females is the need to provide equal opportunities for women in all phases of national life.

Have just two children. If we are facing a population emergency, it should be treated as such. It may be time for a campaign to convince couples everywhere to restrict their childbearing to replacement-level fertility.

About the Authors

Lester R. Brown is founder, president, and a senior researcher at the Worldwatch Institute, 1776 Massachusetts Avenue, N.W., Washington, D.C. 20036. Telephone 1-202-452-1999; Web site www.worldwatch.org.

Gary Gardner is a senior Worldwatch researcher and has written on agriculture, waste, and materials issues for *State of the World* and *World Watch* magazine.

Brian Halweil is a Worldwatch staff researcher and writes on issues related to food and agriculture, HIV/AIDS, cigarettes, and biotechnology.

This article is drawn from their report *Beyond Malthus: Sixteen Dimensions of the Population Problem*. Worldwatch Institute. 1998. 98 pages. Paperback. $5.

SPECIAL REPORT • GLOBAL WARMING

FEELING THE HEAT
LIFE IN THE GREENHOUSE

Except for nuclear war or a collision with an asteroid, no force has more potential to damage our planet's web of life than global warming. It's a "serious" issue, the White House admits, but nonetheless George W. Bush has decided to abandon the 1997 Kyoto treaty to combat climate change—an agreement the U.S. signed but the new President believes is fatally flawed. His dismissal last week of almost nine years of international negotiations sparked protests around the world and a face-to-face disagreement with German Chancellor Gerhard Schröder. Our special report examines the signs of global warming that are already apparent, the possible consequences for our future, what we can do about the threat and why we have failed to take action so far.

By MICHAEL D. LEMONICK

There is no such thing as normal weather. The average daytime high temperature for New York City this week should be 57°F, but on any given day the mercury will almost certainly fall short of that mark or overshoot it, perhaps by a lot. Manhattan thermometers can reach 65° in January every so often and plunge to 50° in July. And seasons are rarely normal. Winter snowfall and summer heat waves beat the average some years and fail to reach it in others. It's tough to pick out overall changes in climate in the face of these natural fluctuations. An unusually warm year, for example, or

even three in a row don't necessarily signal a general trend.

Yet the earth's climate does change. Ice ages have frosted the planet for tens of thousands of years at a stretch, and periods of warmth have pushed the tropics well into what is now the temperate zone. But given the normal year-to-year variations, the only reliable signal that such changes may be in the works is a long-term shift in worldwide temperature.

And that is precisely what's happening. A decade ago, the idea that the planet was warming up as a result of human activity was largely

theoretical. We knew that since the Industrial Revolution began in the 18th century, factories and power plants and automobiles and farms have been loading the atmosphere with heat-trapping gases, including carbon dioxide and methane. But evidence that the climate was actually getting hotter was still murky.

Not anymore. As an authoritative report issued a few weeks ago by the United Nations-sponsored Intergovernmental Panel on Climate Change makes plain, the trend toward a warmer world has unquestionably begun. Worldwide temperatures have climbed more than 1°F over the past

MAKING THE CASE THAT OUR CLIMATE IS CHANGING

From melting glaciers to rising oceans, the signs are everywhere. Global warming can't be blamed for any particular heat wave, drought or deluge, but scientists say a hotter world will make such extreme weather more frequent—and deadly.

EXHIBIT A

Thinning Ice

ANTARCTICA, home to these Adélie penguins, is heating up. The annual melt season has increased up to three weeks in 20 years.

MOUNT KILIMANJARO has lost 75% of its ice cap since 1912. The ice on Africa's tallest peak could vanish entirely within 15 years.

LAKE BAIKAL in eastern Siberia now feezes for the winter 1.1 days later than it did a century ago.

VENEZUELAN mountaintops had six glaciers in 1972. Today only two remain.

EXHIBIT B

Hotter Times

TEMPERATURES SIZZLED from Kansas to New England last May.

CROPS WITHERED and Dallas temperatures topped 100°F for 29 days-sstraight in a Texas hot spell that struck during the summer of 1998.

INDIA'S WORST heat shock in 50 years killed more than 2,500 people in May 1998.

CHERRY BLOSSOMS in Washington bloom seven days earlier in the spring than they did in 1970.

EXHIBIT C

Wild Weather

HEAVY RAINS in England and Wales made last fall Britain's wettest three-month period on record.

FIRES due to dry conditions and record-breaking heat consumed 20% of Samos Island, Greece, last July.

FLOODS along the Ohio River in March 1997 caused 30 deaths and at least $500 million in property damage.

HURRICAN FLOYD brought flooding rains and 130-m.p.h. winds through the Atlantic seabord in September1999, killing 77 people and leaving thousands homeless.

EXHIBIT D

Nature's Pain

PACIFIC SALMON populations fell sharply in 1997 and 1998, when local ocean temperatures rose 6°F.

POLAR BEARS in Hudson Bay are having fewer cubs, possibly as a result of earlier spring ice breakup.CORAL REEFS suffer from the loss of algae that color and nourish them. The process, called bleaching, is caused by warmer oceans.DISEASES like dengue fever are expanding their reach northward in the U.S.

BUTTERFLIES are relocating to higher latitudes. The Edith's Checkerspot butterfly of western North America has moved almost 60 miles north in 100 years.

EXHIBIT E

Rising Sea Levels

CAPE HATTERAS Lighthouse was 1,500 ft. from the North Carolina shoreline when it was built in 1870. By the late 1980s teh ocean had crept to within 160 ft., and the lighthouse had to be moved to avoid collapse.

JAPANESE FORTIFICATIONS were built on Kosrae Island in the southwest Pacific Ocean during World War II to guard against U.S. Marines' invading the beach. Today the fortifications are awash at high tide.

FLORIDA FARMLAND up to 1,000 ft. inland from Biscayne Bay is being infiltrated by salt water, rendering the land too toxic for crops. Salt water is also nibbling at the edges of farms on Maryland's Eastern Shore.

BRAZILIAN SHORELINE in the region of Recife receded more than 6 ft. a year from 1915 to 1950 and more than 8 ft. a year from 1985 to 1995.

century, and the 1990s were the hottest decade on record. After analyzing data going back at least two decades on everything from air and ocean temperatures to the spread and retreat of wildlife, the IPCC asserts that this slow but steady warming has had an impact on no fewer than 420 physical processes and animal and plant species on all continents.

Glaciers, including the legendary snows of Kilimanjaro, are disappearing from mountaintops around the globe. Coral reefs are dying off as the seas get too warm for comfort. Drought is the norm in parts of Asia and Africa. El Niño events, which trigger devastating weather in the eastern Pacific, are more frequent. The Arctic permafrost is starting to melt. Lakes and rivers in colder climates are freezing later and thawing earlier each year. Plants and animals are shifting their ranges poleward and to higher altitudes, and migration patterns for animals as diverse as polar bears, butterflies and beluga whales are being disrupted.

Faced with these hard facts, scientists no longer doubt that global warming is happening, and almost nobody questions the fact that humans are at least partly responsible. Nor are the changes over. Already, humans have increased the concentration of carbon dioxide, the most abundant heat-trapping gas in the atmosphere, to 30% above pre-industrial levels—and each year the

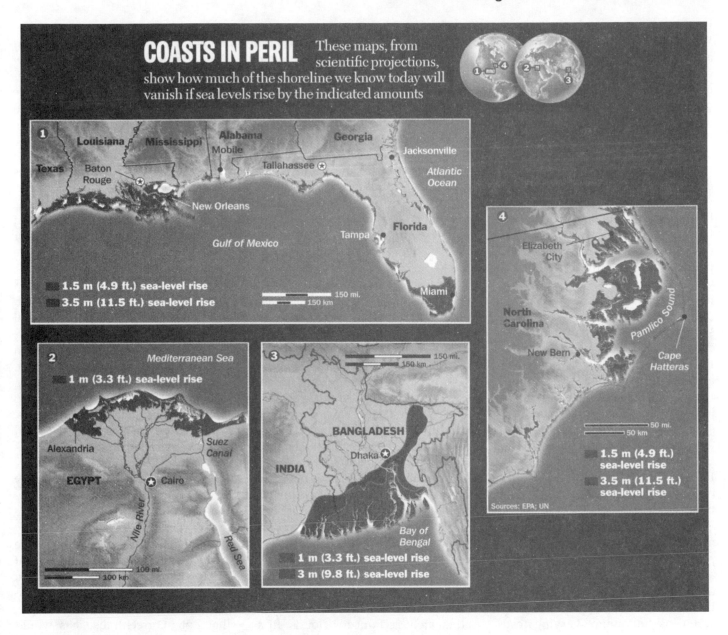

COASTS IN PERIL These maps, from scientific projections, show how much of the shoreline we know today will vanish if sea levels rise by the indicated amounts

rate of increase gets faster. The obvious conclusion: temperatures will keep going up.

Unfortunately, they may be rising faster and heading higher than anyone expected. By 2100, says the IPCC, average temperatures will increase between 2.5°F and 10.4°F—more than 50% higher than predictions of just a half-decade ago. That may not seem like much, but consider that it took only a 9°F shift to end the last ice age. Even at the low end, the changes could be problematic enough, with storms getting more frequent and intense, droughts more pronounced,

coastal areas ever more severely eroded by rising seas, rainfall scarcer on agricultural land and ecosystems thrown out of balance.

But if the rise is significantly larger, the result could be disastrous. With seas rising as much as 3 ft., enormous areas of densely populated land—coastal Florida, much of Louisiana, the Nile Delta, the Maldives, Bangladesh—would become uninhabitable. Entire climatic zones might shift dramatically, making central Canada look more like central Illinois, Georgia more like Guatemala. Agriculture would be

thrown into turmoil. Hundreds of millions of people would have to migrate out of unlivable regions.

Public health could suffer. Rising seas would contaminate water supplies with salt. Higher levels of urban ozone, the result of stronger sunlight and warmer temperatures, could worsen respiratory illnesses. More frequent hot spells could lead to a rise in heat-related deaths. Warmer temperatures could widen the range of disease-carrying rodents and bugs, such as mosquitoes and ticks, increasing the incidence of dengue fever, malaria, encephalitis,

Lyme disease and other afflictions. Worst of all, this increase in temperatures is happening at a pace that outstrips anything the earth has seen in the past 100 million years. Humans will have a hard enough time adjusting, especially in poorer countries, but for wildlife, the changes could be devastating.

Like any other area of science, the case for human-induced global warming has uncertainties—and like many pro-business lobbyists, President Bush has proclaimed those uncertainties a reason to study the problem further rather than act. But while the evidence is circumstantial, it is powerful, thanks to the IPCC's painstaking research. The U.N.-sponsored group was organized in the late 1980s. Its mission: to sift through climate-related studies from a dozen different fields and integrate them into a coherent picture. "It isn't just the work of a few green people," says Sir John Houghton, one of the early leaders who at the time ran the British Meteorological Office. "The IPCC scientists come from a wide range of backgrounds and countries."

Measuring the warming that has already taken place is relatively simple; the trick is unraveling the causes and projecting what will happen over the next century. To do that, IPCC scientists fed a wide range of scenarios involving varying estimates of population and economic growth, changes in technology and other factors into computers. That process gave them about 35 estimates, ranging from 6 billion to 35 billion tons, of how much excess carbon dioxide will enter the atmosphere.

Then they loaded those estimates into the even larger, more powerful computer programs that attempt to model the planet's climate. Because no one climate model is considered definitive, they used seven different versions, which yielded 235 independent predictions of global temperature increase. That's where the range of 2.5°F to 10.4°F (1.4°C to 5.8°C) comes from.

The computer models were criticized in the past largely because the climate is so complex that the limited hardware and software of even a half-decade ago couldn't do an adequate simulation. Today's climate models, however, are able to take into account the heat-trapping effects not just of CO_2 but also of other greenhouse gases, including methane. They can also factor in natural variations in the sun's energy and the effect of substances like dust from volcanic eruptions and particulate matter spewed from smokestacks.

That is one reason the latest IPCC predictions for temperature increase are higher than they were five years ago. Back in the mid-1990s, climate models didn't include the effects of the El Chichon and Mount Pinatubo volcanic eruptions, which threw enough dust into the air to block out some sunlight and slow down the rate of warming. That effect has dissipated, and the heating should start to accelerate. Moreover, the IPCC noted, many countries have begun to reduce their emissions of sulfur dioxide in order to fight acid rain. But sulfur dioxide particles, too, reflect sunlight; without this shield, temperatures should go up even faster.

The models still aren't perfect. One major flaw, agree critics and champions alike, is that they don't adequately account for clouds. In a warmer world, more water will evaporate from the oceans and presumably form more clouds. If they are billowy cumulus clouds, they will tend to shade the planet and slow down warming; if they are high, feathery cirrus clouds, they will trap even more heat.

Research by M.I.T. atmospheric scientist Richard Lindzen suggests that warming will tend to make cirrus clouds go away. Another critic, John Christy of the University of Alabama in Huntsville, says that while the models reproduce the current climate in a general way, they fail to get right the amount of warming at different levels in the atmosphere. Neither Lindzen nor Christy (both IPCC authors) doubts, however, that humans are influencing the climate. But they question how much—and how high temperatures will go. Both scientists are distressed that only the most extreme scenarios, based on huge population growth and the maximum use of dirty fuels like coal, have made headlines.

It won't take the greatest extremes of warming to make life uncomfortable for large numbers of people. Even slightly higher temperatures in regions that are already drought- or flood-prone would exacerbate those conditions. In temperate zones, warmth and increased CO_2 would make some crops flourish—at first. But beyond 3° of warming, says Bill Easterling, a professor of geography and agronomy at Penn State and a lead author of the IPCC report, "there would be a dramatic turning point. U.S. crop yields would start to decline rapidly." In the tropics, where crops are already at the limit of their temperature range, the decrease would start right away.

Even if temperatures rise only moderately, some scientists fear, the climate would reach a "tipping point"—a point at which even a tiny additional increase would throw the system into violent change. If peat bogs and Arctic permafrost warm enough to start releasing the methane stored within them, for example, that potent greenhouse gas would suddenly accelerate the heat-trapping process.

By contrast, if melting ice caps dilute the salt content of the sea, major ocean currents like the Gulf Stream could slow or even stop, and so would their warming effects on northern regions. More snowfall reflecting more sunlight back into space could actually cause a net cooling. Global warming could, paradoxically, throw the planet into another ice age.

Even if such a tipping point doesn't materialize, the more drastic effects of global warming might be only postponed rather than avoided. The IPCC's calculations end with the year 2100, but the warming won't.

World Bank chief scientist, Robert Watson, currently serving as IPCC chair, points out that the CO_2 entering the atmosphere today will be there for a century. Says Watson: "If we stabilize (CO_2 emissions) now, the concentration will continue to go up for hundreds of years. Temperatures will rise over that time."

That could be truly catastrophic. The ongoing disruption of ecosystems and weather patterns would be bad enough. But if temperatures reach the IPCC's worst-case levels and stay there for as long as 1,000 years, says Michael Oppenheimer, chief scientist at Environmental Defense, vast ice sheets in Greenland and Antarctica could melt, raising sea level more than 30 ft. Florida would be history, and every city on the U.S. Eastern seaboard would be inundated.

In the short run, there's not much chance of halting global warming, not even if every nation in the world ratifies the Kyoto Protocol tomorrow. The treaty doesn't require reductions in carbon dioxide emissions until 2008. By that time, a great deal of damage will already have been done. But we can slow things down. If action today can keep the climate from eventually reaching an unstable tipping point or can finally begin to reverse the warming trend a century from now, the effort would hardly be futile. Humanity embarked unknowingly on the dangerous experiment of tinkering with the climate of our planet. Now that we know what we're doing, it would be utterly foolish to continue.

Reported by David Bjerklie,
Robert H. Boyle and
Andrea Dorfman/New York and
Dick Thompson/Washington

The secret nuclear war

The equivalent of a nuclear war has already happened. Over the last half-century, millions have died as a result of accidents, experiments, lies and cover-ups by the nuclear industry. **Eduardo Goncalves** pulls together a number of examples, and counts the fearful total cost.

Hugo Paulino was proud to be a fusilier. He was even prouder to be serving as a UN peacekeeper in Kosovo. It was his chance to help the innocent casualties of war. His parents did not expect him to become one.

Hugo, says his father Luis, died of leukaemia caused by radiation from depleted uranium (DU) shells fired by NATO during the Kosovo war. He was one of hundreds of Portuguese peacekeepers sent to Klina, an area heavily bombed with these munitions. Their patrol detail included the local lorry park, bombed because it had served as a Serb tank reserve, and the Valujak mines, which sheltered Serbian troops.

In their time off, the soldiers bathed in the river and gratefully supplemented their tasteless rations with local fruit and cheeses given to them by thankful nuns from the convent they guarded. Out of curiosity, they would climb inside the destroyed Serbian tanks littering the area.

Hugo arrived back in Portugal from his tour of duty on 12 February 2000, complaining of headaches, nausea and 'flu-like symptoms'. Ten days later, on 22 February, he suffered a major seizure. He was rushed to Lisbon's military hospital, where his condition rapidly deteriorated. On 9 March, he died. He was 21.

The military autopsy, which was kept secret for 10 months, claimed his death was due to septicaemia and 'herpes of the brain'. Not so, says Luis Paulino. 'When he was undergoing tests, a doctor called me over and said he thought it could be from radiation.'

It was only then that Luis learnt about the uranium shells—something his son had never been warned about or given protective clothing against. He contacted doctors and relatives of Belgian and Italian soldiers suspected of having succumbed to radiation poisoning.

'The similarities were extraordinary', he said. 'My son had died from leukaemia. That is why the military classified the autopsy report and wanted me to sign over all rights to its release.'

Today, Kosovo is littered with destroyed tanks, and pieces of radioactive shrapnel. NATO forces fired 31,000 depleted uranium shells during the Kosovo campaign, and 10,800 into neighbouring Bosnia. The people NATO set out to protect—and the soldiers it sent out to protect them—are now dying. According to Bosnia's health minister, Boza Ljubic, cancer deaths among civilians have risen to 230 cases per 100,000 last year, up from 152 in 1999. Leukaemia cases, he added, had doubled.

Scientists predict that the use of DU in Serbia will lead to more than 10,000 deaths from cancer among local residents, aid workers, and peacekeepers. Belated confessions that plutonium was also used may prompt these estimates to be revised. But while NATO struggles to stave off accusations of a cover-up, the Balkans are merely the newest battlefield in a silent world war that has claimed millions of lives. Most of its victims have died not in war-zones, but in ordinary communities scattered across the globe.

The hidden deaths of Newbury

Far away from the war-torn Balkans is Newbury, a prosperous white-collar industrial town in London's commuter belt. On its outskirts is Greenham Common, the former US Air Force station that was one of America's most important strategic bases during the Cold War. The base was closed down after the signing of the INF (Intermediate Nuclear Forces) Treaty by Ronald Reagan and Mikhail Gorbachev. The nuclear threat was over. Or so people thought.

In August 1993, Ann Capewell—who lived just one mile away from the base's former runway—died of acute myeloid leukaemia. She was 16 when she passed away, just 40 days after diagnosis. As they were coming to terms with their sudden loss, her parents—Richard and Elizabeth—were surprised to find a number of other cases of leukaemia in their locality.

The more they looked, the more cases they found. 'Many were just a stone's throw from our front door,' says Richard, 'mainly cases of myeloid leukaemia in young people.' What none of them knew was that they were the victims of a nuclear accident at Greenham Common that had been carefully covered up by successive British and American administrations.

'It is believed that the estimated 1,900 nuclear tests conducted during the Cold War released fallout equivalent to 40,000 Hiroshimas in every corner of the globe.'

On February 28 1958, a laden B-47 nuclear bomber was awaiting clearance for take-off when it was suddenly engulfed in a huge fireball. Another bomber flying overhead had dropped a full fuel tank just 65 feet away. The plane exploded and burnt uncontrollably for days. As did its deadly payload.

A secret study by scientists at Britain's nearby nuclear bomb laboratory at Aldermaston documented the fallout, but the findings were never disclosed. The report showed how radioactive particles had been 'glued' to the runway surface by fire-fighters attempting to extinguish the blazing bomber—and that these were now being slowly blown into Newbury and over other local communities by aircraft jet blast.

'Virtually all the cases of leukaemias and lymphomas are in a band stretching from Greenham Common into south Newbury,' says Elizabeth. However, the British government continues to deny the cluster's existence, whilst the Americans still insist there was no accident.

Yet this was just one of countless disasters, experiments and officially-sanctioned activities which the nuclear powers have kept a closely-guarded secret. Between them, they have caused a global human death toll which is utterly unprecedented and profoundly shocking.

Broken Arrows

In 1981, the Pentagon publicly released a list of 32 'Broken Arrows—official military terminology for an accident involving a nuclear weapon. The report gave few details and did not divulge the location of some accidents. It was prepared in response to mounting media pressure about possible accident cover-ups.

But another US government document, this time secret, indicates that the official report may be seriously misleading. It states that 'a total of 1,250 nuclear weapons have been involved in accidents during handling, storage and transportation', a number of which 'resulted in, or had high potential for, plutonium dispersal.'[1]

Washington has never acknowledged the human consequences of even those few accidents it admits to, such as the Thule disaster in Greenland in 1968. When a B-52 bomber crashed at this secret nuclear base, all four bombs detonated, and a cloud of plutonium rose 800 metres in the air, blowing deadly radioactive particles hundreds of miles. The authorities downplayed the possibility of any health risks. But today, many local Eskimos, and their huskies, suffer from cancer, and over 300 people involved in the clean-up operation alone have since died of cancer and mysterious illnesses.

We may never know the true toll from all the bomb accidents, as the nuclear powers classify these disasters not as matters of public interest but of 'national security' instead. Indeed, it is only now that details are beginning to emerge of some accidents at bomb factories and nuclear plants that took place several decades ago.

Soviet sins

In 1991, Polish film-maker Slawomir Grunberg was invited to a little-known town in Russia's Ural mountains that was once part of a top-secret Soviet nuclear bomb-making complex. What he found was a tragedy of extraordinary dimensions, largely unknown to the outside world, and ignored by post-Cold War leaders.

His film—*Chelyabinsk: The Most Contaminated Spot on the Planet*—tells the story of the disasters at the Soviet Union's first plutonium factory, and the poisoning of hundreds of thousands of people. For years, the complex dumped its nuclear waste—totalling 76 million cubic metres—into the Techa River, the sole water source for scores of local communities that line its banks. According to a local doctor, people received an average radiation dose 57 times higher than that of Chernobyl's inhabitants.

In 1957, there was an explosion at a waste storage facility that blew 2 million curies of radiation into the atmosphere. The kilometre-high cloud drifted over three

The cancer epidemic

Scientists at St Andrew's University recently found that cells exposed to a dose of just two alpha particles of radiation produced as many cancers as much higher doses of radiation. They concluded that a single alpha particle of radiation could be carcinogenic.

Herman Muller, who has received a Nobel Prize for his work, has shown how the human race's continuous exposure to so-called 'low-level' radiation is causing a gradual reduction in its ability to survive, as successive generations are genetically damaged. The spreading and accumulation of even tiny genetic mutations pass through family lines, provoking allergies, asthma, juvenile diabetes, hypertension, arthritis, high blood cholesterol conditions, and muscular and bone defects.

Dr Chris Busby, who has extensively researched the low-level radiation threat, has made a link between everyday radiation exposure and a range of modern ailments: 'There have been tremendous increases in diseases resulting from the breakdown of the immune system in the last 20 years: diabetes, asthma, AIDS and others which may have an immune-system link, such as MS and ME. A whole spectrum of neurological conditions of unknown origin has developed'.[10]

Around the world, a pattern is emerging. For the first time in modern history, mortality rates among adults between the ages of 15 and 54 are actually increasing, and have been since 1982. In July 1983, the US Center for Birth Defects in Atlanta, Georgia, reported that physical and mental disabilities in the under-17s had doubled—despite a reduction in diseases such as polio, and improved vaccines and medical care.

Defects in new-born babies doubled between the 1950s and 1980s, as did long-term debilitating diseases. The US Environmental Protection Agency adds that 23 per cent of US males were sterile in 1980, compared to 0.5 per cent in 1938.

Above all, cancer is now an epidemic. In 1900, cancer accounted for only 4 per cent of deaths in the US. Now it is the second leading cause of premature mortality. Worldwide, the World Health Organisation (WHO) estimates the number of cancers will double in most countries over the next 25 years.

Within a few years, the chances of getting cancer in Britain will be as high as 40 per cent—virtually the toss of a coin.

Soviet provinces, contaminating over 250,000 people living in 217 towns and villages. Only a handful of local inhabitants were ever evacuated.

10 years later, Lake Karachay, also used as a waste dump, began to dry up. The sediment around its shores blew 5 million curies of radioactive dust over 25,000 square kilometres, irradiating 500,000 people. Even today, the lake is so 'hot' that standing on its shore will kill a person within one hour.

Grunberg's film tells of the terrible toll of these disasters on local families, such as that of Idris Sunrasin, whose grandmother, parents and three siblings have died of cancer. Leukaemia cases increased by 41 per cent after the plant began operations, and the average life span for women in 1993 was 47, compared to 72 nationally. For men it was just 45.

The secret nuclear war

Russia's nuclear industry is commonly regarded as cavalier in regard to health and safety. But the fact is that the nuclear military-industrial complex everywhere has been quite willing to deliberately endanger and sacrifice the lives of innocent civilians to further its ambitions.

The US government, for example, recently admitted its nuclear scientists carried out over 4,000 experiments on live humans between 1944 and 1974. They included feeding radioactive food to disabled children, irradiating prisoners' testicles, and trials on new-born babies and pregnant mothers. Scientists involved with the Manhattan Project injected people with plutonium without telling them. An autopsy of one of the victims reportedly showed that his bones 'looked like Swiss cheese'. At the University of Cincinnati, 88 mainly low-income, black women were subjected to huge doses of radiation in an experiment funded by the military. They suffered acute radiation sickness. Nineteen of them died.

'Scientists predict that millions will die in centuries to come from nuclear tests that happened in the 1950s and 1960s.'

Details of many experiments still remain shrouded in secrecy, whilst little is known of the more shocking ones to come to light—such as one when a man was injected with what a report described as 'about a lethal dose' of strontium-89.[2]

In Britain too, scientists have experimented with plutonium on new-born babies, ethnic minorities and the disabled. When American colleagues reviewed a British proposal for a joint experiment, they concluded: 'What is the worst thing that can happen to a human being as a result of being a subject? Death.'[3]

They also conducted experiments similar to America's 'Green Run' programme, in which 'dirty' radiation was released over populated areas in the western states of Washington and Oregon contaminating farmland, crops and water. The 'scrubber' filters in Hanford's nuclear stacks were deliberately switched off first. Scientists, posing as agriculture department officials, found radiation contamination levels on farms hundreds of times above 'safety' levels.

But America's farmers and consumers were not told this, and the British public has never been officially told about experiments on its own soil.

Forty thousand Hiroshimas

It is believed that the estimated 1,900 nuclear tests conducted during the Cold War released fallout equivalent to 40,000 Hiroshimas in every corner of the globe. Fission products from the Nevada Test site can be detected in the ecosystems of countries as far apart as South Africa, Brazil, and Malaysia. Here, too, ordinary people were guinea pigs in a global nuclear experiment. The public health hazards were known right from the beginning, but concealed from the public. A 1957 US government study predicted that recent American tests had produced an extra 2,000 'genetically defective' babies in the US each year, and up to 35,000 every year around the globe. They continued regardless.

Ernest Sternglass's research shows how, in 1964, between 10,000 and 15,000 children were lost by miscarriage and stillbirth in New York state alone—and that there were some 10 to 15 times this number of foetal deaths across America.[4]

'Over the years, the Harwell, Aldermaston and Amersham plants have pumped millions of gallons of liquid contaminated with radioactive waste into the River Thames.'

Those who lived closest to the test sites have seen their families decimated. Such as the 100,000 people who were directly downwind of Nevada's fallout. They included the Mormon community of St George in Utah, 100 miles away from 'Ground Zero'—the spot where the bombs were detonated. Cancer used to be virtually unheard of among its population. Mormons do not smoke or drink alcohol or coffee, and live largely off their own home-grown produce.

Mormons are also highly patriotic. They believe government to be 'God-given', and do not protest. The military could afford to wait until the wind was blowing from the test site towards St George before detonating a device. After all, President Eisenhower had said: 'We can afford to sacrifice a few thousand people out there in defence of national security.'[5]

When the leukaemia cases suddenly appeared, doctors—unused to the disease—literally had no idea what it was. A nine-year-old boy, misdiagnosed with diabetes, died after a single shot of insulin. Women who complained of radiation sickness symptoms were told they had 'housewife syndrome'. Many gave birth to terribly deformed babies that became known as 'the sacrifice babies'. Elmer Pickett, the local mortician, had to learn new embalming techniques for the small bodies of wasted children killed by leukaemia. He himself was to lose no fewer than 16 members of his immediate family to cancer.

By the mid-1950s, just a few years after the tests began, St George had a leukaemia rate 2.5 times the national average, whereas before it was virtually non-existent. The total number of radiation deaths are said to have totalled 1,600—in a town with a population of just 5,000.

The military simply lied about the radiation doses people were getting. Former army medic Van Brandon later revealed how his unit kept two sets of radiation readings for test fallout in the area. 'One set was to show that no one received an [elevated] exposure' whilst 'the other set of books showed the actual reading. That set was brought in a locked briefcase every morning.'[6]

Continuous fallout

The world's population is still being subjected to the continuous fallout of the 170 megatons of long-lived nuclear fission products blasted into the atmosphere and returned daily to earth by wind and rain—slowly poisoning our bodies via the air we breathe, the food we eat, and the water we drink. Scientists predict that millions will die in centuries to come from tests that happened in the 1950s and 1960s.

But whilst atmospheric testing is now banned, over 400 nuclear bomb factories and power plants around the world make 'routine discharges' of nuclear waste into the environment. Thousands of nuclear waste dumping grounds, many of them leaking, are contaminating soil and water every day. The production of America's nuclear weapons arsenal alone has produced 100 million cubic metres of long-lived radioactive waste.

The notorious Hanford plutonium factory—which produced the fissile materials for the Trinity test and Nagasaki bomb—has discharged over 440 billion gallons of contaminated liquid into the surrounding area, contaminating 200 square miles of groundwater, but concealed the dangers from the public. Officials knew as early as the late 1940s that the nearby Columbia River was becoming seriously contaminated and a hazard to local fishermen. They chose to keep information about discharges secret and not to issue warnings.

In Britain, there are 7,000 sites licensed to use nuclear materials, 1,000 of which are allowed to discharge wastes. Three of them, closely involved in Britain's nuclear bomb programme, are located near the River Thames. Over the years, the Harwell, Aldermaston and Amersham plants have pumped millions of gallons of liquid contaminated with radioactive waste into the river.

They did so in the face of opposition from government ministers and officials who said 'the 6 million inhabitants of London derive their drinking water from this source. Any increase in [radio-]activity of the water supply would increase the genetic load on this comparatively large group.'[7] One government minister even wrote of his fears that the dumping 'would produce between 10 and 300 severely abnormal individuals per generation'.

Public relations officers at Harwell themselves added: 'the potential sufferers are 8 million in number, including both Houses of Parliament, Fleet Street and Whitehall'. These discharges continue to this day.

Study after study has uncovered 'clusters' of cancers and high rates of other unusual illnesses near nuclear plants, including deformities and Down Syndrome. Exposure to radiation among Sellafield's workers, in northwest England, has been linked to a greater risk of fathering a stillborn child and leukaemia among off-spring. Reports also suggest a higher risk of babies developing spina bifida in the womb.

Although the plant denies any link, even official MAFF studies have shown high levels of contamination in locally-grown fruit and vegetables, as well as wild animals. The pollution from Sellafield alone is such that it has coated the shores of the whole of Britain—from Wales to Scotland, and even Hartlepool in north-eastern England. A nationwide study organised by Harwell found that Sellafield 'is a source of plutonium contamination in the wider population of the British Isles'.[8]

> **'Study after study has uncovered 'clusters' of cancers and high rates of other illnesses near nuclear plants, including deformities and Down Syndrome. Exposure to radiation among Sellafield's workers, in NW England, has been linked to a greater risk of fathering a stillborn child and leukaemia among off-spring.'**

Those who live nearest the plant face the greatest threat. A study of autopsy tissue by the National Radiological Protection Board (NRPB) found high plutonium levels in the lungs of local Cumbrians—350 per cent higher than people in other parts of the country. 'Cancer clusters' have been found around nuclear plants across the globe—from France to Taiwan, Germany to Canada. A joint White House/US Department of Energy investigation recently found a high incidence of 22 different kinds of cancer at 14 different US nuclear weapons facilities around the country.

Meanwhile, a Greenpeace USA study of the toxicity of the Mississippi river showed that from 1968-83 there were 66,000 radiation deaths in the counties lining its banks—more than the number of Americans who died during the Vietnam war.

Don't blame us

Despite the growing catalogue of tragedy, the nuclear establishment has consistently tried to deny responsibility. It claims that only high doses of radiation—such as those experienced by the victims of the Hiroshima and Nagasaki bombs—are dangerous, though even here they have misrepresented the data. They say that the everyday doses from nuclear plant discharges, bomb factories and transportation of radioactive materials are 'insignificant', and that accidents are virtually impossible.

The truth, however, is that the real number and seriousness of accidents has never been disclosed, and that the damage from fallout has been covered up. The nuclear establishment now grudgingly (and belatedly) accepts that there is no such thing as a safe dose of radiation, however 'low', yet the poisonous discharges continue. When those within the nuclear establishment try to speak out, they are harassed, intimidated—and even threatened.

John Gofman, former head of Lawrence Livermore's biomedical unit, who helped produce the world's first plutonium for the bomb, was for years at the heart of the nuclear complex. He recalls painfully the time he was called to give evidence before a Congressional inquiry set up to defuse mounting concern over radiation's dangers.

'Chet Holifield and Craig Hosmer of the Joint Committee (on Atomic Energy) came in and turned to me and said: "Just what the hell do you think you two are doing, getting all those little old ladies in tennis shoes up in arms about our atomic energy program? There are people like you who have tried to hurt the Atomic Energy Commission program before. We got them, and we'll get you."'[9]

Gofman was eventually forced out of his job. But the facts of his research—and that of many other scientists—speak for themselves.

The final reckoning

But could radiation really be to blame for these deaths? Are the health costs really that great? The latest research suggests they are.

It is only very recently that clues have surfaced as to the massive destructive power of radiation in terms of human health. The accident at Chernobyl will kill an estimated half a million people worldwide from cancer, and perhaps more. 90 per cent of children in the neighbouring former Soviet republic of Belarus are contaminated for life—the poisoning of an entire country's gene pool.

Ernest Sternglass calculates that, at the height of nuclear testing, there were as many as 3 million foetal deaths, spontaneous abortions and stillbirths in the US alone. In addition, 375,000 babies died in their first year of life from radiation-linked diseases.[11]

The final reckoning

How many deaths is the nuclear industry responsible for? The following calculations of numbers of cancers caused by radiation are the latest and most accurate:*

from nuclear bomb production and testing: 385 million

from bomb and plant accidents: 9.7 million

from the 'routine discharges' of nuclear power plants
(5 million of them among populations living nearby):   6.6 million

likely number of total cancer fatalities worldwide: 175 million

[Added to this number are 235 million genetically damaged and diseased people, and 588 million children born with diseases such as brain damage, mental disabilities, spina bifida, genital deformities, and childhood cancers.]

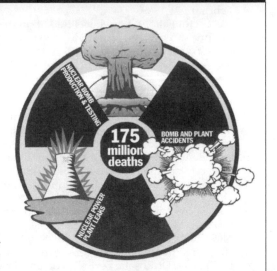

Calculated by Rosalie Bertell, using the official 'radiation risk' estimates published in 1991 by the International Commission on Radiological Protection (ICRP), and the total radiation exposure data to the global population calculated by the UN Scientific Committee on the Effects of Atomic Radiation (UNSCEAR) in 1993.

Rosalie Bertell, author of the classic book *No Immediate Danger*, now revised and re-released, has attempted to piece together a global casualty list from the nuclear establishment's own data. The figures she has come up with are chilling—but entirely plausible.

Using the official 'radiation risk' estimates published in 1991 by the International Commission on Radiological Protection (ICRP), and the total radiation exposure data to the global population calculated by the UN Scientific Committee on the Effects of Atomic Radiation (UN-SCEAR) in 1993, she has come up with a terrifying tally:

- 358 million cancers from nuclear bomb production and testing
- 9.7 million cancers from bomb and plant accidents
- 6.6 million cancers from the 'routine discharges' of nuclear power plants (5 million of them among populations living nearby).
- As many as 175 million of these cancers could be fatal.

Added to this number are no fewer than 235 million genetically damaged and diseased people, and a staggering 588 million children born with what are called 'teratogenic effects'—diseases such as brain damage, mental disabilities, spina bifida, genital deformities, and childhood cancers.

Furthermore, says Bertell, we should include the problem of nonfatal cancers and of other damage which is debilitating but not counted for insurance and liability purposes'[12]—such as the 500 million babies lost as stillbirths because they were exposed to radiation whilst still in the womb, but are not counted as 'official' radiation victims.

It is what the nuclear holocaust peace campaigners always warned of if war between the old superpowers broke out, yet it has already happened and with barely a shot being fired. Its toll is greater than that of all the wars in history put together, yet no-one is counted as among the war dead.

> ## 'It is the nuclear holocaust that peace campaigners always warned of if war between the old superpowers broke out, yet it has already happened and with barely a shot being fired.'

Its virtually infinite killing and maiming power leads Rosalie Bertell to demand that we learn a new language to express a terrifying possibility: 'The concept of species annihilation means a relatively swift, deliberately induced end to history, culture, science, biological reproduction and memory. It is the ultimate human rejection of the gift of life, an act which requires a new word to describe it: omnicide'.[13]

---

*Eduardo Goncalves is a freelance journalist and environmental researcher. He is author of tile reports **Broken Arrow—Greenham Common's Secret Nuclear Accident** and **Nuclear Guinea Pigs—British Human Radiation Experiments**, published by CND (UK), and was researcher to the film **The Dragon that Slew St George**. He is currently writing a book about the hidden history of the nuclear age.*

Notes

1. 'Report of the safety criteria for plutonium-bearing weapons—summary', US Department of Energy, February 14, 1973, document RS5640/1035.

2. Strontium metabolism meeting, Atomic Energy Division–Division of Biology and Medicine, January 17,1954.

3. memorandum to Bart Gledhill, chairman, Human Subjects Committee. LLNL, from Larry Anderson, LLNL, February 21,1989.

4. see 'Secret Fallout, Low-Level Radiation from Hiroshima to Three-Mile Island'. Ernest Sternglass, McGraw-Hill, New York, 1981.

5. see 'American Ground Zero; The Secret Nuclear War', Carole Gallagher, MIT Press. Boston, 1993.

6. Washington Post, February 24, 1994.

7. see PRO files AB 6/1379 and AB 6/2453 and 3584.

8. 'Variations in the concentration of plutonium, strontium-90 and total alpha-emitters in human teeth', RG. O'Donnell et al, Sd. Tot. Env, 201 (1997) 235–243.

9. interview with Gofman, DOE/OHRE Oral History Project, December 1994, pp 49-50 of official transcripts.

10. 'Wings of Death—nuclear pollution and human health', Dr. Chris Busby, Green Audit, Wales, 1995

11. see 'Secret Fallout, Low-Level Radiation from Hiroshima to Three-Mile Island', Ernest Sternglass, McGraw-Hill, New York, 1981.

12. from 'No Immediate Danger— Prognosis for a Radioactive Earth', Dr Rosalie Bertell. Women's Press. London 1985 (revised 2001)

13. pers. Comm. 4 February 2001

Further reading:

'No Immediate Danger—Prognosis for a Radioactive Earth', Dr Rosalie Bertell, Women's Press, London (revised 2001)

'Deadly Deceit—low-level radiation, high-level cover-up', Dr. Jay Gould and Benjamin A. Goldman, Four Walls Eight Windows, New York, 1991

'Wings of Death—nuclear pollution and human health', Dr. Chris Busby, Green Audit, Wales, 1995

'American Ground Zero: The Secret Nuclear War', Carole Gallagher, MIT Press, Boston, 1993

'Radioactive Heaven and Earth—the health effects of nuclear weapons testing in, on, and above the earth', a report of the IPPNW International Commission, Zed Books, 1991 'Secret Fallout. Low-Level Radiation from Hiroshima to Three-Mile Island', Ernest Sternglass, McGraw-Hill, New York, 1981

'Clouds of Deceit—the deadly legacy of Britain's bomb tests', Joan Smith, Faber and Faber, London, 1985

'Nuclear Wastelands', Arjun Makhijani et al (eds), MIT Press, Boston, 1995 'Radiation and Human Health', Dr. John W. Gofman, Sierra Book Club, San Francisco, 1981

'The Greenpeace Book of the Nuclear Age—The Hidden History, the Human Cost', John May, Victor Gollancz, 1989

'The Unsinkable Aircraft Carrier—American military power in Britain', Duncan Campbell, Michael Joseph, London 1984

From *The Ecologist,* April 2001, pp. 28-33. © 2001 by The Ecologist, *www.theecologist.org.* Reprinted by permission.

GRAINS OF HOPE

GENETICALLY ENGINEERED CROPS could revolutionize farming. Protesters fear they could also destroy the ecosystem. You decide

By J. MADELEINE NASH

ZURICH

AT FIRST, THE GRAINS OF RICE that Ingo Potrykus sifted through his fingers did not seem at all special, but that was because they were still encased in their dark, crinkly husks. Once those drab coverings were stripped away and the interiors polished to a glossy sheen, Potrykus and his colleagues would behold the seeds' golden secret. At their core, these grains were not pearly white, as ordinary rice is, but a very pale yellow—courtesy of beta-carotene, the nutrient that serves as a building block for vitamin A.

Potrykus was elated. For more than a decade he had dreamed of creating such a rice: a golden rice that would improve the lives of millions of the poorest people in the world. He'd visualized peasant farmers wading into paddies to set out the tender seedlings and winnowing the grain at harvest time in handwoven baskets. He'd pictured small children consuming the golden gruel their mothers would make, knowing that it would sharpen their eyesight and strengthen their resistance to infectious diseases.

And he saw his rice as the first modest start of a new green revolution, in which ancient food crops would acquire all manner of useful properties: bananas that wouldn't rot on the way to market; corn that could supply its own fertilizer; wheat that could thrive in drought-ridden soil.

But imagining a golden rice, Potrykus soon found, was one thing and bringing one into existence quite another. Year after year, he and his colleagues ran into one unexpected obstacle after another, beginning with the finicky growing habits of the rice they transplanted to a greenhouse near the foothills of the Swiss Alps. When success finally came, in the spring of 1999, Potrykus was 65 and about to retire as a full professor at the Swiss Federal Institute of Technology in Zurich. At that point, he tackled an even more formidable challenge.

Having created golden rice, Potrykus wanted to make sure it reached those for whom it was intended: malnourished children of the developing world. And that, he knew, was not likely to be easy. Why? Because in addition to a full complement of genes from Oryza sativa—the Latin name for the most commonly consumed species of rice—the golden grains also contained snippets of DNA borrowed from bacteria and daffodils. It was what some would call Frankenfood, a product of genetic engineering. As such, it was entangled in a web of hopes and fears and political baggage, not to mention a fistful of ironclad patents.

For about a year now—ever since Potrykus and his chief collaborator, Peter Beyer of the University of Freiburg in Germany, announced their achievement—their golden grain has illuminated an increasingly polarized public debate. At issue is the question of what genetically engineered crops represent. Are they, as their proponents argue, a technological leap forward that will bestow in-

HOW TO MAKE GOLDEN RICE
A four-step process to feed the poor

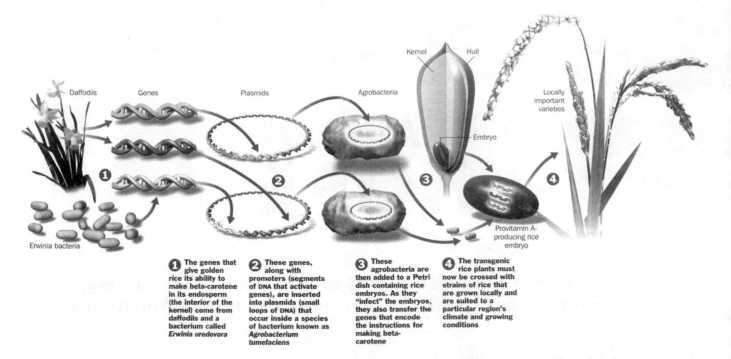

① The genes that give golden rice its ability to make beta-carotene in its endosperm (the interior of the kernel) come from daffodils and a bacterium called *Erwinia uredovora*

② These genes, along with promoters (segments of DNA that activate genes), are inserted into plasmids (small loops of DNA) that occur inside a species of bacterium known as *Agrobacterium tumefaciens*

③ These agrobacteria are then added to a Petri dish containing rice embryos. As they "infect" the embryos, they also transfer the genes that encode the instructions for making beta-carotene

④ The transgenic rice plants must now be crossed with strains of rice that are grown locally and are suited to a particular region's climate and growing conditions

SOURCE: DR. PETER BEYER, CENTER FOR APPLIED BIOSCIENCES, UNIVERSITY OF FREIBURG

calculable benefits on the world and its people? Or do they represent a perilous step down a slippery slope that will lead to ecological and agricultural ruin? Is genetic engineering just a more efficient way to do the business of conventional crossbreeding? Or does the ability to mix the genes of any species—even plants and animals—give man more power than he should have?

The debate erupted the moment genetically engineered crops made their commercial debut in the mid-1990s, and it has escalated ever since. First to launch major protests against biotechnology were European environmentalists and consumer-advocacy groups. They were soon followed by their U.S. counterparts, who made a big splash at last fall's World Trade Organization meeting in Seattle and last week launched an offensive designed to target one company after another (see accompanying story). Over the coming months, charges that transgenic crops pose grave dangers will be raised in petitions, editorials, mass mailings and protest marches. As a result, golden rice, de-spite its humanitarian intent, will probably be subjected to the same kind of hostile scrutiny that has already led to curbs on the commercialization of these crops in Britain, Germany, Switzerland and Brazil.

The hostility is understandable. Most of the genetically engineered crops introduced so far represent minor variations on the same two themes: resistance to insect pests and to herbicides used to control the growth of weeds. And they are often marketed by large, multinational corporations that produce and sell the very agricultural chemicals farmers are spraying on their fields. So while many farmers have embraced such crops as Monsanto's Roundup Ready soybeans, with their genetically engineered resistance to Monsanto's Roundup-brand herbicide, that let them spray weed killer without harming crops, consumers have come to regard such things with mounting suspicion. Why resort to a strange new technology that might harm the biosphere, they ask, when the benefits of doing so seem small?

FROM THE TRANSGENIC GARDEN

COTTON
BEAUTIFUL BOLL: This plant has been given a bacterial gene to help it fight off worms that infest cotton crops

CORN
HEALTHY KERNEL: These corn seeds are protected by the same bacterial gene, one that ecologists fear could harm butterflies

PAPAYA
VIRAL RESISTANCE: Fruit carrying a gene from the ringspot virus are better able to withstand ringspot outbreaks

CANOLA
PROBLEM POLLEN: When transgenic seeds contaminated a non-transgenic shipment from Canada, European farmers cried foul

SOYBEANS
ROUNDUP READY: Will crops designed to take frequent spraying with Monsanto's top weed killer lead to Roundup-resistant weeds?

Taking It to Main Street

By MARGOT ROOSEVELT SAN FRANCISCO

It WAS THE SORT OF KITSCHY STREET THEATER YOU EXPECT IN A city like San Francisco. A gaggle of protesters in front of a grocery store, some dressed as monarch butterflies, others as Frankenstein's monster. Signs reading HELL NO, WE WON'T GROW IT! People in white biohazard jumpsuits pitching Campbell's soup and Kellogg's corn-flakes into a mock toxic-waste bin. The crowd shouting, "Hey, hey, ho, ho—GMO has got to go!" And, at the podium, Jesse Cool, a popular res-taurant owner, wondering what would happen if she served a tomato spliced with an oyster gene and a customer got sick. "I could get sued," she says.

But just as the California activists were revving up last week, sim-ilar rants and chants were reverberating in such unlikely places as Grand Forks, N.D., Augusta, Maine, and Miami—19 U.S. cities in all. This was no frolicking radical fringe but the carefully coordinated start of a nationwide campaign to force the premarket safety testing and labeling of those GMOs, or genetically modified organisms. Seven organizations— including such media-savvy veterans as the Sierra Club, Friends of the Earth and the Public Interest Research Groups— were launching the Genetically Engineered Food Alert, a million-dol-lar, multiyear organizing effort to pressure Congress, the Food and Drug Administration and individual companies, one at a time, start-ing with Campbell's soup.

The offensive represents the seeds of what could grow into a seri-ous problem for U.S. agribusiness, which had been betting that sci-ence-friendly American consumers would remain immune to any "Frankenfood" backlash cross-pollinating from Europe or Japan. Af-ter all, this is (mostly) U.S. technology, and it has spread so quickly and so quietly that the proportion of U.S. farmland planted in geneti-cally altered corn now stands at nearly 25%. Some 70% of processed food in American supermarkets, from soup to sandwich meat, con-tains ingredients derived from transgenic corn, soybeans and other plants. Yet all of a sudden, activists are "yelling fire in a movie the-ater," says Dan Eramian, spokesman for the Biotechnology Industry Organization (BIO).

How widespread is this protest movement? And how deep are its roots? We may soon find out, for it's emergence is a study in the warp-speed politics of the age of the Internet. This is a time when a Web de-signer named Craig Winters can start an organization called the Cam-paign to Label Genetically Engineered Food with a staff of one (himself), mount a website and sell 160,000 "Take Action Packets" in nine weeks. Want to know what the Chileans are doing about trans-genic grain shipments? How South Korean labeling laws work? Just subscribe to one of the four biotech e-mail lists of the Institute for Ag-riculture and Trade Policy, based in Minneapolis, Minn.

Even so-called ecoterrorists who have uprooted scores of univer-sity test plots across the country in the past year use the Net to orga-nize their lawbreaking protests. In an Internet posting from Santa Cruz last week, Earth First! beckons, "You're all invited to sunny Cal-ifornia for a weekend of workshops, training and fun! We also have plenty of [genetically engineered] crops waiting for your night time gardening efforts." Says Carl Pope, the Sierra Club's executive direc-tor: "I've never seen an issue go so quickly."

It started about two years ago, when the buzz from European anti-biotech protest groups began to ricochet throughout the Net, reaching the community groups that were springing up across the U.S. Many were galvanized by proposed FDA regulations that would have al-lowed food certified as "organic" to contain genetically modified in-gredients—an effort shouted down by angry consumers. Meanwhile, Greenpeace began to target U.S. companies such as Gerber, which quickly renounced the use of transgenic ingredients, and Kellogg's, which

has yet to do so. With so-called Frankenfoods making headlines, sev-eral other companies cut back on biotech: McDonald's forswore genet-ically engineered potatoes, and Frito-Lay decreed it would buy no more genetically modified corn.

But the issue that is now on the front burner dates back to 1992, when the FDA decided that biotech ingredients did not materially al-ter food and therefore did not require labeling. Nor, the agency de-clared, was premarket safety testing required, because biotech additives were presumed to be benign. Last March the Center for Food Safety and 53 other groups, including the Union of Concerned Scien-tists, filed a petition to force the FDA to change its policy.

Meanwhile, the biotech issue is gathering steam in Congress, where safety and labeling bills have been introduced by Democratic Representative Dennis Kucinich of Ohio and 55 co-sponsors in the House, and by Daniel Patrick Moynihan and Barbara Boxer in the Sen-ate. Similar statewide bills are pending in Maine, Colorado and Ore-gon. Shareholder resolutions demanding safety testing and labeling have targeted a score of companies from life-science giants to super-market chains.

Surveys indicate that between two-thirds and three-quarters of Amer-icans want biotech food to be labeled. Then why not do it? Because com-panies fear such disclosure could spell disaster. "Our data show that 60% of consumers would consider a mandatory biotech label as a warning that it is unsafe," says Gene Grabowski, spokesman for the Grocery Man-ufacturers of America. "It is easier," BIO's Eramian points out, "to scare people about biotechnology than to educate them."

The labeling threat finally spurred a hitherto complacent industry into action. Last April, Monsanto, Novartis and five other biotech companies rolled out a $50 million television advertising campaign, with soft-focus fields and smiling children, pitching "solutions that could improve our world tomorrow."

But by then the opposition was morphing from inchoate splinter groups into something that looks like a mainstream coalition. In July 1999, some 40 environmentalists, consumer advocates and organic-food activists met in Bolinas, Calif., to map a national campaign. Rather than endorse a total ban on genetically modified foods that Greenpeace was pushing, says Wendy Wendlandt, political director of the state Public Interest Research Groups, "it was more practical to call for a moratorium until the stuff is safety tested and labeled, and companies are held responsible for any harmful effects."

In May the FDA announced that in the fall it would propose new rules for genetically engineered crops and products. Instead of safety testing, it would require only that companies publicly disclose their new biotech crops before they are planted. Labeling would be voluntary.

The critics' response came last week: a campaign to muster public opposition to the FDA's new rules and to target individual companies and their previous trademarks. The mock advertisements for "Camp-bull's Experimental Vegetable Soup," with the advisory, "Warning: This Product Is Untested," is only the first salvo. Some 18 other brand-name U.S. companies are on a tentative hit list, including General Mills, Coca-Cola and Kraft.

Will the companies succumb to the pressure, as they have in Eu-rope? As of last week, Campbell claimed to be unfazed, with few cus-tomers registering concern, despite the spotlight. Even at the San Francisco rally, there was some ambivalence. "I may not eat Campbell's soup as much," offered Shanae Walls, 19, a student at Contra Costa Col-lege who was there with her Environmental Science and Thought class. But as the protesters tossed products from Pepperidge Farm—a Camp-bell subsidiary—into the toxic-waste bin, she had second thoughts. "I love those cookies," she said wistfully. "That might take some time."

THE GLOBAL FOOD FIGHT

① BRUSSELS, 1998
France, Italy, Greece, Denmark and Luxembourg team up to block introduction of all new GM products in the European Union—including those approved by E.U. scientific advisory committees and even a few developed in these five countries. Several E.U. countries have also banned the importation and use of 18 GM crops and foods approved before the blockade went into effect. New safety rules could eventually break this logjam.

② SEATTLE, NOVEMBER 1999
Taking to the streets to protest the spread of "Frankenfoods," among other issues, demonstrators trying to disrupt the World Trade Organization summit are tear-gassed and beaten by police.

③ MIDWESTERN U.S., 1999
A coalition of agricultural groups calls for a freeze on government approval of new GM seeds in light of dwindling markets in anti-GM European countries. Planting of GM corn drops from 25 million acres (10 million hectares) in 1999 to 19.9 million acres (8 million hectares) in 2000.

④ MONTREAL, JANUARY 2000
130 nations, including Mexico, Australia and Japan, sign the Cartagena Protocol on Biosafety, which requires an exporting country to obtain permission from an importing country before shipping GM seeds and organisms and to label such shipments with warnings that they "may contain" GM products.

Key

▶ Strongly in favor of GM foods
▷ Somewhat in favor of GM foods
▶ Opposed to GM foods

—By Michael D. Lemonick. With reporting by Yudhijit Bhattacharjee and Max Rust/New York, with other bureaus

Canada

POPULATION
31,147,000

ATTITUDE
Generally pro, though consumers are wary

Grains make up 24.8% of diet

REASON
Second biggest producer of GM products, after the U.S., and a major food exporter.

U.S.

POPULATION
278,357,000

ATTITUDE
Cautiously pro

REASON
As a major food exporter and home to giant agribiotech businesses, led by Monsanto, the country stands to reap huge profits from GM foods.

Grains make up 23.6% of diet

Argentina

POPULATION
37,031,000

ATTITUDE
Pro

REASON
Third largest producer of biotech crops in the world, after the U.S. and Canada.

Grains make up 29.5% of diet

Brazil

POPULATION
170,116,000

ATTITUDE
Very cautiously pro

REASON
The country is eager to participate in the potentially profitable biotech revolution but is worried about alienating anti-GM customers in Europe.

Grains make up 30.9% of diet

Britain

POPULATION
58,830,000

ATTITUDE
Strongly anti

REASON
"Mad cow" disease in beef and a report that GM potatoes caused immune-system damage in rats have alarmed most Brits. Markets ban GM foods, and experiments are tightly controlled.

Grains make up 22.8% of diet

France

POPULATION
59,079,000

ATTITUDE
Strongly anti

REASON Like Britain, France has been stung by incidents with tainted food. Its attitude is also colored by hostility to U.S. imports and a desire to protect French farmers.

Grains make up 24.3% of diet

(continued)

(conTinued)

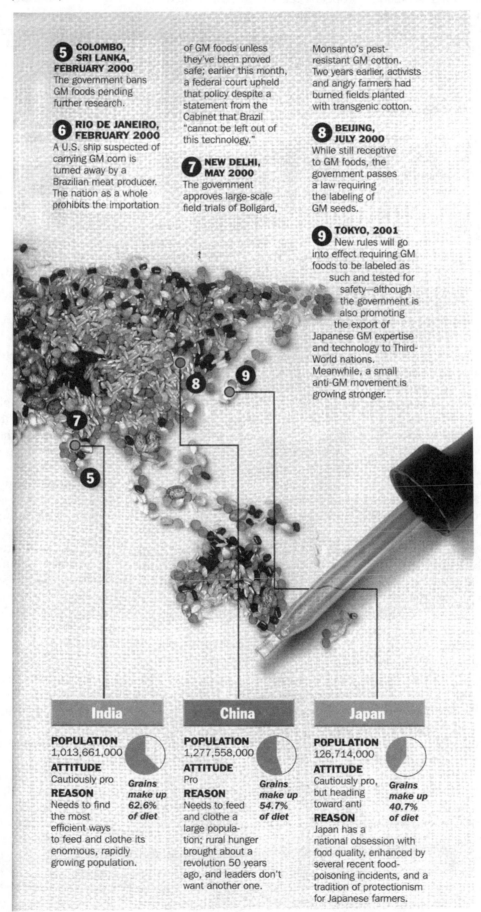

5 COLOMBO, SRI LANKA, FEBRUARY 2000
The government bans GM foods pending further research.

6 RIO DE JANEIRO, FEBRUARY 2000
A U.S. ship suspected of carrying GM corn is turned away by a Brazilian meat producer. The nation as a whole prohibits the importation of GM foods unless they've been proved safe; earlier this month, a federal court upheld that policy despite a statement from the Cabinet that Brazil "cannot be left out of this technology."

7 NEW DELHI, MAY 2000
The government approves large-scale field trials of Bollgard,

Monsanto's pest-resistant GM cotton. Two years earlier, activists and angry farmers had burned fields planted with transgenic cotton.

8 BEIJING, JULY 2000
While still receptive to GM foods, the government passes a law requiring the labeling of GM seeds.

9 TOKYO, 2001
New rules will go into effect requiring GM foods to be labeled as such and tested for safety—although the government is also promoting the export of Japanese GM expertise and technology to Third-World nations. Meanwhile, a small anti-GM movement is growing stronger.

India	China	Japan
POPULATION 1,013,661,000	**POPULATION** 1,277,558,000	**POPULATION** 126,714,000
ATTITUDE Cautiously pro	**ATTITUDE** Pro	**ATTITUDE** Cautiously pro, but heading toward anti
REASON Needs to find the most efficient ways to feed and clothe its enormous, rapidly growing population.	**REASON** Needs to feed and clothe a large population; rural hunger brought about a revolution 50 years ago, and leaders don't want another one.	**REASON** Japan has a national obsession with food quality, enhanced by several recent food-poisoning incidents, and a tradition of protectionism for Japanese farmers.
Grains make up **62.6%** *of diet*	*Grains make up* **54.7%** *of diet*	*Grains make up* **40.7%** *of diet*

Indeed, the benefits have seemed small—until golden rice came along to suggest otherwise. Golden rice is clearly not the moral equivalent of Roundup Ready beans. Quite the contrary, it is an example—the first compelling example—of a genetically engineered crop that may benefit not just the farmers who grow it but also the consumers who eat it. In this case, the consumers include at least a million children who die every year because they are weakened by vitamin-A deficiency and an additional 350,000 who go blind.

No wonder the biotech industry sees golden rice as a powerful ally in its struggle to win public acceptance. No wonder its critics see it as a cynical ploy. And no wonder so many of those concerned about the twin evils of poverty and hunger look at golden rice and see reflected in it their own passionate conviction that genetically engineered crops can be made to serve the greater public good—that in fact such crops have a critical role to play in feeding a world that is about to add to its present population of 6 billion. As former President Jimmy Carter put it, "Responsible biotechnology is not the enemy; starvation is."

Indeed, by the year 2020, the demand for grain, both for human consumption and for animal feed, is projected to go up by nearly half, while the amount of arable land available to satisfy that demand will not only grow much more slowly but also, in some areas, will probably dwindle. Add to that the need to conserve overstressed water resources and reduce the use of polluting chemicals, and the enormity of the challenge becomes apparent. In order to meet it, believes Gordon Conway, the agricultural ecologist who heads the Rockefeller Foundation, 21st century farmers will have to draw on every arrow in their agricultural quiver, including genetic engineering. And contrary to public perception, he says, those who have the least to lose and the most to gain are not well-fed Americans and Europeans but the hollow-bellied citizens of the developing world.

GOING FOR THE GOLD

IT WAS IN THE LATE 1980S, AFTER HE became a full professor of plant science at the Swiss Federal Institute of Technology, that Ingo Potrykus started to think about using genetic engineering to improve the nutritional qualities of rice. He knew that of some 3 billion people who depend on rice as their major staple, around 10% risk some degree of vitamin-A deficiency and the health problems that result. The reason, some alleged, was an overreliance on rice ushered in by the green revolution. Whatever its cause, the result was distressing: these people were so poor that they ate a few bowls of rice a day and almost nothing more.

The problem interested Potrykus for a number of reasons. For starters, he was attracted by the scientific challenge of transferring not just a single gene, as many had already done, but a group of genes that represented a key part of a biochemical pathway. He was also motivated by complex emotions, among them empathy. Potrykus knew more than most what it meant not to have enough to eat. As a child growing up in war-ravaged Germany, he and his brothers were often so desperately hungry that they ate what they could steal.

Around 1990, Potrykus hooked up with Gary Toenniessen, director of food security for the Rockefeller Foundation. Toenniessen had identified the lack of beta-carotene in polished rice grains as an appropriate target for gene scientists like Potrykus to tackle because it lay beyond the ability of traditional plant breeding to address. For while rice, like other green plants, contains light-trapping beta-carotene in its external tissues, no plant in the entire *Oryza* genus—as far as anyone knew—produced beta-carotene in its endosperm (the starchy interior part of the rice grain that is all most people eat).

It was at a Rockefeller-sponsored meeting that Potrykus met the University of Freiburg's Peter Beyer, an expert on the beta-carotene pathway in daffodils. By combining their expertise, the two scientists figured, they might be able to remedy this unfortunate oversight in nature. So in 1993, with some $100,000 in seed money from the Rockefeller Foundation, Potrykus and Beyer launched what turned into a seven-year, $2.6 million project, backed also by the Swiss government and the European Union. "I was in a privileged situation," reflects Potrykus, "because I was able to operate without industrial support. Only in that situation can you think of giving away your work free."

That indeed is what Potrykus announced he and Beyer planned to do. The two scientists soon discovered, however, that giving away golden rice was not going to be as easy as they thought. The genes they transferred and the bacteria they used to transfer those genes were all encumbered by patents and proprietary rights. Three months ago, the two scientists struck a deal with AstraZeneca, which is based in London and holds an exclusive license to one of the genes Potrykus and Beyer used to create golden rice. In exchange for commercial marketing rights in the U.S. and other affluent markets, AstraZeneca agreed to lend its financial muscle and legal expertise to the cause of putting the seeds into the hands of poor farmers at no charge.

No sooner had the deal been made than the critics of agricultural biotechnology erupted. "A rip-off of the public trust," grumbled the Rural Advancement Foundation International, an advocacy group based in Winnipeg, Canada. "Asian farmers get (unproved) genetically modified rice, and AstraZeneca gets the 'gold.'" Potrykus was dismayed by such negative reaction. "It would be irresponsible," he exclaimed, "not to say immoral, not to use biotechnology to try to solve this problem!" But such expressions of good intentions would not be enough to allay his opponents' fears.

WEIGHING THE PERILS

BENEATH THE HYPERBOLIC TALK OF Frankenfoods and Superweeds, even proponents of agricultural biotechnology agree, lie a number of real concerns. To begin with, all foods, including the transgenic foods created through genetic engineering, are potential sources of allergens. That's because the transferred genes contain instructions for making proteins, and not all proteins are equal. Some—those in peanuts, for example—are well known for causing allergic reactions. To many, the possibility that golden rice might cause such a problem seems farfetched, but it nonetheless needs to be considered.

Then there is the problem of "genetic pollution," as opponents of biotechnology term it. Pollen grains from such wind-pollinated plants as corn and canola, for instance, are carried far and wide. To farmers, this mainly poses a nuisance. Transgenic canola grown in one field, for example, can very easily pollinate nontransgenic plants grown in the next. Indeed this is the reason behind the furor that recently erupted in Europe when it was discovered that canola seeds from Canada—unwittingly planted by farmers in England, France, Germany and Sweden—contained transgenic contaminants.

The continuing flap over Bt corn and cotton—now grown not only in the U.S. but also in Argentina and China—has provided more fodder for debate. Bt stands for a common soil bacteria, *Bacillus thuringiensis*, different strains of which produce toxins that target specific insects. By transferring to corn and cotton the bacterial gene responsible for making this toxin, Monsanto and other companies have produced crops that are resistant to the European corn borer and the cotton bollworm. An immediate concern, raised by a number of ecologists, is whether or not widespread planting of these crops will spur the development of resistance to Bt among crop pests. That would be unfortunate, they point out, because Bt is a safe and effective natural insecticide that is popular with organic farmers.

SQUEEZE ME: Scientists turned off the gene that makes tomatoes soft and squishy

Even more worrisome are ecological concerns. In 1999 Cornell University entomologist John Losey performed a provocative, "seat-of-the-pants" laboratory experiment. He dusted Bt corn pollen on plants populated by monarch-butterfly caterpillars. Many of the caterpillars died. Could what happened in Losey's laboratory happen in cornfields across the Midwest? Were these lovely butterflies, already under pressure owing to human encroachment on their Mexican wintering grounds, about to face a new threat from high-tech farmers in the north?

The upshot: despite studies pro and con—and countless save-the-monarch protests acted out by children dressed in butterfly costumes—a conclusive answer to this question has yet to come. Losey himself is not yet convinced that Bt corn poses a grave danger to North America's monarch-butterfly population, but he does think the issue deserves attention. And others agree. "I'm not anti biotechnology per se," says biologist Rebecca Goldberg, a senior scientist with the Environmental Defense Fund, "but I would like to have a tougher regulatory regime. These crops should be subject to more careful screening before they are released."

Are there more potential pitfalls? There are. Among other things, there is the possibility that as transgenes in pollen drift, they will fertilize wild plants, and weeds will emerge that are hardier and even more difficult to control. No one knows how common the exchange of genes between domestic plants and their wild relatives really is, but Margaret Mellon, director of the Union of Concerned Scientists' agriculture and biotechnology program, is certainly not alone in thinking that it's high time we find out. Says she: "People should be responding to these concerns with experiments, not assurances."

And that is beginning to happen, although—contrary to expectations—the reports coming in are not necessarily that scary. For three years now, University of Arizona entomologist Bruce Tabashnik has been monitoring fields of Bt cotton that farmers have planted in his state. And in this instance at least, he says, "the environmental risks seem minimal, and the benefits seem great." First of all, cotton is self-pollinated rather than wind-pollinated, so that the spread of the Bt gene is of less concern. And because the Bt gene is so effective, he notes, Arizona farmers have reduced their use of chemical insecticides 75%. So far, the pink bollworm population has not rebounded, indicating that the feared resistance to Bt has not yet developed.

ASSESSING THE PROMISE

ARE THE CRITICS OF AGRICULtural biotechnology right? Is biotech's promise nothing more than overblown corporate hype? The papaya growers in Hawaii's Puna district clamor to disagree. In 1992 a wildfire epidemic of papaya ringspot virus threatened to destroy the state's papaya industry; by 1994, nearly half the state's papaya acreage had been infected, their owners forced to seek outside employment. But then help arrived, in the form of a virus-resistant transgenic papaya developed by Cornell University plant pathologist Dennis Gonsalves.

In 1995 a team of scientists set up a field trial of two transgenic lines—UH SunUP and UH Rainbow—and by 1996, the verdict had been rendered. As everyone could see, the nontransgenic plants in the field trial were a stunted mess, and the transgenic plants were healthy. In 1998, after negotiations with four patent holders, the papaya growers switched en masse to the transgenic seeds and reclaimed their orchards. "Consumer acceptance has been great," reports Rusty Perry, who runs a papaya farm near Puna. "We've found that customers are more concerned with how the fruits look and taste than with whether they are transgenic or not."

Viral diseases, along with insect infestations, are a major cause of crop loss in Africa, observes Kenyan plant scientist Florence Wambugu. African sweet-potato fields, for example, yield only 2.4 tons per acre, vs. more than double that in the rest of the world. Soon Wambugu hopes to start raising those yields by introducing a transgenic sweet potato that is resistant to the feathery mottle virus. There really is no other option, explains Wambugu, who currently directs the International Service for the Acquisition of Agri-biotech Applications in Nairobi. "You can't control the virus in the field, and you can't breed in resistance through conventional means."

To Wambugu, the flap in the U.S. and Europe over genetically engineered crops seems almost ludicrous. In Africa, she notes, nearly half the fruit and vegetable harvest is lost because it rots on the way to market. "If we had a transgenic banana that ripened more slowly," she says, "we could have 40% more bananas than now." Wambugu also dreams of getting access to herbicide-resistant crops. Says she: "We could liberate so many people if our crops were resistant to herbicides that we could then spray on the surrounding weeds. Weeding enslaves Africans; it keeps children from school."

In Wambugu's view, there are more benefits to be derived from agricultural biotechnology in Africa than practically anywhere else on the planet—and this may be so. Among the genetic-engineering projects funded by the Rockefeller Foundation is one aimed at controlling striga, a weed that parasitizes the roots of African corn plants. At present there is little farmers can do about striga infestation, so tightly intertwined are the weed's roots with the roots of the corn plants it targets. But scientists have come to understand the source of the problem: corn roots exude chemicals that attract striga. So it may prove possible to identify the genes that are responsible and turn them off.

The widespread perception that agricultural biotechnology is intrinsically inimical to the environment perplexes the Rockefeller Foundation's Conway, who views genetic engineering as an important tool for achieving what he has termed a "doubly green revolution." If the technology can marshal a plant's natural defenses against weeds and viruses, if it can induce crops to flourish with minimal application of chemical fertilizers, if it can make dryland agriculture more productive without straining local water supplies, then what's wrong with it?

Of course, these particular breakthroughs have not happened yet. But as the genomes of major crops are ever more finely mapped, and as the tools for transferring genes become ever more precise, the possibility for tinkering with complex biochemical pathways can be expected to expand rapidly. As Potrykus sees it, there is no question that agricultural biotechnology can be harnessed for the good of humankind. The only question is whether there is the collective will to do so. And the answer may well emerge as the people of the world weigh the future of golden rice.

—*With reporting by Simon Robinson/Nairobi*

The New Terrorism

Securing the Nation against a Messianic Foe

By Steven Simon

In the minds of the men who carried them out, the attacks of September 11 were acts of religious devotion—a form of worship, conducted in God's name and in accordance with his wishes. The enemy was the infidel; the opposing ideology, "Western culture." That religious motivation, colored by a messianism and in some cases an apocalyptic vision of the future, distinguishes al-Qaida and its affiliates from conventional terrorists groups such as the Irish Republican Army, the Red Brigades, or even the Palestine Liberation Organization. Although secular political interests help drive al-Qaida's struggle for power, these interests are understood and expressed in religious terms. Al-Qaida wants to purge the Middle East of American political, military, and economic influence, but only as part of a far more sweeping religious agenda: a "defensive jihad" to defeat a rival system portrayed as an existential threat to Islam.

The explicitly religious character of the "New Terrorism" poses a profound security challenge for the United States. The social, economic, and political conditions in the Arab and broader Islamic world that have helped give rise to al-Qaida will not be easily changed. The maximalist demands of the new terrorists obviate dialogue or negotiation. Traditional strategies of deterrence by retaliation are unlikely to work, because the jihadists have no territory to hold at risk, seek sacrifice, and court Western attacks that will validate their claims about Western hostility to Islam. The United States will instead need to pursue a strategy of containment, while seeking ways to redress, over the long run, underlying causes.

trality of sacrifice in their liturgical traditions establish the legitimacy of killing as an act of worship with redemptive qualities. In these narratives, the enemy must be eradicated, not merely suppressed.

In periods of deep cultural despair, eschatology—speculation in the form of apocalyptic stories about the end of history and dawn of the kingdom of God—can capture the thinking of a religious group. History is replete with instances in which religious communities—Jewish, Christian, Islamic—immolated themselves and perpetrated acts of intense violence to try to spur the onset of a messianic era. Each community believed it had reached the nadir of degradation and was on the brink of a resurgence that would lead to its final triumph over its enemies—a prospect that warranted and required violence on a massive scale.

Such episodes of messianic zeal are not restricted to the distant past. In the mid-1980s, a group of Israeli settlers plotted to destroy the Dome of the Rock, the 8th-century mosque atop the Haram al Sharif in Jerusalem. The settlers appeared to believe that destroying the mosque would spark an Arab invasion, which would trigger an Israeli nuclear response—the Armageddon said by the Bible to precede the kingdom of God. The plot was never carried out, because the conspirators could not get a rabbinical blessing. Analogous attempts have characterized Christian apocalypticists and even a Buddhist community whose doctrine was strongly influenced by Christian eschatology—Aum Shinrikyo.

The Fabric of New Terrorism

Religiously motivated terrorism, as Bruce Hoffman of the RAND Corporation first noted in 1997, is inextricably linked to pursuit of mass casualties. The connection is rooted in the sociology of biblical religion. Monotheistic faiths are characterized by exclusive claims to valid identity and access to salvation. The violent imagery embedded in their sacred texts and the cen-

The Doctrinal Potency of al-Qaida

Similar thinking can be detected in narrative trends that inform al-Qaida's ideology and actions. Apocalyptic tales circulating on the Web and within the Middle East in hard copy tell of cataclysmic battles between Islam and the United States, Israel, and sometimes Europe. Global battles seesaw between infidel and Muslim victory until some devastating act, often the destruction of New York by nuclear weapons, brings Armageddon to an end and leads the world's survivors to convert to Islam.

The theological roots of al-Qaida's leaders hark back to a medieval Muslim jurisconsult, Taqi al Din Ibn Taymiyya, two of whose teachings have greatly influenced Islamic revolutionary movements. The first was his elevation of jihad—not the spiritual struggle that many modern Muslims take it to be, but physical combat against unbelievers—to the rank of the canonical five pillars of Islam (declaration of faith, prayer, almsgiving, Ramadan fast, and pilgrimage to Mecca). The second was his legitimization of rebellion against Muslim rulers who do not enforce *sharia*, or Islamic law, in their domains.

Ibn Taymiyya's ideas were revived in the 1960s in Egypt, where they underpinned 25 years of violence, including the assassination of Anwar Sadat in 1981. When the Egyptian government vanquished the militants, survivors fled abroad, taking advantage of European laws regarding asylum or of the lawlessness of Yemen, Afghanistan, and Kashmir.

Ibn Taymiyya's teachings have even deeper roots in Saudi Arabia. They became part of the founding ideology of the Saudi state when Muhammad Ibn Abd al Wahhab formed an alliance with Ibn Saud in 1744.

Al-Qaida embodies both the Egyptian and the Saudi sides of the jihad movement, which came together in the 1960s when some Egyptian militants sought shelter in Saudi Arabia, which was locked in conflict with Nasserist Egypt. Osama bin Laden himself is a Saudi, and his second-in-command, Ayman al Zawahiri, is an Egyptian who served three years in prison for his role in Sadat's assassination.

The jihadist themes in Ibn Taymiyya's teachings are striking an increasingly popular chord in parts of the Muslim world.

Al-Qaida's Geopolitical Reach

Religiously motivated militants have now dispersed widely to multiple "fields of jihad." The social and economic problems that have fueled their discontent are well known—low economic growth, falling wages and increasing joblessness, poor schooling, relentless but unsustainable urban growth, and diminishing environmental resources, especially water. Political alienation and resentment over the plight of the Palestinians and the intrusion into traditional societies of offensive images and ideas compound these problems and help account for the religious voice given to these primarily secular grievances. The mobilization of religious imagery and terminology further transforms secular issues into substantively religious ones, putting otherwise negotiable political issues beyond the realm of bargaining and making violent outcomes more likely.

The political power of religious symbols has led some pivotal states—in particular, Egypt and Saudi Arabia—to use them to buttress their own legitimacy. In so doing they perversely confer authority on the very clerical opposition that threatens state power and impedes the modernization programs that might, over the long haul, materially improve quality of life. Although the jihadists are unable to challenge these states, Islamists nevertheless dominate public discourse and shape the

debate on foreign and domestic policy. For the jihadists, the "near enemy" at home once took precedence over the "far enemy," which now includes the United States and the West. Thanks to bin Laden's doctrinal creativity, in Egypt and Saudi Arabia, Islamists have inextricably intertwined the near and far enemies. The governments' need to cater to the sentiments aroused within mosques and on the Islamist airwaves to keep their regimes secure dictates their tolerance or even endorsement of anti-American views. At the same time, strategic circumstances compel both states to provide diplomatic or other practical support for U.S. policies that offend public sensitivities. It is small wonder that Egyptians and Saudis are the backbone of al-Qaida and that Saudi Arabia spawned most of the September 11 attackers.

The fields of jihad stretch far and wide. In the Middle East, al-Qaida developed ties in Lebanon and Jordan. In Southeast Asia, Indonesians, Malaysians, and Singaporeans trained in Afghanistan, or conspired with those who had, to engage in terror, most horrifically the bombing in Bali. In Central Asia, the Islamic Movement of Uzbekistan became a full-fledged jihadist group. In Pakistan, jihadists with apocalyptic instincts nearly provoked a nuclear exchange between India and Pakistan. East Africa remains a field of jihad four years after the bombings of U.S. embassies in Kenya and Tanzania. Videotapes of atrocities of the Algerian Armed Islamic Group circulate in Europe as recruitment propaganda for the global jihad.

Given its role as a springboard for the September 11 attacks, Europe may be the most crucial field of jihad. Lack of political representation and unequal access to education, jobs, housing, and social services have turned European Muslim youth against the states in which they live. In the United Kingdom, the Muslim prison population, a source of recruits for the radical cause, has doubled in the past decade. Close to a majority of young Muslims in Britain have told pollsters that they feel no obligation to bear arms for England but would fight for bin Laden.

The United States remains al-Qaida's prime target. Suleiman Abu Ghaith, the al-Qaida spokesman, has said that there can be no truce until the group has killed four million Americans, whereupon the rest can convert to Islam.

The Recalcitrance of the Jihadists

How should the United States respond to the jihadist threat? To the extent one can speak of the root causes of the new terrorism, they defy direct and immediate remedial action. Population in the Middle East is growing rapidly, and the median age is dropping. The correlation between youth and political instability highlights the potential for unrest and radicalization. In cities, social welfare programs, sanitation, transportation, housing, power, and the water supply are deteriorating. In much of the Muslim world, the only refuge from filth, noise, heat, and, occasionally, surveillance is the mosque. Economists agree that the way out of the morass is to develop institutions that facilitate the distribution of capital and create opportunity; how to do that, they are unsure. The West can offer aid but cannot as yet correct structural problems.

Improving public opinion toward the United States is also deeply problematic. Decades of official lies and controlled press have engendered an understandable skepticism toward the assertions of any government, especially one presumed hostile to Muslim interests. Trust is based on confidence in a chain of transmission whose individual links are known to be reliable. Official news outlets or government spokespersons do not qualify as such links. Nor, certainly, do Western news media.

Moreover, highly respected critics of the United States in Saudi Arabia demonstrate an ostensibly profound understanding of U.S. policies and society, while offering a powerful and internally consistent explanation for their country's descent from the all-powerful, rich supplier of oil to the West to a debt-ridden, faltering economy protected by Christian troops and kowtowing to Israel. These are difficult narratives to counter, especially in a society where few know much about the West.

The prominent role of clerics in shaping public opinion offers yet more obstacles. The people who represent the greatest threat of terrorist action against the United States follow the preaching and guidance of Salafi clerics—the Muslim equivalent of Christian "fundamentalists." Although some Salafi preachers have forbidden waging jihad as harmful to Muslim interests, their underlying assumptions are that jihad qua holy war against non-Muslims is fundamentally valid and that Islamic governments that do not enforce *sharia* must be opposed. No authoritative clerical voice offers a sympathetic view of the United States.

The prognosis regarding root causes, then, is poor. The world is becoming more religious; Islam is the fastest-growing faith; religious expression is generally becoming more assertive and apocalyptic thinking more prominent. Weapons of mass destruction, spectacularly suited to cosmic war, will become more widely available. Democratization is at a standstill. Governments in Egypt, Saudi Arabia, Pakistan, and Indonesia are unwilling or unable to oppose anti-Western religiously based popular feeling. Immigration, conversion, and inept social policies will intensify parallel trends in Europe.

At least for now, dialogue does not appear to be an option. Meanwhile, global market forces beyond the control of Western governments hasten Western cultural penetration and generate ever-greater resentment. Jihadists could conceivably argue that they have a negotiable program: cessation of U.S. support for Israel, withdrawal from Saudi Arabia, broader American disengagement from the Islamic world. But U.S. and allied conceptions of international security and strategic imperatives will make such demands difficult, if not impossible, to accommodate.

Reducing Vulnerability to New Terrorism

Facing a global adversary with maximal goals and lacking a bargaining option or means to redress severe conditions that may or may not motivate attackers, the United States is confined primarily to a strategy of defense, deterrence by denial, and, where possible and prudent, pre-emption. Deterrence through the promise of retaliation is impossible with an adversary that controls little or no territory and invites attack.

> The United States remains al-Qaida's prime target. Suleiman Abu Ghaith, the al-Qaida spokesman, has said that there can be no truce until the group has killed four million Americans.

Adjusting to the new threat entails disturbing conceptual twists for U.S. policymakers. After generations of effort to reduce the risk of surprise attack through technical means and negotiated transparency measures, surprise will be the natural order of things. The problem of warning will be further intensified by the creativity of this adversary, its recruitment of Europeans and Americans, and its ability to stage attacks from within the United States. Thinking carefully about the unlikely—"institutionalizing imaginativeness," as Dennis Gormley has put it—is by definition a paradox, but nonetheless essential for American planners.

With warning scarce and inevitably ambiguous, it will be necessary to probe the enemy both to put him off balance and to learn of his intentions. The United States has done so clandestinely against hostile intelligence agencies. Against al-Qaida, a more difficult target, the approach will take time to cohere. Probes could also take the form of military action against al-Qaida–affiliated cantonments, where they still exist. The greater the movement's virtuality, however, the fewer the targets available for U.S. action. Preemptive strikes could target sites that develop, produce, or harbor weapons of mass destruction.

A decade of al-Qaida activity within the United States has erased the customary distinction between the domestic and the foreign in intelligence and law enforcement. The relationship between the Central Intelligence Agency and the Federal Bureau of Investigation must change. Only a more integrated organization can adapt to the seamlessness of the transnational arenas in which the terrorists operate.

Civil liberties and security must be rebalanced. How sweeping the process turns out to be will depend largely on whether the nation suffers another attack or at least a convincing attempt. Americans will have to be convinced that curtailing civil liberties is unavoidable and limited to the need to deal with proximate threats. They will need to see bipartisan consensus in Congress and between Congress and the White House and be sure that politicians are committed to keeping the rebalancing to a minimum.

The distinction between public and private sector has also been blurred. Al-Qaida has targeted the American population and used our infrastructure against us. A perpetual state of heightened readiness would impose unacceptable opportunity costs on the civilian world, so vulnerabilities must be reduced. Civilian ownership of the infrastructure is a complication. What the U.S. government does not own, it cannot completely defend. Private owners do not necessarily share the government's perception of the terrorist threat and are often able to resist regulation. Where they accept the threat, they view it as a national security issue for which the federal government should bear the cost. The idea of public-private partnership is only now finding acceptance in the cybersecurity realm as concerns over litigation have brought about a focus on due diligence. The pursuit of public-private partnership will have to be extended to all potentially vulnerable critical infrastructures by a government that does not yet understand perfectly which infrastructures are truly critical and which apparently dispensable infrastructures interact to become critical.

> ## Governments in Egypt, Saudi Arabia, Pakistan, and Indonesia are unwilling or unable to oppose anti-Western religiously based popular feeling.

Defending these infrastructures will also present unprecedented challenges. The U.S. government is not on the lookout for military formations, but for a lone, unknown person in a visa line. Technology—biometrics, data mining, super-fast data processing, and ubiquitous video surveillance—will move this needle-in-the-haystack problem into the just-possible category by providing the means to collect and store detailed and unique characteristics of huge numbers of people and match them to the person in the visa line. The cost will be the need to archive personal information on a great mass of individuals.

The United States must also devise ways to block or intercept vehicles that deliver weapons of mass destruction. It cannot do that alone. The cruise missile threat, for instance, requires the cooperation of suppliers, which means an active American role in expanding the remit of the Missile Technology Control Regime (MTCR). Weapons components themselves must be kept out of terrorists' hands. The recent adoption of MTCR controls on cheap technologies for transforming small aircraft into cruise missiles shows what can be accomplished. Washington has been buying surplus fissile materials from Russia's large stock and helping Russians render them useless for weapons; it will be vital to continue generous funding for that effort.

Remote detection of weapons, especially nuclear ones, that have reached the United States is crucial. Emergency response teams will need to be able to pinpoint the location of a device, identify its type, and know in advance how to render it safe once it has been seized. Local authorities will have to detect and identify biological and chemical agents that have been released. Genetically engineered vaccines must be rapidly developed and produced to stop local attacks from becoming national, and ultimately global, epidemics. Special medical units must be on standby to relieve local health care personnel who become exhausted or die.

Offensive opportunities will be limited but not impossible. They do, however, require impeccable intelligence, which has been hard to come by. The Afghan nexus in which jihadis initially came together and the cohesion of the groups that constitute the al-Qaida movement have made penetration forbiddingly complicated. But as al-Qaida picks up converts to Islam and Muslims who have long resided in Western countries,

penetration may become easier. The more they look like us, the more we look like them.

Another source of potentially vital information is the jihadis picked up by local authorities abroad on the basis of U.S. intelligence and then shipped to their countries of origin for interrogation. Transfers of this sort were carried out frequently during the 1990s and sometimes produced life-saving intelligence on imminent terrorist attacks. In some cases, the authorities where a suspect resides will not wish to make an arrest, fearing terrorist retaliation, political problems, or diplomatic friction. The United States has asserted the authority to conduct these operations without the consent of the host government but has generally refrained from acting. In the wake of September 11, Washington may want to reassess the risks and benefits of these actions.

Without revoking the long-standing executive order prohibiting assassination, the United States should also consider targeted killing, to use the Israeli phrase, of jihadists known to be central to an evolving conspiracy to attack the United States or to obtain weapons of mass destruction. As a practical matter, the intelligence value of such a person alive would generally outweigh the disruptive benefits of his death, assuming that U.S. or friendly intelligence services could be relied on to keep him under surveillance. But this will not always be so. When it is not, from a legal standpoint, targeted killing falls reasonably under the right to self-defense. Such a policy departure is unsavory. But in a new strategic context, with jihadis intent on mass casualties, unsavory may not be a sensible threshold. The killing of al-Qaida operatives in Yemen by missiles fired from a CIA-controlled aerial drone suggests that this threshold may already have been crossed.

Allied Cooperation

As the al-Qaida movement dissolves into virtuality in 60 countries worldwide, international cooperation becomes ever more indispensable to countering the threat.

Many countries that host al-Qaida will cooperate with the United States out of self-interest; they do not want jihadis on their soil any more than Americans do on theirs. A durable and effective counterterrorism campaign, however, requires not just bare-bones cooperation, but political collaboration at a level that tells the bureaucracies that cooperation with their American counterparts is expected. Such a robust, wholesale working relationship is what produces vital large-scale initiatives—a common diplomatic approach toward problem states; a sustainable program of economic development for the Middle East; domestic policy reforms that lessen the appeal of jihadism to Muslim diaspora communities; improved border controls; and tightened bonds among the justice ministries, law enforcement, customs, and intelligence agencies, and special operations forces on the front lines.

Whether this level of burden sharing emerges, let alone endures, depends on the give-and-take among the players. Since September 11, the United States has fostered allied perceptions that Washington is indifferent to their priorities. The United

States has not yet paid a serious penalty in terms of allied cooperation. The scale of the attacks and the administration's blend of resolve and restraint in the war on terrorism have offset allies' disappointment in its go-it-alone posture. But as the war grinds on, good will is certain to wear thin. The United States would be wise to adopt a more flexible posture to ensure allied support in the crises that will inevitably come. Washington's willingness to seek a new Security Council resolution on Iraq was a good start.

Washington's interests would also be well served by modifying what appears at times to be a monolithic view of terrorist networks that equates the Arafats and Saddams of the world with bin Laden (or his successors). Several European partners regard Arafat and his ilk as considerably more controllable through diplomacy than bin Laden. Greater American flexibility may prove essential for ensuring European capitals' military, law-enforcement, and intelligence cooperation. And the fact remains that al-Qaida has killed more Americans than have Iraq, Iran, or Palestinian groups and would use weapons of mass destruction against the United States as soon as it acquired them. A good case can be made for a preventive war against Iraq to stave off the prospect of a nuclear-armed Saddam regime. We should recognize, though, that dealing with this strategic challenge may galvanize the equally dangerous threat of mass casualty attacks by Sunni terrorists.

Israel and the Palestinians

Since the heyday of the Middle East peace process under Ehud Barak's Labor government, jihadists have exploited the Israeli-Palestinian conflict to boost their popularity. The strategem has worked: jihadists are seen as sticking up for Palestinian rights, while Arab governments do nothing. Direct, energetic U.S. diplomatic intervention in the conflict would lessen the appeal of jihadi claims and make it marginally easier for regional governments to cooperate in the war on terrorism by demonstrating American commitment to resolving the Israeli-Palestinian conflict.

The Bush administration, for good reason, fears becoming entangled in a drawn-out, venomous negotiation between irreconcilable parties. They see it distracting them from higher priorities and embroiling them in domestic political disputes over whether Washington should pressure Israel. Still, the administration has been drawn in by degrees and has announced its support for creating a Palestinian state. If the war on terrorism is now the highest U.S. priority, then more vigorous—and admittedly risky—involvement in the Israeli-Palestinian conflict is required. The jihadi argument that the United States supports the murder of Palestinian Muslims must be countered.

Democratization in the Middle East

As it continues to engage with the authoritarian regimes in Cairo and Riyadh, Washington should try to renegotiate the implicit bargain that underpins its relations with both. The current bargain is structured something like this: Egypt sustains its commitment to peace with Israel, Saudi Arabia stabilizes oil prices, and both proffer varying degrees of diplomatic support for American objectives in the region, especially toward Iraq. In return, Washington defers to their domestic policies, even if these fuel the growth and export of Islamic militancy and deflect public discontent onto the United States and Israel. With jihadis now pursuing nuclear weapons, that bargain no longer looks sensible.

Under a new bargain, Cairo and Riyadh would begin to take measured risks to lead their publics gradually toward greater political participation by encouraging opposition parties of a more secular cast and allowing greater freedom of expression. Saudi Arabia would throttle back on its wahhabiization of the Islamic world by cutting its production and export of unemployable graduates in religious studies and reducing subsidies for foreign mosques and madrasahs that propagate a confrontational and intolerant form of Islam while crowding out alternative practices. Both countries would be pushed to reform their school curricula—and enforce standards—to ensure a better understanding of the non-Islamic world and encourage respect for other cultures. With increased financial and technical assistance from the West, regimes governing societies beset by economic problems that spur radicalism would focus more consistently on the welfare of their people. In this somewhat utopian conception, leaders in both countries would use their new legitimacy to challenge Islamist myths about America and Western hostility toward Islam. In sum, Cairo and Riyadh would challenge the culture of demonization across the board, with an eye toward laying the groundwork for liberal democracy.

In the framework of this new bargain, the United States would move more boldly to establish contacts with moderate opposition figures in Egypt, Saudi Arabia, and perhaps other countries. The benefit would be twofold. Washington would get a better sense of events on the ground and would also gain credibility and perhaps even understanding on the part of critics. For this effort to bear fruit, however, the United States would have to use regional media efficiently—something for which it has as yet no well-developed strategy. Washington would also have to engage in a measure of self-scrutiny, examining how its policies contribute—in avoidable ways—to Muslim anti-Americanism. "Re-branding" is not enough.

Change will be slow. The regimes in Cairo and Riyadh face largely self-inflicted problems they cannot readily surmount without serious risks to stability. Nor is the United States entirely free to insist on the new bargain: it will need Saudi cooperation on Iraq as long as Saddam Hussein is in power, if not longer, given the uncertainties surrounding Iraq's future after Saddam leaves the stage. Egyptian support for a broader Arab-Israeli peace will also remain essential. But change has to start sometime, somewhere. It will take steady U.S. pressure and persistent attempts to convince both regimes that a new bargain will serve their countries' long-term interests. The sooner the new deals are struck, the better.

Hazardous but Not Hopeless

Western democracies face a serious, possibly transgenerational terrorist threat whose causes are multidimensional and difficult to address. The situation is hazardous, but not hopeless. The United States possesses enormous wealth, has capable allies, and stands on the leading edge of technological development that will be key to survival. A strategy that takes into account the military, intelligence, law-enforcement, diplomatic, and economic pieces of the puzzle will see America through. For the next few years, the objective will be to contain the threat, in much the same way that the United States contained Soviet power throughout the Cold War. The adversary must be prevented from doing his worst, while Washington and its allies wear down its capabilities and undermine its appeal to fellow Muslims. Success will require broad domestic support and a strong coalition abroad.

Prospects are, in many respects, bleak. But the dangers are not disproportionate to those the nation faced in the 20th century. America's initial reaction to September 11 was and indeed had to be its own self-defense: bolstering homeland security, denying al-Qaida access to weapons of mass destruction, dismantling its networks, and developing a law-enforcement and intelligence capacity to cope with the new adversary. Not all vulnerabilities can be identified and even fewer remedied, and al-Qaida need launch only one attack with a weapon of mass destruction to throw the United States into a profound crisis. Washington and its partners must convince Muslim populations that they can prosper without either destroying the West or abandoning their own traditions to the West's alien culture. That is a long-term project. American and allied determination in a war against apocalyptic—and genocidal—religious fanatics must be coupled with a generous vision about postwar possibilities. Militant Islam cannot be expected to embrace the West in the foreseeable future. But the United States can lay the foundation for a lasting accommodation by deploying its considerable economic and political advantages. It is not too late to begin.

Steven Simon is a senior fellow at the International Institute for Strategic Studies and coauthor, with Daniel Benjamin, of The Age of Sacred Terror *(Random House, October 2002).*

A New Strategy for the New Face of Terrorism

L. Paul Bremer, III

"THE THIRD World War was begun on Tuesday, September 11, on the East Coast of the United States"—so began the French magazine *L'Express* two days later. Whether these words turn out to be prediction or exaggeration will depend on how the world now reacts to the new face of terrorism represented by the vicious attacks of that day.

The September 11 atrocities made for the most dramatic day in American history, dwarfing even the events at Pearl Harbor sixty years ago. Three times as many Americans died in New York and Washington as died at Pearl Harbor. And this time innocent civilians, not military men, were the intended targets. But this was not just an attack on America. Citizens of at least eighty countries died in the collapsed World Trade towers. We are all, in a direct way, victims of the new terrorism.

The Changing Nature of Terrorism

WHILE THE attacks were shocking for their audacity and effectiveness, they should have surprised no serious student of terrorism. A large-scale attack on American soil has been widely predicted by experts. For years they have drawn attention to a disturbing paradox: while the number of international terrorist incidents has been declining over the past decade, the number of casualties has risen. This trend reflects the changing motives of terrorists.

During the 1970s and 1980s, most terrorist groups had limited political motives. For them, terrorism was a tactic mainly to draw attention to their "cause." These groups reasoned that many people would sympathize with that cause if only they were made aware of it. Designing their tactics to support this objective, these "old-style" terrorists rarely engaged in indiscriminate mass killing. They rightly concluded such attacks would disgust the very audiences they were trying to convert to their cause. So most terrorist groups designed their attacks to kill enough people to draw in the press but not so many as to repel the public. Often they used terror to force negotia-

tions on some issue, such as the release of jailed comrades. As one terrorism expert put it, these groups were seeking a place at the negotiating table.

Eventually, most terrorist groups in Europe overplayed their hands and the publics turned against them. But anti-terrorism policies helped win the day. With vigorous American leadership, European countries and the United States developed a counter-terrorist strategy to deal with this threat. At the heart of that strategy were three principles: make no concessions to terrorists; treat terrorists as criminals to be brought to justice; and punish states that support terrorism. On balance, this strategy worked.

Over the past decade, however, it has become clear that many terrorist groups are motivated less by narrow political goals and more by ideological, apocalyptic or religious fanaticism. Sometimes their goal is simply hatred or revenge, and tactics have changed to reflect these motives. Rather than avoiding large-scale casualties, these terrorists seek to kill as many people as possible. They are unconstrained by the respect for human life that undergirds all the world's great religions. including Islam.

Beginning with the downing of Pan Am Flight 103 in December 1988, through the first World Trade Center bombing in 1993, to the chemical attacks in the Tokyo subways in 1995 and the attacks on two U.S. embassies in East Africa in 1998, terrorist actions have resulted in increasing numbers of casualties. The September 11 attacks killed more than 5,000 people, making it the single worst terrorist attack in world history.

Things could get even worse. During the 1990s, concerns arose that terrorists might use chemical, biological, radiological or nuclear agents. In the 1980s, terrorist groups could have developed such weapons, but they did not do so, apparently calculating that their use would make public support for their causes less likely. But far from steering away from such agents, the new terrorists might find these weapons attractive precisely because they can kill tens of thousands. This was the goal, fortunately unrealized, of Aum Shinrikyo's chemical attack on the Tokyo subway. Indeed, there is evidence that some new terrorist groups, including bin Laden's Al-Qaeda, have tried to acquire nuclear, biological and chemical agents. It is known that the terrorist states of North Korea, Iraq, Iran, Libya and Syria all have tried to develop nuclear, chemical and biological weapons. Moreover, in the 1990s, information about chemical and biological agents became widely available on the Internet. The recent anthrax attacks may foreshadow a major escalation to bioterrorism by Islamist and perhaps other terrorists.

The changed motives of these "new-style" terrorists mean that at least two-thirds of the West's old strategy is out-moded. One pillar of that strategy, not making concessions to terrorists, remains valid. But it may be irrelevant when faced with groups like Al-Qaeda. Such groups are not trying to start negotiations. They make no negotiable "demands" that the West can comply with to forestall further attacks. These men do not seek a seat at the table; they want to overturn the table and kill everybody at it.

It is an honorable reflection of the basic friendliness of the American people that most of us find it difficult to believe that anybody hates Americans. Many find it especially confusing that men who lived among us, sometimes for years, attending our schools and shopping in our malls, should hate the very society whose freedoms they enjoyed. That they somehow must not understand us is the first reaction of many.

But this reaction reflects a misunderstanding about the new terrorists. They hate America precisely because they *do* understand our society; they hate its freedoms, its commitment to equal rights and universal suffrage, its material successes and its appeal to so many non-Americans. Thus, the question of whether or not to make concessions in the face of such hatred is simply irrelevant. Nothing America can say or do, short of ceasing to exist, will satisfy these terrorists.

Our long-standing objective of "bringing terrorists to justice", the second pillar of U.S. strategy, is also irrelevant to the new fight. During the past decade, an increasing percentage of terrorist attacks, especially those conducted by Middle Eastern groups, have involved suicides. This underscores the perpetrators' extraordinary commitment to terror, but it also shows the futility of relying on the concept of using criminal justice to punish them. Men who are prepared to die in an airplane crash are not going to be deterred by the threat of being locked in a prison cell. We need to revise our thinking; now our goal should be, as President Bush has suggested, "bringing justice to the terrorists."

Terrorism—The New Face of War

IN THE BROADER sense, the September 11 attacks preview the kind of security threat America will face in the 21st century. Terrorism allows the weak to attack the strong. It is relatively inexpensive to conduct, and devilishly difficult to counter.

Relative to all the other powers in the world, America is stronger than any country has ever been in history. The Gulf War showed that even a lavishly equipped conventional force (at the time, Iraq possessed the world's fifth largest army) was no match for America. The lesson for would-be tyrants and terrorists was clear: America could only be attacked by unconventional means, and terrorism is a fundamental tactic of asymmetrical warfare.

Terrorists take advantage of two important asymmetries. First, in the fight against terrorism, defenders have to protect all their points of vulnerability around the world; the terrorist has only to attack the weakest point. This lesson was brought home to the U.S. government when Al-Qaeda attacked the American embassies in Nairobi and Dar es-Salaam in August 1998, two embassies thought to be in little danger and thus ill-protected.

Secondly, the costs of launching a terrorist attack are a fraction of the costs required to defend against it. To shoot up an airport, a terrorist needs only an AK-47 assault rifle; defending that same airport costs millions of dollars. The September 11 attacks probably cost less than $2 million and caused over $100 billion in damage and business interruption. Thus, the new terrorism reverses the conventional wisdom that, in military operations, the offense must be three times as strong as the defense.

How, then, are we to fight this new and increasingly dangerous threat?

The proper objective of a counter-terrorist policy is to prevent attacks before they happen. So, more than in any other field of foreign and national security affairs, success in the fight against terrorism depends on having good intelligence. But there is no more difficult or dangerous kind of intelligence to collect. The surest way to know about an attack ahead of time is to have somebody tell you the plans. That means having a spy in the terrorist group itself.

Inserting an agent inside a terrorist group is among any intelligence agency's most difficult task. These groups are by nature clandestine and suspicious, even paranoid. Membership is often based on ethnic, tribal, clan or family ties, so Western intelligence agencies can rarely use their own nationals to infiltrate such groups.

There are two other possibilities for getting this valuable "human intelligence." Our agencies can, and do, work with friendly intelligence agencies in the Middle East. Often those organizations can use their own nationals to infiltrate terrorist cells. And if we handle such a relationship properly, our government can get useful and timely information about terrorist plans that enables us to disrupt them before they can be carried out. Such a relationship helped foil Al-Qaeda's planned millennium celebration attacks.

The second path is for the CIA itself to recruit a member of the group. This is exceptionally dangerous since the penalty, if caught spying, is certain death. We have also made the task more difficult for ourselves. Over the past 25 years, the United States has seriously undermined its capability to acquire "human intelligence." In the mid-1970s, politicized attacks by Congress damaged CIA operations and morale. In the late 1970s, a large number of the Agency's best officers specializing in collecting human intelligence were fired. These trends were exacerbated when, in 1995, the Clinton Administration imposed rigid and bureaucratic procedures governing the Agency's recruitment of spies who themselves have been involved with terrorist organizations. These new guidelines had the effect of making such recruitments even more difficult than they already were.

The bipartisan National Commission on Terrorism, which I chaired, carefully investigated the effect of these 1995 "guidelines." During our work in 2000, we heard testimony from serving CIA officers, at home and abroad, from first-tour case officers to station chiefs. Their testimony was unambiguous, unanimous and conclusive: the "guidelines" were an obstacle to the recruitment of effective spies in the struggle against terrorism. We strongly recommended their immediate cancellation.

The CIA's response to this recommendation was curious. Its leaders stated that they had never turned down a proposal *presented to them* to recruit a terrorist spy. But this entirely misses the point. By the time a proposed recruitment makes it to the CIA's leadership, it has already passed through a welter of rules, regulations, procedures, committees and lawyers that essentially guarantees that only the least suspect person will be suggested (assuming that after this tortuous and time-consuming process the terrorist is still around to recruit).

As the Bremer Commission noted, the major problem with the "guidelines" is the effect they have in the field. Officer after officer confirmed to our commissioners that the prospect of having to navigate Washington's bureaucratic jungle-gym was a clear disincentive even to begin the process of such recruitments. Many officers told us that they simply decided to go after easier targets. The "guidelines" have become an effective, though undesirable, bureaucratic prophylactic against risk-taking. They must be changed.

A New Strategy for Countering Terrorism

THE ELEMENTS of a new strategy to deal with the new threat are at hand. We need only the will to implement that strategy.

Our strategic objective must be to deny terrorist groups safe havens from which they can operate and garner various kinds of support from governments. As President Bush stated in his September 20 address, America intends to punish not just the terrorists but any group or state that has in any way supported them.

We must apply this strategy ruthlessly and creatively. Our tactics should range across the entire spectrum of activity from diplomacy, political pressure and economic measures, to military, psychological and covert operations. As the President has emphasized, this will be a long campaign demanding patience and cunning. The battle will be less like an American football game, with its fixed "battle lines" and clearly defined moves (as in the Gulf War), and more like European football: open, fluid and improvisational.

American actions must move beyond the episodic and limp-wristed attacks of the past decade, actions that seemed designed to "signal" our seriousness to the terrorists without inflicting any real damage on them. Naturally, their feebleness demonstrated the opposite. This time the terrorists and their supporters must be eliminated.

Our strategy should operate in three concentric circles. In the first and innermost circle, we must deal decisively with those most immediately responsible for the September attack. This means destroying all the terrorist camps, personnel and infrastructure in Afghanistan and getting rid of the Taliban regime. We must avoid thinking that the fight is only about bin Laden. It is one of the habitual failings of U.S. policy to over-emphasize one individual terrorist and ignore the broader dangers. In the late 1970s, Libya's Muammar Qaddafi was America's enemy number one. In the mid-1980's, Abu Nidal took his place. Ten years later, it was, and remains today, bin Laden.

There are two dangers with this approach. First, it tends to build up the terrorist leader, in his own eyes and in the eyes of his supporters. The concentration on one individual may thus paradoxically make it easier for him to find new recruits. Secondly, over-emphasis on one man may mislead the public into thinking that if only the "bad guy" could be eliminated, the terrorist problem would go away. It's just not so. Even if bin Laden were to die today, our problems would not end, for Afghanistan has become a cesspool of terrorism, much as Lebanon was in the 1980s. At least a half dozen other terrorist groups have training camps and facilities in the country, all welcomed by the Taliban. That is why our initial actions must go beyond destroying the terrorist camps. As long as the Taliban rule in Afghanistan, the terrorists' infrastructure can be quickly reconstituted.

It would be preferable if the Afghan people, who have suffered greatly under the harsh rule of the Taliban, could throw that regime out themselves. Certainly, the West should encourage this by supporting the exiled king, Mohammed Zahir, in his call for an uprising. Still popular among the Afghan people, the king is a Pashtun and thus has a crucial role to play in the establishment of a credible alternative government (though we must respect his need to avoid being seen as an American puppet).

This political strategy must be wedded to a three-pronged military plan. Our military forces and those of our allies must first degrade the Taliban's military capabilities. This will bring about a new balance of forces on the ground. Then we must encourage the creation and arming of an effective Pashtun military force, using as its core those Taliban commanders who have already defected. Finally, we and our allies should support the Northern Alliance, which still controls 10 to 15 percent of the country and which has support among the Tajik, Uzbek and Hazara communities.

The harsh reality is that any campaign that does not result in a change of regime in Kabul will be a failure. This is the *sine qua non* of our entire strategy. We therefore cannot exclude the possibility that it may be necessary to introduce ground troops into this hostile topography.

America's seriousness of purpose in the new war on terrorism will be demonstrated by U.S. and allied actions in this first phase. If we are weak, hesitant or ineffective, we will pay a heavy price later.

Ending State Support for Terrorism

THE SECOND objective of our strategy must be to deny terrorists operating bases. This means rooting out terrorist camps, bases and cells wherever they are, including the United States. It is likely that some of the Al-Qaeda terrorists will escape us in Afghanistan. They will try to relocate elsewhere, perhaps seeking out friendly governments or weak states in the Middle East, Central Asia or in Africa. We must pursue them and destroy them, with or without the help of the relevant governments.

The President made clear in his address to the American people on September 20 that any state that harbors or supports terrorist groups will be henceforth considered "a hostile regime." This statement has important implications beyond the obvious countries of Iran and Iraq. Syria, with which our European allies and we have regular diplomatic relations, still hosts over a dozen terrorist groups. So do Sudan and Lebanon.

Yet for too long American policy has contented itself with merely identifying states that support terrorism without forcing any serious consequences upon them in turn. Our European allies have been even less forceful, seeming to ignore state involvement in terrorism, often in the hopes of winning commercial advantage. For example, the European Union's long running "constructive dialogue" with Iran may have won European firms handsome contracts to develop Iranian energy resources, but it has not in any respect altered Iran's continued and open support for Middle East terrorist groups. Iran remains the world's leading state sponsor of terrorism. Groups such as Hamas, the Palestinian Islamic Jihad and Hizballah, which regularly target innocent civilians, all depend on Iranian support. In fact, as the State Department has pointed out, Iranian involvement in terror has actually increased since the election of Mohammad Khatemi as president four years ago.

Some commentators argue that the new terrorism is caused by discontent with America's role in supporting Israel. The implication is that if America would just weaken that support, the terrorism would end. This argument is wrong on two counts. First, bin Laden has made clear in his own words, for years, that he attacks America because he hates who we are, not because of whom we support. Secondly, dealing effectively with radical Islam is the prerequisite to moving toward a broader regional peace, not the other way around. It was America's decisive (though incomplete) victory over Iraq in 1991 that was the necessary precondition for the Oslo peace process. Now as then, countries in the Middle East and Europe will pay attention to American ideas for regional security when we have shown that we are prepared to act decisively against threats to that security.

A War on Islam?

PRESIDENT BUSH and all his senior advisors have been clear: We do not consider the American response to the September 11 attacks to be a war against Islam. He is right. Bin Laden and his allies in the Taliban are a fringe minority far removed from the teachings of mainstream Islam. But there is a real danger now that "moderate" Muslims are allowing these radicals to hijack Islam, and thus to define Islam as an enemy of the West. Until now, we have heard too few voices of restraint from the Islamic world. Quite the contrary. For example, through their controlled media, the Palestinians and even some "moderate" Arab governments have spewed out anti-American hatred with impunity for years. On the very day of the suicide attacks, the newspaper of the Palestinian Authority, *al-Hayat al-Jadida*, praised suicide bombers as "noble… the salt of the earth, the engines of history.… They are the most honorable among us." Inflammatory articles like this have contributed to an enviromment that made possible the appalling spectacle of schoolchildren in Gaza and Ramallah cheering the news of the American tragedies.

Europeans, who provide the bulk of money to the Palestinians, should make clear that until such inflammatory rhetoric stops, there will be no more euros for Yasir Arafat. Nor should American taxpayers be expected to send another penny to the Palestinian Authority until Arafat roots out, expels or imprisons the Hamas, Hizballah and Islamic Jihad terrorists who oeprate from his territory.

In Pakistan, Islamic *madrassas* regularly indoctrinate young boys to hate America. At one school, after the September 11 attack, eight year-old boys vied with one another to be the one who would grow up to bring down the Sears Tower in Chicago. Here in America, some Islamic leaders have said that the September 11 attacks violate the Quran. But several have then made the astonishing statement that, this being the case, Israelis or Americans themselves must have conducted the attacks.

Moderate Islam is on the front line now. Its leaders have a solemn responsibility to make clear, in public, that the purposeful slaughter of innocent civilians is anathema to Islamic beliefs and that those who commit such acts are apostates who will go to hell, not to heaven. Unless they speak out now, there is a real risk that Islam will be defined by the radicals at war with the West. And then this *will* become a war with Islam, delcared *by* Islam.

Delegitimizing Terror

FINALLY, American strategy must have as a broader objective rebuilding the international consensus against terrorism that flourished briefly during the 1980s, but then fell into neglect. If done effectively, this can delegitimize terror.

There are many areas where better cooperation will prove useful. Intelligence cooperation is the most urgent need. Clearly, no matter how good its intelligence organization, no one nation alone can hope to gather enough specific information on a worldwide terrorist network. In the wake of the September 11 attacks, it has become clear that America's intelligence failure was mirrored in many other countries: none seemed to be taking seriously enough the clear declarations of war by bin Laden, and none was sufficiently attentive to the activities of suspicious people. Sharing intelligence with friendly countries is an essential step in developing a common strategy. As noted, during the 1980s America and its European partners found ways to deepen cooperation in this vital area. This effort must now be accelerated and broadened to include cooperation with friendly Muslim states.

There must also be more vigorous and persistent efforts to track terrorist funds. Too often, terrorist groups have been able to use front organizations, nongovernmental organizations and willing dupes to raise and distribute money. Out of ignorance, laziness or cowardice, most governments have looked the other way. The recent U.S. decision to seize terrorist assets is a good first step. So is the UN Security Council resolution calling on all states to take robust action against terrorist finances.

To maintain broad support for the struggle against terrorism, the United States will have to accept that the problem goes beyond those terrorist groups with a "global reach." While such groups are the proper objective of our initial strategy, we will have to show that we share the concerns of our allies who are subjected to Irish and Basque terrorism, for example, if we are to get continuing support from Britain and Spain in the fight.

As to legal matters, no doubt there will be proposals for new international conventions and treaties concerning terrorism and state support for it. Each of these should be examined on its merits and pursued where useful. But we should not let the search for an illusive international legal consensus stop us from vigorous action against known terrorist groups or states.

WE HAVE seen the face of the new threat to our security in the 21st century. Under Article 51 of the United Nations Charter, the United States is fully justified in taking any and all means of self-defense against that threat. The United States has made clear that it welcomes the assistance of any country in anti-terrorist military operations, and so far the American government has done a masterful job of assembling broad support for the initial phase of the campaign in Afghanistan. The challenge will be to sustain that support as the battle wears on, and especially when the campaign enters the second phase, after we have dealt with Afghanistan.

We must destroy the terrorists before they destroy us. They hate us and are so dangerous that they must be stopped before they can take the battle to a still higher plane of lethality. We must disrupt, dismantle or destroy terrorist groups wherever they are and deny them safe havens. Americans should therefore be under no illusions about the campaign we have embarked upon. There will be war with more than one country. As in all wars, there will be civilian casualties. America will win some battles but lose others. More Americans will die. But neither our allies nor our enemies should be in any doubt: We shall prevail.

"The Martyr"

There is sobbing of the strong,
And a pall upon the land;
But the People in their weeping
Bare the iron hand:
Beware the People weeping
When they bare the iron hand.

—Herman Melville

Ambassador L. Paul Bremer, III is chairman and chief executive officer of Marsh Crisis Consulting. He served as chairman of the National Commission on Terrorism.

Between Two Ages

GET USED TO IT

Address by WILLIAM VAN DUSEN WISHARD, *President, World Trends Research*
Delivered to the Coudert Institute, Palm Beach, Florida, December 1, 2001

Your topic of study "Living in an age of transition" couldn't be more appropriate to what we have been, are, and will continue to be living through probably for the rest of our lives.

In 2000, I published a new book, Between Two Ages. On the front cover appears this sentence: "The next three decades may be the most decisive 30 year period in the history of mankind." Then there's another sentence describing how the book examines that suggestion.

Nothing so dramatizes living between two ages as does the image of the fireball engulfing the World Trade Center, an image burned into the world's psyche September 11th. I'm not going to dwell on that event, except to say this. The image of the imploding World Trade Center must be seen as part of a panorama of images for its full significance to best be understood. The image, for instance, of death camps and crematoriums in Central Europe. The image of a mushroom cloud rising over the Pacific. Of Neil Armstrong stepping onto the Moon. Of Louise Brown, the first human to be conceived outside of the human body. Of a man standing near the summit of Mt. Everest talking on his cell phone to his wife in Australia. Of the first human embryo to be cloned. Of a computer performing billions of calculations in a second, calculations that could not have been performed by all the mathematicians who ever lived, even in their combined lifetimes. These are some of the images, representing both human greatness and depravity, that mark the end of one age and the approach of a new time in human experience.

It was in 1957 that Peter Drucker, who, more than any other person, defined management as a discipline, wrote: "No one born after the turn of the 20th century has ever known anything but a world uprooting its foundations, overturning its values and toppling its idols." So today I'm going to pursue Drucker's thought and suggest why I believe we're living at probably the most critical turning point of human history.

Between two ages. How are we to visualize the difference between those two ages? I offer some contrasts. From the dom-

inance of print communication, to the emergence of electronic communication. From American immigration coming primarily from Europe, to immigration coming mainly from Asia and Latin America. From a time of relatively slow change, to change at an exponential rate. From economic development as a national endeavor, to economic development as part of a global system. From ultimate destructive power being confined to the state, to such power available to the individual. We could continue, but I think you see what I mean. We're in what the ancient Greeks called Kairos—the "right moment" for a fundamental change in principles and symbols.

Exactly what kind of era is opening up is far from clear. The only obvious fact is that it's going to be global, whatever else it is.

In the next few minutes I want to comment on three trends that are part of this shift between two ages. Let me start by stating my bias: I am bullish on the future. We've got unprecedented challenges ahead, clearly the most difficult humanity has ever faced. But I believe in the capacity of the human spirit to surmount any challenge if given the vision, the will and the leadership.

With this in mind, let's look at some trends that are moving us from one age to the next.

First trend: For the first time in human history, the world is forging an awareness of our existence as a single entity. Nations are incorporating the planetary dimensions of life into the fabric of our economics, politics, culture and international relations. The shorthand for this is "globalization."

We all have some idea of what globalization means. In my view, globalization represents the world's best chance to enrich the lives of the greatest number of people. The specter of terrorism, however, raises the question as to globalization's future. Will the 1990's "go-go" version be one of the casualties of terrorism? Yes and no. The economic pace of globalization may slow down, and certainly reaction to America's "soft power"— what other nations see as the "Americanization" of world culture—will continue to grow. But other aspects may actually accelerate. For example, we're already seeing the increased globalization of intelligence, security and humanitarian concerns.

Aside from that, globalization is far more than just economics and politics: more than non-western nations adopting free markets and democratic political systems. At its core, globalization means that western ideas are gradually seeping into the social and political fabric of the world. And even deeper, globalization is about culture, tradition and historic relationships; it's about existing institutions and why and how they evolved. In short, globalization goes to the very psychological foundations of a people.

Look at what's happening. Nations are adopting such ideas as the sanctity of the individual, due process of law, universal education, the equality of women, human rights, private property, legal safeguards governing business and finance, science as the engine of social growth, concepts of civil society, and perhaps most importantly, the ability of people to take charge of their destiny and not simply accept the hand dealt them in life. For millions of people these concepts are new modes of thought, which open undreamt of possibilities.

Is this good? From our perspective it is. But what do other nations feel as America's idea of creative destruction and entrepreneurship press deeper into the social fabric of countries such as China and India; as American cultural products uproot historic traditions?

In the Middle East, American culture as exemplified by a TV program such as Baywatch generates a unique resentment. Such a program presents Islamic civilization with a different nuance of feminine beauty and the dignity of women. Baywatch, and American culture in general, lure Muslims into an awkward position. On the one hand, their basic human appetites respond at a primal level. So it becomes part of them. Yet on another level, they fear the invasion of this new culture is undermining something sacred and irreplaceable in their very social fabric. Yes, it's their own fault; they don't have to import such entertainment. Yet it all seems to be part of so-called "modernization."

All of which illustrates how hard it is for us Americans to appreciate the underlying differences between western ideas and the foundations of other nations. Take some of the basic contrasts between Asia and the west. The west prizes individuality, while the east emphasizes relationships and community. The west sees humans dominating nature, while the east sees humans as part of nature. In the west there is a division between mind and heart, while in the east mind and heart are unified.

I mention this to illustrate the deep psychological trauma nations are experiencing as they confront the effects of globalization. We Americans, raised on the instinct of change, say, "Great. Let tradition go. Embrace the new." But much of the world says, "Wait a minute. Traditions are our connection to the past; they're part of our psychic roots. If we jettison them, we'll endanger our social coherence and stability."

Remember, it took centuries for our political, social and economic concepts to evolve in the West. They are the product of a unique western psychology and experience. Thus we cannot expect non-western nations to graft alien social attitudes onto an indigenous societal structure overnight.

Part of the upheaval created by globalization is the largest migration the world has ever seen, which is now under way. In China alone, 100 million people are on the move from the countryside to the city. In Europe, the OECD tells us that no country is reproducing its population; that the EU will need 180 million immigrants in the next three decades simply to keep its population at 1995 levels, as well as to keep the current ratio of retirees to workers.

As European population growth declines, and as immigration increases, the historic legends that are the basis of national identities tend to wane. As one British historian put it, "A white majority that invented the national mythologies underpinning modern European culture lives in an almost perpetual state of fear that it and its way of life are about to disappear." You realize what he means when you hear that the Church of England expects England to have more practicing Muslims than practicing Anglicans by next year. In Italy, the Archbishop of Bologna recently warned Italy is in danger of "losing its identity" due to the immigration from North Africa and Central Europe. This fear is the subtext for everything else we see happening in Europe today.

The question of identity is at the core of the world problem as globalization accelerates. It came sharply into focus in the 1960's when, for the first time in human history, we saw Earth from space, from the moon. An idea that had only existed in the minds of poets and philosophers suddenly became geopolitical reality—the human family is a single entity. We began to see national, cultural and ethnic distinctions for what they are—projections in our minds. We lost the clarity of identity—Herder's "collective soul"—that had given birth and meaning to nations and civilizations for centuries.

In my view, it's this continuing loss of identity—or the threat of it—that helps fuel terrorism. Granted, there's an individual psychotic aspect to any terrorist. But the context in which they live is a loss of a personal sense of identity, as well as a subsequent psychological identification with the God-image.

One aspect of globalization we sometimes find irritating is America's global role and the resulting world perception of America. This perception is shaped by many factors, some of which we control, many of which we don't. For example, nations have historically felt a natural antipathy toward the world's strongest empire, whoever it happened to be at the time. And make no mistake, we are perceived, at a minimum, as an empire of influence. That said, in my view no great nation has used its power as generously and with as little intention of territorial gain as has America. Nonetheless, if we don't understand what other nations feel about America, globalization will not succeed, and neither will the war on terrorism.

Consider a comment by the Norwegian newspaper, Aftenposten: "in Norway, Nepal, and New Zealand, all of us live in a world that is increasingly shaped by the United States." Now let's play with that thought for a moment and consider a hypothetical situation.

Imagine how we would feel if the world were increasingly shaped by, say, China. Suppose China had produced the information technology that is the engine of globalization, technology that we had to buy and incorporate into our social structure. Picture Chinese currency as the medium of world trade. Further envision Chinese as the international language of commerce. What if Chinese films and TV programs were flooding global entertainment markets, undermining bedrock American beliefs and values. Suppose China were the dominant military and economic world power. Imagine the Chinese having troops stationed for security and peacekeeping in over thirty countries around the world. What if the IMF and World Bank were primarily influenced by Chinese power and pressure. Suppose China had developed the economic and management theories that we had to adopt in order to compete in the global marketplace.

If this were the case, how would Americans feel? I'm not suggesting there's anything inherently wrong with U.S. world influence, I'm trying to illustrate the all pervasiveness of America's reach in the world in order to suggest why even our allies manifest uneasy concerns about America. Understanding this, and adjusting where warranted, is essential to the success of globalization, to say nothing of the future of America.

Consider another example. Think what it looks like to the rest of the world when we judge other nations on the basis of human rights and democracy, while at the same time systematically feeding our children a cultural diet considered by all religions and civilizations throughout history to be destructive of personal character and social cohesion. Two of America's foremost diplomats have commented on this anomaly. Zbigniew Brzezinski, former National Security Advisor to the president, writes, "I don't think Western secularism in its present shape is the best standard for human rights." He mentions consumption, self-gratification and hedonism as three characteristics of America's definition of the "good life," and then says, "The defense of the political individual doesn't mean a whole lot in such a spiritual and moral vacuum."

George F. Kennan, one of the giant U.S. diplomatic figures of the past half century, says simply, "This whole tendency to see ourselves as the center of political enlightenment and as teachers to a great part of the rest of the world strikes me as unthought-through, vainglorious and undesirable." I might add these comments were made before September 11th.

Such comments perhaps seem almost unpatriotic. But America's ability to provide world leadership may depend on whether we have the capacity to consider such reactions, and see what truth there may be in them. It's what the Scottish poet Robert Burns wrote: "Oh would some power the gift to give us, to see ourselves as others see us!"

I emphasize these points because if we're going to build a global age, it's got to be built on more than free markets and the Internet. Even more, it's got to be built on some view of life far broader than "my nation," "my race" or "my religion" is the greatest. Such views gave dynamism and meaning to the empires of the past. But the task now is to bring into being a global consciousness. It must have as its foundation some shared psychological and, ultimately, spiritual experience and expression. At the end of the day, globalization must have a legitimacy that validates itself in terms of a true democratic and moral order.

The second trend moving us between two ages is a new stage of technology development. This new phase is without precedent in the history of science and technology.

At least since Francis Bacon in the 1600's we have viewed the purpose of science and technology as being to improve the human condition. As Bacon put it, the "true and lawful end of the sciences is that human life be enriched by new discoveries and powers."

And indeed it has. Take America. During the last century, the real GDP, in constant dollars, increased by $48 trillion, much of this wealth built on the marvels of technology.

But along with technological wonders, uncertainties arise. Let me interject here that in 1997 I had a quadruple heart bypass operation using the most sophisticated medical technology in the world. So I'm a believer. Nonetheless, the question today is whether we're creating certain technologies not to improve the human condition, but for purposes that seem to be to replace human meaning and significance altogether.

The experts tell us is that by the year 2035, artificial robotic intelligence will surpass human intelligence. (Let's leave aside for a moment the question of what constitutes "intelligence.") And a decade after that, we shall have a robot with all the emotional and spiritual sensitivities of a human being.

Not long after that, computers—will go at such a speed that the totality of human existence will change so dramatically that it's beyond our capability to envision what life will be like. But never fear, we're told. The eventual marriage of human and machine will mean that humans will continue as a species, albeit not in a form we would recognize today.

Thus arrives what some would-be scientific intellectuals call the "Post-human Age." I emphasize, this is not science fiction. It is the projection of some of our foremost scientists.

Let's move from the general to the specific. Consider a remark by the co-founder of MIT's artificial intelligence lab and one of the world's leading authorities on artificial intelligence: "Suppose that the robot had all of the virtues of people and was smarter and understood things better. Then why would we want to prefer those grubby, old people? I don't see anything wrong with human life being devalued if we have something better." Now just absorb that thought for a moment. One of the world's leading scientists ready to "devalue human life" if we can create something he thinks is better. Setting aside the question of who decides what "better" is, to me, devaluing human life is a form of self-destruction.

The editor of Wired magazine says we're in the process of the "wiring of human and artificial minds into one planetary soul." Thus, he believes, we,ll be the first species "to create our own successors." He sees artificial intelligence "creating its own civilization."

These are not "mad scientists." They're America's best and brightest, and they believe they're ushering in the next stage of evolution.

In sum, we're creating technology that forces us to ask what are humans for once we've created super intelligent robots that can do anything humans can do, only do it a thousand times faster? Why do we need robots with emotional and spiritual capability, and what does that have to do with the seventy percent of humanity that simply seeks the basic necessities of life? What will it mean to be able to change the genetic structure not just of an individual child, but also of all future generations? Do we really want to be able to make genetic changes so subtle that it may be generations before we know what we've done to ourselves?

What we're talking about is a potential alteration of the human being at the level of the soul. This is a work proceeding absent any political debate, certainly without the assent of elected leaders. Yet it will change the definition of what it means to be a human being. It's the silent loss of freedom masquerading as technological progress.

Many other questions come to mind, but two in particular. Will it happen, and what is driving this self-destructive technological imperative?

On the first question—will it happen—my guess is probably not. In my judgment, there is a major issue the technological visionaries disregard. That is the question of how much manipulation and accelerated change the human being can take before he/she disintegrates psychologically and physiologically.

What we're experiencing is not simply the acceleration of the pace of change, but the acceleration of acceleration itself. In other words, change growing at an exponential rate. The experts tell us that the rate of change doubles every decade; that at today's rate of change, we'll experience 100 calendar years of change in the next twenty-five years; and that due to the nature of exponential growth, the 21st century as a whole will experience almost one thousand times greater technological change than did the 20th century.

I hasten to add that these are not my projections. They are the views of some of America's most accomplished and respected experts in computer science and artificial intelligence.

Onrushing change is already producing mounting dysfunction. The suicide rate among women has increased 200% in the past two decades. Thirty years ago, major corporations didn't have to think much about mental health programs for employees. Now, mental health is the fastest growing component of corporate health insurance programs. Think of the corporations that now provide special rooms for relaxation, naps, music or prayer and meditation. The issue now for corporations is not so much how to deal with stress; it's how to maintain the psychological integrity of the individual employee.

Other indicators of dysfunction tell us that teen suicide jumped 300% between 1960-90. Books are now written for eight and nine year old children advising them how to recognize the symptoms of stress, and to deal with it in their own lives. Anti-depressants and other character-controlling drugs are taken like aspirin. Rage has assumed a culture-like place in the national fabric, whether rage on the road, in stores, in schools and even in a popular video game called "Primal Rage," and, most tragically, in families.

Now, project forward the predicted increased speed of computers and the resulting ratcheting up of the pace of life over the next decades, and you end up asking, "How much more of this can the human metabolism take?" It's not the case that sooner or later something will give way. The multiplying social pathol-

ogies indicate that individual and collective psychological integrity is already giving way.

The second question is, what's driving this self-destructive activity? Certainly we as consumers are a major part of it. We're addicted to the latest electronic gizmo; whether it's the ubiquitous cell phone to keep us in touch with everyone everywhere, or one of those Sharper Image CD players you hang on the shower head so you can listen to Beethoven while taking a shower.

But let me offer three views that suggest a deeper story. Consider the comment of a former Carnegie-Mellon University computer scientist hired by Microsoft as a researcher. In an interview with the Washington Post, the good professor said, "This corporation is my power tool. It is the tool I wield to allow my ideas to shape the world."

My power tool. What clearer expression of ego-inflation could there be?

A second comment comes from the editor of Wired magazine, who famously wrote, "We are as gods, and we might as well be good at it." The Greeks had a word for identifying ourselves with the gods—hubris, pride reaching beyond proper human limits.

Perspective on all this comes from within the scientific community itself.

Freeman Dyson is one of the world's preeminent theoretical physicists. He talks about the "technical arrogance" that overcomes people "when they see what they can do with their minds."

My power tool; we are as gods; technical arrogance. The Greeks had another word that was even stronger than hubris. Pleonexia. An overweening resolve to reach beyond the limits, an insatiable greed for the unattainable. It is what one writer terms the "Masculine Sublime," which he describes as the "gendered characteristics out of which the myths of science are molded- myths of masculine power, control, rationality, objectivity."

From the earliest times, everything in human myth and religion warns us about overreaching. From the myths of Prometheus in ancient Greece, to the Hebrew story of Adam and Eve; from the Faust legend to Milton's Paradise Lost; from Mary Shelly's Frankenstein to Stevenson's Dr. Jekyll and Mr. Hyde; from Emily Dickinson to Robert Oppenheimer's lament that "in some sort of crude sense, the physicists have known sin"; through all these stories and experiences that come from the deepest level of the human soul, there has been a warning that limits exist on both human knowledge and endeavor; that to go beyond those limits is self-destructive.

No one knows exactly where such limits might be. But if they don't include the effort to create some technical/ human life form supposedly superior to human beings, if they don't include the capacity to genetically reconfigure human nature, if they don't include the attempt to introduce a "post-human" civilization, then it's hard to imagine where such limits would be drawn.

Keep in mind that myths are more than fanciful stories left over from the childhood of man. They emanate from the unconscious level of the psyche; that level which connects us to whatever transpersonal wisdom may exist. It's a level at which, as quantum physics suggests, there may exist some relationship between the human psyche and external matter. There may be some fundamental pattern of life common to both that is operating outside the understanding of contemporary science. In other words, we may be fooling around with phenomena that are, in fact, beyond human awareness; possibly even beyond the ability of humans to grasp. For at the heart of life is a great mystery which does not yield to rational interpretation. This eternal mystery induces a sense of wonder out of which all that humanity has of religion, art and science is born. The mystery is the giver of these gifts, and we only lose the gifts when we grasp at the mystery itself. In my view, Nature will not permit arrogant man to defy that mystery, that transcendent wisdom. In the end, Nature's going to win out.

Some people are already searching for the wisest way to approach such potential challenges as the new technologies present. Bill Joy, co-founder and former chief scientist of Sun Microsystems, suggests we've reached the point where we must "limit development of technologies that are too dangerous, by limiting our pursuit of certain kinds of knowledge." His concerns are based on the unknown potential of genetics, nanotechnology and robotics, driven by computers capable of infinite speeds, and the possible uncontrollable self-replication of these technologies this might pose. Joy acknowledges the pursuit of knowledge as one of the primary human goals since earliest times. But, he says, "If open access to, and unlimited development of, knowledge henceforth puts us all in clear danger of extinction, then common sense demands that we re-examine even these basic, long-held beliefs."

The third trend moving us between two ages is a longterm spiritual and psychological reorientation that's increasingly generating uncertainty and instability. This affects all of us, for we're all part of America's collective psychology, whether we realize it or not.

The best measure of America's psychological and spiritual life is not public opinion polls telling us what percentage of the population believes in God. Rather, it's the content and quality of our culture. For culture is to a nation what dreams are to an individual—an indication of what's going on in the inner life.

In my judgment, what's really going on is that the world is experiencing a long-term spiritual and psychological reorientation similar to what happened when the Greco-Roman era gave way to the start of the Feudal Age. That was a time of great disorientation and searching. The cry "Great Pan is dead," was heard throughout the ancient world as the traditional gods lost their hold on the collective psyche. The Greco-Roman world became awash in countless new religions and sects vying for supremacy.

Not too different from our times, beginning with Nietzsche's cry, "God is dead." When we look at what's happening today we see 1500 religions in America, including such anomalies as "Catholic-Buddhists." Beyond that, we see a smorgasbord of spiritual/psychological fare as seen in the popularity of books such as The Celestine Prophecy or the Chicken Soup series, in the rise of worldwide fundamentalism, in numerous cults such as "Heaven's Gate," in the New Age phenomenon, in interest in Nostradamus, in crop circles, in the supposed "Bible Code," in conspiracy theories, in fascination with the "other" as seen in movies such as "Planet of the Apes" or "Tomb Raiders," in the search for some extraterrestrial intelligence to save us from ourselves, and last but certainly not least, in terrorism, which, at its core, is a demonic hatred expressed in spiritual terms.

What happened in the Rome—early Feudal Age shift was played out over centuries. What's happening today has, yes, been evolving over the past few centuries. We see it first manifested in the emergence of the Faust legend; then in the Enlightenment's enthronement of the Goddess of Reason in Notre Dame and the ensuing acceptance of rationalism as life's highest authority; and in our own time in the ethos of "meaninglessness" that has virtually defined 20th century Western culture. But what's happening today—due to the 20th century electronic information technologies—is probably unfolding at a more rapid pace than the shift in the fourth-fifth-sixth centuries. For information technologies transmit not only information, but psychological dynamics as well.

While there are millions of devout Christians and Jews in America and Europe, the Judeo-Christian impulse is no longer the formative dynamic of Western culture, especially among the so-called "creative minority." Even so calm a journal as the Economist opines, "The West is secular." One need only look at the changing relationship between the roles of the priest and the psychologist to see what has been happening. Earlier in the 20th century, if someone had personal problems, he or she went to the priest for advice. Gradually that changed, and people started going to their psychologist. Recently, the leader of the Roman Catholic Church in England and Wales said that as a background for people's lives, Christianity "has almost been vanquished." His language mirrored a statement by the Archbishop of Canterbury who declared Britain to be a country where "tacit atheism prevails." Newsweek recently described Europe as a "post-Christian civilization." Throughout the continent, Newsweek reported, "churches stand empty."

Part of the psychological reorientation taking place is the breakup of our collective inner images of wholeness. For example, we used to talk about "heaven," which denoted the transcendent realm, eternity, the dwelling place of the gods. Now we just speak of "space," which has no spiritual connotation. We used to talk of "mother earth," which had a vital emotional association. From time immemorial, nature was filled with spirit. Now we just speak of "matter," a lifeless nature bereft of gods.

Thus transcendent meaning—which is the source of psychological wholeness is diminished. The function of symbolic language-words like "heaven" and "mother earth"— is to link our consciousness to the roots of our being, to link our consciousness to its base in the unconscious. When that link is devalued or discarded, there is little to sustain the inner life of the individual. So, few people are inwardly fed by any primal source of wholeness. In effect, our symbolic life and language have been displaced by a vocabulary of technology, a vocabulary that's increasingly devoid of transcendent meaning. The effect is a weakening of the structures that organize and, regulate our life-religion, self-government, education, culture and the family.

As a result, the soul of America—indeed, of the world—is in a giant search for some deeper and greater expression of life. Despite the benefits of modernization, technological society offers no underlying meaning to life. Thus the search taking place is both healthy and normal—given the seminal shift to an entirely new epoch that is occurring as we speak.

What we're discussing is at the core of the crisis of meaning that afflicts not only America and Europe, but Asia as well. For example, the Washington Post reports from Beijing, "Across China people are struggling to redefine notions of success and failure, right and wrong. The quest for something to believe in is one of the unifying characteristics of China today." A report from the East/West Center in Hawaii notes the decline in family and authority in Asia, and concludes by saying, "Eastern religion no longer is the binding force in Asian society." So it's a global crisis of meaning we're talking about.

Let me briefly summarize what we've been discussing. (1) Globalization possibly the most ambitious collective human experiment in history; (2) a new stage of technology the objective of which is to supplant human meaning and significance; and (3) a long-term psychological and spiritual reorientation. These are only three of the basic changes determining the future. And it's because of the magnitude and significance of such trends that I suggest the next three decades may be the most decisive thirty-year period in human history.

How do we respond to such a situation? We're already responding in the most sweeping redefinition of life America has ever known. We're redefining and restructuring all our institutions. Corporations are redefining their mission, structure and modus operandi. In education, we're trying countless new experiments, from vouchers to charter schools to home schooling. Alternative dispute resolution is helping lift the burden off the back of our legal system. Civic and charitable organizations are assuming functions formerly undertaken by local governments. More people are involved in efforts to help the elderly and those in poverty. In fact, it's estimated that well over fifty percent of all adult Americans donate a portion of their time to non-profit social efforts. Most importantly, there are countless efforts underway to redress the severe environmental imbalance we've created.

Against the background of the three trends I mentioned, perhaps this is a modest start, but at least it's a start. Clearly, there's another level of effort to move to, As Bill Joy suggests, such efforts must include a decision whether or not to continue research and development of technologies that could, in Joy's words, "bring the world to the edge of extinction." Obviously, such an examination must be done in a global context if it's to be valid.

But another question is, how are you and I to live in a world that's changing faster than individuals and institutions can assimilate? How do we maintain anchorage and balance when we're in between two ages?

I believe the starting place is understanding; simply to understand the fundamental changes taking place. That takes time and work.

As the most basic change taking place is in us as individuals, we must understand ourselves at a wholly new level. For the individual is the carrier of civilization. In the West, we tend to think in abstract categories of generality, such as civilizations, nations, historic trends, economic imperatives, social theories and philosophical concepts. These, we say, are the factors that make history. In my view, they're not. People make history, and all our concepts, theories and imperatives are projections of one kind or another that emanate from deep within the human psyche. It's what we are as individuals that shapes the future. So the issue boils down to how well do we know ourselves, both as individuals and as a nation?

We all know Socrates advice, "Know thyself." And most of us, if we pay any attention to that suggestion, think of knowing ourselves as knowing our conscious self. We think in terms of ego-consciousness. We think in terms of our persona, the mask we present to the world. The persona, however, is not the true, individual "me." The persona is usually a social identity—being a teacher, lawyer, banker or businessperson. As such, the persona derives from the collective psyche, not from any individual uniqueness.

But who we really are does not derive from our social role, from the work we do or our position on the social scale. Most of what we truly are resides in the unconscious, in the shadow side of our lives. My persona is who I like to think I am. My shadow is who I really am. My persona is the conscious "me." The shadow is the unconscious me. So getting to know the shadow is a prerequisite to knowing ourselves and who we truly are.

By and large, the shadow is a collection of repressed desires and "uncivilized" impulses. It's that part of our character we're not especially proud of and we'd rather not admit to. The British psychiatrist Anthony Stevens suggests that if you want to know what your shadow looks like, just write down a description of the sort of person you simply cannot stand. That description is your shadow. Everyone has a shadow. The problem is we easily see the other person's shadow, but not our own.

So what do we do with our shadow? Because we don't want to confront it, we usually project it on to others. We see our own devils in other people. This projection has been going on for millennia. It caused Christ to say, "And why do you see the mote that is in your brother's eye, but fail to see the beam that is in your own eye?" It's a form of denial, and there can be national denial as well as individual denial.

This failure to see our shadow is responsible for any amount of acrimony in relationships in a family, between friends or in an organization. On a collective level, it gives rise to political polarization, racial tension and international conflict. Hitler's projected shadow was a prime cause of the Holocaust. Every international conflict is, to some extent, a shadow projection. One reason we fail to resolve such international crises is because we don't recognize the critical dimension that is at the center of every crisis—the human psyche and its archetypal shadow. So how can you and I deal with our shadow, something that is unconscious?

The best way I've discovered is to study my reactions to other people. Reactions have two parts: First, an objective assessment of another person's character or actions; and second, the emotional intensity with which I react. No matter how accurate my assessment may be, that emotional intensity represents my shadow. So the instructive question to ask is not, "Why did the other person do what he or she did?" It's "Why am I reacting the way I am? What can my reaction tell me about my shadow?"

Let me make it personal. I have constant reactions to my wife. We've been married forty-four years, and I love her dearly. But that doesn't alter the fact that we react to each other. It's human nature. So when I react to her, no matter what the issue, I've learned to ask myself, "Where's the emotional steam coming from? Why am I reacting so strongly?" And I usually get an answer. And more often than not, the answer has to do with my loss of control of some particular situation. Something has happened that has taken away my control of my plan.

There's another feature of our shadow: the shadow includes aspects of ourselves that contain our unlived life-talents and abilities that, for various reasons, have been buried or never been made conscious. So the more we understand our shadow, the more likely these positive attributes are to develop.

As we confront our shadow, over time our negative qualities can be integrated with our positive qualities to make us more complete personalities. Becoming complete personalities is the whole object of life. That's what healing is all about; it's what growth is all about. It's a process of making conscious what has been unconscious. It's what one author wrote: "The full and joyful acceptance of the worst in oneself may be the only way of transforming it."

My task as a human being is to discover who I really am, and that means getting behind the persona and confronting the shadow. We can live on our persona only so long before life becomes stale and inauthentic, at which point we turn to trivia for distraction and entertainment. The same is true for nations. And while we Americans see our persona, the rest of the world sees our shadow. Indeed, Hollywood has made our shadow America's primary cultural export to the world.

Between two ages. There's a new epoch of human meaning struggling to take shape. Through the chaos and the killing, through the heartache and inner emptiness, the birth of a heightened consciousness is fighting its way out of the womb into the light.

The womb that nurtures this New Time is nothing less than the human unconscious, especially the deepest strata that is common to all humankind, the collective unconscious. The key to unlocking this deeper realm is to know ourselves in a new and deeper way; to become aware of life's opposites—the persona and the shadow, the good and evil, the loves and hatreds — that dwell within each of us, all of which constitute the totality of who we really are. The task is to strengthen the dialogue between consciousness and the limitless creative powers of the collective unconscious, wherein resides life's highest meaning.

A new time in history requires a fresh affirmation of the meaning and coherence of the human journey. That will not come from a speechwriter's pen or Madison Avenue. It must be born in the depths of the psyche of each one of us as we individually seek our own deeper meaning and relevance at a time of opportunity and danger unequaled in history. As we do this, we affirm that the sacred continuity of life continues. But it does not continue in a way we think of as normal. A new epoch will not emerge from conventional attitudes and habits. Living between two ages requires us to redefine what constitutes normalcy. A new normalcy can only come if we face our shadow so it can—over time—be integrated into a greater wholeness of personality. That's the price that must be paid in order that a new spiritual dispensation, a fresh expression of life's highest meaning, can come into being, and can shape the era that is to be.

Some eternal, infinite power is at work in each of us, as well as in the universe. This power is the source of renewal of all man's most vital and creative energies. With all our problems and possibilities, the future depends on how we—each in his or her own unique way-tap into that eternal renewing dynamic that dwells in the deepest reaches of the human soul.

In my view, this is some of what it means to live in an age of transition. Thank you.

From *Vital Speeches of the Day*, January 15, 2002, pp. 203-211. © 2002 by City News Publishing Company, Inc.

Across the Great Divide

**Our world: Capitalism and democracy are the two great forces of the age.
They unleash creativity and human potential. But they can be destructive too;
they challenge the old order. Are we ready for the wild ride of tomorrow?**

By Fareed Zakaria

December 6, 1999
It has been only 10 years since the fall of the Berlin wall, but we are in a new age. In 1986 people would have seen their world of Reagan and Thatcher and Gorbachev as closely linked to the world of 1976 or, for that matter, of 1966 or 1956 or 1946. But today events, just 10 years old, are dim and quaint memories—remember the Nicaraguan contras? Having crossed a great historical divide, events on the other side of that chasm are like ancient history.

For almost a half century, the West has struggled mightily to spread capitalism and democracy around the world. Now it has gotten what it wanted—unbridled market and people power—and they will prove harder to handle than anyone imagined. Capitalism and democracy are the two dominant forces of modern history; they unleash human creativity and energy like nothing else. But they are also forces of destruction. They destroy old orders, hierarchy, tradition, communities, careers, stability and peace of mind itself. Unsentimental about the world as it exists, they surge forward, changing everything they encounter. The challenge of the West in the next century will be to find ways to channel the sweeping power of these two—the last surviving big ideas—as they reorganize all human activity. Otherwise for much of the world, it may be too fast a ride.

Things seem so different now because they are so different. For three genera-tions, the world was defined by great political struggles: the Depression, World War II, the cold war, decolonization. Politics and diplomacy held center stage. Today the air is filled with a new sort of energy. "To get rich is glorious," goes a famous, recent tag line. It is the perfect sound bite for our age—because it was said by the leader of China's Communist Party. The heroes of the past may have been soldiers and statesmen, artists and writers: today they are entrepreneurs. Even countries like China, India and Brazil that once scoffed at the crass commercialism of the West now search desperately for ways to create export zones and high-tech corridors. Napoleon once derided England for being "a nation of shopkeepers." We are now a world of shopkeepers.

Intellectuals like to remind us that globalization is actually not that new. At the turn of the 20th century, free trade, free markets and democratic politics flourished. Today one does not need a visa to travel through much of Europe; then you did not even need a passport.

The point of this comparison is, of course, how it ended—badly. In the early 20th century prominent liberal thinkers believed that prosperity and interdependence had made war unthinkable. And yet it happened. World War I brought an end to the first great age of globalization.

But there are crucial differences between this turn of a century and the last one. Globalization today describes a far more pervasive and deep phenomenon than has ever existed before. Thousands of goods, services and even ideas are manufactured globally, creating complex interconnections between states. A book, for example, can be written in New York, copy-edited in India, typeset in the Caribbean, printed in Singapore and then shipped worldwide. The Internet has made global manufacturing, distribution and communication simple and cheap.

There is another crucial difference between the last round of globalization and this one: the nature of the superpower. An open world economy rests upon the broad edifice of peace, which usually requires a great global hegemony—Britain in 1900, America in 2000. But in 1900 Britain was a declining power; World War I simply accelerated that trend. The picture today could not be more different. Not only is the United States securely the leading power in the world, its advantage is widening. For the past decade, American journalists, politicians and scholars have been searching for a new way to describe the post-cold-war world. It has been staring us in the face: we are living in the American Age.

The American economy has become the envy of the world, spearheading a series of technological breakthroughs that have defined a new post–Industrial Revolution. America's military outpaces any other by leaps and bounds. The Pentagon spends more on defense than the next five great powers combined. It spends more on defense research than *the rest of the world* put together. And Washington has no grand illusions that war is obsolete or that globalization does not require political stability. Whatever Bill Clinton's polemical rhetoric might suggest, there is no groundswell for isolationism in America.

America's edge is as visible in other sectors of society. The gap between American universities and foreign ones is fast widening. Harvard University recently announced that it had completed its $2 billion fund-raising drive months ahead of schedule. Oh, and by the way, it missed its target, overshooting by $0.3 billion. That's $300 million of spare change, which is more than the endowment of many of the best foreign universities. The World Bank recently calculated that the three richest men in America had a combined net worth that exceeds the total GDP of the 48 poorest countries in the world.

Of course, today's tranquil times could be upset by war. A stock-market crash could unnerve the booming economy. Bad foreign policy could bungle many of these extraordinary advantages. But none of these crises is likely to throw up a new superpower. In fact, when a crisis hits, America only becomes more indispensable—think of the East Asian economic collapse, or the Balkan wars. Even in lands where the backlash against America has deep roots, Americanization is pervasive. Listen to a 21-year-old woman, forced to attend an anti-American rally in Tehran: "It's a joke," she told *The New York Times*, pointing at the women clad in black chadors with bright blue colors flashing underneath. "How can you shout, 'Death to America!' when you're wearing blue jeans?" Or consider China. In November, Beijing compromised its gradual approach to economic

reform when it agreed to join the World Trade Organization, largely under U.S. terms.

What can we expect in this new era? The short answer is, more of the same. More of global capitalism but also more of that other distinctive American export, democracy and popular power. Over the last 30 years, a great wave of democratization has swept the world. From Portugal and Greece in the 1970s to Latin America in the 1980s and Central Europe in the 1990s, elections have become a global phenomenon. The pressure will only get more intense. These two forces—capitalism and democracy—will hurl societies into modernity with all its glories and seductions. The companies of tomorrow will be efficient, but will also face brutal competition. Citizens will be able to enjoy culture from all over the world—from opera to Jerry Springer. Teenagers, at the click of a mouse, already have access to great encyclopedias—and racist propaganda.

It is a heady mix and it will only keep getting headier. The forces of creative destruction are beginning to operate at warp speed, creating new companies, careers and communities—but wrecking old ones at an equally dizzying pace. America has gotten used to this high-speed ride. Americans accept the chaos that comes from an ever-changing economy and a chaotic political system. They believe that in the end, it all works out for the best. But will the rest of the world be so understanding? Some countries will close themselves off from this world and stagnate. The wisest will find a balance between their own values and the requirements of modernity.

Most countries recognize the need to tame the fires of capitalism—in fact, they probably do so too much. It will be harder for them to determine how best to

handle democratic populism. Some countries have already begun to see its dangers. They recognize that democracy without the rule of law, minority protections, property rights—what I have called illiberal democracy—can be a hollow shell. It was elections that fueled the fires of nationalism that still rage in the Balkans. It has been elections that have legitimized all manner of thugs from Venezuela to Belarus to Pakistan. In Russia, a well-functioning democracy has been combined with the wholesale corruption of economic reform, law, liberty and political institutions. The result: most Russians now dislike capitalism. They may soon come to dislike democracy.

The United States, the world's greatest democracy, has always kept its own popular pressures on a leash. Its court system is free from public oversight, its Bill of Rights designed to thwart majority rule and its regulatory apparatus keeps tabs on rogue traders and large corporations. Indeed, one could argue that the American way is so successful because both capitalism and democracy are tightly regulated by the rule of law. If the world wishes to learn a lesson about America, this should be the one it takes to heart.

Most difficult of all, societies must make these adjustments as the forces of change swirl around with gathering fury. Whatever the balance countries arrive at, they will still be riding farther, faster than they have ever done. The only advice one can give as we enter a brave new world is this: fasten your seat belts. It's going to be a bumpy ride.

Zakaria is managing editor of Foreign Affairs and author of a forthcoming book on the past, present and future of democracy.

Index

Index

Test Your Knowledge Form

We encourage you to photocopy and use this page as a tool to assess how the articles in *Annual Editions* expand on the information in your textbook. By reflecting on the articles you will gain enhanced text information. You can also access this useful form on a product's book support Web site at *http://www.dushkin.com/online/*.

NAME: DATE:

_____

TITLE AND NUMBER OF ARTICLE:

_____

BRIEFLY STATE THE MAIN IDEA OF THIS ARTICLE:

_____

LIST THREE IMPORTANT FACTS THAT THE AUTHOR USES TO SUPPORT THE MAIN IDEA:

_____

WHAT INFORMATION OR IDEAS DISCUSSED IN THIS ARTICLE ARE ALSO DISCUSSED IN YOUR TEXTBOOK OR OTHER READINGS THAT YOU HAVE DONE? LIST THE TEXTBOOK CHAPTERS AND PAGE NUMBERS:

_____

LIST ANY EXAMPLES OF BIAS OR FAULTY REASONING THAT YOU FOUND IN THE ARTICLE:

_____

LIST ANY NEW TERMS/CONCEPTS THAT WERE DISCUSSED IN THE ARTICLE, AND WRITE A SHORT DEFINITION:

We Want Your Advice

ANNUAL EDITIONS revisions depend on two major opinion sources: one is our Advisory Board, listed in the front of this volume, which works with us in scanning the thousands of articles published in the public press each year; the other is you—the person actually using the book. Please help us and the users of the next edition by completing the prepaid article rating form on this page and returning it to us. Thank you for your help!

ANNUAL EDITIONS: Sociology 04/05

ARTICLE RATING FORM

Here is an opportunity for you to have direct input into the next revision of this volume.
We would like you to rate each of the articles listed below, using the following scale:

1. **Excellent: should definitely be retained**
2. **Above average: should probably be retained**
3. **Below average: should probably be deleted**
4. **Poor: should definitely be deleted**

Your ratings will play a vital part in the next revision.
Please mail this prepaid form to us as soon as possible.
Thanks for your help!

RATING	ARTICLE
	1. The Kindness of Strangers
	2. The Mountain People
	3. More Moral
	4. American Culture Goes Global, or Does It?
	5. What's So Great About America?
	6. What Makes You Who You Are
	7. The New Sex Scorecard
	8. The Criminal Menace: Shifting Global Trends
	9. Parents or Prisons
	10. Enough Is Enough
	11. The American Family
	12. Divorce and Cohabitation: Why We Don't Marry
	13. The Parent Trap
	14. Now for the Truth About Americans and Sex
	15. The War Over Gay Marriage
	16. She Works, He Doesn't
	17. Where Everyone's a Minority
	18. Community Building: Steps Toward a Good Society
	19. For Richer: How the Permissive Capitalism of the Boom Destroyed American Equality
	20. The Real Face of Homelessness
	21. Corporate Welfare
	22. Requiem for Welfare
	23. What's At Stake
	24. Why We Hate
	25. The Past and Prologue
	26. Human Rights, Sex Trafficking, and Prostitution
	27. The New Gender Gap
	28. Who Rules America?
	29. Off the Books
	30. Establishing Rules for the New Workplace
	31. Where the Good Jobs Are Going
	32. Schools That Develop Children
	33. The Doctor Won't See You Now
	34. Sixteen Impacts of Population Growth
	35. Feeling the Heat: Life in the Greenhouse
	36. The Secret Nuclear War
	37. Grains of Hope

RATING	ARTICLE
	38. The New Terrorism: Securing the Nation against a Messianic Foe
	39. A New Strategy for the New Face of Terrorism
	40. Between Two Ages
	41. Across the Great Divide

(Continued on next page)

ANNUAL EDITIONS: SOCIOLOGY 04/05

NO POSTAGE
NECESSARY
IF MAILED
IN THE
UNITED STATES

BUSINESS REPLY MAIL
FIRST CLASS MAIL PERMIT NO. 551 DUBUQUE IA

POSTAGE WILL BE PAID BY ADDRESEE

McGraw-Hill/Dushkin
2460 KERPER BLVD
DUBUQUE, IA 52001-9902

ABOUT YOU

Name   Date

Are you a teacher? ❏   A student? ❏
Your school's name

Department

Address   City   State   Zip

School telephone #

YOUR COMMENTS ARE IMPORTANT TO US!

Please fill in the following information:
For which course did you use this book?

Did you use a text with this ANNUAL EDITION? ❏ yes ❏ no
What was the title of the text?

What are your general reactions to the *Annual Editions* concept?

Have you read any pertinent articles recently that you think should be included in the next edition? Explain.

Are there any articles that you feel should be replaced in the next edition? Why?

Are there any World Wide Web sites that you feel should be included in the next edition? Please annotate.

May we contact you for editorial input? ❏ yes ❏ no
May we quote your comments? ❏ yes ❏ no